P9-DFJ-241

THE BORDERLINE CHILD

24.95

THE BORDERLINE CHILD

Approaches to Etiology, Diagnosis, and Treatment

EDITED BY
Kenneth S. Robson, M.D.

McGRAW-HILL BOOK COMPANY
New York   St. Louis   San Francisco
Bogotá   Hamburg   Johannesburg   London   Madrid
Mexico   Montreal   New Delhi   Panama   Paris
São Paulo   Singapore   Sydney   Tokyo   Toronto

Copyright © 1983 McGraw-Hill Book Co. All rights reserved. Printed in the
United States of America. Except as permitted under the Copyright Act of
1976, no part of this publication may be reproduced or distributed in any form
or by any means, or stored in a data base or retrieval system, without the prior
written permission of the publisher.

Thomas H. Quinn and Michael Hennelly were the editors of this book.
Christine Aulicino was the designer. Thomas G. Kowalczyk supervised the
production. It was set in English by B.P.E. Graphics, Inc.

Printed and bound by R.R. Donnelley and Sons, Inc.

Library of Congress Cataloging in Publication Data
Main Entry under title:
The Borderline child.
Bibliography: p.
Includes index.
1. Borderline personality disorder in children.
I. Robson, Kenneth. [DNLM: 1. Personality disorders—In infancy and child-
hood. WS 350.8.P3 B728]
RJ506.B65B67   1982   618.92'89   82-9894
ISBN   0-07-053346-6   AACR2
ISBN 0-07-053346-6

TO
TANYA
with Love and Gratitude

CONTENTS

PREFACE

To the untutored eye, the recognition of serious psychiatric disturbance in adults poses little difficulty. Yet there seems a curious reluctance to acknowledge similar levels of disturbance in children; to attribute grief, depression, or insanity to the young runs counter to ordinary and more reassuring perceptions of childhood. This reluctance may have slowed the study of such children and limited the quality of care delivered to them. This book is intended to offer a comprehensive examination of one population of troubled children—those exhibiting characteristics of borderline syndromes.

To date, the literature on borderline conditions in childhood has been limited in both size and scope (see Shapiro, this volume). Many existing studies deal with small populations of children pooled without benefit of reliable diagnostic criteria. While such criteria have been elaborated for adult borderline states, comparable data in childhood are only beginning to emerge (see Vela et al., this volume). Furthermore, if one adds to the inherent instability of the diagnostic process in childhood a concept as vague as "borderline" there is a risk of insult being added to heuristic injury! In my opinion, ultimately most borderline children described in the literature and this volume will turn out to be at biogenetic risk for major mental illnesses and their variants (see Kestenbaum, this volume). Nonetheless, the concept of the borderline child is with us for the present and deserves more fundamental clinical and biological study—hence, this book.

Current models in child psychiatry oscillate within the poles of *psychodynamic, descriptive,* and *biological* orientations. Such ambiguity appears to be healthy and true to existing data. This book reflects an effort to provide the reader, whether practitioner or investigator, with a thorough and scholarly exposure to an "ecumenical" examination of borderline states in childhood. Loosely speaking, the contributions are in sequence. Chapters 1, 2 and 3 deal with conceptual and nosological issues while Chapter 4 addresses both a working classification of borderline syndromes and sound clinical descriptions. Chapters 6 through 8 are devoted to diagnostic and etiological issues while Chapters 9 through 12 explore approaches to treatment.

It has been apparent in editing this book that certain critical kinds of information are badly needed to further extend our understanding of these children. Family studies, careful genetic research, and long-term follow-up reports seem especially important. A broader and deeper appraisal of biochemical processes will surely be underway. And, of course, "markers" that will facilitate reliable identification of these conditions in infancy and early childhood may initiate preventive strategies. It is my hope that this book will both improve existing clinical skills with this seriously impaired population of children and encourage more and better research into the nature and causes of their psychopathology.

KENNETH S. ROBSON, M.D.
Boston, Massachusetts

THE BORDERLINE CHILD

The Borderline Child in an Overall Perspective

E. James Anthony, M.D., F.R.C. Psy., D.P.M.
BLANCHE F. ITTLESON PROFESSOR OF CHILD PSYCHIATRY
AND DIRECTOR OF THE EDISON CHILD DEVELOPMENT RESEARCH CENTER
WASHINGTON UNIVERSITY SCHOOL OF MEDICINE
ST. LOUIS, MISSOURI

ONE OF THE PLEASURES OF WRITING an introduction to a comprehensive and well-constructed book is that the difficult spadework has already been done, leaving one in the omniscient position of surveying the field and regarding it *sub specie aeternatitis*. The strong implication is that the borderline child is here to stay and that clinicians should hone up on nosological issues, the etiological and diagnostic considerations, the various modalities of treatment that have been instituted to relieve this serious condition, and the outcome for such children when they enter adult life. This represents the classical approach to a disease entity within the ambience of the medical model. One is presented with the careful delineation of its "natural history," and the approach is flexible enough to include both neurochemistry and psychoanalysis within the same general framework, presumably on the authority of the physical thesis of complementarity that permits us to look at phenomena in widely divergent ways without assuming rightnesses and wrongnesses.

Diagnosis in psychiatry is a notoriously treacherous business. Whenever one feels at ease with a cherished and cultivated entity, someone is very likely to come along and stab it in the back. But the idea of a book fashioned in this way is to protect as many flanks of the new entity as possible. One can protect it on its neurological, the neurophysiological, and the neurochemical facets; one can bolster it on its nosological, the psychological, and the psychoanalytic sides; and one can buttress it by a series of therapeutic tests that range from the biological to the psychodynamic with the implication that if the condition responds to the treatment given, it must be a reality. Finally, if the picture holds true over time, as in a follow-up, then one has every reason to believe that one is dealing with a diagnostically demarcated state.

The problem of the label "borderline" itself begs a large number of questions. It is neither this nor that but something in-between, something marginal but not necessarily transitional. It is both changeable in its manifestations and stable enough to be considered a definite entity. It is not in the process of changing from one condition to another unless there has been a misdiagnosis. Thus we are dealing with something that changes but remains approximately and recognizably the same, at least during the childhood period. (There is some evidence to suggest that in adult life it can undergo a profound transformation and emerge as a major psychiatric disorder. This raises the crucial question as to which borderline children are on their way to becoming adult psychotics.)

How will this book go down in the clinical history of child psychiatry?

Will it be remembered for its pioneer effort of collecting and collating much of the widely scattered and disconnected data on the borderline child? Or will its fate be similar to that of early compilations on hysteria that blossomed in one era and then faded into relative nonexistence in the next? It is hard to predict psychiatric fashion: What I can say is that the text crystallized my own nebulous thinking in this area and has provided me with added confidence in making the diagnosis.

My own experience of borderline states comes in part from prolonged clinical experience and from my own research on high-risk children of psychotic parents (represented in this book by Kestenbaum's chapter) who have now begun to show, in the course of their development, what seem to be borderline characteristics. This was most striking in one case in which the child was the offspring of a manic-depressive father and a schizophrenic mother.

One should mention that scientific workers from other disciplines have also been intrigued by conditions that were intermediary between major groups. Darwin, for example, in 1832, wrote of "a poor specimen of a bird which to my unornithological eyes appears to be a happy mixture of lark, pigeon and snipe . . . an inosculating creature." This was his first use of this unusual word defined by the dictionary as having "characteristics intermediate between those of two similar or related taxonomic groups" (Anthony & Gilpin, 1981). Since then, taxonomists from all disciplines have been alerted to the "inosculate" as a bridging class. Darwin spoke of a "happy mixture," but more generally the inosculate has been regarded as a "poor specimen" incorporating the less favorable elements from different major groups.

In the psychiatric literature of the last century, the term "borderline" was used to indicate a transitional phase of disorder on its way to becoming a clear-cut psychosis, but with increasing clinical experience, this concept of transition has become less acceptable because cases appeared to maintain a curious identity of their own. I have spoken of the "psychopathology of intermediacy" (Anthony & Gilpin, 1981), indicating an overall concern with the unpleasant human predicament of falling between two psychological stools. I envisioned this borderline condition as an intermediate, not a transitional state. It was not something on the way to becoming something else. Except under certain circumstances of risk, it *was* something in its own right. Schmideberg (1959) referred to its "stable instability," Pine (1974) to its "predictable unpredictability," and Grinker (1975) to its "vacillating eccentricity." For clinicians, it was altogether an elusive concept, characterized by shifting developmental levels, changing clinical manifestations, and a varying ego organization, all suggesting a high degree of structural fluidity. The individual appeared to live with one foot solidly fixed in reality and the other loosely steeped in fantasy with no firm links between the two. To "catch" this disorder diagnostically was comparable to the hopeless proverbial task of putting salt on the bird's tail. As one approached, it took wing to the opposite end of the spectrum. One had two alternatives: either to consider it a fixed disease entity with a physiological niche of its own or to recognize it as basically metamorphic and quite unexpectedly subject to changes of character, appearance, state, and development. But then came the vexing question: How can one do consistent clinical work on such an inconsistent clinical entity? And what does one treat when phenomena run the gamut from primitive states of being with primitive mechanisms of defense to almost good-enough reality and relatedness. Moreover, the connections seem to be missing. The links between inside and outside, between thought and things, and between signs and objects signified are not established within any firm system of representation, and so the child is unable to respond consistently to both internal and external events. The clinician himself has to live with a degree of "certain uncertainty" which may be disconcerting but, at the same time, challenging to our clinical acumen and skill.

I should say something about the language of borderline children which is often a primary or prelogical process and heavily imbued with magical thinking. I am reminded of an Eskimo myth dealing with their particular cosmology in which a brother falls in love with his sister and pursues her unceasingly until she finally takes refuge in the sky and becomes the moon. He, in turn, is transformed into the sun and continues the chase, sometimes managing to catch up as in an eclipse and embrace her. The sister, in her anger, deprives the brother of food, offering him instead her severed breast. "If you desire me, eat me!" But the boy refuses. A new transformation occurs: the girl becomes the sun and the boy the moon who gradually wanes from lack of food until the sun reaches out and feeds it from the breast that had previously been rejected. The cycle is then repeated every month. The myth establishes connections between animism, incest, and cannibalism and speaks to the people at all levels.

At times, it seems to the clinician as if the borderline child has also created a personal myth that is so privately formulated that it becomes difficult for anyone from the outside to penetrate into its meaning. In order to investigate these idiosyncratic communications, we must do as Levi-Strauss (1969) did when dealing with phenomena in production: we must first examine the "raw material" before we "cook" it, and in doing so, we must keep in mind the often forgotten fact that "cooking" transforms the real ingredients and renders them artificial.

What then can we say about a child "who is never the same child; who goes his own peculiar way irrespective of circumstance; who lags behind in some ways and seems forward in others; whose behavior is marked by fluctuations; who does not know how to deal with things that are inside or outside him; and who apparently experiences the universe in a Pascalian-Kierkegaardian manner, as remote, terrifying, and inexplicable?'' (Anthony & Gilpin, 1981).

To understand this clinical idiosyncracy fully, one cannot come upon it in the flower of its evolution and draw retrospective conclusions about its beginnings. One needs to understand the borderline children developmentally, to follow them prospectively over time and record the kaleidoscopic changes as they occur both spontaneously and in response to therapeutic interventions.

The clinician in close therapeutic contact with this type of child is often struck by the upsurge of "unthinkable anxiety" of which Winnicott (1965) spoke: the feeling that one is falling to pieces, losing one's supports, lacking direction, unable to relate to one's self, one's body, or to others. Phenomeno-logically, the child feels peculiarly "skinless." It took an individual of genius, Virginia Woolf, to describe her borderline state as a child: her anxiety over feelings of discontinuity and fragmentation and her frantic attempts to bring about unity within herself. As she herself put it, she had "never been able," since early childhood, "to become part of life; as if the world was complete and I was outside of it being blown forever outside the loop of time. Other people seemed to live in a real world but I often fell down into nothingness. I had to bang my head against some hard door to call myself back to the body." (Bell, 1972) Some of the patients in Laing's book *The Divided Self* (1970) described less articulately the feelings of merging or being engulfed by the outside world. The oneness would result in a strange terror at the loss of identity and fusion of self. What was dreaded most was also most longed for. One patient described how if she stared long enough at the environment, she would blend with it and disappear, while another explained that she had to die to keep from dying. These are the paradoxes of this in-between world that pulls at the person from both the upper and lower borders (Pine, 1974), at times drawing the patient toward normality, conflict, and identity, and at other times leaning toward madness. What better term is there to describe the borderline case than Darwin's "inosculate?" (Anthony & Gilpin, 1981)

I would like to say something about the first borderline child to be described in the psychiatric literature. Freud treated the Wolf Man between the years 1910–1914 and furnished us, as Blum (1974) reminds us, with a dramatic and vivid account of a borderline disturbance in childhood. There seemed to be a continuity between the borderline childhood and its extension into adolescence and adulthood. The Wolf Man never became frankly psychotic. Nevertheless, throughout his development, he was subject to uncontrolled regression. When seen in continuity, there was clearly a paranoid core to the disorder and the persecutory anxieties were always in evidence. After his nightmare at the age of four years, he could not bear to be looked at and would scream if he thought that someone was staring at him. Later he became erythrophobic and obsessed hypersensitively about his nose and skin. Still later, his social anxieties pushed him further into seclusion. The borderline constellation, described by Freud during childhood, included attacks of panic, fantasies of torture, screaming reactions, and uncontrolled, flooding rages suggesting a marked ego deviation (Weil, 1953). In adult life, the ego deficiency manifested itself in narcissistic sensitivity, detachment, disturbed object relations, affective impoverishment, poor impulse control, and a tendency to severe regressive responses. At times the neurotic elements were more prominent than the borderline ones, but there was never a period when the Wolf Man was entirely asymptomatic.

When one undertakes a "talking" therapy with the borderline child, one soon discovers limitations on both sides: the therapist may be unable to reach the child or the child may be too severely disturbed to be reached. Ekstein (1981) has pointed out that there will always be those who cannot reach the borderline child for various reasons and that it is wise for them to find this out as early as possible and not waste their own precious, professional time as well as the patient's time. The language of the borderline child may be too difficult for them to learn, in that they may have no talent for primary-process thinking or communicating; they may be far too rational for this type of child and too immersed in logical processes. In working with borderline children, one needs to be flexibly "bilingual"; one must be able to think in both primary- and secondary-process modes, speak through the medium of play and symbolism, and understand the communicative uses of "acting out." The cognitively oriented therapist may be intolerant of the endless disappointments that accompany the treatment of borderline children, the sudden and severe regressions that occur unexpectedly at any time, and the very small therapeutic gains that seem to be made. Consultations with colleagues from time to time are valuable in dealing with the numerous countertransference reactions that arise.

Some authors have attempted to describe various subgroups of the borderline spectrum in the adult, and a similar attempt has been made by Pine (1974) and Morales (1981) with respect to children. The latter has postulated five groups. The first is characterized by a severe regression with collapse; the second, with severe aggression; the third, by highly dependent and clinging behavior; the fourth, by a devastating degree of separation anxiety; and the last, and most stable, the borderline personality with a narcissistic veneer. Morales has correlated these groups with those of Grinker who has differentiated cases that border on neurosis, cases that border on psychosis, a core borderline syndrome (corresponding to the separation syndrome of Morales), and a well-defended, affectless, "as if" character, corresponding to the fifth group described by Morales. With Pine, correspondences are fewer: his cases of internal disorganization in response to external disorganization are roughly similar to group two in the Morales classification, and his cases demonstrating shifting levels of ego organization are not dissimilar from the separation and core borderline syndromes of Morales and Grinker.

Morales also examined his spectrum in relation to ego and self-organization, differentiating them on the basis of the signal function of anxiety, the degree and quality of regression, the amount of activity and passivity in relation to adaptive capacities, and the extent to which the self is integrated or fragmented. These are useful clinical varieties to consider in relation to particular cases, but it is almost contradictory to attempt to pin down a borderline child into any definable pigeonholes when the very essence of the syndrome is fluid, even though all cases present with some ego defect of poor reality testing and illogical thinking. Gilpin's (1981) use of the terms "true-fluid," "non-fluid," and "miscellaneous-fluid" are not only semantically confusing but nosologically crude, even though they have been helpful to a particular clinical investigator with respect to her understanding of the psychodynamics, the treatability, or the prognosis. What Gilpin and Morales have both emphasized is the difficulty that the parents of borderline children face in child management, especially when they themselves not only lack certain essential inner resources but aggravate the child's development because of their own near-borderline states. They want their own passive-dependent needs to be met, their own traumatized lives to be healed, and their own narcissistic aspirations to be fulfilled. For the most part, they are unable to separate the children from themselves, and, not having been the recipients of good enough mothering themselves, they prove inept at mothering even normally responsive children.

To what extent does it help the clinician to broaden the dimensions of a syndrome that eludes description? Does the use of a "diagnosis cube" such as Stone (1980) put forward flesh out a ghostly structure with theoretical considerations stemming from genetic and constitutional research, psychoanalysis, phenomenology, and research on the biogenetic psychoses. At best, it provides a map that helps us to follow the borderline psychopathology into many different terrains and gives us, I think, an illusional sense of knowing the landscape better. We do need to build bridges between the different constructs that we use, and we can at least assure ourselves that this most enigmatic of all mental disorders is at last beginning to emerge as a fairly recognizable nosological entity.

My own view of the borderline syndrome is that it is "typically atypical," and I therefore find Kernberg's definition (a characterological organization identifiable by *typical* symptom constellations, by *typical* ego defenses, by a *typical* pathology of internal object relationships, and by *typical* genetic-dynamic features) somewhat difficult to accept. I have never, at least in children, seen a *typical* borderline case. I have seen and diagnosed cases in which there was an absence of phase dominance, a regression to primary identification, a tendency to panic, a fluidity of organization, a heavy reliance on splitting mechanisms, and an early failure in the separation-individuation process. But, like Pine, I find some relief in not being compelled to isolate a single unifying mechanism. Yet many clinicians make the diagnosis with some confidence on positive features that are present and not by a simple process of eliminating neurosis and psychosis. Pine feels that what is common to a large number of children in this group is failure along one or another line of development, but even this does not account for the fluidity. On the whole, I am inclined to agree with Dickes (1974) that borderline states, whether in children or in adults, are best considered as a conglomerate of several syndromes of differing etiologies. By saying this, we avoid the procrustean approach.

My own understanding of the borderline child remains on an intuitive, preoperational level, and I am constantly puzzled by its manifestations. I react at times like D. H. Lawrence who once said in a moment of exasperation at the demand for clear-cut evidence, "I feel it in my belly." What makes me suspect that I am dealing with a borderline case? I must confess I often "feel it in my belly" rather than in my brain.

> These children do not make sense to us at the beginning, and frustrate our omnipotence and omniscience very easily; they test us out to the full and beyond; they challenge our capacity for forming a stable alliance; if we are intolerant of regression or acting out, they can make us suffer; they can fill us with guilt for their emptiness and despair and hopelessness. They can make the long road to trust a hazardous one, but in the face of the steadiness and reliability of the therapist and his availability, a working, if erratic, partnership can be effected. The transference stages can oscillate among murderous and self-destructive impulses and wishes that occasionally frighten the therapist. (Anthony & Gilpin, 1981)

These are undoubtedly "belly feelings." One fine day they will be supplemented by biochemistry!

REFERENCES

Anthony, E.J., & Gilpin, D. *Three further clinical faces of childhood.* New York: Spectrum, 1981.

Bell, Q. *Virginia Woolf.* New York: Harcourt Brace Jovanovich, 1972.

Blum, H. P. The borderline childhood of the Wolf Man. *Journal of American Psychoanalytic Association,* 1974, *22* (4), 721–742.

Dickes, Robert. The concepts of borderline states: An alternative proposal. *International Journal of Psychoanalysis and Psychotherapy,* 1974, *3* (1), 1–27.

Ekstein, R. The concept of borderline: A fresh perspective. In *Three further clinical faces of childhood.* New York: Spectrum, 1981.

Grinker, R. S., Sr. Neurosis, psychosis and the borderline states. In A. M. Friedman, H. I. Kaplan, B. J. Sadock (Eds.), *Comprehensive textbook of psychiatry* (Vol. 2). Baltimore: Williams & Wilkins, 1975.

Laing, R. D. *The divided self.* Baltimore: Penquin, 1970.

Levi-Strauss, C. *The raw and the cooked* (J. D. Weightman, trans.). New York: Harper & Row, 1969.

Masterson, James F. *Treatment of the borderline adolescent.* New York: Wiley, 1972.

Morales, J. The borderline spectrum in children. In *Three further clinical faces of childhood.* New York: Spectrum, 1981.

Pine, F. On the concept of "borderline" in children. *The Psychoanalytic Study of the Child,* 1974, *29,* 341–368.

Pine, F. On phase-characteristics pathology of the school child: Disturbances of personality, development and organization (borderline conditions) of learning, and of behavior. In S. Greenspan & E.H. Pollack (Eds.), The course of life: Psychoanalytic contribution toward understanding personality development (Vol. 2, *Latency, adolescence and youth*). Bethesda: NIMH, 1980.

Schmideberg, M. The borderline patients. In S. Arieti (Ed.), *The American handbook of psychiatry.* New York: Basic Books, 1967.

Stone, Michael H. *The borderline syndromes.* New York: McGraw-Hill, 1980.

Weil, A. Certain severe disturbances of ego development in childhood, *The Psychoanalytic Study of the Child, 1953, 8,* 271–287.

Winnicott, D. W. The effect of psychotic parents on the emotional development of the child. In *The child and individual development.* London: Tavistock, 1965.

CHAPTER 1

The Borderline
Syndrome
in Children:
A Critique

Theodore Shapiro, M.D.
PROFESSOR OF PSYCHIATRY
PROFESSOR OF PSYCHIATRY IN PEDIATRICS
DIRECTOR, CHILD AND ADOLESCENT PYSCHIATRY
CORNELL UNIVERSITY MEDICAL COLLEGE
NEW YORK, NEW YORK

INTRODUCTION

EVER SINCE ADAM was admonished by God to name all the beasts of the field, human beings have taken the suggestion as a serious, if not full-time, activity. Even more distressing, the request seems to have been confused with the further admonition to go forth and multiply. As we move along in history, we notice an increase in the proliferation of names, some of which point to little.

Any discussion of the borderline syndrome has to take into account both the problems and virtues of *classification as knowledge* while acknowledging that useful nosologies have been designed for easy communication between professionals when they share a common frame of reference. The difficulties that arise in clarifying the boundaries of the borderline syndrome arise from the fact that uncertainty about the frames of reference used by investigators exists and their application by clinicians vary. Indeed, the definition of borderline syndrome or borderline personality organization that is currently preferred by some is beset with special problems in childhood that arise from different conceptual backgrounds and also from uncertainty about the existence of such disorders early in life. The use of the term in childhood gives rise to all of the hazards of early designation of personality type within the developmental span and the assumption of persistence of disorder into later life.

Those who considered these problems of classification for DSM-III wisely noted that there is "no right way or natural way to classify psychiatric disorders" (Cantwell, 1980), thus, emphasizing the arbitrariness of any classification system. More importantly, they opted "not to classify children but disorders of children" (Cantwell, 1980). This approach represents a departure from nosological principles that address disease processes and etiological factors.

I not only address the issues that have made DSM-III the document that it is, I also use some of the rhetoric around the support of that document in order to understand what clinicians are struggling with in their attempts to designate borderline disorders. I direct my review especially toward the problems of using the designations *borderline personality disorders* and *borderline syndrome* for children while ample confusion in the use of these terms for the designation of adults already exists. When any term is applied to children, the problems are multiplied many fold.

Mental health professionals who work with children are legion and from a legion of disciplines, but what has been called the "medical model" is still

12

of interest to us, especially regarding the classification of disorder. Diagnosis in medicine has long sought descriptive clarity, but it yearns longingly for etiological certainty. Terms such as "schizophrenia" and "depression" imply process and disease but lack etiological certainty. Epidemiological terms such as "handicap" and "disorder" carry fewer presuppositions but are beset with suppositions nonetheless. Some argue that an etiological approach to child psychiatric disorders may not be the best approach given our current knowledge. Cantwell suggests that a descriptive phenomenological approach may be more useful for treatment of fractures, which he cites as an analogy to mental disorder, than knowledge of the nature of the cause. His reasoning here is based on the fact that material cause, in an Aristotelean sense, offers no help for treatment because the task is to reduce the fracture, not to reestablish the circumstance of injury. His analogy, however, is flawed.

Historically, the medical model produced descriptive categories which later bore functional and etiological fruit. Physicians long have recorded their observations and constructed conglomerates of signs and symptoms into syndromes; these syndromes were and are then linked to pathophysiological organ systems and later to etiologies. Cushing's syndrome, for example, received a new level of understanding and impetus to research when the relationship of its signs to adrenocortical hormones was addressed. Caution is warranted even for Cushing's syndrome, however; although the adrenocortical steriods are surely involved, the original series of cases included some basophylic tumors of the hypophysis, rather than hypersecretion of the organ of focus, the suprarenal glands. So we must admit that syndromes, per se, while they may be descriptively sound, do not point to etiology directly. However, the more we learn about substrate correlation and pathophysiology, the more we can then point to aspects of the interplay of biological processes as a means of explicating disease process.

Clearly, the model for disorder or disease is *organismic* in its vantage point rather than *person-oriented.* On the other hand, psychiatrists, especially child psychiatrists, are significantly directed toward the humanistic enterprise of describing deviations in the development of the *person* and the establishment of a set of categories which pertain to maladaptation of such persons as well as presumed organismic dysfunction. Some offer that this focus may be discontinuous with medical diagnosis. I believe that we cannot lose sight of the fact that in the severe disorders of childhood (which to my thinking includes the borderline disorders), inborn, genetic, perinatal, and congenital factors have proven to be a significant part of our expectations. Similar thoughts have been catalogued by Stone (1980) regarding adult borderlines. While there is a tendency to follow the nineteenth-century implications of the medical model in seeking organic or substrate malfunction, psychiatrists also seek functional and psychosocial determinants of disorder. But such a view is not exclusive of organismic factors. We have become accustomed to complementarity along with overdetermination and multiaxial approaches.

To continue the analogy to the medical model as expanded for use in psychiatry, we can approach nomenclature from the three standpoints of *description, dynamics,* and *genetics.* At the *descriptive* level, we seek face validity and descriptive validity, but that which is reliable and repeatedly recognizable does not always provide prognostic predictive validity. Moreover, construct validity would require that once there is an airtight system of observation with reliable reproducibility, specific follow-up and organismic features might be sought as external to psychiatric clinical methods to provide support for certainty.

A *dynamic* vantage point maintains that it is possible to classify on the basis of *how* the person and his or her presumed mental apparatus is organized in its intrapsychic balances. The Freudian mental apparatus of the structural theory has been most relevant to many clinician's considerations of borderline conditions, especially with the addition of an object-relations model that has been employed with impressive pragmatic value.

The *genetic* point of view, of course, suggests that retrospective factors can account for the phenomenology of the current descriptive disorder. We are well acquainted with the psychoanalytic genetic nomenclature that has produced designations such as anal or oral character and narcissistic character. The central premise of this system is that the descriptors which emerge are to be anticipated because they result from the viscissitudes of maturation of the mind's content and have common genetic roots, but this premise is not descriptive. By contrast, it would not be possible for a behaviorist to come up with a dynamic formulation on the basis of concepts such as defense and impulse, nor would it be possible for an epidemiologist to come up with a set of genetic propositions from descriptive criteria, except as the empirical correlates to subgroups defined by descriptive exclusion criteria. Thus, genetics and dynamics are theory-specific unless one were to test the validity of one system against that of another, ignoring the theoretical subsystem that gave rise to each formulation.

I have belabored a number of theoretical issues in introducing my discussion of borderline personality organization in childhood because I would like to make a central belief clear. Different techniques of observation and presuppositions produce different nosologies, and it is possible for a single individual to look at varying nomenclatures for their strengths, while at the same time recognizing that each nomenclature is operationally bound— that is, it can describe no more than the techniques that its own observations permit. Against this difficulty, child psychiatrists are in a very special position because they place developmental propositions at the center of their work. This tends to bind them together, though never so perfectly as to prevent controversy.

A second problem that troubles child psychiatry rests on the fact that historically the discipline has frequently taken its lead from adult psychiatry. While the genetic point of view which attributes the origins of symptoms to past experience may direct adult psychiatrists to childhood, it is often a different childhood than that seen directly by child psychiatrists. Nonetheless, childhood nomenclatures traditionally have been built by analogy to adult systems. Thus are we beset by the term *borderline syndrome,* born in adulthood and transposed to childhood. Now we are challenged to tell the world how the adult became who he or she is or what it was in the child or the environment of the child that permitted this outcome in personality. With these factors in mind, I shall finally embark on a discussion of the borderline syndrome, or borderline personality organization, in childhood, presenting the uncertainties and problems that plague us in its delineation. Other contributors to this volume, more certain than I, may appeal more to the convinced reader. However, I hope that what follows permits a more persistent skepticism with which the reader may temper his enthusiasm.

BORDERLINE ADULTS

Clinicians do not doubt that there is a group of patients who have an exacerbating and remitting course characterized by impulsivity, deviance in thinking, difficulties within their human relationships, and affective storms alternating with emptiness which has been called the "borderline syndrome." When we were residents at NYU-Bellevue during the late 1950s, we used to designate them by the ward to which they were directed—an acute care, "mildly disturbed" ward. We called them "PQ-1 schizophrenics." At New York Psychiatric Institute, a similar tendency to make somewhat overinclusive diagnoses also existed. We at Bellevue playfully, if not competitively, called them "Psychiatric Institute schizophrenics". Such designations were our way of saying to colleagues: "We know what you're talking about; the patients do not fit all of the criteria for a deteriorating schizophrenic disorder, nor are they simply severe neurotics—but we do know some things about them." And indeed, we did know some things—even at that time. This was a group of patients who tended to improve with dynamic interpretative therapies so long as the contact was kept. It was unclear initially whether interpretation was relatively useless as compared to a sustaining relationship. Acting out was prominent, we thought, and separations frequently gave rise to angry storms, or "vacation babies," and self-destructive histrionic behavior. Post-therapeutic behavior tended to be just the same as prior behavior with little aftereffect. They also were likely to respond badly to the newly introduced phenothiazines and were more likely to tolerate meprobamate.

This was a group who might enter with a variety of clinical pictures that were designated in various ways by varying people during the 1950s and 1960s. Some of the first clinical differentiations segregated such patients as "borderline schizophrenics." Zilboorg (1957) referred to his cases as "ambulatory schizophrenics." Hoch and Polatin (1949) discussed the myriad of neurotic symptoms, the pan-sexuality and pan-anxiety they saw as a reflection of defective ego structures and designated their patients as "pseudoneurotic schizophrenics." These are but a few of the terms that were and have been popular. By now these cases and names are part of history, documenting the fact that clinicians were struggling to achieve some consensus and face validity about a group of patients that they could recognize—but did not have a name for. The boundaries were not descriptively clear because of attempts to include such patients within disease categories. Some sentiment held that in labelling them schizophrenics we did these patients a social and administrative disservice. On the other hand, clinicians had to catalogue their knowledge and help families and patients to anticipate difficulties in life and prognosis. Such needs create an impetus to create new names.

John Frosch (1960) made a valiant attempt at a descriptive designation by calling his patients "psychotic characters." He tried to establish a common dynamic core and projected inferences about common genetic experiences characterized by out-of-phase traumata. He established criteria that these are people who have major difficulties in reality sense and in relationship to reality but only intermittent difficulties in reality testing without the tendency to dementia. He called them psychotic characters because he felt that the analogy of the relationship of character disorders to neuroses was apt. It was an attempt that was clear in its descriptive, dynamic, and genetic propositions, although it remained untested for reliability and validity in large groups of patients. Parenthetically, during the same time we all discussed patients with acute schizophrenic episodes without recurrence as well and were concerned about what they were to be called in remission. The concept of "schizophrenia without psychosis" was a nomenclatural anathema because schizophrenia was a subclass under the heading psychosis in our nosology.

A strong research movement arose that argued for stronger distinctions between the biological and the family determinants of disorder. While biochemists worked on serotonin and catecholamines, others such as Singer and Wynne (1965) and Lidz (1968) dealt with families and communicative styles within families. Ample evidence now shows that both groups were working on complementary views of the same people. However, the shading into borderline communicative styles from purely schizophrenic functioning is worth noting. Meehl's (1962) concept of schizotypy allowed individuals with a genetic propensity to schizophrenia to exist without symptomatic illness but with expression of the postulated genetic tendency in borderline behavior. The struggle to find etiology thus gave rise to new clinical information and ideas.

Moving forward rapidly into the modern era, strong support for the borderline condition in adults has come from a number of sources. In some ways these data are indeed somewhat divergent. In their genetic studies of schizophrenia, Kety, Rosenthal, and Wender (1971a, b) have adopted a vantage point which is not dissimilar to that put forth originally by Meehl suggesting that borderline syndromes may be genetically continuous with schizophrenia. Gunderson (1977) borrowed from the earlier work by Grinker, Werble, and Drye (1968) in attempting to define and segregate the descriptive characteristics of borderlines while ignoring biological postulates.

Earlier descriptions included the following features: anger, depression, and loneliness, along with a poorly coherent self-identity and anaclitic dependency. Gunderson (1977) was able to isolate a group of hospitalized patients between sixteen and thirty-five without evidence of organicity who could be identified using his diagnostic interview for the borderline (DIB). He noted that the patients so identified looked socially like neurotics but were vocationally more like schizophrenics. Reports of depression, anger, and anxiety were frequent, and a significant number reported impatience and demandingness prior to admission. Depression was the most common affect. All observations indicated that psychotic percepts were not as bizarre as in schizophrenia and that depersonalization was likely.

Spitzer, Endicott, and Gibbon (1979) recently provided further support for the suggestion that this group can be distinguished from schizophrenics and those with other character disorders. They showed that good sensitivity could be claimed for item sets that distinguished 808 borderlines from 808 control patients. DSM-III distinguishes between borderline personality disorder and schizotypal personality in accord with Spitzer et al.'s segregation, but the discreteness is descriptive, without claims for etiological significance. Moreover, half the patients had both diagnoses, confounding our notion of discreteness. Thus, the differences from schizophrenia are reasonably recognizable to trained clinicians, but "the borderline concept" is not unitary—it is best conceptualized as consisting of at "least two major dimensions that are relatively independent within a borderline group." (p. 23) Sheehy, Goldsmith, and Charles (1980) support Spitzer et al.'s findings in a study of outpatients with the added suggestion that impairment of reality testing remains a useful parameter to distinguish the group from the schizophrenias.

Such recent work points to the idea that borderline condition may not be appropriately related to schizophrenia as it has been historically. Rather, it may be more closely related to unstable personality disorders and affective disorders as suggested by Stone (1980). Klein (1975) indicated prior to Stone that the borderline conditions may be closer to histrionic disorders and affective problems than to schizophrenia.

The concept of borderline conditions in adults would be incomplete without mentioning Otto Kernberg's important work (1977a,b). The central premise of his view is that the diagnosis of "borderline personality organization" (his preferential term) is best made on a "structural basis" rather than by a descriptive approach which he feels is limiting. Although seeking phenomenological and descriptive criteria, he is more interested in inferred categories derived from the object-relations-theory/psychoanalytic vantage point. He notes, as do others, that borderline patients tend to be anxious and to have polysymptomatic neuroses, including phobias, obsessive-compulsive symptoms, multiple elaborate or bizarre conversion symptoms, and dissociative reactions. They also may be hypochondriacal and even paranoid. Polymorphous perverse sexual trends and classical prepsychotic personality structures, such as paranoid, schizoid, or hypomanic variants, are seen. Borderline patients tend to be impulsive and/or addictive. Dynamically, they prefer to use mechanisms of splitting and projective identification as central features of their primitive defensive organization. These latter factors come from observations gained in the therapeutic situation over time and are thus method specific, but no more method specific than approaches that insist on descriptive checklists.

Prior to turning to borderline conditions of childhood, I would like to indicate that the adult pictures have been discussed and criticized no less frequently than the concept in childhood. Rich (1978) argues that premature closure in settling on the borderline diagnosis is unhealthy because it may lead to denial of appropriate therapies for patients. He thus echoes Guze's caution that misdiagnosis gives one a false sense of complacency even as a useful therapy may be being withheld. Rich notes that borderline personality disorder points to a continuum where formerly many argued that a clear neurotic-psychotic boundary exists. He also describes the multiple uses of the word "borderline"—he reviewed 20 patient charts where 9 different borderline diagnoses were used (borderline, borderline states, borderline personality, borderline syndrome, borderline psychosis, borderline schizophrenia, borderline schizoid personality, borderline hysterical character, and borderline character). Borderline mental retardation is also mentioned, leading to even greater confusion. Moreover, most critics argue that there must be systematic criteria for exclusion as well as for inclusion to verify the existence of a discrete group.

A more recent discussion by Frances (1980) claims that borderline personality disorder is most unclear with respect to what it borders on, especially since schizotypal and cyclothymic disorders occupy the borders of schizophrenia and affective disorders. The misfortune of the word itself is evident in its implied commonsense meaning, rather than its technical sense to the clinician. He notes that *descriptively* the term "borderline" has been used to define a symptomatic picture similar to unstable personalities while *psychodynamically* it is used to define an inferred level of personality organization, and that, in addition, it is sometimes used as a tacit rating of impairment and severity. The latter fact draws attention to the use of the term as a *dimension* rather than as a *category*. He suggests that the syndrome might have been more categorical and precise had the criteria included that such patients have displayed transient but self-limited deficits in reality testing. So much for the concept of borderline personality in adults.

THE BORDERLINE SYNDROME IN CHILDHOOD

An old psychiatric "saw" is that when one has difficulties in adult diagnosis, one should anticipate even greater difficulties for similar dispositions in childhood. This anticipation of problems is sometimes true, but, at times, clearly designated distinctive disorders of childhood do not show up in as distinctive an adult form. Without apology, I would suggest that there is no way to discuss the borderline conditions without discussing the diagnosis of childhood schizophrenia. This notion mimics our prior historical review of adult schizophrenia in relation to the adult borderline condition.

While descriptions of schizophrenia in childhood were in the literature prior to 1942, Bender's (1942) seminal article of that year describing it as a biological disorder with varying clinical behaviors had an overriding impact on a generation of child psychiatrists. She described childhood schizophrenia as an encephalopathy expressed at all levels of outflow of the central nervous system, including vegetative, motor, perceptual, affective, and cognitive channels. Moreover, the deficits in functioning were ascribed to a disorder in timing of development, and defect was not to be found in the cytoarchitecture of the brain, given the available techniques. The biological tendency to disorganizing anxiety provided a fulcrum for psychosocial deviance. Bender saw schizophrenia as a disease concept discontinuous from neuroses rather than as a syndrome description (Kanner's early infantile autism, for example). Phenomenologically, the disorder would be available to view in varied clinical pictures that changed in accordance with the child's developmental status. This left open the possibility for the concept of a "core disorder" as well as a disposition towards schizophrenia on biological grounds, without clear clinical manifestations being evident all the time. The notion of schizophrenia without psychosis was no problem for child psychiatrists of Bender's persuasion.

Her biological orientation was met with enthusiasm by some and skepticism from others—she also left open the possibility for further evidence to be discovered in the biodevelopmental integrative system as new techniques were developed. Fish (1957, 1978), who worked with Bender initially and then on her own, took up Bender's vantage, examining the integration and sequencing of neuromotor and sleep/wake patterns in infants as observable windows to CNS integration and using such observations as a means of predicting later onset of childhood schizophrenia in high-risk and genetically loaded populations. Shapiro (1969, 1970, 1972, 1974a,b, 1976, 1977a,b) tracked language behavior in young severely disordered children in order to achieve a similar window during the two- to six-year-old period. Goldfarb (1961, 1974a, 1974b) took a course which resulted in splitting the disorder into those who had organic (O) and nonorganic (NO) features. His idea was that, in the multi-etiological pool of influence, children might have heavier loading on either biological or experiential sides with similar results. This distinction was already in the air as an implied feature of Bender's vantage point.

Having set this concept of a core disorder or disease in motion, child psychiatrists became accustomed to the possibility that psychosis in childhood might appear without secondary symptoms. They thus followed more closely the model outlined by Bleuler, invoking the notion that whatever piloted development provided disharmonies in behavior that could be witnessed clinically at both organismic and person levels.

On the other hand, some psychoanalytic dynamic psychiatrists early on disclaimed the possibility of schizophrenia in childhood (see Katan, 1950). Many now feel that that view was based on a misreading of Freud's emphasis on the importance of bisexual conflict in the Schreber case generalized too broadly to all psychoses. From a more practical vantage based on direct clinical contact, David Beres, a psychoanalyst and former pediatrician, was instrumental in bringing to the analytic community the fact that one did see psychotic children. He worked at a residential center for children, many of whom had been seen earlier by Bender in New York. Beres (1956) suggested that instead of using the diagnosis of childhood schizophrenia, it might be more valid and therapeutically instructive to look at the varying ego functions that were affected during the acute psychotic phase. The task then was to determine how rapidly the affected functions changed, how evanescent they were, and how embedded they were in the defects in the child's adaptive style. This approach would provide a better picture of the child's overall functioning on a dimensional scale rather than as a categorical diagnosis. Beres proposed a functional assessment which had therapeutic and educational prognostic value, guaranteeing also that children were not prematurely labelled. He also provided a possibility that clinicians might look at the field of forces which affect ego reality functioning on a temporary basis rather than as a permanent impairment or disposition. Esman (1960), concurring with Beres, suggested the more general term "childhood psychosis" rather than the discrete entities being touted. Beres also rejected the idea that the disorders of childhood were necessarily continuous with adult schizophrenia on the grounds that some of the severe regressions and deviations seen were temporary.

Bender clearly opposed the new dimensional approach because she claimed that the extent of the pathology seen was not understandable except as an expression of more severe biological deviance. She consequently sought continuity with adult schizophrenia and her own follow-up studies (1942) confirmed the evolution of disorder into adolescence and adulthood, as did others.

The interplay between Bender's view and that of a psychoanalyst who saw severely disordered children is not idle history. The onset of interest and curiosity in the borderline syndrome in childhood rests very heavily on dynamically oriented psychoanalytic structural models of deviant personality and has to be seen in the context of the interplay between academic child psychiatry and psychoanalytic approaches. Indeed, most of the early papers concerning borderline children are dynamic rather than descriptive statements. (I discuss the reasons for this later.)

The most direct route to the concept of borderline disorder in children derives from both Bender and Beres in the work of Annemarie Weil (1970) who bridges the disparate views. Dr. Weil worked with and studied Bender and Fish. They also were significantly concerned with Weil's clinical work. In addition, Weil is a psychoanalyst and devoted to psychoanalytic models and treatment. She took seriously the notion of biological incursions on ego development and proposed the concept of a "basic core." She advanced the proposition that such an abstract core could be damaged and not foster the integration of new stimuli into coherent and well-timed adaptive functions (Weil, 1970). Her interest in Bender's biological propositions and her experience with children who were moderately to severely disordered turned her away from naive environmental determinism. Instead, she proposed both biological vulnerability and difficulties in the child's attunement to his or her mother's ministrations. Her view allowed for an integration of Mahler and

Bender and also permitted consideration of temperamental style (Chess et al., 1963).

One of the earliest statements from a psychoanalyst about borderline children per se was made by Elisabeth Geleerd (1958), who also had experience with psychosis of childhood and was significantly influenced by Beata Rank, Annemarie Weil, and Margaret Mahler. She gave extensive credit to Mahler's 1949 discussion of clinical studies in benign and malignant cases of childhood psychosis. Themes of body ego and withdrawal to inner states of apathy and stupor where confident expectation of rescue and relief are given up were repeated by Geleerd. Mahler (1949) designated both autistic and symbiotic psychoses and described the desperate clinging of the symbiotically psychotic child. But she also described a *third group*, characterized by a more benign picture, with low tolerance for frustration and poor emotional differentiation from their mothers, who are beset by a series of neurotic-like defense mechanisms. High anxiety is a feature of these cases as well as disturbances in a number of central functional areas. (One can only speculate whether these were cases similar to Bender's nonpsychotic phase of childhood schizophrenia.) Geleerd classified her cases showing features described as *borderline* in accord with other publications about adults at the time. She stressed the maintenance of the fantasy of omnipotence as a central dynamic cause of the psychological and behavioral manifestations of this disorder and ascribed *specialness* to the anxiety, describing it as discontinuous from neurotic anxiety, much as Bender had.

Following Geleerd's observations, Rosenfeld and Sprince (1963, 1965) attempted to formulate the borderline concept more comprehensively. They stated: "We have noticed a very wide divergence in the use of the concept borderline even among those of us with similar training and approach." (1963, p. 605) They then outlined four central themes: (1) bisexual conflict is always present but is not central; (2) faulty ego apparatuses should be evident early in life; (3) anxiety is characterized by primitive feelings of disintegration; and (4) there is precarious maintenance of object cathexis and easy slippage of such cathexes into identifications. (p. 634) Their case descriptions shade over significantly into characteristics that other investigators might consider to be within the spectrum of childhood schizophrenia. Indeed, acute, excessive, and seemingly illogical anxiety is the sixth criterion in the childhood schizophrenic syndrome according to British Working Party criteria modeled after Bender's original contribution. Moreover, hallucinations and delusions were also present in some cases described by the psychoanalytic authors.

Perhaps the most careful descriptive material available on childhood borderline disturbances was provided by Pine (1974). In this earlier paper and a later presentation at the meeting of the Tufts University Symposium in Boston (printed in this volume), he elaborated his generalizations gleaned from years of clinical experience. He would describe the borderline condition, like the group of schizophrenias, as "borderline conditions." His aim, he suggested, was to identify the larger *developmental* and *pathological commonalities* as a *class of disorders* with *subclasses* which were *neither psychotic nor nonpsychotic,* i.e. neurotic. (Italics his.) The failures to be noted are (1) in achieving an appropriate level in developmental lines; (2) major ego-function deficits; and (3) object-relations problems. As in Rosenfeld and Sprince's case reports his descriptions include a variety of children, some of whom have suffered many environmental stresses, a number of whom have a tendency towards splitting, and some of whom have hallucinatory experiences. The generalization is offered that they are *stable in their instability,* and that notion is the hallmark of his discussion.

Paulina Kernberg (unpublished manuscript) has also tried to outline the clinical features of these disorders. Aware of the problems that accrue from mixing theoretical frames, she assumes a common psychoanalytic framework and prior work with severely regressed young patients as well as a commitment to investigation. Her criteria include having multiple neurotic symptoms; out-of-phase persistence and liability of symptoms; an incapacity to anticipate gratification; and poorly established object constancy. Worries about the bodily self are prominent, with fears of disintegration and annihilation with the need to be hooked to mother for survival. Fears of merging, anxiety, and rage attacks are associated with significant deficits in ego function. A wide array of children with a variety of organic-like symptoms and even diagnoses of ADD and perceptual difficulties are included. Kernberg echoes Geleerd, stating that the reality span is brief and that there are nonspecific ego deficits, poor impulse control, and poor frustration and anxiety tolerance. Omnipotent projections, splitting, denial, and ego regression accompanied by shifting ego states characterize the defensive strategies inferred from behavior.

On a dynamic level, psychoanalysts project a genetic anlage for the borderline syndrome within Mahler's separation-individuation process, designating the rapprochment crisis as the crucial period. During that phase of development, the child is said to suffer a weakened integration of good and bad images. The tendency to maintain split representations leads to a poor protective barrier for the affects anxiety and rage. Lack of basic trust and constitutional defects that interfere with normal integration lead to a clinical picture of sensory difficulties, attention deficits, and so forth, all of which may also aid in perpetuating splitting.

Masterson (1972), who has worked with adolescents extensively, also utilizes a Mahlerian framework to understand the problems of borderlines. His central idea includes the proposition that the parents of his patients are also borderline—a finding which has not as yet been replicated by others. His therapeutic maneuvers follow directly from his developmental propositions, and his attempts to readapt the children without confusing interactions with their families as an initial therapeutic approach are consonant with his formulations.

Edward Shapiro (1978) has reviewed the developmental and family issues of the adult borderline patient with appropriate consideration of the dangers in extrapolating from adult report and family data to infantile circumstance. He nonetheless ventures to elaborate on developmental failures as described by Kernberg with the claim that they occur after self-object differentiation but prior to the development of object constancy. Such formulations, he believes, are heuristic to work with adult borderlines.

The reader should be aware at this juncture, and in reviewing the literature on borderline conditions in childhood (including the recent description in the *Handbook of Child Psychiatry,* 1979), that this is a new and young field of inquiry. All of the papers are clinical case descriptions that include recognizable children but present all the problems of case reports. The cards are stacked in line with the observer's vision of the message to be delivered. Each presentation attempts to clarify the picture, but the investigator also wishes to make a clinical point. The method is time-honored but hazardous unless a next step can be planned to lend veridical strength to good clinical observation. No recorded systematic studies have addressed the following issues. (1) There are no attempts to achieve simple systematic descriptive clarity, as in the recent adult literature. Exclusion criteria are broad and not as well spelled out as inclusion criteria. (2) Symptom-by-symptom analysis does not lead to clear and distinct groups—e.g., some writers insist that there be no secondary symptoms, such as hallucinations, while others permit the inclusion of hallucinatory experiences. (3) There is a major mix in frame of reference in the collective writing, with a predominating emphasis on dynamic formulations geared to the very important role of dynamic therapy with such children. However, some formulations resemble Freud's attempt at a genetic nosology (e.g., anal character), this time with emphasis on a Mahlerian genetic theory. (4) As of this writing, there are but few follow-up studies of children who have been designated as borderline.

Reports from Denmark by Dahl (1976), and Aarkrog (1977) and Wergeland (1979) from Norway are somewhat confusing because their reporting categories do not correspond exactly with those used in the United States. Both groups use the diagnosis *borderline* to mean *borderline psychosis,* and their groupings suggest less severe variants of pervasive development disorder. Wergeland's report of 29 children, five to twenty years of age following discharge from hospital, suggests that psychotherapy is useful, but no useful prognostic criteria were found to suggest continuity of form in later life. Thus we cannot at current writing say that children designated as borderline in childhood are destined to emerge with a similar condition in adulthood. We are reminded of the intramural battle that has been waged around the issue of whether childhood schizophrenia leads to adult schizophrenia, and, if not, what does the designation point to that is discreet and meaningful? It has been omitted from DSM-III largely on such descriptive and follow-up grounds. Moreover, most investigators who are interested in borderline conditons in childhood are also skittish about the notion of schizophrenia in childhood.

Designation of children by analogy to adult diagnoses ought to be considered a poor way of classifying. That the child is a relatively unformed organism and a person still in developmental flux places difficulties in the path of accurate, reliable diagnosis that will withstand time and maturation. From a descriptive standpoint, we have become more certain that while temperamental styles do persist, other evidence also indicates that environments affect expression of disorder and handicap and influence emerging clinical pictures. For this reason, among others, multi-axial approaches have been adopted. However, we can be sure that the more seriously disordered children who appear at clinic very early are likely to have the worst prognosis. The clinical manifestation, however, may change as development proceeds. On the other hand, children in middle childhood and early adolescence where borderlines have begun to be identified may be subject also to acute stress that may lead to temporary decompensations that descriptively fit borderline criteria without the hypothesized substructure. One may note in this argument similarities to Beres' position versus Bender's argument that children who break down are different from more resilient children. However, applying Weil's criterion of a core factor or Mahler's regression-progression ratio as standards for the borderline condition would help us to invoke both biological and developmental postulates. This moves us to a dynamic viewpoint that postulates capacity to maintain an internal object and attain and maintain an adaptive level.

As the reader must by now recognize, each frame of reference has its own etiologic presuppositions: one suggests an innate thrust; the other suggests that that innate thrust may in some way be influenced by interactional variables with mother or other caretakers. The notion of ego stability despite varying contexts at each stage is something that may be considered too, but it is a psychoanalytic proposition that merely paraphrases the person's capacity to keep an even keel, despite strong winds of fortune or misfortune. While useful for therapeutic judgments, the inferences are not as useful for reliable and valid diagnostic categorization of disorder or disease, and without age-stage norms for various behaviors and tendencies toward regression, we become uncertain about variants on the normal versus pathology.

From analogy to borderline features in adults, one might look toward establishing descriptive criteria along the following dimensions in childhood: (1) depression-loneliness; (2) stability-instability; (3) problems with core identity; (4) variable work-school history; and (5) unstable inner relation to object. However, even if one found evidence of the symptoms or constellations suggested, would they be discriminating and exclusive? School reluctance also includes a clinging relation to mother because of problematic object status, difficulties with stable identity, and work inhibitions. However, we do not use this as a nosological entity anymore, although perhaps those children parcel out into a few borderlines. Childhood depression, a newly defined area in childhood, might also appear as a variant on the themes mentioned. Even the notion of "early adolescent identity diffusion" might include loneliness and depression, a poor identity core, instability in relation to the next developmental step, and work inhibition. Children with attention-deficit disorders also show unstable and impulsive behavior, often feel depressed and lonely, and have work difficulties. There are recent suggestions that borderlines were earlier diagnosed as ADD. Moreover, childhood schizophrenia, as formerly described, might have all of the features mentioned, with or without Schneiderian secondary symptoms. Whether DSM-IV will reintroduce that disorder remains moot.

Child psychiatrists should consider other disadvantages accruing to the designation of childhood borderline conditions. One might echo Rich's concern about the adult diagnosis: diagnosis of any variety provides a false sense of safety in having a name that then precludes treatment and educational interventions that advance development and even cure. A childhood schizophrenic, for example, misdiagnosed as a borderline child might be deprived of pharmacotherapy that might help in his or her adaptation. Research might be impeded if diagnostic lines were drawn on inadequate criteria. It seems to me that premature closure could be brought to issues pertaining to the often-asked query, "Borderline to what?" While we would like to recognize the manifestations of the adult disorder earlier in life, the usual rules of description and dynamic and genetic formulations must be considered. We also have to decide how we wish to build our nomenclature and whether it will be research significant or clinically significant. The current adoption of DSM-III does direct us away from dynamic-structural propositions, but it should not prevent those who wish to test such notions by empirical methods from doing so. The forces within child psychiatry that lean toward descriptive clarity do not restrict the use of empirical studies that would test and validate dynamic propositions, were the effort to be expended by analysts.

CONCLUSIONS

The general objections to the concept of borderline disorders in childhood rest on the fact that data are currently inadequate to designate a discreet diagnostic entity. Moreover, it would be advisable to seek a better term for the disorder unless we believe very strongly, despite this inadequate data, that this new disorder represents a continuity with the *adult borderline personality disorder*. One will also have to determine how exclusive a group is to be so constituted.

William James suggested that to be a difference, a difference has to make a difference. In a similar mood, I would suggest that therapeutic goals, dynamic understanding, etiological discoveries, and descriptive clarity all have different aims. Insofar as they overlap in the medical model, we should be pleased, but those working with children who have some characteristics of borderline disorder ought to be considering empirical studies that will lead to elaboration and validation. At the same time, clinicians require guideposts in diagnostic clarity to maintain a balance between optimism and pessimism towards their patients and their patients' families. They also have to make distinctions that will direct their therapeutic efforts, appropriately and in accord with what is known thus far.

R E F E R E N C E S

Aarkrog, T. Borderline and psychotic adolescents: Borderline symptomatology from childhood—actual therapeutic approach. *Journal of Youth and Adolescence,* 1977, *6* (2).

Bender, L. Childhood schizophrenia. *Nervous Child,* 1942, *1,* 138–140.

Beres, D. Ego deviation and the concept of schizophrenia. *The Psychoanalytic Study of the Child.* 1956, *101,* 164–235.

Cantwell, D. The diagnostic process and diagnostic classification in child psychiatry—DSM III. Introduction, *Journal of the American Academy of Child Psychiatry,* 1980, *19* (3), 345–355.

Chess, S., Thomas, A., Birch, H., Hertzig, M., & Korn, S. Behavioral individuality in early childhood. New York: New York University Press, 1963.

Dahl, V. A follow-up study of a child psychiatric clientele with special regard to the diagnosis of psychosis. *Acta Psychiatric Scandanavica,* 1976, *54,* 106–112.

Esman, A. Childhood psychosis and "childhood schizophrenia." *The American Journal of Orthopsychiatry,* 1960, *30,* (2), 391–396.

Fish, B. The detection of schizophrenia in infancy: A preliminary report. *Journal of Nervous and Mental Disease,* 1957, *125,* 1–24.

Fish, B. Neurologic antecedents of schizophrenia in children. Part 8. Childhood psychosis. In S. Chess and A. Thomas (Eds.), *Annual progress in child psychiatry and child development.* New York: Brunner/Mazel, 1978.

Frances, A. The DSM III personality disorders section: A commentary. *American Journal of Psychiatry,* 1980, *137* (9), 1050–1054.

Freedman, A.M., & Bender, L. When the childhood schizophrenic grows up. *American Journal of Orthopsychiatry,* 1957, *27* (3).

Frosch, J.A specific problem in nosology: The psychotic character disorder. *Journal of the American Psychoanalytic Association,* 1960, *8* (1–4), 544–551.

Geleerd, E.R. Borderline states in childhood and adolescence. *Journal of the American Psychoanalytic Association,* 1958, *2,* 279–295.

Goldfarb, W. *Childhood schizophrenia.* Cambridge, Mass.: Harvard University Press, 1961.

Goldfarb, W. *Growth and change of schizophrenic children: A longitudinal study.* Washington, D.C.: V.H. Winston & Sons, 1974.

Grinker, R.R., Sr., Werble, B., & Drye, R.C. *The borderline syndrome.* New York: Basic Books, 1968.

Gunderson, J.G. Characteristics of borderline. In P. Hartocollis (Ed.), *Borderline personality disorders: The concept, the syndrome, the patient.* New York: International Universities Press, 1977.

Hoch, P.H., & Polatin, P. Pseudoneurotic forms of schizophrenia. *Psychiatric Quarterly,* 1949, *23,* 248–276.

Katan, M. Structural aspects of a case of schizophrenia. *The Psychoanalytic Study of the Child,* 1950, *5,* 175–211.

Kernberg, O. The structural diagnosis of borderline personality organization. In P. Hartocollis (Ed.), *Borderline personality disorders: The concept, the syndrome, the patient.* New York: International Universities Press, 1977a.

Kernberg, O. Structural change and its impediments. In P. Hartocollis (Ed.), *Borderline personality disorders: The concept, the syndrome, the patient.* New York: International Universities Press, 1977b.

Kernberg, P. Borderline children. Unpublished manuscript.

Kety, S.S., Rosenthal, D., & Wender, P.H., et al. Mental illness in the biological and adaptive families of adopted schizophrenics. *American Journal of Psychiatry,* 1971a, *128,* 302–306.

Kety, S.S., Rosenthal, D., & Wender, P.H. The adopted way of offspring of schizophrenics. *American Journal of Psychiatry,* 1971b, *128,* 307–311.

Klein, D. Psychopharmacology and the borderline patients. In J.E. Mack (Ed.), *Borderline states in psychiatry.* New York: Grune & Stratton, 1975.

Lidz, T. *The person, his development throughout the life cycle.* New York: Basic Books, 1968.

Mahler, M., Ross, J.R., Jr., & DeFries, Z. Clinical studies in benign and malignant cases of childhood psychosis. *American Journal of Orthopsychiatry,* 1949, *19,* 295–305.

Mahler, M.S., & Gosliner, B.J. Symbiotic child psychoses: Genetic dynamic and restituted aspects. *The Psychoanalytic Study of the Child,* 1955, *10,* 00–00.

Masterson, J. *Treatment of the borderline adolescent: A developmental approach.* New York: Wiley, 1972.

Meehl, P.E. Schizotaxia, schizotypy, schizophrenia. *American Psychologist,* 1962, *17* (12), 827–838.

Pine, F. On the concept "borderline" in children: A clinical essay. *The Psychoanalytic Study of the Child,* 1974, *29,* 341–368.

Pine, F. The borderline disturbance of childhood: Developmental diagnosis and therapeutic perspectives. Presented at Tufts University School of Medicine Symposium: The Borderline Child, Nov. 9, 1979. See also Chap. 4, this volume.

Rich, C.L. Borderline diagnoses. *The American Journal of Psychiatry,* 1978, *135* (11), 1399–1401.

Rosenfeld, S.K., & Sprince, M.P. An attempt to formulate the meaning of the concept "borderline." *The Psychoanalytic Study of the Child,* 1963, *18,* 603–635.

Rosenfeld, S.K., & Sprince, M.P. Some thoughts on the technical handling of borderline children. *The Psychoanalytic Study of the Child,* 1965, *20,* 495–516.

Schizophrenic syndrome in childhood. Progress report of a working party (April 1961). *Cerebral Palsy Bulletin*, 1961, *3* (5), 501–504.

Shapiro, T. Language behavior as a prognostic indicator in schizophrenic children under 42 months. *Infant Psychiatry*, 220–226. New Haven: Yale University Press, 1976.

Shapiro, T. The quest for a linguistic model to study the speech of autistic children. *Journal of the American Academy of Child Psychiatry*, 1977a, *16* (4), 608–619.

Shapiro, T. The speech act: A linguistic frame of reference to study ego adaptation of a psychotic child. In N. Freedman & S. Grand (Eds.), *Communicative structures and psychic structures*. New York: Plenum, 1977b.

Shapiro, E.R. The psychodynamics and developmental psychology of the borderline patient: A review of the literature. *The American Journal of Psychiatry*, 1978, *135* (11), 1305–1315.

Shapiro, T., Chiarandini, I., & Fish, B. Thirty severely disturbed children: Evaluation of their language development for classification and prognosis. *Archives of General Psychiatry*, 1974a, *30*, 819–825.

Shapiro, T., & Fish, B. A method to study language deviation as an aspect of ego organization in young schizophrenic children. *Journal of the American Academy of Child Psychiatry*, 1969, *8*, 36–56.

Shapiro, T., Fish, B., & Ginsberg, G. The speech of a schizophrenic child from 2–6. *American Journal of Psychiatry*, 1972, *128*, 1408–1413.

Shapiro, T., Huebner, H., & Campbell, M. Language behavior and hierarchic integration in a psychotic child. *Journal of Autism & Childhood Schizophrenia*, 1974b, *4*, 71–90.

Shapiro, T., & Lucy, P. Echoing in autistic children: A chronometric study of semantic processing. *Journal of Child Psychology/Psychiatry*, 1977, *19*, 373–378.

Shapiro, T., Roberts, A., & Fish, B. Imitation and echoing in young schizophrenic children. *Journal of the American Academy of Child Psychiatry*, 1970, *9*, 548–567.

Singer, M.T., & Wynne, L.C. Thought disorder and family relations of schizophrenics: Results and implications. *Archives of General Psychiatry*, 1965, *12*, 201–212.

Spitzer, R.L., Endicott, J., & Gibbon, M. Crossing the border into borderline personality and borderline schizophrenia. *Archives of General Psychiatry*, 1979, *36*, 17–24.

Stone, M.H. *The borderline syndromes: Constitution, Personality, and Adaptation*. New York: McGraw-Hill, 1980.

Weil, A.P. The basic core. *The Psychoanalytic Study of the Child*, 1970, *25*, 442–460.

Wergeland, H. A follow-up study of 29 borderline psychotic children 5 to 20 years after discharge. *Acta Psychiatrica Scandinavica*, 1979, *60*, 465–476.

Zilboorg, G. Further observation on ambulatory schizophrenia. *American Journal of Orthopsychiatry*, 1957, *27*, 667–682.

CHAPTER 2

Borderline Syndromes in Childhood:
A Critical Review

Ricardo M. Vela, M.D.
CHIEF PHYSICIAN
CHILD AND ADOLESCENT SERVICES
BRONX LEBANON HOSPITAL CENTER
ASSISTANT CLINICAL PROFESSOR
ALBERT EINSTEIN COLLEGE OF MEDICINE

Esther H. Gottlieb, M.D.
HENRY ITTLESON CENTER FOR CHILD RESEARCH
RIVERDALE, NEW YORK

Howard P. Gottlieb, M.D.
DIRECTOR, EARLY CHILDHOOD PROGRAM AND
ASSOCIATE CHIEF PHYSICIAN, CHILD AND ADOLESCENT PROGRAM
BRONX LEBANON HOSPITAL CENTER
ASSISTANT CLINICAL PROFESSOR
ALBERT EINSTEIN COLLEGE OF MEDICINE

INTRODUCTION

DURING THE LAST THIRTY YEARS, a considerable amount of literature on borderline disorders has been published. Following Robert Knight's 1953 paper on borderline states, many authors have expanded on the diagnosis of borderline disorders in adults. Concomitantly, after Weil's 1953 publication describing children with severe ego-development disturbances, many authors have expanded on the diagnostic, psychodynamic, and psychotherapeutic issues presented by children with borderline disorders.

This chapter discusses diagnostic issues as they pertain to borderline conditions in childhood. There are a variety of opinions regarding the definition and nature of these disorders. Some clinicians believe that the syndrome is synonymous with borderline personality disorder, while others see it as a continuous spectrum going from neurotic to psychotic disorders. Still others feel that it is a useless concept of questionable value. That the term "borderline" as applied to children represents a meaningful category is unclear. If it does, what does it imply in terms of etiology, treatment, and prognosis?

Diagnostic criteria for adults with "borderline personality disorder" have been defined and incorporated into the recently published DSM-III, and the disorder has been recognized as a valid psychiatric entity. Although the DSM-III stipulates that any appropriate adult diagnosis can be used for diagnosing a child, some of the listed items may not be appropriate for children under twelve years of age (e.g., spending, sex, gambling, shoplifting, long-term goals, career choice). In addition, borderline personality disorder in adults may not be continuous with borderline conditions in children. When one looks up "borderline child" in the DSM-III index, reference is made to schizotypal personality disorder, but the rationale for this is not clear. The other DSM-III diagnosis that might be significant is childhood-onset pervasive developmental disorder. The diagnostic criteria for this disorder identify only some aspects of borderline conditions in childhood. Many items, such as resistance to change in the environment, oddities of motor development, abnormalities of speech, and self-mutilation, seem to be absent in the great majority of children with borderline disorders.

The literature on borderline conditions in childhood focuses primarily on therapeutic, theoretical, and psychodynamic considerations. The clinical usefulness of the concept has not been systematically examined. In fact, one must wonder if the various authors are using the term in the same way.

32

DIAGNOSTIC ISSUES

No doubt exists in general medicine that a diagnosis, as accurate as possible, is required for adequate treatment of an illness. Ideally, a diagnosis should imply information about the etiology, the prognosis, and the appropriate treatment of the illness. Even in medicine many diagnostic categories fall short of this ideal, but in psychiatry the ideal is approached less often and the situation is more complicated.

Some clinicians doubt the applicability of the medical model to mental or interpersonal problems, and the categorization of mental illness as a disease state has been questioned (Szasz, 1961). Further, the problems encountered in psychiatry are more complex than those disorders categorized in general medicine. The interaction between a person and his social as well as his physical environment must be considered in order to assess the problem, its causes, and complicating factors. Research is more difficult in psychiatry because of the need to control variables and the intangibility of many theoretical formulations.

Although the medical model cannot be applied rigidly in psychiatry, it forms the basis for an organized approach to the classification and management of psychiatric problems. As pointed out by Spitzer and Wilson (1975), even when it works poorly, the medical model should not be abandoned unless some other model works more effectively in organizing information and phenomena.

Several researchers have addressed the problems of classification in child psychiatry (Rutter, 1965, 1977; Rutter et al., 1975; Cromwell et al., 1975; Spitzer & Cantwell, 1980), and the following points have emerged.

First, as Rutter (1965, 1975) points out, a diagnostic classification should be based on observable facts, not concepts, and symptomatology should be described operationally. One difficulty encountered in reviewing the literature on borderline conditions in children is the absence of descriptions of the child's actual behavior. As a consequence, observed symptoms tend to be reported as inferred metapsychological formulations. For example, an author may use the term "primary identification" (Ekstein & Wallerstein, 1954) without describing how the child imitates the behavior of another person, or the term "shifting levels of ego organization" (Pine, 1974) without describing what direct observations led to the formulation. These formulations may be useless to psychiatrists of nonpsychoanalytic orientation.

Second, face validity must be established. As defined by Spitzer and Williams (1980) and Spitzer and Cantwell (1980), face validity is the first step toward identifying a diagnostic category. It refers to the extent to which experts agree on the identification of a particular disorder. This consensus has not been established for borderline conditions in children, but, we hypothesize, it can be obtained from the literature.

Third, the diagnostic category must be reliable. This refers to the extent to which different clinicians can agree on diagnoses as applied to a series of cases (Spitzer & Williams, 1980; Rutter et al, 1975; Cromwell et al, 1975; Rutter, 1977). The problem here is that adequate reliability studies cannot be undertaken before the use of the term "borderline" is operationally defined and agreed upon by clinicians.

Fourth, any diagnosis ideally should also have descriptive and predictive validity. It should differ from other categories in etiology, symptomatology, prognosis, and response to treatment. The present lack of diagnostic criteria precludes the establishment of these kinds of validity for borderline conditions in childhood.

Fifth, in addition to the establishment of reliability and validity, there should be logical consistency, that is, the diagnostic decision rules for making identification should be stated clearly, precisely, and explicitly (Cromwell et al., 1975). No such rules exist for the diagnosis of borderline conditions in children.

Finally, the process of making the diagnosis of borderline conditions in children must be practicable in ordinary clinical practice (Rutter et al., 1975; Rutter, 1977). It is clear from the literature that many of the symptoms described in children with borderline conditions were obtained after long periods of intensive psychotherapy. As pointed out by Kanner (1948), psychoanalytic diagnosis, in contrast to medical diagnosis, depends on inferred complex mechanisms which emerge during the course of analysis. It does not constitute a step between examination and treatment. Although long-term involvement with the child should be helpful in clarifying the diagnosis, symptoms should ideally be obtainable from clinical interviews with the parents and the child, complemented by information from teachers and other sources, and should offer the best basis for making the diagnosis. The problem here is that children with borderline disorders manifest a wide variety of unusual behavioral symptoms that are often difficult for lay persons to describe, especially if questions are not addressed specifically enough.

A review of a number of classification systems in child psychiatry (Beller, 1962; Brown et al., 1937; Cameron, 1955; Chess, 1969; Group for the Advancement of Psychiatry, 1966; Henderson & Gillespie, 1932; Kanner, 1948; Pearson, 1936; Rutter, 1965, 1977; Rutter et al., 1975; Settlage, 1964; Strecker & Ebaugh, 1931) show that only Beller (1962) includes the diagnosis of "borderline disturbance" in children. Drawing material mostly from Geleerd, Weil, and Mahler, Beller describes these children as having low frustration tolerance, withdrawing into fantasy at the slightest provocation, displaying uneven function and development, having severe temper tantrums with loss of contact with reality, and showing infantile fantasies of omnipotence. In addition, such children exhibit uncontrollable impulsivity, mood swings, tenuous relationships, poor judgment, and "all kinds of neurotic traits." Beller differentiates children with borderline conditions from those with childhood psychosis by their ability to remain in contact with reality, to function more effectively, and to regress less.

BORDERLINE CONDITIONS IN ADULTHOOD, ADOLESCENCE, AND CHILDHOOD

Confusion about the use of the term "borderline" has plagued both adult and child psychiatry. Although a great deal has recently been written about its application to adults and some clarification of the issues has been achieved with the advent of DSM-III, the meaning of the term in childhood and adolescence, as well as the presence or absence of continuity of its usage in these three groups, remains unclear. As one looks at the various clinical descriptions moving from adulthood through adolescence to childhood, the "borders" of borderline become increasingly blurred, especially with regard to psychosis.

ADULTS

The history of the use of the term "borderline" as well as a plethora of diagnostic criteria have been extensively reviewed elsewhere (Stone, 1980; O. Kernberg, 1975; Schwartzberg, 1978; Perry & Klerman, 1978) and are beyond the scope of this chapter. Here we briefly review current thinking about the condition. Liebowitz (1979) distinguished four usages of the term: (1) a clinical disorder described by behavioral criteria; (2) a mild form of schizophrenia; (3) a nonspecific use which may include atypical affective disorders; and (4) a psychostructural entity. Using the St. Louis approach to diagnostic validity, Liebowitz concludes that borderline conditions are distinct from schizophrenia but require further distinction from the affective disorders.

Stone (1980) points out three ways in which borderline is currently used: (1) to describe conditions seen from the psychoanalytic perspective as midway between neurosis and psychosis; (2) to describe conditions intermediate between schizophrenia and the affective disorders; and (3) to describe a mild or latent form of schizophrenia.

Perry and Klerman (1978) compared the diagnostic criteria for borderline conditions of four authors: Knight, Grinker, Kernberg, and Gunderson and Singer. They found a lack of agreement in the various criteria: out of 104 items, 55 were noted by only one author, 36 by two, 12 by three, and 1 by all four. They suggest that the existing criteria be tested more adequately.

Finally, Spitzer et al. (1979) reviewed the literature and developed diagnostic criteria for the two major conditions the term is used to identify: borderline schizophrenia and borderline personality organization. These criteria, for which high specificity and sensitivity were demonstrated, are used in the DSM-III for the categories of schizotypal personality disorder and borderline personality disorder.

In summary, while further research needs to be done on borderline conditions, whether in the sense of borderline personality organization (Borderline Personality Disorder) or of borderline schizophrenia (Schizotypal Personality Disorder), their separation in DSM-III is a major step forward. However, as Stone (1980) and Leibowitz (1979) state, further investigation of their relationship to affective disorders is necessary.

ADOLESCENTS

Kernberg (1978) discusses the difficulties of diagnosing borderline personality organization in adolescence, pointing out that the disorganization resulting from severe neurosis in adolescence may mimic the more severely inadequate functioning of the borderline. Conversely, the borderline may be mistakenly diagnosed as a neurotic. The distinction between psychosis and borderline conditions in adolescents is difficult as well because adolescents are entering the at-risk age for schizophrenia and manic-depressive illness (Stone, 1980).

Kernberg (1978) describes borderline conditions in adolescence much as he describes borderline personality organization in adults. He lists the following criteria: (1) identity diffusion; (2) primitive defensive operations; (3) intact reality testing; (4) severe character pathology; and (5) polysymptomatic neurosis.

Masterson's (1980) concept of borderline conditions in adolescence parallels in most respects Kernberg's description of borderline personality organization in adults. Masterson describes the most common picture as one in which the adolescent is aggressively acting out. His diagnostic scheme takes five issues into account: (1) the present illness, in which severe acting out is seen as a defense against abandonment depression and which can include antisocial behavior, drinking or drug abuse, promiscuity, or acting like a hippie; (2) a precipitating environmental separation experience, obvious as in death or divorce, or more subtle, as in parental illness or depression; (3)

past history of narcissistic oral fixation, where developmental history might reveal prolonged dependency, poor frustration tolerance, poor impulse control and faulty reality testing, which could be expressed in a variety of symptoms (Masterson suggests that the clinician look for a history of trauma, such as maternal depression, between the ages of eighteen months and three years); (4) borderline symptoms in the parents themselves; (5) faulty family communication, with an emphasis on action rather than verbal communication.

Rinsley (1972) describes a heterogeneous group of patients whom he diagnoses as having symbiotic psychosis of adolescence which overlaps with Masterson's borderline group. He feels that on careful scrutiny the majority of these adolescents present with subtle or overt classical thought disorders which would point to a schizophrenic diagnosis. Rinsley's criteria are: (1) Masterson's criteria; (2) overt or latent thought disorder; and (3) a need for inpatient treatment.

Giovacchini (1978) uses "borderline" in a different sense than Masterson, Rinsley, or Kernberg. He sees the borderline state as a pathological exaggeration of the borderline characteristics of normal adolescent development and uses it to describe patients who easily regress to psychotic thinking and who have a "borderline" adjustment (unstable functioning).

CHILDREN

When we reviewed the literature on borderline conditions in childhood in an attempt to develop diagnostic criteria (see below), the limitations of current knowledge about the meaning and usefulness of this concept were strikingly evident. While a great deal has been written about the symptomatology from the psychoanalytic perspective and while there is general agreement on the idea that these children are severely disturbed, with ego deficits and disordered functioning in many areas, other aspects of its meaning have been neglected. Some authors (Frijling-Schreuder, 1969; Geleerd, 1958; Rosenfeld & Sprince, 1965; Pine, 1974) use the term to mean borderline on a psychotic-neurotic continuum, with the possibility of frank psychosis always present. Others (Chethik, 1979; Weil, 1953) view it as a precursor to severe character pathology in adulthood. For some it is a unitary concept, while some describe subgroups.

REVIEW OF FOLLOW-UP STUDIES

Most of the data on the course of borderline conditions in childhood and adolescence is anecdotal, and variable outcomes are reported. For example,

Weil (1953) reports that some of her cases developed frank psychosis, some developed "as if" personalities, and others developed severe character disorders. Prospective studies on outcome have not been published.

The available studies are flawed. Wergeland (1979) reports a follow-up study on 29 cases diagnosed as borderline at ages ranging from two to thirteen with a follow-up range of five to twenty years. Five cases remained borderline psychotic, 4 were manifestly psychotic, 6 were severely neurotic, 3 were moderately neurotic, and 11 were symptom free. The criteria for diagnosis, both when first diagnosed and later, are not clearly specified. Also age at follow-up is not related to follow-up diagnosis.

Aarkrog (1977) reviewed 100 admissions to an adolescent psychiatric unit. Fifty of the adolescents were diagnosed as borderline and 50 as psychotic. Again criteria for diagnosis are not stated. Fifty-three of these adolescents suffered from some type of psychiatric problem in childhood; 21 of the 53 had been diagnosed as borderline in childhood. The later diagnosis of these 21, whether borderline psychotic or psychotic, is not stated.

Dahl (1976) followed up 322 admissions to a child psychiatric inpatient service at twenty years and reported that 6 were originally diagnosed as borderline psychotic. At twenty years, 3 of the 6 had had no further psychiatric admissions, 2 were diagnosed as borderline schizophrenic, and one as schizoid character disorder.

What is clear from this discussion is that the relationship between borderline conditions in childhood, adolescence, and adults has not been established. Because of the different meanings of the concept, comparisons of various authors' diagnostic criteria for the conditions in adulthood, adolescence, and childhood are of limited usefulness at this point.

DIAGNOSTIC CRITERIA

In an attempt to develop operational diagnostic criteria for borderline conditions in childhood, Vela, Gottlieb, and Gottlieb (1980) reviewed the literature on borderline conditions in childhood with special attention to the description of symptoms. Eight authors were reviewed: (1) Chethik (1979); (2) Ekstein and Wallerstein (1954); (3) Frijling-Schreuder (1969); (4) Geleerd (1958); (5) Marcus (1963); (6) Pine (1974); (7) Rosenfeld and Sprince (1963); and (8) Weil (1953).

A total of seven sets of symptoms was obtained from the review of eight monographs. The monograph by Ekstein was excluded from the results because no agreement could be reached on descriptive symptomatology. Table 2-1 shows a summary of the symptoms extracted from the remaining seven authors.

Table 2-1
COMPOSITE LIST OF SYMPTOMS AND CORRELATION BETWEEN DIFFERENT AUTHORS

	CHETHIK	FRIJLING-S.	GELEERD	MARCUS	PINE	ROSENFELD	WEIL	CORRELATION	% AGREEMT.
1. Disturbed interpersonal relat.	X	X	X	X	X	X	X	7	100
2. Disturbed sense of reality	X	X	X	X	X	X	X	7	100
3. Panic anxiety	X	X	X	X	X	X	X	7	100
4. Impulsivity	X		X	X	X	X	X	6	86
5. Neurotic-like symptoms	X	X	X	X		X	X	6	86
6. Abnormal development	X	X	X	X		X	X	6	86
7. Motoric disturbances	X			X		X		3	43
8. Autoerotic/fetish		X		X			X	3	43
9. Poor judgment				X	X			2	29
10. Fluctuating functioning		X			X			2	29
11. Character traits	X							1	14
12. Feelings of loneliness		X						1	14
13. Mood swings				X				1	14
14. Hallucinations					X			1	14
15. Inappropriate/lack of affect					X			1	14
16. Inadequacies					X			1	14
17. Bizarre behavior						X		1	14
18. Bizarre language						X		1	14
19. Identity disturbance						X		1	14

Out of a total of 19 symptoms (See Table 2-1), 6 symptoms were agreed upon by six or more of the authors. Of the remaining 13 symptoms, 2 were mentioned by three authors, 1 by two authors, and the remaining 10 by only one of the authors.

The high agreement on the 6 symptoms suggests that the borderline syndrome in childhood may be a valid entity, at least on the level of face validity. The low agreement on the 13 remaining symptoms may indicate that (1) these symptoms are irrelevant; (2) some authors did not report important behaviors, yielding false negatives; (3) these may be associated symptoms; (4) there may be subgroups within the major category; or (5) nonborderline cases were included by some of the authors. Clinical application of the preliminary criteria must be done in order to answer this question.

The 6 symptoms agreed upon by at least six of the authors reviewed were designated as "consensus symptoms" and operationally defined. They are shown in Table 2-2.

Table 2-2
CONSENSUS SYMPTOMS FOR BORDERLINE CONDITIONS IN
CHILDREN

1. Disturbed interpersonal relationships characterized by the following:
    a. Behaving in a controlling, overdemanding, extremely possessive, clinging, overdependent way with adults in a relationship in which the child constantly demands to have his needs satisfied.
    b. Excessively outgoing social interactions without appropriate discrimination of the situation.
    c. Periods of being extremely withdrawn and aloof.
    d. Extreme outburst of love and hate toward the same person or exaggerated but superficial love for one parent and outbursts of hate toward the other parent.
    e. Frequent exaggerated copying of another person's behavior, e.g., imitating every action, gesture, or movement the person makes.
    f. Isolation from peers and lack of friends.
2. Disturbances in the sense of reality manifested by the following:
    a. Fantasies of being all-powerful, including not only believing them, but behaving as if they were true, e.g., the child behaves as if he were a superhero, and engages in dangerous behavior.
    b. Withdrawal into fantasy more often than would be appropriate for a child of the same age. The fantasies are too idiosyncratic, too sustained, or appear at inappropriate moments.
    c. Excessive self-absorption in pretend play to the degree that the child has difficulty differentiating play from reality, e.g., playing with toy soldiers and reacting to the other person as if the person were actually an enemy.
    d. Paranoid ideation, but not delusions, involving the belief that the child is being harrassed or unfairly treated, e.g., "The kids are always out to get me."
    e. Excessive use of magical thinking, with the fear that their thoughts will

actually come true, e.g., fearing the mother will be hurt as a result of the child's thinking it.

3. Excessive, intense anxiety manifested by the following:
   a. Chronic, constant anxiety, often diffuse and free floating which interferes in most areas of the child's functioning and which may be manifested by driven restlessness, sleeplessness, and inability to concentrate.
   b. Panic states manifested by intense anxiety reaching panic proportions which the child may verbalize as fear of body disintegration, a major catastrophe, or fear of becoming another person. These states may also be demonstrated by the child's appearing frantic, disorganized, and severely agitated, with striking facial immobility, dead still or stiffened body, mechanical movements, and disturbed and unintelligible speech.
   c. Excessive anxiety to a wide variety of stimuli or new situations. Anxiety resulting from the child perceiving the world as a dangerous place to the point that it interferes with the child's functioning.
   d. Intense fear of separation from other persons, clinging to adults for protection, and getting very anxious when contact with them is temporarily broken.

4. Excessive and severe impulsive behavior, resulting from minimal provocation or frustration, occurring in a child past the age when this behavior would be normal and characterized by the following:
   a. Repetitive, unmitigated fits of rage.
   b. Loss of control, e.g., biting others, destroying objects indiscriminately.
   c. Total unmanageability due to aggressive behavior.
   d. Loss of contact with reality during these episodes.
   e. Tantrums lasting for an hour or more.
   f. Paranoid ideation during the tantrum, e.g., the child shouts "Let go of me" when no one is touching him.

5. "Neurotic-like symptoms, e.g., rituals, somatic concerns, obsessions, multiple phobias, or intense self-imposed restrictions and inhibitions which are fleeting and interchangeable.

6. Uneven or distorted development characterized by the following:
   a. Deviant or erratic physiologic patterning, e.g., hypertonic states, erratic feeding and sleeping patterns, hypo- or hypersensitivity to stimuli, or vomiting and diarrhea without demonstrable medical cause.
   b. Apathy, never crying to show their needs, poor sucking, lack of response to mother's face for months, poor molding into mother's arms, or lack of anticipatory gesture when picked up.
   c. Excessive rubbing, rolling, or head banging.
   d. Delay in motor or language areas.

These consensus symptoms were compared with the criteria for several DSM-III diagnoses and met the criteria for separation anxiety disorder, oppositional disorder, attention deficit disorder, and schizotypal personality disorder. With the exception of schizotypal personality disorder, each of these diagnoses addresses only one aspect of the multiple dysfunction described by borderline conditions in childhood.

The DSM-III criteria for overanxious disorder, avoidant disorder, schizoid disorder of childhood and adolescence, schizophrenia, major depressive disorder, and panic disorder were not fulfilled by the consensus criteria. Although the consensus symptoms did not meet the criteria for borderline personality disorder and childhood-onset pervasive developmental disorder, there was considerable overlap with both these disorders.

According to the consensus criteria, borderline conditions fit the diagnostic criteria for schizotypal personality disorder and present with many features of borderline personality disorder and childhood-onset pervasive developmental disorder. In the case of schizotypal personality disorder, the consensus symptoms met the following criteria: magical thinking, social isolation, inadequate rapport, and paranoid ideation. For borderline personality disorder, the overlapping criteria were: unstable interpersonal relationships, inappropriate anger, intolerance of being alone, and impulsivity. The last two were met by re-interpreting the behavioral examples to apply to children. When childhood-onset pervasive developmental disorder was considered, overlap occurred in the following areas: impaired social relations, excessive anxiety, and inappropriate affect.

The overlap with these three disorders is confirmed by Petti and Law's (1980) report of a retrospective application of DSM-III criteria to the charts of 11 children diagnosed as borderline. One case fulfilled the criteria for borderline personality disorder, schizotypal personality disorder, and childhood-onset pervasive developmental disorder. Two patients fit the criteria for both schizotypal personality disorder and childhood-onset pervasive developmental disorder. Another 2 cases fulfilled the criteria for borderline personality disorder and childhood-onset pervasive developmental disorder. Three patients were diagnosed only as borderline personality disorder, and 3 only as schizotypal personality disorder.

These three disorders have multiple areas of dysfunction which in general are similar to those described in borderline conditions in children. None of these DSM-III disorders, by itself, fulfills all of the areas of dysfunction that are considered significant and defining of borderline conditions as proposed in the consensus criteria. Furthermore, any conclusions reached by comparison with DSM-III are tentative because some categories, especially those for childhood, were included on the basis of face validity only (Spitzer & Cantwell, 1980).

DIFFERENTIAL DIAGNOSIS

As described by the consensus criteria, children with borderline syndromes may present with the following symptoms: extreme anxiety, impulsive behavior, distortions in the sense of reality, disturbances in interpersonal relations, multiple neurotic-like traits, and uneven or distorted development. A child presenting with these symptoms must be evaluated to distinguish whether his pathology can best be described as a borderline condition, as a more or less severe disorder, or as the co-occurrence of a borderline condition with another disorder. The need to differentiate which diagnostic category best describes the child's areas of disturbance is not a simple labeling exercise, but one which has therapeutic and prognostic significance.

As an example, a child presenting with clinging behavior, hyperactivity, and severe temper tantrums may on evaluation be found to have multiple areas of dysfunction as in borderline conditions. Another child may present with the same symptoms but have a severe developmental language disorder as the cause of his symptomatology. The intervention one makes would be very different in these two cases, even though the presenting symptomatology is similar. A symptom alone, without an understanding of its severity, duration, and possible etiology, is meaningless.

The following DSM-III disorders are discussed as diagnoses which must be considered when a child presents with one or more of the symptoms of borderline conditions as defined by the consensus criteria: schizophrenia, borderline personality disorder, schizotypal personality disorder, childhood-onset pervasive developmental disorder, attention deficit disorder, developmental language disorder, schizoid disorder of childhood and adolescence, narcissistic personality disorder, and avoidant disorder of childhood and adolescence.

Separation anxiety disorder, oppositional disorder, overanxious disorder, obsessive-compulsive disorder, and panic states may all have specific features in common with borderline conditions in childhood, but they lack the multiple areas of disturbance, as well as the overall severity of disturbance, character-istic of borderline conditions in childhood.

Schizophrenia

When a child presents with idiosyncratic fantasies, temper tantrums during which he is out of contact with reality, and severely disturbed interpersonal relationships, the diagnosis of schizophrenia must be consid-ered. Although children with borderline conditions have a disturbed "sense" of reality, delusions, hallucinations, and thought disorders are not present. If there are psychotic symptoms, they are briefly present, with a quick return to previous functioning.

Borderline Personality Disorder

Borderline personality disorder overlaps with borderline conditions of childhood in the areas of disturbed interpersonal relationships, inappropriate anger, impulsivity, and intolerance to being alone. Clinging and separation anxiety are the childhood equivalents of intolerance to being alone. The DSM-III definition of borderline personality disorder may identify some aspects of borderline conditions in children, but it does not address the disturbed sense of reality and distorted development which seem to be important characteristics of the child with a borderline condition.

Schizotypal Personality Disorder

Magical thinking, bizarre fantasies, paranoid ideation, social isolation, and inadequate rapport in face-to-face interaction are symptoms in common between schizotypal personality disorder and borderline conditions of childhood. The level of overall disturbance in schizotypal personality disorder is similar to that described in borderline conditions of childhood, and this disorder may represent one subtype of borderline conditions. Severe impulsive behavior, panic states, multiple neurotic-like symptoms, and clinging and demanding behavior which are seen in many children with borderline conditions are not part of the criteria for schizotypal personality disorder.

Childhood-Onset Pervasive Developmental Disorder

Childhood-onset pervasive developmental disorder and borderline conditions of childhood may each present with excessive anxiety, unexplained panic attacks, constricted or inappropriate affect, unexplained rage reactions, and impaired social relationships. The overall impairment described by the DSM-III criteria for childhood-onset pervasive developmental disorder appears to be greater, and these children are described as having no inner language, imaginary play, or warm relationships. These features are absent in children with borderline conditions.

Attention Deficit Disorder

Attention deficit disorder, both with and without hyperactivity, has a number of symptoms in common with borderline conditions in childhood. The common features include restlessness, inability to concentrate, impulsivity, poor frustration tolerance, and poor peer relationships. In borderline conditions, restlessness and poor concentration are presumed to be secondary to anxiety and/or preoccupation with fantasy material. The impulsivity, poor frustration tolerance, and poor peer relationships are usually more prominent in the borderline syndrome than in attention deficit disorder. Many symptoms of borderline conditions in childhood—that is, panic anxiety, distorted sense of reality, and severely disturbed interpersonal relationships—are not described as criteria for attention deficit disorder, and this disorder addresses only some aspects of the disturbance seen in borderline conditions in childhood.

Developmental Language Disorder

Children with developmental language disorder, expressive and receptive type, may present with hyperactivity, distractibility, immaturity, aggressiveness, social withdrawal, and intense clinging relationships. These symptoms are similar to some aspects of borderline conditions. However, these disorders may co-occur, and any child who appears to have a language disorder coupled with severe behavioral symptoms should be assessed to determine if the behavioral disturbance is secondary to the language impairment or a co-occurring borderline condition.

Schizoid Disorder of Childhood and Adolescence

In schizoid disorder of childhood and adolescence, the deficit in the capacity to form social relationships does not distress the child because he or she has no desire for them. Because a child with a borderline syndrome has poor peer relationships and may be withdrawn and aloof, there appears to be some overlap. However, many of these children seek contact with others as evidenced by clinging and controlling behavior. The withdrawn and aloof child with borderline features may not be persistently withdrawn and may feel his isolation acutely. Furthermore, in borderline conditions of childhood, more areas of dysfunction exist than the criteria for schizoid disorder describe.

Narcissistic Personality Disorder

Narcissistic personality disorder describes many of the characteristic disturbances in interpersonal relationships of borderline conditions of childhood, but it does not address the other areas of dysfunction seen in borderline conditions. Common features include extreme self-centeredness and self-absorption, fantasies of being all-powerful, need for constant attention, feelings of rage if others are indifferent, overidealization and devaluation, feelings of entitlement, and lack of empathy. Narcissistic features are prominent in children with borderline conditions.

Avoidant Disorder of Childhood and Adolescence

In avoidant disorder, there is a persistent and excessive shrinking from contact with strangers coupled with poor peer relationships and clinging behavior. However, the child exhibits a desire for warm relationships and in general has good relationships within his or her family. Children with borderline conditions, on the other hand, may be withdrawn and aloof in all spheres, or inappropriately outgoing with strangers. The disturbance in interpersonal relationships seen in borderline conditions is more pervasive than the social anxiety in avoidant disorder.

CONCLUSIONS

Do borderline conditions in childhood represent a valid entity? This question remains unanswered. As Chiland and Libovici (1977) state, this diagnosis may reflect an evolving process of variable potential. Kestenbaum's (1983) experience confirms this. She reports case histories and 14- to 30-year follow-ups of seven children diagnosed as borderline, noting adult diagnoses including anxiety neurosis, schizophrenia, bipolar illness, schizotypal personality disorder, schizoid personality disorder, and sociopathic behavior.

One problem with classifying disorders on the basis of descriptive symptomatology is that varying psychopathological processes may superficially appear the same, yet have different etiologies, prognoses, and implications for treatment. Further research should include follow-up studies with the inclusion of genetic data and investigations using a behavioral rating scale to test the usefulness of the consensus criteria.

Finally, unless a relationship between borderline conditions in childhood and borderline syndromes in adulthood can be established (an unlikely event), the use of the term "borderline child" should be abandoned in order to avoid unneccessary confusion.

R E F E R E N C E S

Aarkrog, T. Borderline and psychotic adolescent: Borderline symptomatology from childhood— actual therapeutic approach. *Journal of Youth and Adolescence,* 1977, *6* (2), 187–197.

American Psychiatric Association. *Diagnostic and statistical manual of mental disorders* (DSM-III) (3d ed.). Washington, D.C.: 1980.

Beller, E.K. *Clinical process: A new approach to the organization and assessment of clinical data.* Glencoe, Ill.: The Free Press, 1962.

Brown, S., Pollock, H., Potter, H.W., & Cohen, D.W. *Outline for psychiatric classification of problem children* (Rev. ed.). Utica, N.Y.: State Hospital Press, 1937.

Cameron, K. Diagnostic categories in child psychiatry. *British Journal of Medicine and Psychology,* 1955, *28* (1), 67–71.

Chess, S. *An introduction to child psychiatry* (2d ed.). New York: Grune & Stratton, 1969.

Chethik, M. The borderline child. In J. Noshpitz, (Ed.), *Basic handbook of child psychiatry.* New York: Basic Books, 1979.

Chiland, C., & Libovici, S. Borderline or prepsychotic conditions in childhood: A French point of view, In P. Hartocollis, (Ed.), *Borderline personality disorders.* New York: International Universities Press, 1977.

Cromwell, R.L., Blashfield, R.K., & Strauss, J.S. Criterion for classification systems. In N. Hobbs (Ed.), *Issues in the classification of children.* San Francisco: Jossey-Bass, 1975.

Dahl, V. A follow-up study of a child psychiatric clientele with special regard to the diagnosis of psychosis. *Acta Psychiatrica Scandanavica,* 1976, *54,* 106–112.

Ekstein, R., & Wallerstein, J. Observations on the psychology of borderline and psychotic children. *The Psychoanalytic Study of the Child,* 1954, *11,* 303–311.

Frijling-Schreuder, E. Borderline states in children. *The Psychoanalytic Study of the Child,* 1969, *24,* 307–327.

Geleerd, E. Borderline states in childhood and adolescence, *The Psychoanalytic Study of the Child,* 1958, *13,* 279–295.

Giovacchini, P. The borderline aspects of adolescence and the borderline state. In S. Feinstein & P. Giovacchini (Eds.), *Adolescent psychiatry* (Vol.6). Chicago: University of Chicago Press, 1978.

Group for the Advancement of Psychiatry. *Psychopathological disorders in childhood.* New York: 1966. CAP report No. 62.

Henderson, D.K., & Gillespie, R.D. *A textbook of psychiatry* (3d ed.). London: Oxford University Press, 1932.

Kanner, L. *Child psychiatry* (2d ed.). Springfield, Ill.: Charles C Thomas, 1948.

Kernberg, O. *Borderline conditions and pathological narcissism.* New York: Jacob Aronson, 1975.

Kernberg, O. The diagnosis of borderline conditions in adolescence. In S. Feinstein & P. Giovacchini (Eds.), *Adolescent Psychiatry (Vol. 6).* Chicago: University of Chicago Press, 1978.

Kestenbaum, C. The concept of the borderline child as a child at-risk for major psychiatric disorder in adult life. In K.S. Robson (Ed.), *The borderline child: Approaches to etiology, diagnosis, and treatment.* New York: McGraw-Hill, 1983.

Knight, R. Borderline states. *Bulletin of the Menninger Clinic,* 1953, *17,* 1–12.

Liebowitz, M. Is borderline a distinct entity? *Schizophrenia Bulletin,* 1979, *5,* (9), 23–38.

Marcus, J. Borderline states in childhood, *Journal of Child Psychology/Psychiatry,* 1963, *4,* 207–217.

Masterson, J. *From borderline adolescent to functioning adult: The test of time.* New York: Brunner Mazel, 1980.

Pearson, G.H.J. Classification of psychological problems of children. In H.A. Christian (Ed.), *The Oxford medicine* (Vol. 7), *Psychiatry for practitioners.* New York: Oxford University Press, 1936.

Perry J., & Klerman G. The borderline patient. *Archives of General Psychiatry,* 1978, *35,* 141–150.

Petti, T., & Law, W. Borderline psychotic behavior in hospitalized children: Approaches to assessment and treatment. Paper presented at the 27th annual meeting of the American Academy of Child Psychiatry, Chicago, October, 1980.

Pine, F. On the concept "borderline" in children. *The Psychoanalytic Study of the Child,* 1974, *29,* 341–368.

Rinsley, D. A contribution to the nosology and dynamics of adolescent schizophrenia. *Psychiatric Quarterly,* 1972, *46,* 159–186.

Rosenfeld, S., & Sprince, M. An attempt to formulate the meaning of the concept "borderline." *The Psychoanalytic Study of the Child,* 1963, *18,* 603–635.

Rosenfeld, S., & Sprince, M. Some thoughts on the technical handling of borderline children. *The Psychoanalytic Study of the Child,* 1965, *20,* 495–517.

Rutter, M. Classification and categorization in child psychiatry, *Journal of Child Psychology/Psychiatry.* 1965, *6,* 71–83.

Rutter, M. Classification. In M. Rutter & L. Hersov (Eds.), *Child psychiatry.* Oxford: Blackwell Scientific Publications, 1977.

Rutter, M., Shaffer, D., & Sheperd, M. *A multiaxial classification in child psychiatric disorders.* Geneva: World Health Organization, 1975.

Schwartzberg, A. Overview of the borderline syndrome in adolescence. In S. Feinstein, & P. Giovacchini (Eds.), *Adolescent psychiatry* (Vol. 6). Chicago: University of Chicago Press, 1978.

Settlage, C. F. Psychologic disorders. In W.E. Nelson (Ed.), *Textbook of pediatrics* (8th ed.). Philadelphia: W.B. Saunders, 1964.

Spitzer, R., & Cantwell, D. The DSM III classification of the psychiatric disorders of infancy, childhood, and adolescence. *Journal of the American Academy of Child Psychiatry,* 1980, *19,* 356–370.

Spitzer R., Endicott, J., & Gibbon, M. Crossing the border into borderline personality and borderline schizophrenia. *Archives of General Psychiatry,* 1979, *36,* 17–24.

Spitzer, R. L., & Williams, J.B. Classification of mental disorders and DSM III. In H.I. Kaplan, A.M. Freedman, & B.J. Sadock, (Eds.), *Comprehensive textbook of psychiatry III.*Baltimore: Williams & Wilkins, 1980.

Spitzer, R. L., & Wilson, P. T. Classification in psychiatry, In A.M. Freedman, H.I. Kaplan, and B.J. Sadock (Eds.), *Comprehensive textbook of psychiatry II.* Baltimore: Williams & Wilkins, 1975.

Stone, M. *The borderline syndromes,* New York: McGraw-Hill, 1980.

Strecker, E. A., & Ebaugh, F. G. *Practical clinical psychiatry for students and practitioners* (3d ed.). Philadelphia: Blakiston, 1931.

Szasz, T.S. *The myth of mental illness.* New York: Harper & Row, 1961.

Vela, R., Gottlieb, H., & Gottlieb, E. Diagnostic criteria for borderline conditions in children. Paper presented at the 27th Annual Meeting of the American Academy of Child Psychiatry, Chicago, October, 1980.

Weil, A. Certain severe disturbances of ego development in childhood. *Psan. St. C.,* 1953, *8,* 271–286.

Wergeland, H. A follow-up study of 29 borderline psychotic children, *Acta Psychiatrica Scandanavica,* 1979, *60,* 465–476.

CHAPTER 3

The Borderline Child at Risk for Major Psychiatric Disorder in Adult Life: Seven Case Reports with Follow-up

Clarice J. Kestenbaum, M.D.
DIRECTOR, CHILD AND ADOLESCENT PSYCHIATRY
ST. LUKE'S ROOSEVELT HOSPITAL CENTER
ST. LUKE'S SITE
NEW YORK, NEW YORK
CLINICAL PROFESSOR OF PSYCHIATRY
COLUMBIA UNIVERSITY

INTRODUCTION

FOR THE PAST THIRTY YEARS, the concept of the borderline child has appeared in the literature as an outgrowth of diagnostic considerations about the borderline adult. Several authors reported on severely disturbed children whose symptoms did not fit neatly into neurotic or psychotic categories. Bergman and Escalona (1949) described five cases of children who demonstrated unusual visual, auditory, or tactile sensitivity, along with marked unevenness in cognitive development. They noted that the children could not tolerate change, were negativistic, had frequent rage outbursts, and were excessively vulnerable to stress.

Rudolf Ekstein (1954) used the term "schizophrenoid" to describe the case of a child with atypical development in whom there were marked, sudden fluctuations in ego states without observable cause. He commented on the quality of relatedness to the therapist which was of a tenuous nature and easily disrupted.

The term "borderline" has acquired several different meanings, usually referring to the no-man's land between neurotic and psychotic mental functioning. Vela, Gottlieb, and Gottlieb have observed that "although there is considerable literature on borderline conditions in childhood, the syndrome has not been adequately defined and distinguished from other disorders" (page 31ff., this volume). They point out, furthermore, that the focus has been primarily on theoretical, psychodynamic, and therapeutic issues; a systematic examination of the clinical usefulness of the concept has not been attempted.

In my discussion of borderline children, I shall state the conclusion, derived from clinical observations, that the diagnostic label "borderline child" embraces a heterogeneous group of overlapping syndromes that lead to a variety of psychiatric conditions in adult life.

Many authors consider borderline conditions in adulthood to be spectrum illnesses on a continuum from neurotic to psychotic. Furthermore, many believe that genetic factors are involved. In a broad review of the history of the term, Stone (1980) has demonstrated

that patients called borderline by almost any of the popular definitions appear in many instances to have a hereditary predisposition to mental illness. The suggestion of a hereditary factor is no new discovery. It was, if anything, taken for granted by the psychiatric and psychoanalytic communities until the second generation of psychoanalysts began to adopt a more linear and purely psychological model of causation. (p.7)

I would like to state the hypothesis that the seriously disturbed child who is not psychotic may be exhibiting the prodromata of a future major psychiatric disorder that may have constitutional underpinnings. It is better, in my opinion, to consider such a child as "on the way to becoming" schizophrenic for example, or manic-depressive, rather than "borderline." He or she may, of course, outgrow those symptoms and enter the normal maelstrom of life, develop antisocial features, and become involved with penal institutions, or the person may retain the borderline label as a borderline adult throughout life.

The importance of early assessment has preventive implications. If diagnoses in childhood were more precise, we might be able to identify the constitutionally vulnerable child and provide specific treatment modalities best suited to avert or ameliorate the condition. Studies of the histories of individuals who later became psychotic (including genetic data and early childhood psychopathology) have shed light on a hitherto darkened area.

HIGH-RISK RESEARCH IN SCHIZOPHRENIA

The past twenty years have produced increasing numbers of research projects which have focused attention on those individuals who have a high probability of developing a major psychiatric disorder in adult life. "These studies were subsumed under the rubric 'risk research' and have been directed toward determining which people are most vulnerable to eventual schizophrenic illness" (Kestenbaum, 1981). Various etiological models have been reviewed in the current psychiatric literature (Garmezy, 1974; Kety, 1975; Erlenmeyer-Kimling, 1968) which include psychogenic, genetic, and gene-environment interaction theories.

Erlenmeyer-Kimling (1978) has gathered evidence in support of hereditary factors which includes the following: prevalence throughout the world is 0.8–5 percent; male-female ratio is 1:1; risk figures are compatible with a genetic hypothesis, that is, that first degree relatives of schizophrenics are at greater risk of becoming schizophrenic compared to the general population— 5.5% for parents, 10% for siblings, 11% for children. (Monozygotic-twin concordance rates for twins reared apart are approximately the same as for twins reared together; they are three times as high as the concordance rates for fraternal twins.)

Watt (1972) in a follow-back study of children who were hospitalized for schizophrenia as adults found that preschizophrenic individuals displayed particular symptomatology. Boys demonstrated primary evidence of unsocialized aggression and secondary evidence of internal conflict, overinhibition, and depression. Preschizophrenic girls demonstrated primary evidence of oversensitiveness, conformity, and introversion. He proposed, moreover, three additional postdictive indices of schizophrenia which differentiated subjects from controls: (1) parental death; (2) severe organic handicap; and (3) extreme emotional instability. In a subsequent follow-up study, Waring and Ricks (1965) noted that differences between the early histories of schizophrenic parents and normal controls involved perinatal complications in 60 percent of the cases and reports of neurological dysfunction. Chronic schizophrenic patients were characterized by a family history of schizophrenia and a schizoid premorbid personality, with few close peer relationships. Ricks and Berry (1970) noted that the chronic schizophrenic has biological and social equipment which offers small margin for error in development, such as low IQ, low vocational success, and the presence of biological handicap.

RESULTS OF PROSPECTIVE-LONGITUDINAL STUDIES

In 1962, Mednick and Schulsinger (1970), using more sophisticated methodology, began a Danish longitudinal study of children of schizophrenic mothers. The investigators believed that such children demonstrated a particular vulnerability to schizophrenia which is a joint function of genetic loading and pregnancy and birth complications. This combined liability, they contend, results in an infant who demonstrates a labile pattern of autonomic responsivity. McNeil and Kaij (1978) reported significantly more obstetrical and neonatal complications in a Swedish high-risk sample. There is high agreement among investigators about the neurological soft signs noted in the offspring of schizophrenics (B. Fish, 1962; Marcus, 1974). Marcus and his co-workers in the Jerusalem Infant Development Project (1980) were able to identify a subgroup of infants born to schizophrenics who demonstrated the same dysmaturation in motor functions as well as in perceptual development.

L. Erlenmeyer-Kimling and her colleagues at the New York State Psychiatric Institute (1976) have been investigating the children of schizophrenic parents since 1971. In addition to corroboration of positive neurological findings in the index cases consistent with findings of other investigators, a study of attentional tasks has emerged which differentiates the high-risk group from the controls at early ages. The high-risk subjects scored lower on the tests of neuropsychological development as well. The same subgroup has also been found to show an increasing overlap with the subjects showing behavioral problems as they reach adolescence, a finding noted by parents, teachers, and global assessment. Erlenmeyer-Kimling and her colleagues Cornblatt and Fleiss contend that these findings support the hypothesis that attentional dysfunctions serve as early predictors of later pathology (Erlenmeyer-Kimling et al., 1979).

THE CHILD AT RISK FOR AFFECTIVE DISORDER

Recent advances in the study of individuals at risk for affective disorder demonstrate that serious forms of these disorders in childhood and adolescence not only exist but are commonly encountered (Cytryn & McKnew, 1972). Studies of children at risk for manic-depressive illness are beginning to employ the models used in studying schizophrenic risk. According to Rosenthal (1970), there is a high rate of lifetime prevalence of affective disorders in the first- and second-degree relatives of patients with primary affective disorders as compared with the general population (6–24 percent versus 1–2 percent).

A genetic hypothesis has been supported by Zerbin-Rudin (1972) in a review of six major twin studies. Overall concordance rates for monozygotic twins were consistently higher than for dizygotic twins (74 percent versus 19 percent). A study of adopted-away monozygotic twins also supports a genetic hypothesis (Mendlewicz & Rainer, 1977).

The subject of a juvenile form of manic-depressive illness and similarity or dissimilarity of symptoms occurring in childhood or adult life was explored by Anthony and Scott in a review of manic-depressive psychosis in children (1960). They concluded that manic-depressive psychosis in children is extremely rare, but that the early variety may be due to heavy genetic loading plus intense environmental experience. Such cases were often mislabeled schizophrenic, according to Carlson and Strober (1978), because of the tendency to label young patients "schizophrenic until proven otherwise" (Stone, 1971).

Feinstein and Wolpert (1973) speculated that adult manic-depressive patients may show specific and equivalent behavior in childhood "which is the precursor of the thymocyclic *[sic]* personality and depressive states of the adult, and in some cases, manifest a juvenile version of the illness." (p. 124) Another study described 13 children with a family history of bipolar manic-depressive disorder. Six of the children exhibited the following features:

1. Family history positive for bipolar illness.

2. Specific clinical symptomatology.

3. Specific patterns in psychological test scores (WISC) which reveal verbal scores to be significantly greater than performance scores with considerable subtest scatter.

The clinical symptoms included depressed mood, behavior problems, learning problems, and hyperactivity (Kestenbaum, 1979). A double-blind study of the children of manic-depressive parents has demonstrated that a subgroup of the study cases corroborated these findings (Decina et al., 1981).

William Bunney (1972) has conceptualized the manic depressive adult as a constitutionally vulnerable individual. In the manic phase, the patient may be bombarded by stimuli he or she cannot organize, presenting flight of ideas, pressured speech, and clang associations. The patient may become elated, hyperactive, grandiose, and hypersexual until there is a break with reality and he or she becomes delusional. Likewise, the constitutionally vulnerable child under stress may exhibit an embryonic version of the same clincal features: extreme silliness, hyperactivity, sleep disturbance, pressured speech, and increased magical thinking as attempts to deny social or academic problems.

CLINICAL VIGNETTES

I have presented a brief review of research on children at risk for major psychiatric disorder in order to suggest an approach to more accurate assessment of children who are currently labelled "borderline."

The following case illustrations (with 10- to 25-year follow-up data) demonstrate that people with similar symptomatology early in life have signficantly different clinical outcomes.

Three of the patients in adult life are in the schizophrenic spectrum, two have manic-depressive diagnoses, one became an "antisocial personality-disordered borderline adult," and one is "normal neurotic." I have used the composite list of symptoms for borderline conditions in children (Vela, Gottlieb, & Gottlieb, page 39, this volume) to select the cases. The authors compiled six symptoms (consensus criteria) which obtained 86–100 percent agreement among eight authors: (1) disturbed interpersonal relationships; (2) disturbed sense of reality; (3) panic anxiety; (4) impulsivity; (5) neurotic-like symptoms; and (6) abnormal development. Each of the eight children under discussion exhibited at least five of the six symptoms. The remaining thirteen symptoms (which obtained 14–43 percent agreement) were noted whenever they were indicated.

CONSENSUS CRITERIA FOR DIAGNOSIS 'BORDERLINE CHILD'

		BILLY	MONA	DAN	AMANDA	MILO	VELIA	FRED
1.	Disturbed interpersonal relat.	X	X	X	X	X	X	X
2.	Disturbed sense of reality	X	X	X	X	X	X	X
3.	Panic anxiety	X	X	X	X	X	X	X
4.	Impulsivity	X			X	X	X	X
5.	Neurotic-like symptoms	X	X	X	X		X	X
6.	Abnormal development	X	X	X		X		X
7.	Motoric disturbances	X		X			X	
8.	Autoerotic/fetish							
9.	Character traits				X			
10.	Fluctuating/hysterical functioning	X	X	X	X	X	X	X
11.	Feelings of loneliness	X				X	X	X
12.	Mood swings				X	X		
13.	Hallucinations							
14.	Inappropriate/lack of affect							
15.	Inadequacies	X					X	
16.	Bizarre behavior		X	X	X		X	X
17.	Bizarre language		X					
18.	Identity disturbance	X	X	X	X	X	X	X
19.	Poor judgment	X			X	X	X	
20.	Family history of mental illness	?	?		MD	MD		

MD = Manic Depressive Disorder

Case 1 Billy B. (Follow-up, 19 years)

ADULT DIAGNOSIS: SCHIZOPHRENIA, PARANOID TYPE

Presenting symptoms Billy B. was first evaluated at age seven because of reading failure, short attention span, an articulation problem (a lisp), and severe temper tantrums.

Family history Mr. B., Billy's father, a forty-three-year-old truck driver of Irish descent, was a seventh grade dropout. An alcoholic, he was abusive toward his wife and children. The paternal grandfather had died in an institution (diagnosis unknown), and the paternal grandmother was said to be "simple or retarded."

Mrs. B. was the granddaughter of a physician and the daughter of a Protestant minister. She too dropped out of high school prior to graduation.

Three older male siblings were known as the "neighborhood hoodlums," either suspended from school or in trouble with the law. Home was chaotic, the parents constantly quarrelling or physically fighting.

Developmental history   Billy was the product of a full-term normal delivery. Pathological developmental features included difficulty in sucking, projectile vomiting until fourteen months, food allergies until age two, headbanging until age two-and-a-half, and hospitalization for asthma at age three. Developmental milestones were normal except for delay in sitting up (nine months) and the presence of a lisp when he began to talk (twenty-two months). Although he was toilet-trained at eighteen months, Billy was enuretic until age seven. A sister died from apparent crib death during the time Billy was hospitalized, and Mrs. B. reported being depressed for six months.

None of the children attended nursery school, but Billy was noted to be more clinging and fearful than the others. He refused to go to kindergarten and had to be threatened with force. He needed to have a favorite pillow with him at all times. Terrifying nightmares began when Billy was four. He awakened at night screaming in terror, which resulted in punitive threats from Mr. B. Tantrums could last for an hour.

Clinical course   The initial consultation resulted in Billy's receiving speech therapy for his articulation problem, the only recommendation the family would accept.

Billy was reevaluated at age eleven, once again referred by the school principal for severe academic and social problems. I found Billy to be a pale, anxious, immature eleven-year-old. His teachers reported that he was "inattentive in class, deeply preoccupied by his inner world." He had developed a handwashing compulsion that resulted in twelve to fifteen trips to the sink each day. A quiet loner, Billy had no friends and was frequently called "crybaby." He was often in trouble for truancy and failure to do his homework. Psychological tests revealed a full-scale IQ of 115, with much subtest scatter. According to the psychologist, extreme anxiety interfered with his performance. Moderately poor graphomotor skills were also noted, along with a "fair-to-poor" Bender-Gestalt test. No electroencephalographic abnormalities were detected.

Psychotherapy was begun despite Mr. B.'s protest that his son "should not use therapy as a crutch but should face his problems like a man." Billy was eager to come to sessions, but he was suspicious and showed a definite projective trend. For example, he wondered if I were writing notes specifically to annoy him. He soon began to share his tormented inner world—his fear of the dark, of being alone, of being mugged, knifed, bombed. He half believed in the late-night television monsters that invaded his dreams, but he denied ever having had hallucinations. His dreams were filled with violence and death. "I was embalmed in a glass case, on exhibition," he once reported. "Another corpse rose up and came toward me. It was my father. He was dead, decomposing. I could smell his body even in the dream. He touched me and I died. The whole street was covered with arms and legs and blood.''

During the six months of treatment, Billy developed a love-hate relationship with me. At times he was clinging and childishly demanding; at other times he expressed hatred and rage toward me for seeing other patients or going on vacation. He was doing better in school, however, and his parents decided that he had had enough therapy when the school year ended.

When Billy was sixteen he was once again brought for psychiatric evaluation, but this time he was admitted to the Adolescent Inpatient Unit. A high school dropout with a police record for assaultive behavior, he was hospitalized for suicidal and homicidal preoccupation, with the diagnosis "borderline adolescent." A trial of phenothiazine medication was unsuccessful in curbing his instigation of fistfights on the unit, and he was sent to a state hospital. Released after one year, he was readmitted at age nineteen with a history of auditory hallucinations that were persecutory in nature. He believed that people were trying to kill him. He was diagnosed "schizophrenia with an affective component." A trial of lithium was unsuccessful. During the next seven years, Billy was hospitalized nine times with the diagnosis "schizophrenia, paranoid type." He was never able to complete high school, hold a job, or form an intimate relationship.

CRITERIA FOR DIAGNOSIS "BORDERLINE CHILD"

Billy fulfilled all six of the consensus criteria.

1. Disturbed interpersonal relationships characterized by clinging, demanding possessive attitude, extreme ambivalence, isolation from peers, and lack of friends.

2. Disturbance in the sense of reality manifested by withdrawal into idiosyncratic, frightening fantasies, paranoid ideation, and excessive use of magical thinking.

3. Excessive anxiety manifested by sleeplessness, inability to concentrate, panic states, fear of body disintegration, perception of the world as dangerous, and severe separation anxiety.

4. Excessive and severely impulsive behavior characterized by tantrums and unmitigated fits of rage.

5. Neurotic-like symptoms, such as multiple phobias and handwashing compulsion.

6. Uneven development characterized by a history of poor sucking, headbanging, projectile vomiting, and articulation difficulties.[1]

---

[1]Detailed descriptions for each of the six headings appear on pages 40–41.

Case 2[2] Mona S. (Follow-up, 15 years)

ADULT DIAGNOSIS: SCHIZOTYPAL PERSONALITY DISORDER

Presenting symptoms Mona, the only child of a middle-aged couple, was referred for psychiatric treatment by her parents at age six because of extreme shyness, school refusal, inconsistent work habits, and "joylessness." Additional symptoms included: frequent nocturnal and occasionally diurnal enuresis; multiple fears (of animals, of the dark, of being alone); belief in "supernatural powers" (she was convinced that the eyes in photographs and paintings followed her around the room). She had no friends and spent her time daydreaming or playing with her doll collection.

Family history The parents were Jewish, with an Eastern European family background. Mr. S. was a successful businessman, "obsessional and quiet," by his own report, and psychiatrically well. Mrs. S. had a history of emotional problems. Her father, alcoholic, suspicious, physically abusive, unable to keep steady employment, was known in his family as "the crazy one." Never hospitalized for psychiatric illness, he had a brother who died in a mental institution. Mrs. S. left home at age sixteen and worked as a secretary until her marriage at age thirty-five. A "loner," she was in treatment for agoraphobia, which was so incapacitating at times that she could not attend her psychiatric sessions. She had the habit of sending the therapist many pages of "associations" (described as loose and rambling) in lieu of sessions.

Developmental history Pregnancy and delivery were without incident. Early manifestations of deviance were noted as hypersensitivity to noise and an extremely low pain threshold. Motor development milestones were within normal limits except for language development. Mona was not at all communicative, according to Mrs. S., appearing to understand everything but not speaking. She was intolerant of change (new faces or surroundings) and had more than expectable separation anxiety. "Food fads" and a rejection of all but five or six foods were reported, along with a preoccupation with vomiting (which had occurred infrequently during febrile illness). Other complaints included refusal to dress herself, intense power struggles which resulted in tantrums, and an inability to maintain relationships with other children. The simultaneous death of Mona's grandmother and a month-long hospitalization of her mother for an operable malignancy when Mona was four were crucial traumatic events.

Because of reported "staring spells," Mona had a neurological examination with negative findings. She was left-handed with right-eye dominance. A psychological test revealed a WISC full-scale IQ of 115 "with higher potential." There was considerable subtest scatter, particularly in lower scores for language comprehension. Projective tests were characterized by

---

[2]This case has been discussed previously (Kestenbaum, 1981).

"peculiar percepts: monsters, dragons, skeletons, eyes." The psychologist reported that many reponses revealed a suspicious quality, "much like the repsonses of an adult with paranoid personality."

Clinical course Mona began psychotherapy with biweekly sessions and frequent consultations were held with her parents. Although she was able to be comfortable with me after several weeks, she avoided eye contact for months. She considered eyes to have special powers of control and imagined that her thoughts could kill. When questioned about these beliefs, she admitted that these "worries" were imaginary but told me "it feels the same as if they were real."

Initial therapeutic intervention was in the nature of establishing trust. I tried to serve as an organ of reality, correcting Mona's distortions and interpretations whenever possible. The parents were counseled not to give in to all of Mona's demands—for removal of pictures from the walls or for permission to remain home from school, for example. Her teachers were advised to institute on-site special educational therapy to help her develop language skills and concentration.

Mona enjoyed telling and illustrating stories. Fire, explosion, death, and destruction constituted the themes of her drawings. A well-executed drawing of a smiling girl brought forth the comment, "She's happy because she's eavesdropping on her enemies. Everything about this girl is bad; she has no friends, she is mean and she hates everyone." During doll-play, Mona reenacted events she would not describe in words, giving detailed accounts of what the dolls thought and felt. (For example, doll A explained to doll B, "It's dangerous to eat something you don't like, then you'll vomit and your head will fall off and your stomach will burst out.")

As Mona developed more confidence, she acquired several friends and joined a Junior Girl Scouts Club. New themes continued to emerge involving her low self-esteem, confused body image, and maladaptive defense mechanisms—chiefly denial and projection. As an example, when Mona was eight she enacted the role of eight-year-old Moira "who was born two months ago—she didn't want to come out of her mother's tummy; she has two brains, one which turns itself off when she wants to go into her secret world."

I tried to help Mona work through her feelings of being "queer," different from other children, and to help her evolve better ways of solving problems. In preadolescence, Mona became deeply upset by her budding sexuality. Her thoughts became confused, and she experienced episodes of depersonalization.

The bizarre quality of her imagination and fear of pubertal change and bodily damage is exemplified by one of her 12-year-old stories: "Moira was bad," went to jail, got pregnant, and had an abortion. She stuck the abortus back into her vagina to grow again, but instead, Moira turned herself inside out, upside down, and her ovaries started to walk on two little tube-like legs. She cried, but "instead of tears falling, little eggs dropped out."

I encouraged Mona to use her rich imagination and expressiveness to create stories which could more appropriately be shared with teachers and schoolmates. Mona became editor of the school paper and achieved success and admiration from her peers for her writing skills. Treatment was terminated at age fourteen when Mona's family moved out-of-state.

One follow-up revealed that Mona had made a good adjustment to college life (in a small lowpressure college) and had selected several male teachers as "mentors" to guide her in her literary interests and writing skills. A psychiatric consultant, whom she visited briefly during her senior year, considered her diagnosis to be "schizoid personality" or "schizotypal personality disorder."

Upon completion of college, Mona found employment as a school librarian in a small town near her family. She had acquired several close friends, and had one intimate relationship with a local artist. During a chance meeting on the street one summer, Mona told me, "Sometimes I get those old feelings. The kind I used to have as a child—that people want to hurt me, that statues might move and such. . . . But I always remember what you used to say and I tell myself 'that's make believe.' Besides, I always know there are people I can talk to and where I can call for help if I ever need it."

CRITERIA FOR DIAGNOSIS "BORDERLINE CHILD"

Mona fulfilled five of the six consensus criteria:

1. Disturbed interpersonal relationships characterized by an overdemanding, controlling manner with adults and children, periods of withdrawal, isolation from peers, and lack of friends.

2. Disturbance in the sense of reality manifested by withdrawal into idiosyncratic fantasies, excesive self-absorption in "pretend" play, paranoid ideation short of delusions, and excessive use of magical thinking.

3. Excessive, intense anxiety manifested by panphobias, fear of separation from adults, and perception of the world as so dangerous that her function was impaired.

4. Neurotic-like symptoms, such as multiple phobias and somatic concerns.

5. Uneven development characterized by delay in language expression and unusual sensitivities.

Case 3[3] Dan T. (Follow-up, 30 years)

ADULT DIAGNOSIS: SCHIZOID PERSONALITY DISORDER

Presenting symptoms Dan was first seen by a psychiatrist at the age of

[3]This case has been reported elsewhere (Kestenbaum, 1977).

nine in the mid-1950s. He had been referred by his pediatrician after he had become conspicuously preoccupied with death, with the convictions that he was "stupid" and didn't deserve to live. His parents had noted that he had become increasingly fearful of being alone, of the dark, and of animals, particularly spiders. At a younger age he had been terrified of children's fairy tales, such as Hansel and Gretel and Snow White. These fears had not diminished with time; in fact, he was unable to sit through "The Wizard of Oz" without becoming "hysterical" at the sight of the wicked witch.

Family history Mr. T. was an unsuccessful businessman, considered to be passive and depressed. Mrs. T. was a highly intelligent former nurse who was the controlling member of the household. Both sets of grandparents were European-born, Jewish, and without history of psychotic illness. There were no siblings.

Developmental history Birth and delivery were reportedly normal. Dan was an active, irritable baby. Motor development was delayed, coordination having been poor from the start. Language development was early—he spoke full sentences at age two.

Clinical course Dan achieved an IQ score at the time of that psychiatric evaluation of over 150. He was noted to be small and clumsy, with a lumbering, awkward gait. He exhibited a number of "soft signs" similar to those found in nonmotor brain damage. He behaved more like a miniature adult than a child. He was clearly quite brilliant intellectually, but he alienated all his peers by continually correcting and criticizing them. He had no close friends and was always the last one to be chosen for any team. The parents reported that he had a number of obsessive rituals and, if something prevented him from performing them, he became extremely anxious. He would bow his head, holding his hands in front of him, looking up and down, and praying silently. He felt God would strike him or his mother dead if he did not follow God's wishes, and several times he felt God had "spoken" audibly to command him. He was particularly fearful of contracting cholera which he had read about in school.

The therapist at the time felt that Dan was most likely a childhood schizophrenic, borderline type, whose superior intellectual endowment enabled him to function as well as he did. Psychotherapy was begun on a twice-weekly basis.

The therapist, using techniques of play therapy and story telling, learned that Dan was greatly confused about his gender identity and about sex and reproduction in general. He had interrupted his parents during intercourse when he was four and received from them a long and thorough explanation of the reproductive functions of which he understood nothing. He believed "the man urinates inside the lady, only the pee has invisible bugs in it that makes babies grow." Dan was preoccupied with thoughts of bodily injury. On one occasion he had observed his mother's used menstrual pads in the bathroom and believed his father had hurt her and caused her to bleed. Dan's mother frequently used him as a sounding board for her complaints about the unfairness of men toward women, about her lot in life, and her husband's neglect of her needs. Dan felt close to his mother but was frightened of her angry scolding and the verbal attacks on his father.

After two years of therapy, Dan's symptoms had abated considerably; he was able to adopt a more social attitude toward peers, although he was still considered "odd" or "a brilliant weirdo" by schoolmates. The parents viewed the symptomatic relief as sufficient, and treatment was discontinued against the therapist's advice.

Dan first came to my attention at the age of twenty-eight when he was referred to me for emergency consultation. He had been at a party where a number of friends had smoked marijuana. Dan, who had not previously used marijuana, felt himself suddenly "going mad," as if the marijuana fumes were making his body "disintegrate" and his thoughts fly out of his head. He complained that he had no sensation in his genitals. He had had other episodes of acute anxiety, particularly while traveling, but nothing akin to this episode. Though of average height, he walked stooped over, scanning a newspaper as he walked so that he appeared considerably shorter. His gait was jerky, his movements uncoordinated. His hair was long and unkempt, his mustache untrimmed. He dressed in "counter-culture" jeans. He looked, as a colleague of his commented, "like a fawn who had lost his way." When Dan spoke, he never looked directly at his listener but averted his eyes, usually selecting a spot several feet away. Equally striking was his obvious intelligence: he was a gifted and skillful language instructor, who, despite his mannerisms, could hold his class spellbound—albeit from a distance. He was a respected and creative academician.

He had had, however, some difficulty functioning because his compulsive behavior was severe enough to interfere with many everyday activities. He had, for example, to read every word on a page no matter what the material, want ads, box tops, etc. He had innumerable fears, many persisting from childhood and still not abated (fear of the dark, fear of crowds, fear of flying, fear of being alone—and he lived alone), some of which were distinctly idiosyncratic. He had a morbid fear of contracting cholera and assiduously avoided any trips to tropical climates. He had obsessional thoughts about tarantulas which might sting him to death and so he refused to travel to the Southwest. The psychologist who tested him shortly after his panic reaction felt he had a marked homosexual conflict and sexual confusion about his gender. He had never had overt homosexual experiences of any kind (nor heterosexual either). In fact, he denied ever having masturbated. The idea was repellent to him and, moreover, frightening inasmuch as he believed he could do irreparable harm to his penis.

Despite superior functioning at work, his self-esteem was inordinately low. His successes did not in any way affect this view of himself. On the other hand, he elaborated grandiose fantasies and manifested a strong need to control (as if to compensate for feelings of worthlessness). One had the impression his high intelligence protected him from a more severe break with reality, although under emotionally charged circumstances (such as the marijuana incident) he experienced a brief psychotic episode (schizophrenic in type).

Dan's academic performance had been outstanding throughout his college and postgraduate years, which he completed despite his lack of social relationships. There, as in grade school, he was tolerated as a brilliant "oddball." Following his therapy in childhood, he had not felt the need to seek psychiatric help, but he eventually came to believe he should try to "get at the roots of the problem." He began intensive psychoanalytic psychotherapy with me and continued in treatment for over five years. Dan established a clinging ambivalent transference to me and eventually was able to work through some of his problems in the area of separation-individuation, achieving a greater sense of autonomy. During the course of therapy, he began socializing and dating, at first with difficulty, but eventually he became engaged to a creative woman in his own field. He had lost his stilted mannerisms; the phobias and compulsive habits disappeared as did his bizarre behavior. He terminated treatment when he was offered a professorship at a leading university in a different city. In subsequent letters, he reported an excellent adjustment to his new life.

CRITERIA FOR DIAGNOSIS "BORDERLINE CHILD"

Dan fulfilled five of the consensus criteria:

1. Disturbed interpersonal relationships characterized by isolation from peers and lack of friends.

2. Withdrawal into idiosyncratic fantasy, and excessive use of magical thinking to semidelusional proportions.

3. Excessive intense, chronic anxiety and the perception of the world as a dangerous place.

4. Neurotic-like symptoms, such as somatic concerns, multiple phobias, and obsessions.

5. Uneven or distorted development characterized by motor delay and clumsiness.

Case 4 Amanda S. (Follow-up, 18 years)

ADULT DIAGNOSIS: SCHIZO-AFFECTIVE

Amanda S. was referred for psychiatric evaluation at the age of nine. She was described as "wild, unmanageable, excited, lacking impulse control, and a behavior problem" by the school principal of a well-known progressive school.

Family history Mrs. S. was a wealthy "socialite," recently widowed. She was attractive, nervous, and irritable, with a history of psychiatric treatment for depression. Her childhood and adolescence were stormy. The maternal grandmother had been diagnosed as "psychotic"—she died in a mental institution. The maternal grandfather had boasted that he had amassed a fortune due to his own creative efforts in the world of finance. He was described by contemporaries as hypomanic and full of boundless energy.

Mr. S. was a young professional man who died suddenly from a myocardial infarction when Amanda was seven. There was no reported history of mental illness in his family. All four grandparents were native-born Americans. None had had a particular religious affiliation.

Amanda's only sibling was one brother, aged seven, without apparent problems. Because Mrs. S. was frequently abroad or otherwise engaged, a housekeeper who had lived with the family for many years was the children's chief caretaker.

Developmental history Neonatal history was without incident. Amanda was considered to be a happy, outgoing baby with normal developmental milestones. From the age of two, she demonstrated a bad temper when she didn't get her own way. Nursery school reports were good, other than comments about frequent tantrums and arguments with other children. She was particularly close to her father, and his sudden death affected Amanda more than either her mother or brother. Her school behavior began to deteriorate shortly afterwards.

Clinical course A psychological test obtained prior to starting dynamically oriented psychotherapy revealed a full-scale WISC of 95, with verbal 106 and performance 85. The psychologist noted if tests involving social judgment or motor-visual functioning were excluded, she would have achieved a full-scale score of 120. The Bender-Gestalt was poor. The psychologist concluded that either an organic interference or a schizophrenic disorganization was present even though the absence of autistic distortions or bizarre percepts in the projective data precluded the latter diagnosis. There was evidence of intermittent depression, a serious problem of impulse control, and unusual sexual preoccupation. She noted in the report, moreover, that the child was irritable, sharp-tongued, hostile, and resistive.

Amanda began psychotherapy with surprising eagerness. She rarely missed a session although she had difficulty getting up in the morning and was chronically late for classes. A beautiful child, in constant motion, she was rarely able to sit quietly for more than five minutes. Her speech was pressured, almost staccato, interrupted by squeals and giggles. She spoke incessantly of boys. She had one friend, Mary, with whom she spent most of her time.

Within several months of beginning therapy, the teachers reported that although she was disorganized in school, with individual attention she was handling some subjects better and more easily. She was also less disruptive in class. Amanda lacked social judgment, however, and was overly friendly to strangers and excessively outgoing with adults. In sessions she spoke at length of her father and the shock of his sudden death. Her feelings toward her mother were extremely ambivalent (protestations of love and hate at the same time). Against advice, the family left for a five-month vacation abroad which necessitated discontinuation of the treatment.

When I saw Amanda upon her return she was eleven years old and had acquired several new symptoms, compulsive handwashing and bedtime rituals. She half-believed that if she didn't complete these acts, her mother would die as her father had. Her compulsions concerning arrangements for her clothes and toilet resulted in her spending an hour dressing each morning; she was chronically late for school and began missing sessions. She was extremely impulsive and on several occasions attacked her mother, biting her arm. Mrs. S. was rarely home and was planning to remarry.

A trial regimen of phenothiazine medication proved unsuccessful. Amanda's symptoms, especially her concentration difficulty, worsened. She was never delusional nor did she ever experience hallucinations. Recommendation for hospitalization was refused by the family. Amanda was sent instead to an out-of-state therapeutic boarding school. Her homesickness was so severe that she was removed from the school and sent to her mother's new home in the South. In a less pressured school atmosphere and with the help of a new psychiatrist, Amanda's more flagrant symptoms lessened in intensity.

I heard no word about Amanda for five years, but then Mrs. S. wrote me a letter. Amanda had done reasonably well until age sixteen when she again developed compulsive rituals, including binge eating. She remained in her room for days, fasting and performing her rituals. Once again Amanda was sent to live in New York City with relatives. Extreme disorganizations were evident in the first consultation, manifested by flight of ideas and loosened associations. Her compulsion to have absolute control of her balance necessitated her moving very slowly so that she would always be certain of her position. I arranged for hospitalization, a recommendation which was again refused.

No further word was forthcoming for nine years, at which time I learned that Amanda had eventually completed high school in the South but had had no further educational experience. At age twenty-one she required hospitalization for anorexia nervosa which proved temporarily successful.

At age twenty-four she was hospitalized once again for an acute manic episode following a "wild spending spree." A trial of lithium was instituted, but Amanda reportedly refused all medication. Since that time she has led a marginal existence, gaining employment for brief periods of time as an unskilled office worker or "vacationing" with relatives. She had one or two friends and a relationship with an unskilled office worker deemed unsuitable by her family.

CRITERIA FOR DIAGNOSIS "BORDERLINE CHILD"

Amanda fulfilled five of the six consensus criteria:

1. Disturbed interpersonal relationships characterized by excessively outgoing social interactions without appropriate discrimination and extreme outbursts of love and hate toward the same person.

2. Disturbances in the sense of reality manifested by excessive use of magical thinking with the fear that her thoughts would come true.

3. Excessive anxiety manifested by an inability to concentrate and an intense fear of separation (homesickness).

4. Excessive and severe impulsive behavior resulting from provocation or frustration along with loss of controls (biting others).

5. Neurotic-like symptoms, such as rituals, obsessions, and compulsive behavior.

In addition, she demonstrated poor judgment, histrionic character traits, and mood swings.

Case 5[4] Milo R. (Follow-up, 14 years)

ADULT DIAGNOSIS: BIPOLAR DISEASE, JUVENILE TYPE

Presenting problem Milo was a seven-year-old European-born boy when his parents first sought help. He was repeatedly in difficulty because of undisciplined behavior. He was constantly in the principal's office for offenses such as sounding the firebell, throwing spitballs, and cursing at teachers. Numerous fears of the dark, of monsters, and of large animals constituted additional symptoms. He was considered overactive.

Family history Mr. R. was a forty-five-year-old lawyer, a partner in an international law firm, and very successful, highly competitive, and "driven," according to his wife. European-born, he spoke many languages fluently and had achieved high honors in school. He had been under care for recurrent depression but had never been hospitalized. His own father had been "an explosive, temperamental artist" prone to impulsive fits of behavior. "If he was unhappy with anyone, he'd 'cut him dead' and wouldn't speak to him for twenty-five years." The paternal grandmother had bona fide manic-depressive illness; her first depressive episode at age fifty followed her husband's death. She had four hospitalizations for manic attacks and was eventually treated with lithium carbonate. Several of the grandfather's sib-

[4]This case has been presented elsewhere (Kestenbaum, 1981)

lings had had manic-depressive illness resulting in hospitalization.

Milo's mother was the middle child of a working class family. History of emotional disorder was negative. In addition to Milo, the R.'s had two other boys, a fifteen-year-old who was considered gifted, a brilliant student prone to feelings of shyness and insecurity, and a ten-year-old who had had dyslexia and other learning problems since first grade. He had received special remedial help from that time forward.

Development history Birth and delivery were stated to be within normal limits.

Milo's past history was unusual in that the family moved several times during his first year of life when the father's business took him away from home for many months at a time. Milo, who Mrs. R. felt was "the easiest baby of all three," was frequently left in the care of nursemaids. When Milo was eight months old, the father returned home after a seven-week absence. Milo "shrieked and screamed in fear" when his father tried to pick him up. From that time, Mrs. R. was aware of his extreme sensitivity to noise, trains, fire engines, strangers, and any change in the environment—behavior which lasted until he was two.

Milo was considered a difficult child by his nursery teachers from age three. He was asked to leave kindergarten for being too excitable, active, and independent, "just full of beans" according to his mother. At home he was loving and affectionate with family members and pets, but he developed a series of fears which did not abate. He had tantrums which continued for up to an hour when he did not get his own way. He was concerned about the existence of creatures from outer space. In fact, Mrs. R. noted, he seemed to believe in the Easter Bunny and the Tooth Fairy longer than had her other children. Despite parental warnings, Milo threw rocks at passing cars. On one occasion he impulsively fired his B-B gun in the direction of an automobile, causing the driver to swerve and hit a tree. The police were called. Such examples of "thoughtless behavior" were commonplace. Milo appeared remorseful but would repeat a similar piece of behavior the following week. He cried and promised not to do it again, claiming "I don't know why I do it."

Milo had a brief course of psychotherapy prior to the family's moving to another country when Milo was ten. Milo's academic and social problems continued to cause concern. He was repeatedly in trouble for loss of control, cursing, or fighting. He did well with special tutorial help, but he couldn't seem to work alone. The final move to the United States resulted in a change of schools once again and a second psychiatric consultation.

When I first met Milo he was a thin, blond, handsome, and well-coordinated boy who looked immature for thirteen. He gazed at his shoes most of the time, and his eyes filled with tears when he thought of his friends in Europe. "I wish I could get A's in school like my brother and my parents— they both were straight A students—but I always mess up. I forget to do my homework, I lose my notebooks—I only do well in sports . . . . The kids here are all crumbs. One day they like you and the next day they don't talk to you. My brother bugs me, always giving me a lecture. My father lectures me too. I am a great disappointment to the family.'' Milo noted other problems as well: "I do things I know are bad but I can't stop myself, like telling lies to teachers or kids and taking things.'' He also described feeling frightened when alone in his room in the dark. He imagined monsters of every shape about to attack him. He described a series of rituals he performed nightly to make himself feel better—touching things twice, placing his shoes under the bed at just the right angle—"but I still feel scared.'' He sometimes wished he hadn't been born and often wished he were dead.

Psychological tests were obtained because of Milo's academic performance. His IQ was in the superior range. It was felt that his learning inhibition resulted not only from changing schools but also related to Milo's giving up a task when he could not grasp it immediately. He could not remain with an activity because frustration resulted in his avoiding the task altogether.

His full-scale IQ (WISC) was 120, with a verbal of 128 and a performance of 107. His lowest score was on coding (eye-hand coordination on an alternating timed task); the other scores were average to superior. The psychologist felt that the lower score was due to slower timing rather than poor visual-perceptual or motor performance. The Bender-Gestalt reproductions were good.

Because of the lack of the appropriate school-age skills, remedial education was recommended, along with psychoanalytic psychotherapy.

Milo seemed eager for help. He spent many sessions describing his fears and his inability to fall asleep. "I just toss and turn and think of all the ways I'm a failure.'' His mood fluctuated between black despair and euphoria. Even his choice of colors was gloomy. "I wanted to have my room painted black. I wanted to give black a chance.'' His speech was usually pressured and overinclusive. He described his analysis of a TAT card he was shown during his psychological testing: "It was about Beethoven. His mother made him practice but he really didn't have time to study. Maybe he had a lousy teacher, maybe he was sick or paralysed and couldn't hold the pencil, maybe he had a headache, maybe he was an alcoholic or drug addict, maybe he gets no pleasure in anything, maybe he didn't believe in himself.''

Milo disliked studying his assigned texts but was fascinated by the C.S. Lewis *Tales of Narnia* and Tolkien's *The Hobbit*. "I can go into a secret world of my own and be king.'' He spent hours in such fantasy, winning all the games, taking all the honors.

As Milo began to obtain some relief from the sessions, he became more outgoing in school, but not in ways conducive to academic success. He made friends with some of the local school delinquents and became involved in incidents of minor vandalism, writing obscenities on the board and tossing books around. He was suspended for several days. His friends rarely got caught. He admitted that he often acted on impulse, getting in more trouble than his peers. "I just am sick of feeling low and when I get happy for once my parents scream at me and I get suspended." He was, according to his parents, much happier, but, they complained, "in a childish way—dancing on door stoops, acting like a six-year-old, clowning." He was hyperexcitable in the office on occasion, giggling and telling jokes.

During the summer vacation, without the structure of school or treatment sessions, Milo once again got into trouble. He ran away from home following an incident in which he was caught breaking into a grocery store along with several other boys in search of snacks and beer. Milo's participation had been impulsive. "Since that is all in the past," he told me the following week, "I don't want to think about it." The behavior problem became more severe. Milo became involved in gang fights and acquired the reputation of being a bully. His fantasies about becoming a detective, a shark fisherman, a famous ballplayer occupied his study time. He perceived himself to be helpless in real life; his fantasied omnipotence enabled him to shut out the reality of his failing academic situation. His dreams were full of rageful scenes of torture and revenge. In one dream, he reported, "I was the worst criminal in the world. I was caught and handcuffed. I knew I had special powers and could escape, which I did."

Milo made friends with another aggressive boy who got into fights and enjoyed gambling and other "exciting" activities. Milo began to emulate him in every way. He began to miss sessions with the excuse that he forgot the time. That same month he was nearly expelled from school for striking a boy in the face, seriously injuring him. Following this incident, Milo refused to come for sessions, professing a hatred of me, of the sessions, of being forced to come to the office which was like "jail." He later admitted that all adults, including me, had let him down by not helping him with his confused feelings or magically helping to control himself when he lost control.

Milo made efforts to "hold the line" with his tutor and did improve in most of his subjects. He even wrote an essay describing the effects of psychotherapy on a hypothetical boy: "His getting into trouble was due to the fact that he would act on impulse no matter what the consequences were instead of thinking over the actions and then deciding whether or not they were prudent."

Shortly after his fifteenth birthday Milo was sent to a boarding school. His moods were still unstable, expansive, and gregarious one day, despondent and depressed the next. During the transition period in the new school, fights with schoolmates increased in intensity. On one occasion Milo lost control and struck a boy who had taunted him with a stick, fracturing his leg. An emergency psychiatric consultation was obtained. The psychopharmacologist considered Milo to have a juvenile form of cyclothymic disorder with dyscontrol and recommended a trial of lithium carbonate. The headmaster allowed Milo to complete the semester with the understanding that he would continue taking the drug.

Milo later reported his version of the incident. "I don't remember what happened. It's as if my mind went blank—I just went crazy and when he cursed me out, that's all I remember until I saw the stick in my hand and the guy on the ground."

Milo remained on lithium for a year with excellent results—his marks improved, he made friends, and he had no more "explosive" rage outbursts until the summer of his eighteenth year when he decided to discontinue lithium against medical advice. Within six months he developed a florid mania. He believed that he had special powers, that he was destined to be a great baseball player. He hitchhiked to California in order to be "discovered" by a major league team, but the police brought him back in a disheveled and disorganized state. He was hospitalized briefly and began intensive therapy with the school's consulting psychiatrist.

In a follow-up visit at age twenty, Milo reported that he had completed three years of college, was on the baseball team, was getting good marks, and planned to become a teacher. He had not taken lithium for one year but continued psychotherapy. "I see now that I used to be out of control," he told me, "that I had violent reactions to everything. I feel pretty O.K. now. Most of the time when I get overexcited or blue, I tell myself I'm just like other people, only more so. It helps knowing that it's my physiology; I can always talk to the doc about it, and it helps me understand other people a lot better."

CRITERIA FOR DIAGNOSIS "BORDERLINE CHILD"

Milo fulfilled all six consensus criteria:

1. Disturbed interpersonal relationships characterized by behaving in an excessively controlling and demanding way, excessively outgoing social interactions without appropriate discrimination of the situation.

2. Disturbances in the sense of reality manifested by fantasies of being all-powerful; excessive use of magical thinking.

3. Excessive intense anxiety, manifested by driven restlessness, sleep disturbance, lack of concentration, and excessive stranger and separation anxiety.

4. Excessive and severe impulsive behavior resulting in fits of rage, loss of control, tantrums, aggressive behavior.

5. "Neurotic-like" symptoms such as compulsive rituals and multiple phobias.

6. Uneven development characterized by rocking, headbanging, unusual sensitivity to noise, tantrums, mood swings, fluctuating function, and hyperactivity.

Milo also demonstrated poor judgment.

Case 6 Velia G. (Follow-up 15 years)

*ADULT DIAGNOSIS: BORDERLINE PERSONALITY DISORDER,
ANTISOCIAL BEHAVIOR*

Presenting symptoms Velia was first brought for psychiatric evaluation to a child psychiatric clinic at age seven because of poor academic achievement, fighting, truancy, stealing from children, and lying to teachers. She was often found daydreaming and wandering in the halls of her school.

Family history Mrs. G. was an attractive waif-like twenty-four-year-old woman with a history of emotional problems. A poor historian, she was rambling and vague. She was the daughter of an alcoholic salesman often away from home on binges. His pattern was to return home in order to "dry out," then disappear for weeks at a time. The maternal grandmother was a member of a group which helped wives of alcholics—"like a martyr she put up with everything." Mrs. G. ran away from home at age fifteen without completing school. She was a daredevil and joined a circus as a motorcycle performer. At age sixteen she married a seventeen-year-old auto mechanic who spent most of his time at race tracks. She became pregnant but wouldn't consider abortion because of her Catholic background. No information is available about Mr. G. regarding family background, nor is it clear whether or not there was psychotic illness in Mrs. G's family.

Development history Velia was reared by her grandparents until the age of five. She rarely saw her mother who worked as a theatrical stagehand in another city. She was a premature (seven months) five-pound infant. Reportedly she had been a quiet child who did not demonstrate problems. She walked late (fifteen months) and constantly tripped. She needed special shoes for "pedalic inversion" and slept with a leg brace until age three. In addition to the usual childhood illnesses, she had a history of chronic bronchitis and pneumonia at age five. Velia had no friends and was a lonely child. She was very attached to her grandmother, whom she considered her real mother.

Mrs. G. remarried when Velia was five, and the child went to live with her mother and stepfather. "That was the worst day of my life," she told me. "Even though I had my own room, I hated it." Velia had a hard time adjusting to the apartment and to her new family. She experienced severe, uncontrollable rage episodes and began walking in her sleep. Unable to get along with other children, she abused younger children if she did not get her way. She began lying to her parents, stealing coins from her mother's purse, tearing up her clothes and hiding them. School problems were noted in first grade. Although she had high average intelligence demonstrated on intelligence tests, her lack of concentration kept her from completing homework assignments. She spent her time daydreaming. "I think about my grandmother's dog who died last year, about animals who were killed and brought to the butchershop." She was too clumsy to excel in class sports and games and gave up easily without trying.

Velia began psychotherapy on a twice-weekly basis. She was a beautiful child who related in a charming and compliant manner during the first session. Her voice was high-pitched, and when nervous, she stammered and her speech became pressured. She denied that she had any problems and was only coming because her parents were forcing her. She seemed to enjoy sessions but related in a superficial manner, cooperative and friendly. She behaved like a "good little girl" and betrayed anger or hostility only in verbal statements, like "How would you like it if I put a live rattlesnake on your plate?"

After several months of doll-play and story telling, she announced with the first indication of passion, "I hate growing up. I hate being a woman, women are Halloween witches—so are you." This scene occurred in response to her mother's accusation that Velia had taken $10 from her purse. During the next few sessions, Velia became violently upset—"You're dead, I killed you." When I told her she obviously had something important on her mind which she was afraid to share with me, she screamed, "You're a mind reader and a witch, you make me think of awful things. I like to think of pleasant things." She became wild and threw two dolls against the door. "I could vomit; you're vomited up! There, I vomit you out of me." She put her hands over her ears and ran under the desk. Although sessions during which she lost control and regressed to the point of soiling herself were infrequent, they always followed an incident at home or school she preferred "to forget." There had been a great deal of turmoil at home, and the parents were on the verge of divorce. Mrs. G. noted that her daughter had demonstrated peculiar behavior at home since the arrival of a new puppy. The dog urinated on the floor several times, and Velia wet her underwear twice on the same day.

In session, Velia demonstrated what it was like to lose control. "I just let everything fall out! woosh!" (A puddle appeared on the floor under her feet.) She ran to a closet and pulled out a toy gun, and pointing it at me, she said, "I'm going to kill you. I'm going to shoot out your eyes. It's because you're mad at me." These sessions during which she was verbally abusive and disorganized were interspersed with sessions where she displayed strong positive emotions, telling me she wanted me to adopt her and how she loved me as much as her grandmother.

She continued to show marked ambivalence toward me during the ensuing year although school work was somewhat better. She might hang a doll by the neck for being a thief, run out of the office and hide in closets, or want to sit in my lap and remain overtime in the session. After two years of therapy, the family moved out of town. Velia made a relatively good adjustment to the new home but repeated fourth grade in her new school.

Nothing was heard of Velia for a seven-year period after which a social worker attached to the juvenile court in Velia's town contacted me. Life had not been easy for Velia. Her parents had finally separated. Mrs. G. became depressed to the point of suicide threats. Velia had also made a suicidal gesture after failing two semesters. She had run away from home with the intention of finding her biological father who, she heard, owned a small ranch in the Midwest. She was deeply disappointed by the visit. He had remarried and had a new family and he demonstrated little interest in Velia. A school dropout, Velia became involved with drugs and minor theft. She was on probation for shoplifting and was ordered by the courts to continue psychiatric therapy with a social worker connected to the court system.

I saw Velia at age twenty-one. She had married a drug addict who killed himself with an overdose several months before the birth of their child. Velia's mother was to rear the child while Velia planned to complete her high-school equivalency and find a job.

CRITERIA FOR DIAGNOSIS "BORDERLINE CHILD"

Velia fulfilled five of the six consensus symptoms:

1. Disturbed interpersonal relationships characterized by controlling, clinging behavior with adults, extreme outbursts of love and hate towards the same person, isolation from peers, and lack of friends.

2. Disturbances in sense of reality manifested by a withdrawal into fantasy and excessive absorption in pretend play.

3. Excessive intense anxiety, diffuse and free-floating, particularly in new situations.

4. Excessive and severe impulsive behavior resulting in repetitive fits of rage.

5. Uneven development, characterized by sleeping patterns (somnambulism) and clumsiness.

Case 7 Fred A. (Follow-up, 15 years)

ADULT DIAGNOSIS: ANXIETY NEUROSIS

Presenting symptoms Fred A. was first brought for psychiatric consultation at age ten for compulsive micturition and deteriorating academic performance. The chief symptom consisted of a compulsion to urinate in inappropriate places, such as the corner of an empty schoolroom or his parent's living room. His teachers reported that he seemed preoccupied and had become more isolated from peers during the prior six months.

Family history Mr. A. was a successful lawyer employed by a prestigious firm. He was considered to be a "workaholic" who spent little time with his family. He was authoritarian and controlling at home. The paternal grandparents were Italian-born Jews of modest means. Mrs. A. was a former model, a beautiful woman who bemoaned the passing of her youth. She resented having had to give up her career and avoided home responsibilities whenever possible. She had had several courses of psychotherapy for recurrent neurotic depression. Her parents were American-born Jews from a lower-class background. There was no known family history of psychosis on either side. One sister, age twelve, was reportedly doing well at home and school.

Development history Pregnancy and delivery were without incident. Fred was noted to be less active than his sister and his developmental milestones, including language, were slightly delayed. He was, however, fully toilet-trained by eighteen months. The mother reported that he was always shy, fearful in new situations, and that he clung to her skirts in the presence of strangers. Fred was considered too immature for nursery school at age three. The following year his mother had to remain with him in the schoolroom for a full month becaue of his temper tantrums when she would attempt to leave. He lost control and could not be pacified for hours, according to the teachers.

Academic work proceeded smoothly. Fred was a compliant student who learned quickly. He perpetually worried about his work, however, and would copy an entire page if one word was misspelled. Socially he was aloof, a nonparticipant in games, and until second grade he did not have a single friend. At home he seemed withdrawn, preferring to spend time alone with his mother or his pet dog "Tiger," whom he adored. He spent little time with his sister or the family housekeeper, who seemed to prefer the older child. Other symptoms included nightmares, from which he would awaken screaming and run to his mother's bed, fear of being left alone, and fear of the dark. He always slept with the lights fully turned up. He insisted that there be a direct line of vision from his room to his parents. Both doors were kept open so that Fred would not become frightened.

One night, when Fred was nine he heard his parents quarreling and specifically overheard his mother accuse his father of having an extramarital affair. Fred ran into the room and asked them if they were going to get divorced. His father chased him from the room and threatened to spank him if he returned. From that day Fred seemed to lose interest in school. He stopped seeing his one friend and spent most of his time in his room alone, except for the company of Tiger. Several weeks later the housekeeper noticed his crumpled up soiled underpants hidden under the bed. The teacher began to report his urinating in corners shortly afterwards.

Psychologicals obtained prior to beginning treatment revealed that emotional difficulties interfered with abstract thinking, making for a full scale IQ of 104. The psychologist noted "highly constricted . . . much evidence of regression and denial. Weakness in the ability to test reality . . . great need to avoid and deny conflict . . . ."

"This child allows himself no conscious expression or feelings of hostility whatsoever. . . . He feels extremely dependent on parental approval and cannot allow himself to criticize them. The Rorschach . . . is liberally sprinkled with images of ferocious attacking monsters."

On examination I found Fred to be a slender, timid boy with downcast eyes. He denied feeling sad, but tears welled up in his eyes when asked about the family tensions. He did not want to discuss his problems or his feelings but enjoyed painting or drawing silently. Several weeks after starting therapy, Fred drew a picture of an imaginary beast. "He's called an elebear, half elephant, half bear. No one wanted him because he was so shy, but he thought people who talked a lot and yelled were stupid; they made him mad. He knew if he talked they'd laugh at him. They'd say 'oh here comes that ugly, stupid, disgusting elebear,' so one day he decided he would run away. He knew he was different from everyone; he was ashamed all the time, but he did something to get even—he stomped on their houses."

Fred finally began to discuss his chief problem. He had developed the overbearing urge to urinate in forbidden places in response to the magical belief that if he didn't perform the ritual, his parents would die. He knew it couldn't be true that he was endowed with such power, but he was afraid to take a chance and not complete the act. I offered an explanation for the bizarre behavior which caused him such great pain and isolated him even further from peers while upsetting his parents to the point of distraction. He, like the elebear, was unable to express verbally his anger toward his parents, particularly his father, so he was "messing up their house." His low self-esteem was dealt with in similar terms, using the elebear as a point of departure. Several productive family sessions followed. Within a month, the offending symptom vanished.

I recommended a continuation of psychoanalytic therapy, but the parents were satisfied that the problem was solved and terminated treatment. I did not hear from Fred for twelve years. One afternoon I received a visit from a twenty-two-year-old medical student. Fred was now a good-looking young man on his way to becoming a physician. He remembered his sessions at age eight but had forgotten the symptoms. He had done well in high school. Because of examination anxiety in college, he had begun psychoanalytic treatment and was now in the termination phase. He had several good friends and was intimately involved with a student nurse. He recalled the brief psychotherapeutic experience with fondness and said that it had had a profound influence in his life. He was planning to become a child psychiatrist.

CRITERIA FOR DIAGNOSIS "BORDERLINE CHILD"

Fred fulfilled all six of the consensus criteria:

1. Disturbed interpersonal relationships characterized by behaving in an excessively controlling, possessive, clinging, overdependent way with his mother, periods of withdrawal, isolation from peers and lack of friends.

2. Disturbance in the sense of reality manifested by fantasies of being powerful enough to cause his parents to die, withdrawal into idiosyncratic fantasies, excessive use of magical thinking with the fear that his parents could die.

3. Excessive intense anxiety resulting from separation from parents; nightmares from which he awakened in a panic.

4. Excessive and severe loss of control and tantrums when threatened with separation.

5. "Neurotic-like" symptoms which included obsessions and rituals.

6. Uneven development manifested by delay in motor and language development.

DISCUSSION

Of the seven children whose case vignettes are presented here, all were labeled "borderline" at some point in childhood. Their follow-up diagnoses however, are distinctly different.

The first three cases fit into the schizophrenic spectrum; the next two, affective disorders; and the last two are nonspecific, one with poor and the other good outcome in adult life. Only one, Velia, fits the DSM-III criteria for Borderline Personality Disorder, as outlined by Spitzer; she also fulfills Gunderson's criteria (1977).

Gunderson has been a prominent advocate of the borderline concept and has selected several essential features as criteria for the personality disorder. The five main areas of function include social adaptation, impulse-action patterns, affects, interpersonal relations, and psychosis. Velia, in adult life, demonstrated lowered achievement not commensurate with her intelligence; impulsivity in terms of drug abuse and promiscuity; manipulative suicidal threats; disturbance in close relationships; superficially good socialization beneath which lay a disturbed identity and shifting indentifications with others; a predominance of rageful affect rather than emotional warmth; and brief "micropsychotic episodes" under stress.

SCHIZOPHRENIC SPECTRUM

The first three cases have several features in common and similarities to those reported in the schizophrenia-risk literature.

All three children have histories of pathological early development, features prominent in the histories of children at risk for schizophrenia. Billy demonstrated sucking difficulty, projectile vomiting, delay in motor development, and an articulation problem. Mona exhibited hypersensitivity to noise, and her language development was delayed. Her WISC revealed lower scores for language comprehension (scores similar to those of children at risk) (Erlenmeyer-Kimling et al., 1981). Dan also demonstrated poor coordination and motor developmental delay. All three had marked anxiety to the point of panic. Reality testing was impaired. Billy and Mona had attentional problems severe enough to interfere with school performance.

Family history is probably significant in the first two cases, but a careful genetic history was not taken from any of the families under discussion. The type of mental illness of Billy's and Mona's hospitalized relatives is unknown. If one considers the three cases as part of a schizophrenic spectrum, the diathesis-stress framework becomes an important conceptual model. I believe that all three children were vulnerable to schizophrenia, but only Billy, under the impact of chaotic homelife and parental abuse, became chronically ill. Superior intelligence and early intervention were undoubtedly protective in Dan's case. He fulfills DSM-III criteria for schizoid personality disorder. Mona exhibits all eight inclusion criteria for schizotypal personality disorder: odd communication, ideas of reference, suspiciousness, recurrent illusions, magical thinking, inadequate rapport, hypersensitivity, and social isolation.

Although Mona and Dan do not fulfill the criteria for borderline personality disorder, they would most likely be considered to exhibit borderline features according to Kernberg's diagnostic criteria (1977).

Kernberg describes the borderline case from the psychostructural point of view as the intermediate variant between neurotic and psychotic organization. The critical points in his diagnostic spectrum are: reality testing (adequate capacity to test reality in both interpersonal and nonpersonal realms) and ego integration (sharply contradictory and unassimilated attitudes about important aspects of the self and pathological internalized object relations). Primitive defenses (such as splitting, denial, projective identification) are also prominent features of Kernberg's criteria. Both Dan and Mona exhibit many of these features, although they do not display the lowered achievement and manipulative quality of the person diagnosed borderline personality disorder.

AFFECTIVE SPECTRUM

Family history for affective illness is highly significant in the cases of Amanda and Milo. The developmental histories of both children differ from the first three cases. Developmental milestones were within normal limits, but symptoms such as temper tantrums, overactivity, impulsivity, and lability of mood are noted. The WISC patterns on psychologicals show significant difference between verbal and performance IQ, a finding which may be significant in helping to identify children vulnerable to affective illness.

Viewing Amanda retrospectively, I feel she was constitutionally prone to bipolar disorder. The sudden death of her father and a less than adequate mother catapulted her into an early, unrecognized manic-depressive illness. The severity of her symptoms and the lack of periods of relative health have led to the schizo-affective label, although some diagnosticians would label her symptoms manic-depressive.

Milo's childhood history is typical for individuals with subsequent bipolar disorder. Early psychotherapeutic intervention, as well as lithium management, helped to control his illness, I believe, and may protect against future breakdown.

ENVIRONMENTAL FACTORS

The cases of Velia and Fred are significant in that constitutional features seem to play a relatively small role in the development of childhood psychopathology. Environmental factors seem far more significant.

When Beata Rank first described children with atypical development (1949), she emphasized the mother's role in the child's arriving at a state of marked emotional deprivation. Mahler has placed great emphasis on object relations and internal structure (1971). She sees borderline disorders as the outgrowth of a developmental arrest at the separation-individuation phase when the infant is ordinarily beginning to differentiate himself from the mothering figure (sixteen to twenty-six months, the *rapprochment subphase*).

Mahler does not overlook constitutional factors that may aggravate the tendency in some vulnerable children to fail at the task of making proper self- and object differentiations. She speaks of the interrelated variables of early traumatization of the infant and constitutional predisposition (without identifying the nature of the predisposition.) Dince (1979) has described the psychotherapies of borderline adults in which maternal depression in the early years had a profound impact on subsequent self-object differentiation.

In the case of Velia, chaotic homelife and the abrupt rupture of her relationship with her grandparents constituted a trauma which she was never able to overcome. She fulfills the DSM-III criteria for Borderline Personality Disorder, but she would also satisfy Kernberg's nonspecific diagnostic criteria for borderline structure, namely, low anxiety tolerance (high vulnerability to stress, poor impulse control in terms of self-destructive acts or sexual promiscuity) and poor sublimatory capacity.

Fred perceived his depressed mother as nonnurturing and his father as distant; threat of abandonment due to a possible divorce led to his regressive symptomatology at age eight. Fred was able to resolve his conflicts with the help of brief psychotherapeutic intervention and subsequent psychoanalysis in late adolescence.

CONCLUSION

We can draw no conclusions from this small sample concerning the percentage of so-called "borderline children" who become borderline, psychotic, or neurotic in adult life. Such a study would require a much larger sample and a carefully matched control group for purposes of comparison. If such a study will indeed demonstrate that the majority of individuals labeled borderline in childhood do not become borderline adults, the value of the diagnostic label "borderline child" becomes questionable. The case vignettes illustrate the point that the seriously disturbed child who is not psychotic should be considered "on the way to becoming" a psychiatrically disordered adult, and that in many cases this type of disorder may be recognized early in life. Such recognition could lead to specific interventions of a psychotherapeutic, psychoeducational, and psychopharmacological nature. The reconsideration of the borderline child as a child at risk may further aid in establishing more accurate diagnoses.

R E F E R E N C E S

American Psychiatric Association. *Diagnostic and statistical manual of mental disorders* (DSM-III) (3d ed.). Washington, D.C.: 1980.

Anthony, E.J., & Scott, P. Manic-depressive psychosis in childhood. *Journal of Child Psychology/Psychiatry, 1,* 53–72, 1960.

Bergman, P., & Escalona, S.K. Unusual sensitivities in very young children. *The Psychoanalytic Study of the Child,* 1949, 3–4, 333–352.

Bunney, W.E., Goodwin, F.K., Murphy, D.L., et al. The "switch process" in manic depressive illness, III. Theoretical implications. *Archives of General Psychiatry 1972, 27,* 312–319.

Carlson, G.A., & Stober, M. Manic-depressive illness in early adolescence. *Journal of the American Academy of Child Psychiatrists,* 1978, *17,* 138–153.

Cytryn, L., & McKnew, D.H.J. Proposed classification of childhood depression. *American Journal of Psychiatry*, 1972, *129*, 149–155.

Decina, P., Farber, S., Kestenbaum, C.J., Kron, L., et al. Children of manic-depressive parents—psychological findings. Presented at the American Psychiatric Association Annual Meeting, New Orleans, May 13, 1981.

Dince, P.R. Factors inherent to the treatment of borderline patients. *Journal of American Academy of Psychoanalysis*, 1979, *7* (2), 147–164.

Ekstein, R. The space child's time machine: On reconstruction in the psychotherapeutic treatment of a schizophrenic child. *American Journal of Orthopsychiatry*, 1954, *24*, 492–506.

Erlenmeyer-Kimling, L. Studies on the offspring of two schizophrenic parents. In D. Rosenthal & S.S. Kety, (Eds.), *The transmission of schizophrenia*. New York: Pergamon, 1968.

Erlenmeyer-Kimling, L. Genetic approaches to the study of schizophrenia: The genetic evidence as a tool in research. *Birth Defects: Original Article Series*, 1978, *14*, (5), 59–74.

Erlenmeyer-Kimling, L., Cornblatt, B., & Fleiss, J. High-risk research in schizophrenia. *Psychiatric Annals*, 1979, *9* (1), 38–51.

Erlenmeyer-Kimling, L., Kestenbaum, C.J., Bird, H.R., & Hilldoff, U. Assessment of the New York high-risk project in sample A who are now clinically deviant. In N. Watt et al. (Eds.), *Proceedings of the plenary conference of the high-risk consortium*. In press.

Feinstein, S., & Wolpert, E.A. Juvenile manic-depressive illness: Clinical and therapeutic considerations. *Journal of the American Academy of Child Psychiatry*, 1973, *12*, 123–136.

Fish, B. Abnormal states of consciousness and muscle tone in infants born to schizophrenic mothers. *American Journal of Psychiatry*, 1962, *119*, 439–445.

Garmezy, N. Children-at-risk: The search for the antecedents of schizophrenia. Part I. Conceptual models and research methods. *Schizophrenia Bulletin*, MIMH, 1974, *8*, 14–90.

Gunderson, J.E. Characteristics of borderlines. In P. Hartocollis (Ed.), *Borderline personality disorders*. New York: International Universities Press, 1977.

Kernberg, O.F. The structural diagnosis of borderline personality organization. In P. Hartocollis (Ed.), *Borderline personality disorders*. New York: International Universities Press, 1977.

Kestenbaum, C.J. Psychotherapy of childhood schizophrenia. In B. Wolman, J. Egan, & A. Ross (Eds.), *Handbook of treatment of mental disorders in childhood and adolescence*. Englewood Cliffs, N.J.: Prentice-Hall, 1977.

Kestenbaum, C.J. Children at risk for manic depressive illness: Possible predictors. *American Journal of Psychiatry*, 1979, *136*, 1206–1208.

Kestenbaum, C.J. Children at-risk for schizophrenia. *American Journal of Psychotherapy*, 1980, *34*(2), 164–177.

Kestenbaum, C.J. The child at-risk for major psychotic illness. In S. Arieti (Ed.), *American handbook of psychiatry* (3d ed.). New York: Basic Books, 1981.

Kestenbaum, C.J. Adolescents-at-risk for manic-depressive illness. *Annals of Adolescent Psychiatry* (in press).

Kety, S.S. Studies designed to disentangle genetic and environmental variables in schizophrenia. Some epistemological questions and answers. *American Journal of Psychiatry*, 1975, *132*, 1134–1137.

Mahler, M.S. A study of the separation-individuation process and its possible application to borderline phenomena in the psychoanalytic situation. *The Psychoanalytic Study of the Child*, 1971, *26*, 403–424.

Marcus, J. Cerebral functioning in offspring of schizophrenics: A possible genetic factor. *International Journal of Mental Health*, 1974, *3*(1), 57–73.

Marcus, J. & Mednick, S. Neurologic dysfunctioning in offspring of schizophrenics. *Schizophrenia Bulletin* (in press).

McNeil, T.F., & Kaij, L. Obstetric factors in the development of schizophrenia: Complications in the births of preschizophrenics and in reproduction by schizophrenics. In L.C. Wynne, R.L. Cromwell, & S. Matthysse (Eds.), *The nature of schizophrenia*. New York: Wiley, 1978.

Mendlewicz, J. & Rainer, J. Adoption study supporting genetic transmission of manic-depressive illness. *Nature,* 1977, *268,* 327–329.

Rank, B. Adaptation of the psychoanalytic technique for the treatment of young children with atypical development. *American Journal of Orthopsychiatry,* 1949, *19,* 130–139.

Ricks, D.F., & Berry, J.C. Family and symptom patterns that precede schizophrenia. In M. Roff, & D.F. Ricks (Eds.), *Life History in Psychopathology.* Minneapolis: University of Minneapolis Press, 1970.

Rosenthal, D. An historical and methodological review of genetic studies of schizophrenia. In J. Romano (Ed.), *The origins of schizophrenia.* Rochester, N.Y.: Proceedings of the First Rochester International Conference on Schizophrenia, 1967.

Stone, M.H. Mania: A guide for the perplexed. *Psychotherapy and Social Science Review,* 1971, *5*(10), 14–18.

Stone, M.H. *The borderline syndromes: Constitution, personality, and adaptation.* New York: McGraw-Hill, 1980.

Vela, R., Gottlieb, E., & Gottlieb, H. This volume, Chapter 2.

Waring, N. & Ricks, D.F. Family patterns of children who became adult schizophrenics. *Journal of Nervous and Mental Disease,* 1965, *140,* 351–364.

Watt, N.F. Patterns of childhood and social development in adult schizophrenics. *Archives of General Psychiatry,* 1972, *35,* 160–165.

Zerbin-Rudin, E. The genetics of schizophrenia: An international survey. *Psychiatric Quarterly,* 1972, *46,* 371–383.

CHAPTER 4

Borderline Syndromes in Childhood: A Working Nosology and Its Therapeutic Implications

Fred Pine, Ph.D.
PROFESSOR
DEPARTMENT OF PSYCHIATRY (PSYCHOLOGY)
ALBERT EINSTEIN COLLEGE OF MEDICINE
NEW YORK, NEW YORK

IN RECENT CLINICAL PRACTICE, the flow of children who are given the diagnosis "borderline" has reached flood proportions. Whence the flood? I believe that one source is the decreasing frequency with which the classical symptom psychoneuroses are seen, in childhood as in adulthood. Clinicians are alerted instead to issues of character pathology, a form of pathology which can be essentially neurotic in structure but which shades into more serious conditions at its more disturbed extreme. In addition, the post-World-War-II growth of the child guidance movement, as well as of research utilizing direct child observation, has brought to clinicians an acute awareness of the flagrant "psychopathology of everyday childhood" in the lives of young people growing up. Third, the rapid extension of clinical services to poverty and ghetto populations, following upon the sting to professional and governmental conscience of the civil rights battles of the 60's and represented in the spread of Community Mental Health Centers, brought us in greater contact with children whose lives are blighted by social pathology (crime, addiction, prostitution, violence, hunger, abandonment, and so on) as well as psycho-pathology, and whose overall functioning shows the toll taken by such massive pathological intrusions upon development. And fourth, the writings of a number of individuals (noted below) who have tried to isolate and define key intrapsychic mechanisms and/or failures in what they called "borderline children" (or related entities) gave a sophisticated clinical-intellectual context for formulations in this area.

Whether these be all or any of the sources of the flood, the phenomenon is clear: a high frequency of the labelling of children "borderline" with an associated looseness in the key meaning intended to be attached to the term. A multitude of phenomena—including isolation from others or indiscriminate relationships, nonavailability of stable defenses or rigid reliance on pathologi-cal defenses, panic states or affectlessness, hollow pseudomaturity or infantile behavior, and an assortment of peculiarities of social behavior, thought and language, or motor style, all are used to produce the umbrella diagnosis: borderline. Is there something real here that so many clinicians are grasping at? Can the morass be sorted out? Earlier (Pine, 1974a), I took a stab at answering these questions, as did a number of other writers on child psychopathology (Ekstein & Wallerstein, 1954; A. Freud, 1956; Rosenfeld &

This chapter is taken from a larger work entitled "On phase-characteristic pathology of the school-age child," to be published in *The Course of Life: Psychoanalytic Contributions to Understanding Human Personality Development,* S.I. Greenspan & G.H. Pollack (eds.), U.S. Government Printing Office & NIMH, in press.

Sprince, 1963, 1965; Weil, 1953, 1956). I should like to review some of that work here, attempting also to formulate some of the broad developmental lines that have gone awry in borderline patients, to draw distinctions within the broad borderline domain, and to specify at least some implications of these distinctions for the treatment process.

Some years ago, a group of colleagues and I agreed to meet regularly in a small clinical study group to discuss issues in child psychopathology. Our ready consensus, for reasons already apparent here, was to begin with a look at the borderline child. Influenced by the writers whom we studied, when we looked at children who had been (or could easily be) diagnosed borderline, we kept concepts in mind such as the absence of phase dominance and regression to primary identification (Rosenfeld & Sprince, 1963), the tendency towards panic anxiety (Weil, 1953), fluidity of psychic organization (Ekstein & Wallerstein, 1954), heavy reliance on splitting mechanisms (Kernberg, 1967, 1968), and, from the point of view of Mahler's concept of the separation-individuation process (Mahler, Pine, & Bergman, 1975), early failures in that process (Masterson, 1972). While our group imagination could press clinical and metapsychological constructs into creative forms that would subsume most of the cases we examined, or press cases into forms such that they could be thus subsumed, my own sense was that in so doing we were engaging in a rather forced exercise.

In contrast, shortly thereafter, an enormous freeing of thought took place when we abandoned the word "the" in the phrase "the borderline child" and replaced it by the term "borderline children." That is, we gave up the self-imposed demand to find a single unifying mechanism and considered instead that we were dealing with an array of phenomena, having some larger developmental and pathological commonalities, perhaps, but also having specific variant forms. In this it would be parallel to psychoneurosis, with its commonalities and variant forms. In back of this change also was the idea, still very clear to me, that the term "borderline" is a *concept*—one that *we* can *decide* how to use—and that our job was to specify the phenomena to which we would apply it. This rephrasing of our key term ("borderline child*ren*") also set another aspect of our task: to identify the larger developmental and pathological commonalities that make this a reasonable, if not tight, conceptual grouping, and then to describe its specific variant forms.

Put another way, children described as "borderline" are first defined by a dual negation: they are not (merely) neurotic and they are not (clearly) psychotic. What they *are* remains to be stated. Or, put yet another way, while we could manage to subsume many children who are called "borderline" under one or another clinical construct (e.g., fluidity), we came to see this not as a *gain* in clinical generalization, but as a *loss* in clinical specificity. In short, we felt we could do better with the joint conceptual tools of (1) *broadly defined commonalities* plus (2) *specific variants* in these children than we could do with any single concept, mechanism, or process alone. Let me propose that as a way of thinking here, as well.

What is the *general commonality?* I believe that all of the children who come to be considered borderline show failures in one or another of the developmental lines associated with the development of major ego functions or central aspects of object relationship; the failures may be in the form of developmental arrest, aberrant development, or both. Normally, by the ages of seven or eight to ten or eleven, ego development has proceeded to the point where secondary-process thinking and reality testing are well established and where some capacity for delay and at least some reliable and well-structured defenses have been attained. In addition, object relations have developed more or less normally through the early autistic (objectless) and symbiotic (undifferentiated) stages (Mahler, 1968); some degree of libidinal object constancy (Hartmann, 1952, Pine, 1974b) and of specificity of object attachment have been achieved; and object relations have been subjected to the shaping influences of the drives at each of the psychosexual stages of development. Furthermore, the triadic relations of the Oedipal period have been experienced and dealt with in some manner. Superego development, in addition, has proceeded to the point of at least some degree of internalization of standards—that is, with some experience of guilt for transgression and with some internally powered efforts at control and delay of impulses.

By contrast, the group of children who are generally considered borderline, or severely disturbed, do not show this context of normal development of ego function and of object relationship. In particular, ego malfunction in them may include disturbances in the sense of reality and at times in reality testing, as well as a failure in the development of signal anxiety so that unpleasant affect readily escalates to panic instead of triggering reliably available defenses. Object relations may be characterized by their shifting levels, by too great a dependence of ego structure upon the object contact (Ekstein, 1966), and by regression to primary identification (Rosenfeld & Sprince, 1963). While superego forerunners are also likely to be impaired, this problem is not in fact readily separable in its impact from failures of judgment and affectional attachment that are already implied by pointing to failures in ego function and object relationship. Final superego formation is likely to be secondarily interfered with by prior developmental failures. The precise developmental failures, and their breadth and severity, may vary from one child to another.

Speaking less formally and more descriptively, I suggest that children diagnosed borderline often have in common that they are "peculiar" in some way. Hardly an adequate clinical formulation and, at that, they may seem peculiar only to those who have sufficient familiarity with the quality, the "feel," of normal children of this age. But I do believe there is a phenomenon here that is worth thinking about, and that these peculiarities have something to do with the developmental disturbances in these children. By the school-age years, a fair degree of character stability is ordinarily attained (Pine, 1970), and a certain normative socialization is part of its *external* accompaniment; modes of thinking, speaking, doing, and relating are part and parcel of both character and socialization. The "peculiarities" of these children are often violations of these age-linked, normally fulfilled, expectations. When the (preschool) child's major relationships are within the family, peculiarities of object relation or ego function may go unnoticed by equally peculiar family members or may be compensated for by them in the mix of habitual family interrelatedness. Teachers, peers, and diagnosticians may not be so generous.

Have we now established a clear-cut general category of borderline children all of whom have significant commonalities? Not really; not to my satisfaction at least. On the other hand, while we have such commonality for the various psychoneuroses, we certainly do not have it for the broad array of psychoses either. What we have here is a rather loose, but I believe not fully arbitrary, array of pathologies characterized more or less by one or another failure in the development of ego function and/or object relation. It is clinically useful to start from this point, I believe.

These basic failures in the normal developmental progression of ego functioning and object relationship are what differentiates borderline children from neurotic children. For, though we may define the *classical psycho-neuroses* as involving an unsuccessfully resolved conflict between drive and opposing forces (superego and defense)—unsuccessfully resolved in that it culminates in anxiety and/or formation of compromise symptoms and/or neurotic character traits—we also assume that these features exist in the context of *more or less normal* ego function and object relationship, at least outside the area of focal conflict. That is why, though they involve personal suffering and, at times, impairment of functioning, we generally consider the neuroses to be relatively "healthy" conditions.

In passing, I should also say a bit regarding the distinction of borderline from psychotic conditions. I have discussed this more fully elsewhere (Pine, 1974a) and shall do no more here than to assert what I said there in the interest of saving time and avoiding repetition. In brief then: I believe that some psychotic conditions of childhood—notably infantile autism (Kanner, 1942, 1949), symbiotic psychosis (Mahler, 1952, 1968), some organic conditions, and (though rarely) adult-like schizophrenias involving apparently adequate functioning followed by regressive disorganization—can be fairly clearly differentiated from borderline conditions. But, for the rest, I do not believe a sharp line divides borderline and psychotic conditions. Each of the borderline conditions that I describe below shades into what can be called psychosis at the more severe end of its particular spectrum.

What are some of the specific developmental failures in borderline children? One that is frequently mentioned (Weil, 1953; Rosenfeld & Sprince, 1963) is the failure to achieve the signal function of anxiety (S. Freud, 1933). That is, even rather early on in development, the normal young child begins to anticipate when an anxiety-inducing situation is imminent (based on memory of previous experience). Such anticipation is accompanied by mild anxiety which sets defensive operations into motion, be these flight, a turn to mother, or (later) intrapsychic defense. But the capacity for this (both to anticipate and to have modes of defense available) is a developmental achievement of great moment. For the infant cannot do this and is instead helpless in the face of anxiety (unless mother intervenes), and the intensity of this anxiety can rise to traumatic proportions—that is, well beyond the organism's capacity to master or discharge. For certain children, the failure to develop the capacity to use the anxiety signal to set a reliable array of defenses into operation is both an indicator of past developmental failure and a source of continuing inability to develop mastery. For, if anxiety rapidly escalates to panic, the kinds of new learning, new trials at mastery, that can come at moments of delay in the face of danger, cannot take place.

Early failures in the process of separation and individuation (Mahler et al., 1975) also have consequences for the later stability of ego boundaries and of object attachment under stress. Rosenfeld and Sprince (1963), acknowledging their debt to Anna Freud, find a regression to primary identification to be a characteristic phenomenon in their severely disturbed children. That is, quite the reverse of those later identifications which are basic to the growth of individuality and are a prime form of "adding something" to ourselves, some severely ill children begin to lose their sense of self as they merge into an undifferentiated self-other duo. Masterson's (1972) work on borderline adolescents also draws heavily on concepts of failure in the process of separation and individuation.

Ekstein and Wallerstein (1954; see also Ekstein, 1966) describe the unstable, fluid ego organization characteristic of some severely disturbed children. These are children in whom the developmental achievement of stable personality organization has not taken place but in whom, instead, personality organization varies with (has not achieved autonomy from) changes in affect level and object attachment. Weil (1953, 1956) describes their pervasive unevenness of development and the equally pervasive oddness that follows from it. And Kernberg (1967, 1968), working mostly with adult patients, focuses on the pathological consequences of excessive reliance on certain primitive defenses, most notably "splitting"—that is, the developmental failure of, or the regressive interference with, the integration of representations of the good and bad (both self and other) into more realistic whole images. As I have noted elsewhere (Pine, 1974b), such integration can be conceptualized as fostering a toning down of idealization (via the effect of the "bad" on the "good" images) and a tempering of rage (via the effect of the "good" on the "bad").

I have summarized, and meant to imply basic agreement with, a variety of pathological mechanisms described by a variety of clinicians. Can no *single* mechanism or issue be found in all of these children? That question takes me full circle. That was the idea that our study group discarded, with intellectually freeing effects, as we moved from the term "the borderline child" to the term "borderline children." Personally I might like, for example, to see that failures in the separation-individuation process underlie all of what we call borderline pathology—and that has been suggested. But I myself (Pine, 1979) have just spent considerable time trying (in writing) to preserve the separation-individuation concepts from their perhaps inevitable overextension. In any event, we are dealing with matters that are part clinical and part definitional—and we have to keep them straight.

For the time being, then, I would prefer to hold to the idea that many different core pathological mechanisms are found in borderline children—that is, in children who show the broad defining attributes of developmental failure or aberration in major aspects of ego function and object relationship. In many ways, the persons whose work most closely links to my own views are Knight (1953a, 1953b), writing on borderline adults, and Redl (1951), writing on ego disturbances in children. For Knight emphasizes not single mechanisms, but a general tendency to ego regression in borderline adults; in any particular instance, the specific nature of the regression would still have to be identified. With a shift in emphasis from regression to primary developmental failure, that approach is essentially my own as well. And in his paper on ego disturbances, Redl presents an argument for the value of specificity in identification of pathology within any broad domain. There he indicates that generalized "support" for an ill-defined "weak ego" leaves us high and dry when it comes to choices regarding technique. Rather, careful specification of particular areas of ego pathology permits tailoring of technical interventions to those weaknesses. That clinical philosophy underlies my approach to the specification of particular psychopathological phenomena in the borderline as well (Pine, 1976).

Let me turn, now, to some of the observable clinical entities, the *variant forms,* with which child clinicians are familiar. We can view these entities as subtypes within the borderline domain, in part defined by the ways in which the mechanisms already described, among others, appear in them. I have given case examples of these subtypes elsewhere (Pine, 1974a), and in the interest of avoiding repetition I shall not give them here. What I shall describe may rather be considered as variations in the *phenomena* (rather than *subtypes*); by this I mean to suggest that more than one kind of "borderline phenomenon" can be found in any particular "borderline child." A final prefatory note: I wish to emphasize that this is a *working* nosology—tentative, alterable, incomplete, but useful at our current stage of understanding.

SHIFTING LEVELS OF EGO ORGANIZATION

Some children show remarkable variation in the degree of pathology of their overall mode of functioning, a phenomenon in certain particular children I shall try to capture by the term *shifting levels of ego organization*. At one moment sensitively, often painfully, in touch with their thoughts and feelings, expressed in the context of a stable alliance with a trusted therapist—or simply playing-thinking-behaving in age-appropriate ways in the context of that same alliance and sense of therapeutic presence—these children may at another moment, often suddenly within a single session, become peculiar, voice odd ideas, lose the more mature relatedness to the therapist and instead speak illogically, uncommunicatively, and affectively withdraw. But, in the instances to which I refer, there is no apparent panic; rather, there is a sense of familiarity, of ego syntonicity in the child's move into peculiar functioning.

Ekstein and Wallerstein (1954; Ekstein, 1966) have written on such children, emphasizing how critical is the loss of contact and return to contact with the therapist in setting off or terminating such states. The absence of panic in the "peculiar" state is, I believe, an important key to understanding what is going on. Such children have not simply "broken down"; rather, they have regressively moved to a more primitive level of ego organization (and object relation). In the face of some disturbing (inner or outer) stimulus, anxiety arises—and culminates, not in the triggering of a set of more-or-less adaptive defenses, but in the onset of this single, massive, regressive, maladaptive defense. But maladaptive how? Only to the outside: only for social adaptation. For internally it is highly adaptive—that is, it terminates the anxiety; it truly "works" for the child (hence I refer to it as an ego *organization*) although at a substantial price.

My understanding is that such children have achieved two quite different levels of ego organization. But both are *organizations;* they include modes of thinking, relating, and handling anxiety. The "higher" level is vulnerable, however, and too easily slips away. In terms of the mechanisms described by other writers (and reviewed earlier), these children show marked fluidity of functioning and a pervasive oddness when in their more primitive mode of functioning. Although they do not demonstrate panic anxiety, they avoid it at a major adaptive price by a massive ego regression.

In terms of treatment, my impression is that it is critical to recognize the anxiety-binding functions of the more primitive ego organization. Hence, while work with such children (and all severely disturbed children) must include a very real sense of the benign qualities of the therapist conveyed gently and unobtrusively to the child, a good deal of exploratory, interpretive work is also required. The work is not simply a matter of making up for deficits, educatively of seeing the child through panic supportively, or of fostering delayed growth developmentally. While as any therapist knows, these may all come into play at times, work with these children includes exploration and insight into the source of the anxiety, the function of the regresssion, the secondary gains in it, and the historical basis for its use.

INTERNAL DISORGANIZATION IN RESPONSE TO EXTERNAL DISORGANIZERS

In contrast in many ways to those children just described are those who evidence *internal disorganization in response to external disorganizers.* These are children whose lower-level functioning is not their achievement—it is not an "achievement" at all; it does not "work" for them but reflects instead a true incursion upon their functioning, the result of an invasion that has disrupted it. Hence the descriptive name.

It is my impression that such children are most commonly the product of rearing environments where a high level of social pathology (addiction, criminality, prostitution, violence, and so on) are part of everyday family life. In the children's psychiatric ward of a big city municipal hospital where I have seen them, they are often from ghetto/poverty areas as well, though I see no reason to believe that the same (disorganizing) result cannot be brought about in other settings that include an intense psychological barrage upon the child's functioning. In any event, observation of such children through our ward setting teaches something about the "clinical course" of the illness and, in turn, permits inferences about its structure. These children arrive in the emergency room, sometimes with reported hallucinations or delusions, often with confusion in speech and relatedness, and frequently with reports of recent suicidal or homicidal behavior. On the ward, they rapidly pull together and indeed often come to be seen as more or less normal children. What are we to make of this?

I believe that the rapid recovery in the benign setting of the ward (shielded from their disorganizing environment) suggests that the basic developmental tools of ego function (here reality testing, reliable intrapsychic defense, secondary-process thinking) and for nondestructive, trusting object relationships had indeed been formed, but that they were fragile, unable to withstand the disintegrating effect of chaotic life circumstances. In a benign setting, integration can take place. From a purely descriptive point of view, these children can also be seen as fluid—that is, functioning at different levels at different times. But the "fluidity" is very different here, captured better, I believe, by words like "breakdown" or "collapse" than by a phrase like "shift to a different level of functional ego organization."

Important things can be said from the point of view of treatment. I believe the key first line of treatment is rescue. The first-line rescue is not a fantasy of the therapist, in this instance, but a need of the child. It is essentially the benign setting, including a caring adult, without need for exploration or insight, that fosters integration and use of capacities that are present in seed form. But it would indeed be a rescue fantasy if we were to believe that the work is done at that point. First and most obvious, of course, is the issue of return to the offending environment; and either extensive family work (often impossible to accomplish), or placement, or long-term help for the child in withstanding the barrage is required. But second, and more subtly, the child's tendency to repeat actively what he has experienced passively, both as a form of mastery and as an expression of his continuing love/hate attachment to his parents, can only be forestalled through long-term treatment that both supports and interprets, as needed and as possible, for the particular patient. Obviously such long-term treatment is often more an ideal than a possibility, and so the generational repetition remains.

CHRONIC EGO DEVIANCE

The subgroup of children who show what I call *chronic ego deviance* are not really a group at all, since there is no unifying underlying structural or developmental feature by which all can be characterized. So this is a loose array, perhaps waiting for distinctions within it to be described as our clinical knowledge advances. Described by Weil (1953, 1956) some time ago, these children show any one or more of an assortment of aberrations of logical thought, reality testing, defense, or object relation. Panic anxiety, failure to achieve phase dominance in the course of psychosexual development, and unreliability of object attachment, of self-object differentiation, or of stable defense may, in any one chld, be characteristic. I use the word *chronic* in describing their ego deviance to emphasize that the impairment is part of the child, not reactive as in the group who respond to disorganizing environments, and also to emphasize that the instability of their functioning can be expected to continue to show up—that is, their instability is stably present.

In my own experience, I have discovered one phenomenon in treatment that differentiates these children sharply from the preceding group. Those children (the group disorganized in response to external disorganizers) tend to *heal* rapidly in the setting of a benign environment and a trusting relationship to the therapist; soon, from the point of view of basic ego intactness at least, they appear more-or-less normal. But some of the chronically ego-deviant children show a quite opposite phenomenon. That is, as the trusting relationship to the therapist develops, they permit themselves to *reveal*, perhaps for the first time, isolated bits of bizarre thought or behavior that they have concealed until that time.

Treatment for these children must vary with the nature of the specific failure or aberration of ego development (set, of course, in the context of the patient's whole life). It was Redl (1951) who first argued compellingly that indiscriminate support for a vaguely defined weak ego would get us nowhere; instead we have to specify the area of deficit and tailor intervention techniques to this. In an earlier paper (Pine, 1976), I tried to demonstrate some instances of such work in the context of the implicit parenting function served by the therapist for the ego-deviant patient. Indeed, this chapter has that same intent: to specify pathological conditions more precisely so that we can adapt an essentially psychoanalytically informed treatment approach to the particular patient.

INCOMPLETE INTERNALIZATION OF PSYCHOSIS

Of the borderline children whom I have thus far described, two of the groups (shifting levels of ego organization and chronic ego deviance) carry their pathology within, the former as a pathological defense organization and the latter as the result of developmental failure of various sorts; the current reactive component in the pathology is relatively small. In contrast, the reactive component is more substantial in those children whose internal disorganization is responsive to external disorganizers and in those children who display an *incomplete internalization of psychosis*. In this latter group, however, the reactive component does not simply reflect a destructive intrusion upon the child's functioning but is a core part of the child's attachment to the primary love object, usually the mother (see Anthony, 1971).

I am referring to children, generally children of a psychotic mother, who assimilate parts of the mother's psychosis as a way of being close to mother and of having her within. It involves more than conscious mimicry, and is, hence, pathological. Because the internalization of the mother's psychosis is still incomplete, I call these children borderline rather than psychotic. The incompleteness of the internalization is made clear by the relative speed with which some of the more obvious indicator behaviors drop away when the children are separated from their mothers and other love objects become available (again, see Anthony, 1971). Descriptively, fluidity of functioning is again apparent. Formulatively, since the child moves towards merging with the mother, failures in the separation-individuation process (Mahler et al., 1975) can be inferred, as can the child's reliance on regression to primitive forms of incorporation for defense. There is no question but that treatment is a long and complex process, notwithstanding the gains the child may make if separated from the mother (e.g., by the hospitalization of either one of them). For like the other reactive group of borderline children (internal disorganization in response to external disorganizers), a large residue remains even when the obvious "reaction" terminates. These children require extended work to relive (in the transference), to understand (through exploration), and to work through the relation with the primary love object. Within the essentially analytic/exploratory content of the sessions, the benign presence of the therapist—a differentiated other, who allows individuality and who does not require sharing of pathology as a condition for relatedness—will (whatever his or her theoretical orientation) inevitably provide corrective emotional experience (Alexander, 1956).

EGO LIMITATION

There are other children who, though they vary in the precise area and quality of their pathology of ego function and object relationship, show enough similarity in the developmental route to that pathology to warrant grouping them for purposes of conceptualization and discussion of treatment. I call them children with *ego limitation.* That term *could* be used to refer to inhibited children, dull children, culturally deprived children, or whatever. But let me describe the children for whom I *intend* to use it.

Sometimes, for inner and familial reasons, a child "happens upon" an early adaptive-defensive mode that markedly curtails large areas of subsequent development. If this happens, and if at the same time the defense is "successful" (in *inner* terms—that is, lessening anxiety, allowing gratification, fitting with the family), it may be retained for a long time with ever-growing damage to the developmental process. Thus, a pseudo-imbecilic child (Mahler, 1942; Pine, 1974a) whose inner psychological requirements are *not* to learn, will show effects of that learning stoppage in formal school learning, peer relations, social sense, and everywhere else. Or, to take another example, Youngerman (1979) reports on a child, electively mute fairly continously since age three, the development of whose entire thought process was impaired as a consequence of the refusal to speak. Speech externalizes inner fantasies and permits their correction against the response of others; by verbalizing certain ideas, and seeing that wishes do not always produce effects, the child learns to abandon ideas of the omnipotence of thought; and, of course, speech is the instrument of relationships at a distance—*permitting* distal connection and *not requiring* highly charged body contact and affect and gesture as the continuing modes of communication. The "election" of mutism by this child prevented those developments from taking place.

It is my experience that children showing this early and severe ego limitation bring a wide range of serious failings in ego function and object relation into their later treatment. It is also my impression, however, that a defensive-adaptive style of such long duration and (though pathological) such great "success" (intrapsychically) is not readily renounced. Not only does work with such children require sustained and sophisticated interpretive work to penetrate their heavily relied-upon defense organizations but, and this is critical, once it is penetrated we are still left with a substantially deficient child. That is, the years of nonlearning have taken their toll. Interpretation (of, for example, the basis for the pseudo-imbecility or the mutism) may lead to lesser reliance on the defense, but it does not create what has been missed in development. For this, an extensive educative process is required, along with continuing therapeutic work. But two cautions are in order: first, the educative process cannot be undertaken until the defense barrier is more-or-less abandoned, until the child understands it and is trying to give it up, or the "education" will be greeted with that very same defense style and be cast away; second, optimism about making up for the lost development of years, even after the defense is penetrated and educational supplementation is begun (either within or outside of the therapy), is hardly warranted in such cases where, in my experience at least, the child remains with considerable deficit.

SCHIZOID PERSONALITY

Exactly parallel to its adult form, *schizoid personality* in childhood seems to me to warrant inclusion in the broader group of borderline children. Such personalities, characterized by a sharply constricted and undeveloped affective life with emotional distance in human relationships and preoccupation with their own (often rich but peculiar) fantasy life, can already be seen quite clearly in childhood. The peculiarities of thought and severe limitations of object relationship reflect the developmental aberrations or failures of the general borderline domain.

Like the children with shifting levels of ego organization whose shift to a more primitive organization successfully wards off anxiety (even at the price of often severe disturbance of function), the preoccupation with fantasy in the schizoid children also often works well to avoid anxiety (or indeed *any* affect). Treatment is therefore difficult. Since fantasizing works well for the children, they will not easily give it up; relationships to others are quite cut off, and so the therapist cannot easily become important to the child. And, since the child does not *shift* between in-touch and fantasizing states, but rather stays safely shielded from others by affective distance and fantasy preoccupation, the therapist does not see the variability that allows for even periodic contact or interpretive inroads. Once again a long sustained treatment seems necessary, with all of the patience, restraint, and interpretive skill that is part and parcel of any full treatment, all of which can lead to the slow growth of a therapeutic alliance.

SPLITTING OF GOOD AND BAD IMAGES OF SELF AND OTHER

I should like to describe one more subgroup of borderline children that I had not been able to describe at the time of my earlier paper (Pine, 1974a). Alerted by Kernberg's (1967, 1968) writings on adult borderline patients, I became attuned to certain children who show an omnipresent *splitting of good and bad images of self and other.* Such children, often "sweet" or "good" on the surface, will, in treatment, reveal an absorbing inner preoccupation with hate and violence, often with homicidal or world-destruction fantasies, equally often with scant and precarious control over them. The splitting is evidenced in the lack of connection between the "good" and the "bad" self and other. Hate, unmodified by affectionate images, becomes icy or fiery, devouring of the self or the other (in mental life), and frightening—to the patient, and, at times, to the therapist who learns about it. We are speaking here of a structural flaw and its consequences, a flaw stemming from an early failure to bring good and bad representations together and so defensively keeping them apart. This must be clearly set off from later, far less pathological "splits" of good and bad that are *not* based on the early failure and its consequent structural flaw.

I first became aware of this as a phenomenon in childhood from an adult patient, suffering from her irreconcilable love-hate images toward her adoptive parents, who was able to recall the phenomenon vividly from her childhood. The "teacher's pet" in school, the good girl, she nontheless recalls sitting in class absorbed with violent and destructive fantasy. Hearing it, I was reminded of the recurrent newspaper stories of mass murderers who, as the history unfolds, were "good" children, generally quiet and not too well known to anyone, but well-behaved, disciplined. And then I was reminded of the comment heard among educators, that troublesome (noisy, school-failing) children come to the attention of the school, but that quiet children who may also be in trouble may not be noticed. Might not some of these quiet children not only be "in trouble" as nonlearners but also as instances of the kind of child of which I am now speaking? Not all of them by any means! But surely here and there.

Such were my thoughts at the time, listening to my adult patient speak. Since then, more alert to the issue, I have come across the phenomenon three or four times in a few years through supervision of the work of others or through direct consultation or treatment myself. There is now no question in my mind but that the phenomenon exists in childhood. Its attendant disturbances in thought processes and object relations warrant its being considered another form of the borderline disturbance. Just beginning to work in the area, I do not yet feel comfortable commenting on any repeated issues in the treatment of such children; my impression is, however, that the work is exceedingly difficult, that the "split" modifies only slowly, and that the primitive rage and violence is constantly in danger of either erupting or succumbing to repression rather than undergoing modification. Nonetheless, my first extensive work with a child of this kind has had a very favorable outcome, based in part upon my constantly linking the good and the bad, the love and the hate, my interpreting the function of their being kept separate, and my having repeatedly to "lovingly" absorb the child's rage attacks and "hold" them within the affectionate working relationship.

SUMMARY

I have advanced the idea that a loose, but defensible, conceptual category of "borderline children" can be defined in terms of central developmental failures or aberrations in ego development and object relationship. These disturbances are identifiable in the school-age period because, by that age, one ordinarily expects to see some degree of stability of character and of socialization in the child; the "peculiarities" of the borderline child generally violate that expectation. Within the broad borderline domain, there is a distinct clinical gain from seeking not a single unifying mechanism that is shared by all such patients, but individualized descriptions of subtypes of borderline phenomena—subtypes which *do* have essential commonalities and whose commonalities of etiology and/or structure can lead us to individualized implications for treatment.

In fact, I have not, here, discussed treatment issues in the detail they deserve. But I *have* attempted to discuss, in considerable detail, (1) the range of developmental failures underlying borderline disturbances (and the normal developmental pathways that these children have been unable to follow) and (2) the genetic and structural distinctions in varying presenting pictures within the area. A particular view of the therapeutic process underlies these choices—the choice of detailed discussion of development and of diagnostic specificity, and lesser discussion of treatment technique per se. In that view the two detailed aspects of the discussion are in fact central to the issue of therapeutic technique.

Knowledge of development can be invaluable to the therapeutic enterprise. Elsewhere (Pine, 1976) I have tried to show that therapy (even psychoanalytic therapy *as it is traditionally carried out*) can be viewed in part as a process of facilitating normal development in addition to the more customary view of it as a process of correcting interruptions and aberrations of development. Certainly in childhood, with developmental change still proceeding rapidly, this view is useful. An understanding of the current *developmental tasks* of a child can help us to understand the continuing pathogenic consequences of particular presenting problems (e.g., learning failure and its implications for self-esteem regulation; or school refusal, and its confirmation of attachment to home and mother, making displacement to school, peers, and learning impossible). An understanding of how relevant normal developments that did *not* take place *should* have taken place (e.g., delay of impulse expression, neutralization of the learning process, development of signal anxiety and reliable internal structure) can give us clues to the historical loci of the sources of the presenting pathology. And, though developmental failures can by no means always be reversed by a later re-experiencing of the relevant developmental opportunities, an awareness of those normal modes of development can provide *cues for technical interventions* in individual instances (Pine, 1976).

And finally, knowledge of the specificity of pathological mechanisms is also invaluable to the therapeutic enterprise. When Freud (1912) spoke of the analyst's "evenly suspended attention" to the associative material of the patient, he did not mean that the analyst's mind was blank, unaware of all that had been learned previously. Rather, the analyst should not be precommitted to any single idea, thus permitting new and surprising (or perhaps old and familiar) themes to achieve centrality. Our general theory of human function-ing, our past knowledge of all our patients, and our knowledge of all that has happened and is now happening with the particular patient in our office are all parts of what the therapist's mind should be "evenly suspended" *over*. The same is true for diagnostic specificity. Only when we have the full array in mind, in short, only when we have learned from the accumulation of clinical knowledge, can our evenly hovering (uncommitted) clinical minds light upon and recognize the central phenomena in any particular patient, or in any particular session. The technical attitude of therapists has to be one of exploration and discovery; but one has to be a *prepared* explorer who will recognize relevant variations in the terrain when one sees them. Only then will we understand, and only then will we be able to speak to the patient in descriptive or interpretive words that will help the patient understand, the pathological processes at work. Precision in interpretation ultimately follows from precision in understanding. Hence, an informed view of development and of specific pathological mechanisms makes possible a refined therapeutic technique.

About treatment, one concluding point: once recently, when I was discussing an earlier version of the ideas presented here with a rather unsophisticated group of beginning therapists, the discussion began to turn around the question: should we or should we not make interpretations to borderline patients? Referring to Knight (1953a) in excessively simplistic form, one person concluded that we were not supposed to make interpreta-tions. And another, referring to Kernberg (1968), equally simplistically concluded that indeed we were supposed to interpret. What, they asked, did I think they were "supposed" to do?

I assume by now my answer to that question is clear. With fuller understanding of the range of pathology subsumed under the concept "border-line," one cannot avoid the responsibility of *creating* an answer tailored not only to the events of the moment (as in all dynamic psychotherapy) but also to the *specific* form of the pathology. Sometimes we do one thing, and sometimes another. Shall we interpret? I can only say: it all depends. On what? That is what I have tried to spell out, at least in part, herein.

R E F E R E N C E S

Alexander, F. *Psychoanalysis and psychotherapy.* New York: Norton, 1956.

Anthony, E.J. Folie à deux. In J.B. McDevitt & C.F. Settlage, (Eds.), *Separation-Individuation.* New York: International Universities Press, 1971.

Ekstein, R. *Children of time and space, of action and impulse.* New York: Appleton-Century-Crofts, 1966.

Ekstein, R., & Wallerstein, J. Observations on the psychology of borderline and psychotic children. *The Psychoanalytic Study of the Child*, 1954, *9*, 344–369.

Freud, A. The assessment of borderline cases. In *The writings of Anna Freud* (Vol. 4). New York: International Universities Press, 1969. (Originally published, 1956.)

Freud, S. Recommendations to physicians practicing psychoanalysis. *Standard edition* (Vol. 12). London: Hogarth, 1958. (Originally published, 1912.)

Freud, S. New introductory lectures on psychoanalysis. *Standard edition* (Vol. 22). London: Hogarth, 1964. (Originally published, 1933.)

Hartmann, H. The mutual influences in the development of ego and id. *The Psychoanalytic Study of the Child*, 1952, *7*, 9–30.

Kanner, L. Autistic disturbances of affective contact. *Nervous Child*, 1942, *2*, 217–250.

Kanner, L. Problems of nosology and psychodynamics of early infantile autism. *American Journal of Orthopsychiatry*, 1949, *19*, 416–426.

Kernberg, O. Borderline personality organization. *Journal of the American Psychoanalytic Association*, 1967, *15*, 641–685.

Kernberg, O. The treatment of patients with borderline personality organization. *International Journal of Psychoanalysis*, 1968, *49*, 600–619.

Knight, R. Borderline states. *Bulletin of the Menninger Clinic*, 1953a, *17*, 1–12.

Knight, R. Management and psychotherapy of the borderline schizophrenic patient. *Bulletin of the Menninger Clinic*, 1953b, *17*, 139–150.

Mahler, M.S. Pseudoimbecility. *Psychoanalytic Quarterly*, 1942; *11*, 149–164.

Mahler, M.S. On child psychosis and schizophrenia. *The Psychoanalytic Study of the Child*, 1952, *7*, 286–305.

Mahler, M.S. *On human symbiosis and the vicissitudes of individuation*, (Vol. 1): *Infantile psychosis*. New York: International Universities Press, 1968.

Mahler, M.S., Pine, F., & Bergman, A. *The psychological birth of the human infant*. New York: Basic Books, 1975.

Masterson, J.F. *Treatment of the borderline adolescent: A developmental approach*. New York: Wiley, 1972.

Pine, F. On the structuralization of drive-defense relationships. *Psychoanalytic Quarterly*, 1970, *39*, 17–37.

Pine, F. On the concept "borderline" in children: A clinical essay. *The Psychoanalytic Study of the Child*, 1974a, *29*, 341–368.

Pine, F. Libidinal object constancy: A theoretical note. *Psychoanalysis and Contemporary Science*, 1974b, *3*, 307–313.

Pine, F. On therapeutic change: Perspectives from a parent-child model. *Psychoanalysis and Contemporary Science*, 1976, *4*, 537–569.

Pine, F. On the pathology of the separation-individuation process as manifested in later clinical work: An attempt at delineation. *International Journal of Psychoanalysis*, 1979, *60* (2), 225–241.

Redl, F. Ego disturbances. In S.I. Harrison & J.F. McDermott (Eds.), *Childhood Psychopathology*. New York: International Universities Press, 1972. (Originally published, 1951.)

Rosenfeld, S.K., & Sprince, M.P. An attempt to formulate the meaning of the concept "borderline." *The Psychoanalytic Study of the Child*, 1963, *18*, 603–635.

Rosenfeld, S.K., & Sprince, M.P. Some thoughts on the technical handling of borderline children. *The Psychoanalytic Study of the Child*, 1965, *20*, 495–517.

Weil, A.P. Certain severe disturbances of ego development in childhood. *The Psychoanalytic Study of the Child*, 1953, *8*, 271–287.

Weil, A.P. Certain evidences of deviational development in infancy and early childhood. *The Psychoanalytic Study of the Child*, 1956, *11*, 292–299.

Youngerman, J. The syntax of silence. *International Review of Psychoanalysis*, 1979, *6*, 283–295.

CHAPTER 5

Borderline Conditions: Childhood and Adolescent Aspects

Paulina F. Kernberg, M.D.
DIRECTOR, CHILD AND ADOLESCENT PSYCHIATRY
THE NEW YORK HOSPITAL, CORNELL MEDICAL CENTER
WESTCHESTER DIVISION
ASSOCIATE PROFESSOR OF PSYCHIATRY
CORNELL UNIVERSITY MEDICAL COLLEGE
NEW YORK, NEW YORK

ABOUT TWENTY YEARS AGO, Elisabeth Geleerd (1958) wrote a paper entitled "Borderline States in Childhood and Adolescence." Not unexpectedly at that time, she attempted to understand the special and confusing characteristics of these patients by conceptualizing their psychopathology in terms of psychoanalytic psychology and, most innovatively, by examining these clinical phenomena in relation to Margaret Mahler's description of childhood psychosis. Already in 1949, Mahler and her colleagues had begun to delineate the clinical characteristics of what was later to become the concept of "borderline conditons" in children. Annemarie Weil (1953) followed a different path. Departing from individual differences in constitutional givens, ego, drives, and superego, she delineated the syndrome which was later to be called "ego deviancy." Interestingly, the authors who have contributed to the further elaboration of borderline conditons, both in adults and in children and adolescents, have had a common matrix of experience: (1) psychoanalysis as a theoretical framework, (2) work with severely regressed young or adult patients, and (3) an intense interest in or research commitment to child development. Perhaps many of the barriers to understanding the developmental issues, psychopathology, and most importantly the principles of psychotherapeutic technique in these cases originate in lack of experience in one of these areas.

I have selected a group of authors for study here.[1] In reviewing their publications, I picked out those aspects of borderline pathology described most frequently and where most agreement occurred. I have added, however, some items that also seem to me characteristic and relevant.

The assumption here is that borderline adults represent chronologically older borderline adolescents. The adult borderline does not differ substantially from the adolescent except in the accrual of secondary complications in the course of living (marriage, children, career vicissitudes) which do not essentially modify the borderline personality organization in these patients. Due to the persistence of primitive defense mechanisims (such as splitting and its related defenses) with their ongoing ego-weakening effects, the patient has an inability to integrate experience because of incomplete, distorted relations with external objects. The chronic instability of unintegrated superego components deprives the patient of guidelines for the self- and other-evaluation

---

[1] On borderline children, see Geleerd (1958), Frijling-Schreuder (1969), Mahler (1971), Pine (1974), and Rosenfeld and Sprince (1963). On the adolescent, see Erikson (1959), Grinker et al. (1968), Kernberg (1975, unpublished), Knight (1953), and Masterson (1967, 1971, 1975).

102

and hence of a stable sense of identity. The patient is therefore not basically affected by positive life circumstances because he or she cannot learn from experience. Time has stopped for the patient.

For example, a patient, age forty-five, acknowledged to me quite candidly that she just did not feel her age; she felt she was either a little girl or at the most a budding adolescent. Her three marriages, four children, college education, and wide travels throughout the world had not left much of an imprint on her.

DESCRIPTIVE SYMPTOMATOLOGY

In children, authors describe a characteristic multiple symptomatology with obsessions, phobias, compulsions, and hysterical traits and symptoms. The various neurotic and behavioral symptoms, however, in themselves are not typical. What is characteristic is the persistence of symptoms that should have been outgrown. The fears and phobias of four- to five-year-olds, or the tendency to compulsive behavior of two- to three-year olds, persist with an increased intensity beyond these developmental stages. Also generally described is the lability in levels of functioning. What about adolescents? Knight (1953), Kernberg (1975), and Grinker et al. (1968) describe multiple symptomatology with an assortment of neurotic and character neurotic symptoms; all conclude that none of these symptoms are specific in themselves.

The classic prepsychotic personalities—hypomanic, schizoid, and paranoid—are cited in the descriptive symptomatology of borderline conditions. Schizoid personality in children has been described (Pine, 1971), but paranoid and hypomanic personalities as understood in adult psychopathology are rare and less fixed. A young adolescent described by Geleerd (1958), for example, used her mother to integrate her reality testing. When, during a visit, the mother expressed grief over seeing her daughter full of ideas of reference, the girl corrected these ideas as she noticed her mother's sadness in relation to her.

During adolescence, the differential diagnosis needs to be viewed from the developmental perspective of adolescence. Symptoms such as depression; anxiety; identity crisis, with its rapid shifts of identification with a certain social group or ideology; neurotic conflicts with authority; even activation of primitive defensive operations in the normal identity crisis, including occasionally antisocial behavior and infantile narcissistic object relations—all are far from having the severity and chronicity that they do in the borderline adolescent. The same relation exists between transitory developmental symptoms and traits which normal children present and the multiple severe symptomatology of the borderline child.

SENSE OF SELF

The borderline child does not have the capacity to anticipate gratification, even if previous gratification has been given, because he or she has not achieved object constancy. Instead, there is a disturbed sense of self, with distrust and fear of disintegration (Geleerd, 1958; Mahler, 1971).

A seven-year-old borderline child in analysis, for instance, had the fantasy that he would like to play football, but only under certain conditions. He would wear an inflatable outfit, which would expand with air so as practically to invade the whole field. Thus, anybody who bumped against him would only hit him on the surface, and he would be well-protected. The sense of self includes, of course, the bodily self, and hence the fear of and anxiety in response to potential disintegration and annihilation.

Attempting to verbalize the fantasy systems that some of these children and adolescents experience of the self, one could formulate the following:

1. "I am hooked to my mother and therefore she cannot survive without me or I cannot survive without her." (Fig. 5-2) This would correspond to the stage of differentiation in terms of Mahler's separation-indivuation phases.In contrast, if one were to put it in words, the true symbiotic relation fantasy characteristic of psychosis, where there is fusion of self and object represen-taion with no boundries between them would be: "I and mother are one." (Fig. 5-1)

2. In the early practicing subphase, the experience of self could be verbalized as "I carry mother all around and I don't need her." (Fig. 5-3)

3. In the practicing proper phase, the experience of self could be put into the following words: "Mother is inside and part of me for a while. If she is not around I may cease to exist—lost her inside of me—and therefore I need her around to refuel." (Fig. 5-4)

4. In the rapprochement phase, the experience of self becomes "Mother is not part of me or I am not part of mother, but instead she is under my control or I am under her control." (Fig. 5-5)

In my opinion, what appears descriptively as fear of merging may have therefore a variety of structural implications different from those of the truly symbiotic psychosis, where self and object dissolve into each other and feel like one. In borderline cases, fears and wishes of merging *preserve* the distinction between self- and object images, primitive as these may be. I would like to propose that borderline conditions may stem not only from the rapprochement crisis, but also from fixations or regressions to the earlier differentiation or practicing phases of the separation-individuation process.

Structurally, self- and object images are differentiated from each other, but they have a varying relationship to each other according to the substage of the separation-individuation process in question. In the early differentiation subphase, self- and object image may have still a common partial core (Fig. 5-1). In the next stage, the early practicing subphase, we have a self surrounded by the object image (Fig. 5-2). The practicing phase proper could be represented as a self-image having introjected the object image (Fig. 5-3). Because of the increased capacity to recognize the reality of separateness, there is a need for the external object to reinforce or refuel the engulfed object image.

Lastly, the wish and fear of merging in the rapprochement subphase really means the need to control or coerce the external object or to be controlled and coerced by the external object, with increased need for the external object's presence to reinforce and protect the frail stability of achieved self- and object differentiation in the absence of object constance (Fig. 5-4). The borderline patient's attempts to achieve a sense of identity and autonomous functioning is forever unattainable.

Merger

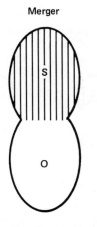

Figure 5--1 Symbiotic phase.

Twinship

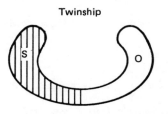

Figure 5-2 Early differentiation.

Mirroring

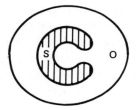

Figure 5–3 Early practicing.

Mirroring

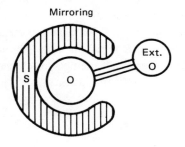

Figure 5–4 Practicing proper.

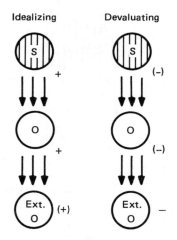

Figure 5–5 Rapprochement. Left, shadowing. Right, coercion.

S = self-image
O = object image
Ext. O = external object
Reprinted with modifications from: Kernberg, P. F. (1979), Psychoanalytic profile of the borderline adolescent.
In: S. C. Feinstein, P. L. Giovacchini (eds). *Adolescent Psychiatry Development and Clinical Studies, Volume VII*. Chicago: University of Chicago Press, pp. 234–256.

OBJECT RELATIONS

This category includes relations to external objects and to transitional objects.

RELATIONSHIP TO MOTHER

The borderline child's relationship to the mother is characterized either by primitive idealization of the object with the patient's sharing in what is perceived as the object's goodness and power or by devaluation and attribution of extreme meanness to the mother (Geleerd, 1958; Mahler, 1971; Weil, 1953; and Rosenfeld & Sprince, 1963). As described by Shapiro et al. (1977) in research on families of borderline adolescents, the parents are perceived as all good or all bad, according to the need to split and separate the good mother of separation from the bad mother of separation.

TRANSITIONAL OBJECTS

Clinical observations seem to indicate that transitional objects in borderline children are absent or may acquire a bizarre quality. In borderline adolescents, the history of transitional objects is nonexistent. The existence of a transitional object presupposes the acquisition of a positive object relation with the mother which can be internalized, so that the child's relation to his internalized object can be reproduced in an intermediate world of experience. It is not surprising that borderline children who have not developed a positive sense of self in relation to a positive object (in the context of soothing and pleasurable experience with the mother) would not have a transitional object at the appropriate age of 8 to 24 months or of the usual quality—that is, an object experienced in the gestalt of the maternal experience, such as a satin blanket edge, diaper, or furry soft toy. Instead, these children tend either to continue clinging to the mother, searching for positive symbiotic experiences or positive refuelings, or to represent their relationship to the bad mother of separation by attaching themselves to inanimate objects—like the child who had as his transitional object a telephone receiver which he took everywhere he went. Moreover, the transitional objects of borderline children characteristically portray self-images or ideal images akin to the imaginary companion, in contrast to the transitional objects reflecting a positive mother-child interaction.

The part object and self-representations are not intergrated. What follows is common to adults, adolescents, and children. Ekstein and Friedman (1967) depict the reversal of self- and object images which Kernberg (1975) describes for adolescent and adult borderlines. No matter how primitive the object relation, however, there is always an object separate from the self. "The external object is usually utilized by the patient as a prop for his projections so that at times the patient experiences himself as the therapist while simultaneously the therapist is induced to reenact an aspect of the personality of the patient."

AFFECTS

Various authors working with children (Pine, 1974; Rosenfeld & Sprince, 1963; Geleerd, 1958) agree that anxiety is of an intense, free-floating nature. This anxiety of total loss and disaster and annihilation has a traumatic quality quite different from the signal anxiety of neurotic patients.

As Mahler et al. observed in 1949, rage is prevalent, with proneness to tantrums. Aggression may reach dangerous proportions, such as poking a pencil in the eye of a schoolmate, throwing a baby brother against the wall, or seriously threatening to jump out of the window.

In quality, affects are sudden, abrupt (see Pine, Rosenfeld, and Sprince) and have all-or-nothing quality, with direct discharge or no discharge at all. One sees immaturity and wide mood swings. We can understand the latter as derivatives of the mood swings in the separation-individuation process—that is, elation in the practicing subphases and depressive moods alternating with a sense of omnipotence in the rapprochement crisis. Thus, an angry coercive attitude and a hypomanic-like elation can be considered as the affective counterpart of the main fixation point of this psychopathology—the separation-individuation subphases, especially the rapprochement crisis. Grinker et al. (1968) refer to similar mood swings in adult borderline patients.

There appears to be a lack of guilt, concern, assessment in depth of others, commitment to a set of values (cultural and artistic), and the possibility of nonexploitative relationships with others. Missing also are the affective modulated derivatives that stem from the integration of positive and negative self-representations into an integrated concept—namely, what Mahler has described as the state of being "on the way to object constancy."

Similar affective qualities are described in borderline adolescents: intense anger, demandingness (an expression of coercion), exploitative behavior, lack of social tact. Grinker et al. (1968) describe mood swings, depression with hostile rage reactions, and self-destructiveness or detached, mute behavior associated with a passive show of anger. This latter characteristic coincides with Geleerd's (1958) observation that there is either aggression or no direct expression of aggression at all.

Borderline children lack the capacity to anticipate and even experience enjoyment and pleasure, as can be observed in their practical inability to use play for these purposes. In a parallel fashion, borderline adolescents lack the capacity to experience true satisfaction and pleasure.

EGO FUNCTIONS

SPECIFIC EGO FUNCTIONS

In regard to apparatuses of secondary autonomy, some children who suffer from minimal brain dysfunction (affecting spatial orientation, memory, verbal abilities), or other physical deficiencies, such as deafness or blindness, are more prone to develop problems of separation-individuation and hence are at high risk for the development of borderline conditions. In fact, there is increasing evidence of minimal brain dysfunction and/or physical deficiencies in some adolescent and adult borderline patients (Hartocollis, 1968).

In relation to motor functions, Weil (1953) has described poor patterning in development, including erratic eating and cleaning habits. Rosenfeld and Sprince (1963) cite unusual movement postures and hyperactivity. A nine-year-old patient of mine, for example, was diagnosed as schizoid personality with borderline features. He had a very unsteady gait and was so hyperactive that he literally fell from his chair during the initial diagnostic interview. He often bumped into things, and objects accidentally fell from his hands. There was no sign of organicity in the neurological examination, and, indeed, his lack of coordination was resolved as he realized that his motor style reflected his identification with his father who had the same pattern of movements.

Borderline adolescents may also have awkward gaits and movements, but it seems these may not be as reversible as those of younger ages.

In terms of *perception,* borderline children are capable of and prone to visual and auditory hallucinations. An important differential diagnosis should be made with the developmentally normal imaginary companion (Nagera, 1969).

Visual and auditory hallucinations in children are determined by partial regression without having the ominous implications of psychosis that adolescents' hallucinations have. Many borderline children hear voices instigating them to jump out of the window or reproaching them, or the voices of dead people who call them. This phenomenon is at times partially supported by the culture—with Puerto Ricans, for example. These hallucinations disappear when anxieties lessen and the child is in a more supportive environment. According to Coren and Saldinger (1967), the conditions for development of hallucinations in children are: (1) intense affect, usually aggression; (2) lack of outlet for this affect; (3) incomplete ego development; (4) poor parental models for reality testing; (5) conflict-laden cathexis of the auditory or visual sphere; (6) a drowsy or tired state; or (7) a traumatic real event which acutely undermines reality testing because it mirrors the child's internal conflict. In borderline children, aggression, incomplete ego development, and poor parental models for reality testing are heavily weighted factors. No author describes the presence of delusions in borderline adolescents other than in schizophrenia or other adolescent psychosis, thus differentiating borderline conditons from schizophrenic reactions.

As to *reality testing,* all of the authors concur that there is always contact with reality, but, although they report no delusions in children, they agree with Geleerd (1958) that "reality span is brief." The child requires the presence of the object to maintain his sense of reality. In cases of stress, the sense of reality fails, as does reality testing (Pine, 1974). Refusal to accept the reality principle makes adaptation to reality inadequate. In the case of reality testing in children, the diagnostic technique has not yet been systematized. By contrast, Otto Kernberg (1977), in his Structual Diagnostic Examination for adolescents, systematically evaluates the patient's capacity to test reality in the here-and-now situation. This is done by asking the patient either to evaluate his or her own behavior and the behavior of the interviewer, or to empathize with the different perception that the interviewer may have about the patient's productions. If the patient shows a capacity to empathize with the interviewer's perspective, with some social norms which he or she may not comply with but at least can recognize, that is an important criterion differentiating borderline conditions (where this capacity exists) from schizophrenia (where this capacity is not present). The capacity for reality testing is assessed in children through the incidence of play disruption, as well as in their capacity to leave their play and come back to everyday life upon termination of the session.

NONSPECIFIC EGO FUNCTIONS

The variable and discrepant levels of ego organization indicate an underlying failure to establish a solid hierarchy of ego states and functions. The synthetic function of the ego is nonoperating. In a way, splitting has a reciprocal relation to the synthetic function of the ego, which involves the synthesis of self- and object images as well as the integration and depersonification of the superego.

Nonspecific ego deficits present are: lack of impulse control, low frustration tolerance, low anxiety tolerance, and, I would add, low depression tolerance. The deficits in these functions are common to children and adolescents. The lack of impulse control seems to be a hallmark of borderline function, with lack of control of the different levels of ego organization. What is important, however, is that this lack of control may not necessarily represent an ego defect in the sense of lack of capacity to control; rather it may be used defensively to bring about different ego states for the purpose of controlling anxiety.

DEFENSE MECHANISMS

Various authors studying children's borderline conditions have talked about brittle defenses and failures in defenses. The same brittleness is described in borderline adolescents. Ekstein and Wallerstein (1954) and Rosenfeld and Sprince (1963), however, describe more significant and specific defenses, such as the use of omnipotence, projections, splitting, denial, ego regression, and shifting ego states.

Weil (1953) discusses the presence of "faulty repression," and Ekstein and Wallerstein (1954) cite the aggression easily elicited by frustration which causes abrupt leaps in the use of different levels of defense mechanisms and occurs in the absence of gross external stimuli. These descriptions of defense mechanisms closely overlap with Kernberg's (1975) statement that repression is not the main mechanism of defense in borderline conditons, but rather splitting is, with all the accompanying mechanisms of omnipotence, primitive forms of projections, and denial.

The concept of failure in defense or brittle defense is based on the assumption that prior to repression and the classical mechanisms of defense there is lack of differentiation and structure. Clinical experience, however, shows that primitive but structured forms of defense are definitely present in borderline states. Primitive forms of denial, idealization, devaluation, and projection become apparent as one observes the patient in individual treatment or in the family context.

SUPEREGO INTEGRATION

There is a unanimous sense that early developmental failures have an impact on superego formation (Pine, 1974; Rosenfeld & Sprince, 1963). Superego development, because of the splitting and lack of synthetic function of the ego, remains at the level of introjects, easily projected onto external objects, which explains the paranoid potential of these patients. The adolescent borderline frequently produces psychotic transference with a paranoid flavor.

PLAY AND WORK

The borderline child does not play normally. He is addicted to pretend play (Weill, 1953) which reveals a compulsion to be active and in control but does not show enjoyment, resolution of conflict, or adaptive expression of fantasy.

Both the child and adolescent can be excellent students. Later in life, at the work or professional career level, the borderline patient usually settles for work actually below his capacities. In graduate school, the borderline also does not do as well as his or her potential had indicated (Gunderson, 1977).

FANTASIES

Geleerd (1958) and Ekstein have discussed the fantasy life of the borderline child. No relinquishment of omnipotent fantasy occurs. The fantasies come from all levels of psychosexual development and are sexual as well as aggressive. The child is easily made anxious and becomes overwhelmed by these fantasies. For example, a seven-year-old patient was afraid to light matches because, if he did, fire would ensue and would invade the entire street and destroy New York City and the United States, and the world, and would only stop short of the north and south poles where there are 7, no 700 feet of ice. He would never play with matches for sure. According to Ekstein, a feeling of external danger usually goes along with the fantasy so that there is very little gratification from fantasies.

Distance fantasies, often oral in character, are typical in regressed ego states, as are fears of separation and abandonment, bodily disintegration, and distortion of body image. A patient age six, for example, swallowed his teeth as his permanent teeth replaced them. Fantasies connected with Oedipal levels may mask problems deriving from earlier stages of development.

Masturbatory fantasies with Oedipal components, combined with fantasies of aggression and fantasies of other perverse activities permeated with aggression, are common in both children and adolescents. There is no clear-cut period of latency. Similarly, compulsive masturbation with perverse fantasies is frequent. One borderline child, for example, had masturbatory fantasies which included the idea of flooding the world with urine. He pictured his mother's dying under his father's beatings. An adolescent patient dreamed she had intercourse with a blade that would cut her so badly she might die.

CHARACTERISTICS OF THE OEDIPAL SITUATION

The borderline child, as well as the adolescent, experiences Oedipal situations which are distorted by the weight of the difficulties in the separation-individuation stages. The phallic stage is unstable. As the inability to separate from the mother enhances incestuous ties, the boy has increased problems of disidentification with the mother and is predisposed to both homosexual behavior and problems of core identity. In the borderline adolescent, fear of annihilation by abandonment on the part of the mother increases the difficulty of separating to invest in another object. In the younger child, this is evidenced in problems with peers; in the adolescent, in difficulties with peers and heterosexual relations, frequently characterized by extreme forms of sadistic control of the partner or the altruistic surrender of shadowing.

PSYCHOSIS IN BORDERLINE CONDITIONS

Both adolescents and children may have brief psychotic episodes related to stress with paranoid symptoms, depersonalization, derealization, dissociation, and suicide attempts.

ETIOLOGY

The etiological factors in borderline syndrome are many-fold. *Problems in the rapprochement crisis* in the separation-individuation process lead to the persistence of splitting, a weakening mechanism of defense, which interferes with the integration of good and bad images, in order to protect the child from anxiety and rage. This seems to be one of the most prevalent theories about borderline conditions (Mahler, 1971). Kernberg (1975) has postulated the role of congenital oral aggression leading to a history of intense frustration and intense aggression.

Constitutional defects that interfere with the normal mode of integration of perceptions, such as blindness, deafness, minimal brain dysfunction, or constitutionally determined lack of anxiety tolerance and excessive aggressive drive, may also cause splitting. These latter factors, however, are not very easily differentiated from the pathology of parent-child interaction.

FAMILY CONTRIBUTIONS

Shapiro et al. (1975) indicate the pervasiveness of pathological interactions within the families of borderline adolescents. In their research on hospitalized borderline adolescents receiving family therapy, they cite the abundant use of projective identification in the family setting which, if not necessarily causal, contributes to maintain borderline functioning. Each member of the family sees himself as "strong and autonomous," without dependent needs, while the designated child is perceived as weak, vulnerable and demanding, and totally dependent. The parents unconsciously perceive the child's independent moves as hostile rejections or his or her needs for nurturing and support as straining demands. Splitting and projective identification impair the child's ego formation. The child is unable to tolerate the parent's or his own anxiety. The child then has to modify its objective experience in accordance with these projections.

A seventeen-year-old was hospitalized two weeks after his own mother was hospitalized for a suicide attempt. In the preceding months, he had wanted to work and was successful in getting employment as a worker on a newspaper. His mother, a chronically depressed woman, became so panicky about his moving out of the home and being more independent that she told him that she would not be around anymore and attempted to commit suicide. After the mother's hospitalization, he became upset, withdrawn, and for two weeks stayed home, doing nothing. Finally he had an abrupt outburst of temper, breaking chairs and furniture, and forcing his father, a passive and withdrawn man, to hospitalize him. Once in the hospital he reorganized, feeling relieved to be away from the family. In those patients where endowment is adequate, the role of the family, and specifically the mother, in the separation-individuation phase seems to be crucial.

Kestenberg has described other forms of pathological communication between the family members—keeping family secrets, contradictory behaviors, narcissistic use of the child, inconsistency, dominant intrusive behavior, and depersonification of the child who is treated as an object to soothe mother's anxieties and not as a subject in his own right. The mother exerts such control over the child that he or she submits to the cruel object in the hope of eventually triumphing and obtaining love. Extreme forms of masochistic surrender to the idealized mother may stem from this mechanism which interferes with the expression of aggression and maintains splitting, thus fostering the formation of borderline personality organization.

ABERRANT DEVELOPMENT VERSUS DEVELOPMENTAL ARREST

Although these concepts are meant to be descriptive, it seems to be more true to the picture one sees in borderline children to conceptualize an aberrant developmental course with accrual of distortions in practically every aspect of the personality than to postulate arrest per se. It is not that development has not proceeded but that it has followed a skewed course. This distinction has ramifications for the treatment approach. With most borderline children, it would be a mistake to base the therapy only on supportive interventions or environmental manipulation. Instead, it is necessary to undo and resolve extreme character pathology and conflict configurations.

IS EGO ORGANIZATION INHERENTLY UNSTABLE?

Some authors have described the instability of the ego, or what is perhaps more readily understood as a fluid ego organization, in borderline patients (Ekstein & Wallerstein, 1954). In my experience, however, the shifting ego states correspond to organized self- and object representations which are activated for defensive purposes, for primary and secondary gains, to deal with frustration or anxiety. As noted above, the more typical defense mechanisms found in neurosis are not so readily observed. Instead, one finds coercion, shadowing, withdrawal, regression, or direct temper outbursts, and each of these corresponds to the activation of different self- and object representations.

To take a clinical example, K., an eight-year-old boy, had broken the window of the garage. He had also been stealing pencils from his peers at school. When confronted with this misbehavior, he blamed two or three children in a rather diffuse manner. He was unable to feel any guilt and, instead, seemed only fleetingly embarrassed. Indeed, he was furious about even being confronted in this manner. When told by his mother that he would not be allowed any Halloween candy, he denied that the punishment was fair and pretended to be in a very good mood. At first, he sucked his thumb and appeared to try to control his reaction in that way. Soon thereafter he assumed a flippant attitude and declared that he was going to get candy anyhow; in fact, the school bus driver had already given him some. In the next half hour, a variety of expressive reactions ensued, including temper outbursts, projection, coercive behavior with the mother, and throwing an object at the therapist. K. tried to deal with the situation inefficiently through mechanisms of denial, omnipotent fantasy regression, and splitting. Yet this shifting behavior did not necessarily arise out of any intrinsic instability of his ego states. In some cases, however, one could speculate that there might be a correspondence here on the affective level to the cognitive "instability" that children with minimal brain dysfunction present in terms of learning something one day and being unable to retrieve that knowledge the next day.

THE QUESTION OF EGO WEAKNESS

An important consideration in treatment is the question of ego weakness. This global concept needs to be spelled out in its particulars. After all, the ego is a system containing many functions, only one of those being object relations. Moreover, one should note that ego weakness in itself can be used for defensive purposes. This certainly adds a most crucial leverage in the interpretative work with these patients. The very expectations of the therapist who postulates an irreversible ego defect, rather than a special form of defense by the ego, may make the child who cannot be reached by therapeutic interaction a self-fulfilling prophecy.

DO BORDERLINE CONDITIONS BLEND WITH PSYCHOTIC CONDITIONS?

An understanding of this question is crucial for the conduct of psychotherapy. Certainly, borderline children may have brief psychotic episodes related to stress, with paranoid symptoms, depersonalization, derealization, dissociation, and suicide attempts. But here I would like to discuss two issues: the nature of defenses and anxieties in the psychotic patient and the lack of differentiation between self and object.

In my opinion, typical psychotic defenses include the most primitive forms of projection, fragmentation, somatic defenses such as extreme hypochondriasis, animation of inanimate objects, deanimation of animate objects, formation of bizarre objects, delusions, and hallucinations. The anxieties do not entail fears of annihilation so much as fears of falling, losing oneself through dissolving, and of total fragmentation. Lack of capacity to test reality given the supports of clarification and confrontation further delineates psychosis from borderline conditions.

A key difference lies in the psychotic patient's regression to a symbiotic state with no boundaries between self and object. In contrast, the fusion fantasies of borderline patients, if looked at carefully, contain the various structural implications that I outline in my description of the experience of self. They illustrate failures in the process of separation-individuation and not regression to an undifferentiated self. It is true that there may be transitory states of regression to and fixation at a pathological symbiotic level, but in most cases the patient can rebound to the differentiation between self and object in one or the other of the constellations I have described. Again, these formulations have practical implications in terms of the specific interpretive work with the transference in the here-and-now and also in the understanding of countertransference reactions.

CONTINUITY OF BORDERLINE STATES

In relation to the continuity of borderline conditions into adulthood, most authors believe there is such a continuity. Pine (1974) describes chronic failures in reality testing and object relations which are silently present at all times in these children and continue into adulthood, making for "the odd adult." Weil (1953) describes the same progression. Blum describes such a continuity convincingly in his paper, "The Borderline Childhood of the Wolf Man" (1974). Mahler (1971) and Kernberg (1975) also support this thesis. And it is indeed justified if we assume that the borderline personality organization is insulated from the effects of the environment unless a therapeutic intervention intense and prolonged enough changes the internal world of the patient and the patient becomes able to modify his inner objects in accordance with external reality.

In conclusion, I have tried to present the differences and similarities between child and adolescent borderline patients, while stressing the continuity of pathology and likelihood of common etiology. The differences stem more from the differences in developmental levels than from the intrinsic psychopathology of the borderline condition with its characteristic lack of integration of the self and of objects and its widespread negative effects on personality and adjustment to external reality.

R E F E R E N C E S

Blum, H.P. Psychoanalytic understanding and psychotherapy of borderline regression. *International Journal of Psychoanalysis and Psychotherapy*, 1972, 1 (1) 46–59.

Blum, H.P. The borderline childhood of the Wolf Man. *Journal of the American Psychoanalytic Association,* 1974, *22,* 721–742.

Coren, H.Z. & Saldinger, J.S. Visual hallucinosis in children. A report of two cases. *The Psychoanalytic Study of the Child,* 1967, *22,* 331–356.

Ekstein, R. & Friedman S. Object constancy and psychotic reconstruction. *The Psychoanalytic Study of the Child,* 1967, *22,* 357–374.

Ekstein, R. & Wallerstein, J. Observations on the psychology of borderline and psychotic children: Report from a current psychotherapy research project at Southard School. *The Psychoanalytic Study of the Child,* 1954, *9,* 344–369.

Erikson, E.H. *Identity and the life cycle. Psychological Issues,* 1959, Monograph 1, No. 1.

Fast, I., & Chethik, M. Some aspects of object relationships in borderline children. *International Journal Of Psycho-Analysis,* 1972, *53,* 479–485.

Fintzy, R.T. Vicissitudes of the transitional object in a borderline child. *International Journal of Psycho-Analysis,* 1971, *52,* 107–114.

Freud, A. Adolescence. *The Psychoanalytic Study of The Child,* 1958, *13,* 255–278.

Frijling-Schreuder, E.C.M. Borderline states in children. *The Psychoanalytic Study of the Child,* 1969, *24,* 307–327.

Frosch, J. The psychotic character: Clinical psychiatric considerations. *Psychiatric Quarterly,* 1964, *38,* 81–96.

Geleerd, E.R. Borderline states in childhood and adolescence. *The Psychoanalytic Study of the Child,* 1958, *13,* 279–295.

Grinker, R.R., Sr., Werble, B., & Drye, R.C. *The borderline syndrome.* New York: Basic books 1968.

Gunderson, J. Characteristics of borderline. In P. Hartocollis. (Ed.), *Borderline personality disorders: The concept, the syndrome, the patient.* New York: International Universities Press, 1977.

Hartocollis, P. The syndrome of minimal brain dysfunction in young adult patients. *Bulletin of the Menninger Clinic,* 1968, *32* (2), 102-104.

Kernberg, O., et al. Psychotherapy and psychoanalysis: Final report of the Menninger Foundation's psychotherapy research project. *Bulletin of the Menninger Clinic,* 1972, *36,* 1–275.

Kernberg, O., *Borderline conditions and pathological narcissism.* New York: Jason Aronson 1975.

Kernberg, O. The diagnosis of borderline conditions in adolescence. Unpublished, 1975.

Kernberg, O. The structural diagnosis of borderline personality of organization. In P. Hartocollis, (Ed.), *Borderline personality disorders: The concept, the syndrome, the patient.* New York: International Universities Press, 1977.

Knight, R.P. Borderline states. In R.P. Knight and C.R. Friedman (Eds.), *Psychoanalytic psychiatry and psychology.* New York: International Universities Press, 1953.

Lewis, M. Transitory or pseudo-organicity and borderline personality in a 7-year-old child. *Journel of the American Academy of Child Psychiatry,* 1976, *15,* 131–138.

Maenchen, A. Object cathexis in a borderline twin. *The Psychoanalytic Study of the Child,* 1968, *23,* 438–456.

Mahler, M.S. A study of the separation-individuation process: Its possible application to borderline phenomena in the psychoanalytic situation. *The Psychoanalytic Study of the Child,* 1971, *26,* 403–424.

Mahler, M.S., & Kaplan, L. Developmental aspects in the assessment and narcissistic or so-called borderline personalities. In P. Hartocollis (Ed.), *Borderline personality disorders: The concept, the syndrome, the patient.* New York: International Universities Press, 1977.

Mahler, M.S, Ross, J.R., Jr., & DeFries, Z. Clinical studies in benign and malignant cases of childhood psychosis. *American Journal of Orthopsychiatry,* 1949, *19,* 295–305.

Masterson, J.F. Treatment of the adolescent with borderline syndrome: A problem in separation-individuation. *Bulletin of the Menninger Clinic,* 1972, *35,* 5–18.

Masterson, J.F., & Rinsley, D.B. The borderline syndrome: The role of the mother in the genesis and psychic structure of the borderline personality. *International Journal Of Psycho-Analysis,* 1975, *56,* 163–177.

Nagera, H. The imaginary companion: Its significance for ego development and conflict solution. *The Psychoanalytic Study of the Child,* 1969, *24,* 165–175.

Pine, F. One the concept "borderline" in children. *The Psychoanalytic Study of the Child,* 1974, *29,* 341–368.

Pine, F. On the separation process, universal trends and individual differences. In J.B. McDevitt & C.V Settlage, (Eds.), *Separation-individuation: Essays in honor of Margaret S. Mahler.* New York: International Universities Press, 1971.

Rosenfeld, K., & Sprince, M. An attempt to formulate the meaning of the concept "borderline." *The Psychoanalytic Study of the Child,* 1963, *18,* 603–635.

Weil, A.M. Certain severe disturbances of ego development in childhood. *The Psychoanalytic Study of the Child,* 1953, *8,* 271-287.

CHAPTER 6

A Clinical Approach to the Psychological Testing of Borderline Children

Martin Leichtman, Ph.D.
DIRECTOR OF PSYCHOLOGY
CHILDREN'S DIVISION
THE MENNINGER FOUNDATION
TOPEKA,KANSAS

Sharon Nathan, Ph.D.
STAFF PSYCHOLOGIST
CHILDREN'S DIVISION
THE MENNINGER FOUNDATION
TOPEKA, KANSAS

INTRODUCTION

IN THE LATE 1940S AND 1950S, clinicians such as Mahler (Mahler, Ross, & DeFries, 1949), Weil (1953, 1956), and Beres (1956) called attention to a group of children who exhibited marked disturbances in ego functions and object relationships which approached, but which were less severe than, those found in the more widely recognized childhood psychoses. The term "borderline children" began to be applied to these children in this period as Ekstein and Wallerstein (1954) used it to designate one group of youngsters who displayed abrupt shifts between psychotic and neurotic levels of ego organization and Geleerd (1958) used it to designate a somewhat broader group characterized by impulsivity, low frustration tolerance, emotional immaturity, erratic developmental patterns, a readiness to withdraw into fantasy, and marked disturbances in the face of rejection or loss of contact with caretaking figures. Over the last two decades, numerous papers (Marcus, 1963; Rosenfeld & Sprince, 1963, 1965; Frijling-Schreuder, 1969; Pine, 1974; Chiland & Lebovici, 1977; Chethik, 1980; Leichtman & Shapiro, 1980a; Rinsley, 1980a, 1980b) have sought to provide a more systematic delineation of these conditions, and the concept of borderline disorders in children has been used extensively by clinicians, although its acceptance is far from universal.

This concept, as it is described in the literature and used in clinical settings such as our own, is distinguished by a number of characteristics. It is applied to children who exhibit a wide, varied, and, at times, bewildering array of presenting problems that include (1) multiple and shifting neurotic symptoms (phobias, compulsions, hysterical and hypochondriacal states, excessive anxiety, and sleep disturbances); (2) pronounced behavioral and characterological problems that lead to major conflicts at home, in school, and in the community; (3) delays in or uneven patterns of development; (4) poor social adaptation; and (5) psychotic-like symptoms. Because of the variability and nonspecificity of many of these symptoms, diagnoses of borderline conditions tend to be based on assessments of development and functioning along structural dimensions drawn from psychoanalytic ego psychology and object-relations theory. Borderline children are held to display early fixations in libidinal development, primitive modes of affect organization, problematic defensive operations, disturbances in thought organization and reality testing, diffuse ego weaknesses, and difficulties in identity formation and object relationships that stand between those encountered in severe neuroses and the psychoses. These difficulties are attributed to arrests in development centering on issues that are salient in the second and third years of life, although they may have roots in earlier periods and reverberations throughout childhood. Accounts of the particular causes and consequences of such developmental disturbances in children are rarely explicit, but they generally seem to agree with those conceptions of similar pathology in adolescents and adults suggesting that borderline conditions result from varying combinations of constitutional, psychological, and familial factors and occur in individuals of differing character types (Kernberg, 1967, 1970, 1972; Rinsley, 1978; Stone, 1980). Consequently, while the term "borderline children" has occasionally been used as if it applied to a single syndrome, most clinicians working with children use it to cover a group of disorders that have noteworthy common features but which may differ substantially in their particular manifestations and etiologies. Apart from Pine (1974) and Rinsley (1980b), however, little has been published on different types of borderline chldren, and no typological scheme is commonly used.[1]

Although much has been written on the use of psychological tests in the diagnosis of borderline conditions in adults (Singer, 1977), and although case studies (Fuller, et al., 1954; Olesker, 1980) have pointed to the value of testing in work with borderline children, the literature on psychological assessment of these children is quite limited. Indeed, it is confined chiefly to a classic paper by Engel (1963); a discussion of the use of the Rorschach to assess reality testing in borderline and psychotic children by Meyer and Caruth (1964); a report on the test patterns of 40 five- to eleven-year-old "prepsychotic" children by Rausch de Traubenberg and Boizou (1980); and two articles of our own describing a clinical approach to the assessment of borderline children (Leichtman & Shapiro, 1980a, 1980b). Drawing upon this literature, this chapter describes the use of psychological testing in the diagnosis of children between the ages of five and thirteen who are currently described as manifesting borderline disorders.

In particular, the chapter examines the process through which a psychoanalytically oriented approach to psychological assessment can be used to gain an understanding of the presenting problems and varied patterns of psychological functioning of a group of children who often respond to testing in distinctive and highly atypical ways. It focuses on the manner in which different aspects of the test situation—children's behavior within it, the test

[1]The approach to differentiating among types of borderline disorders taken in this chapter has been influenced by a promising typological scheme being developed by a colleague, Efrain Bleiberg. On the basis of reality testing and object relations issues, Bleiberg suggests that different borderline conditions may be linked to schizophrenic, narcissistic, and affective and impulse disorders.

process, tests of mental abilities, and projective tests—provide information of diagnostic significance and the ways in which this information may be integrated, used to answer diagnostic questions, and translated into treatment plans. By considering testing from this perspective, we hope to contribute to an appreciation of both the kinds of problems with which clinicians struggle in their efforts to understand borderline children and the rich possibilities psychological evaluations offer for the diagnosis of these conditions.

BEHAVIOR IN THE TEST SITUATION

Borderline children differ from borderline adults as well as from most other children in the extent to which their conflicts and problems are manifested openly in the test situation. Borderline adults can usually manage an apparently adequate adaptation to the demands of everyday life situations (Shapiro, 1978) and show the clearest evidence of their pathology on particular psychological tests (Singer, 1977). Most children can handle testing without unusual displays of disturbed or disruptive behavior. In contrast to normal children, borderline children display their pathology far more openly in daily life. They tend to be anxious, impulsive, and intolerant of frustration; they exhibit pronounced characterological and interpersonal problems; they are subject to abrupt mood swings and sharp regressions; and they are apt to interpret the world around them and to interact with others in idiosyncratic ways. The stressful circumstances surrounding most evaluations exacerbate such problems. Ill-equipped to handle crises, borderline children are frequently seen when not only they, but also their families, are in turmoil; fearful of separations, they are often referred when there is an immediate threat of separation from their family or after a separation has taken place, as in the case of hospitalization. The demanding, affect-arousing, at times threatening nature of psychological tests only increases that stress. As a consequence, the behavior of borderline children in the course of evaluations often provides graphic demonstrations of their conflicts and important insights into their personality organization.

Consideration of this behavior is significant from two standpoints. First, because so much may be revealed about the character and problems of borderline children in this way, behavioral observations usually provide an extraordinarily rich source of clinical data. Second, because much of that behavior is atypical and problematic, the manner in which these children approach and work on tests often has an important bearing on how tests are administered to them and how test data is interpreted.

BEHAVIORAL OBSERVATIONS

In discussing the distinctive quality of the test process with borderline children, Engel (1963) notes: "From the first moment, such children make much more vigorous use of the testing relationship than do others and cast their intrapsychic struggles upon the testing situation in large and bold signals." (p. 433) A review of test reports on children seen in The Menninger Foundation's Children's Division over the last seven years who have been diagnosed as manifesting borderline "conditions," "disorders," "personalities," or "features" amply confirms this point.[2] Although testing in our institution is done as part of a comprehensive evaluation and extratest interactions tend to be kept to a minimum, these reports nonetheless include a wealth of detail about the general behavior of borderline youngsters and striking accounts of dramatic incidents that occurred in the course of the testing. The reports are also written with a vividness frequently lacking in evaluations of other youngsters.

Often it is clear that something about youngsters' appearances, attitudes, or ways of presenting themselves has made a strong and immediate impression on the psychologist. For example, one report begins: "Doug is a wiry, bland youngster, who, although attractive and well-groomed, manages to convey the impression that he is unlikable and disgusting." Another starts: "Bill is a tense, poorly coordinated boy who, while possessing pleasant features, often looks either vague or diabolical." Still another begins: "David approached the testing with a grandiose attitude which, when threatened, quickly turned to smoldering, pent-up anger." The aspects of test behavior which are highlighted vary from child to child. In some cases, attention focuses on the air of helplessness and vulnerability youngsters project; in others, on their extreme provocativeness; in others, on their suspiciousness; and in still others, on their desperate efforts to play roles (e.g., the con man, the comedian, or the tough delinquent) that are usually too much for them to sustain. Some youngsters try desperately to comply with every request psychologists make, while others exhibit constant resistance. What is most striking in the impressions these children convey is less the particular problems noted than the openness with which problems are displayed and the degree to which they compel attention.

A number of different patterns of test behavior are noted frequently in reports on borderline youngsters. One common pattern is that involving a mixture of diffuse ego weaknesses and exaggerated infantile character traits. For example, discussing one such youngster, a psychologist writes:

[2]The clinical material cited in this chapter is drawn from test protocols and reports of these cases.

> A large, loud, hyperactive youngster, Ken resembles a nine-year-old in appearance, but a two-year-old in behavior. Throughout most of the testing, he behaved in a wild, negativistic, infantile manner. He was rarely able to attend to test tasks for more than a few minutes at a time. Instead, he rushed about the room, playing with one toy and then another; climbed on desks and tables; ran through the halls; and engaged in similar forms of wild, aggressive play. When thwarted in such activities, he would shout, kick, thrash about, or, failing to get his way through such actions, insist that he had to go to "the potty."

While in many cases manifestations of impulsivity, distractibility, poor frustration tolerance, and difficulty sustaining goal-directed activity are periodic rather than constant, they appear in most reports of borderline children.

With a second group of youngsters who are able to exhibit more controlled, better organized behavior for a period of time, behavioral observations center on episodes of abrupt regression and marked shifts in ego states. For example, an account of work with one six-year-old reads:

> Johnny's behavior is erratic and poorly integrated. At times in the test situation, he acted like a charming little adult whose speech was surprisingly complex and who was appealing in his sensitivity to nuances in one's response to him. This precocious maturity, however, easily gave way to the dependency of a much younger child. . . . When frustrated or upset, his behavior lost its playful quality and became disorganized. In the final test session, perhaps in the face of concerns about separation, he became preoccupied with fantasies about hospitals, operations, and violence and responded to minor frustrations, such as difficulty around a task involving hand and eye coordination, with outbursts of shrieking, throwing things, and name-calling.

Especially poignant are those cases in which such regression involves disorganization and the children become acutely concerned about their tenuous hold on reality. On the basis of experience with youngsters of the kind described by Ekstein and Wallerstein (1954), Engel (1963) suggests that a hallmark of work with borderline children is the "pivotal interruption" in which, in the face of youngsters' intense anxiety and disorganization, psychologists temporarily discontinue testing to act as therapists.

In other cases, the urgency of youngsters' needs and the intensity of interactions with psychologists are most striking. Describing work with an eight-year-old boy, one psychologist writes:

> Don is an extremely anxious, hyperactive child who seemed constantly in need of oral supplies. . . . When forced to stay with a task, he would become angry and

sullen, demanding that I buy him some pop or give him "something . . . anything!" . . . When I responded to him in a warm, sympathetic way, his behavior deteriorated. He became erratic and demanding as though saying he needed someone firm to control him because he couldn't control himself. However, it was constantly necessary to reassure him that the control was benign by putting my arm around him. Indeed, he craved physical contact and, if controls were not accompanied by it or by indications that my intentions were benign, he would immediately interpret them as signs of anger.

In still other cases, the preference of youngsters for fantasy over reality stands out. Despite efforts to keep them at test tasks, these children may temporarily convert testing into play-therapy sessions in which they dramatize issues of particular concern to them. For example, a report on a recently hospitalized six-year-old notes:

> During the tests, Jack often engaged in fantasy play. For example, at one point, acting out his sense of worthlessness, he managed to get his head into a wastebasket and pretend he was "in the trashcan." In another longer play sequence, he got under the desk and said that he was a lion in a cage who was going to bite my leg. He then put some cardboard between us to keep himself from biting me.

With many youngsters it may be difficult to differentiate play and reality as they present accounts of their talents, achievements, friendships, or life histories that involve transparent and, at times, fantastic fabrications.

As we said more fully in an earlier publication (Leichtman & Shapiro, 1980b), observations of the kind of behavior described in these reports provide a wealth of information on all aspects of borderline pathology. There are frequent demonstrations of conflicts around early developmental issues, poorly modulated impulsive behavior, chronic anxiety that gives rise to regression and desperate action, intense, labile affect states, a readiness to superimpose fantasy on reality, magical thinking and peculiar ideation, and marked disturbances in identity and object relationships. Indeed, so rich are such data that, with those few youngsters whose problems make them virtually untestable, one can often formulate a solid diagnostic picture on the basis of their behavior and interactions in the process of being untestable.

APPROACHES TO PSYCHOLOGICAL TESTING

Three aspects of the behavior of borderline children in the test situation are significant, not only from a diagnostic standpoint but also because of their impact on how testing is conducted and how test data is understood.

First, borderline children are distinguished by the extent to which behavioral and emotional problems of all kinds can disrupt the test process. In the course of testing such youngsters, psychologists are likely to find themselves struggling constantly to cope with impulsivity, attention and concentration problems, angry outbursts in the face of frustration, pervasive anxiety, shifting affective states, abrupt regressions, exaggerated defensive and characterological stances, and a host of other problems. While the types and severity of problems vary from child to child, the sheer volume of these problems and the extent to which they complicate administration of psychological tests is itself diagnostically significant.

Second, borderline children typically adopt a stance toward psychological tests that is qualitatively different from that of less disturbed youngsters, a stance that reflects the degree to which their behavior is still oriented around "the pleasure principle" rather than "the reality principle" (Chethik & Fast, 1970; Chethik, 1980). Whereas most children accept the structure of the tests and the test situation as defined by the psychologist and have as a primary motive performing well on test tasks, borderline children tend to try to impose their own meaning on the evaluation and are guided by quite different motives. Rausch de Traubenberg and Boizou (1980) note: "The test situation represented for these children an opportunity to seek a gratifying relation, not an opportunity to demonstrate their capacities." (p. 400) As seen in the examples noted earlier, the search for gratification may take the form of a hunger for gifts, praise, or attention, efforts to make testing into a game or abandon it for play, or attempts to transform the test situation into a stage on which to play out particular roles and fantasies. Equally important, borderline children approach tests struggling to defend against primitive fears, anxieties, and fantasies centering on concerns about failure, helplessness, attack, and decompensation. These struggles may play an even larger role in their efforts to redefine the test situation and control what occurs within it. To be sure, borderline children are also concerned with performing well on tests, yet frequently, when examined carefully, their concerns center on the image of their performance, on maintaining or warding off fantasies about themselves, or on immediate rewards or punishments rather than on the realistic implications of their work. Needless to say, the more youngsters define test tasks in idiosyncratic ways and the more their primary motivations depart from those that usually guide test performance, the greater the caution that should be exercised in psychometric interpretations of test data.

Finally, borderline children establish relationships with psychologists of a kind rarely encountered in evaluations of other youngsters. These relationships are intense, highly dependent, and often deeply conflicted (Engel,

1963; Leichtman & Shapiro, 1980a, 1980b; Rausch de Traubenberg & Boizou, 1980), although with preadolescents they may involve a degree of hostility and resistance that obscures the dependence. Showing little recognition of psychologists as independent beings, borderline children strive to fit them into preexisting roles. For example, at the beginning of the evaluation, these children may show surprisingly little anxiety about separating from their parents and going off with a stranger. Rather they converse with psychologists as if they were old acquaintances, take over offices as if they owned them, and try vigorously to set the agenda for the session. Often these efforts center on getting psychologists to assume roles that complement ones they are playing out (see Fast & Chéthik, 1972). Perhaps most significant, even with vulnerable, dependent, seemingly compliant children, the relationships have a highly coercive, controlling quality. A sense of anxiety and even desperation pervades them and becomes manifest whenever psychologists do not play expected roles or children feel their sense of control is in jeopardy. From the standpoint of testing, it is noteworthy that these children often ignore and even deny the realistic basis of these relationships—namely, that they are ones in which particular work and an evaluation are to be done. As a consequence, the boundaries of the usual patient-examiner relationship that provides a framework for test administration and interpretation may become blurred.

THE TEST PROCESS

As the description of their behavior in the test situation suggests, borderline children are often difficult to test. While some can be tested in the same manner as other youngsters, most present moderate to severe problems and resistances that require special interventions on the part of psychologists at least periodically in the course of the evaluation. A few exhibit difficulties so severe that it is impossible to complete testing in its standard form. The nature and extent of these problems depend on a number of factors: age, severity of pathology, character organization and defenses, and current stress. As a rule, the younger the child, the more severe the pathology, the more infantile and alloplastic the defensive style, and the greater the present stress, the more the difficulty encountered in the test process. The problems experienced in testing borderline children, particularly the nature of the interventions psychologists make in the test process and the qualities of the emotional responses these children elicit in them, are worth considering in some detail because of their unusual nature and because they are themselves important sources of diagnostic information.

THE CONDUCT OF THE TESTING

Administration of psychological tests is, even under normal circumstances, a complex and varied clinical process. In addition to presenting test items in their standard form and recording reponses, psychologists have other responsibilities which cannot be prescribed so carefully. These responsibilities include: (1) a host of activities described in some test manuals under the heading of "maintaining rapport with children," activities such as making contact with children, setting them at ease, helping them become engaged in test tasks, providing them with reasonable encouragement, and minimizing anxieties and other sources of interference with test performance; (2) maintaining the structure of tests against subtle and none-too-subtle encroachments such as children's efforts to avoid test tasks, to change their meaning, or simply to give superficial or flippant answers rather than make genuine efforts to grapple with test problems; and (3) inquiring into responses when their meaning is unclear or curious or when the process through which they have been arrived at appears significant. Although test manuals define some general boundaries for appropriate behavior toward subjects and provide broad guidelines for responding to and inquiring into test responses, it is generally recognized that there is considerable diversity in such activities because they depend heavily on the style and temperament of individual psychologists, on moment-by-moment assessments of the states of those being tested, and on the responses of youngsters to particular interventions (Terman & Merrill, 1960). With most children, the test process proceeds in so smooth and unremarkable a manner that psychologists' actions warrant little consideration and are usually taken for granted as attention focuses on test results themselves. However, with more disturbed children, and particularly with borderline youngsters who are among the most difficult patients to test, the problems encountered in all areas of test administration are considerable, and psychologists must intervene in the test process in a wide variety of ways.

In order to test borderline children, psychologists frequently have to work extensively to help them cope with the impulsivity, concentration problems, low frustration tolerance, proneness to fatigue, precarious self-esteem, intense anxiety, vulnerability to regression, and tenuous hold on reality that can, in any number of combinations, seriously interfere with their ability to engage in test tasks. With younger and especially disturbed children, offices may be rearranged or seating changed to reduce stimulation, remove distractions, or increase controls. Test sessions may be shortened or breaks taken more frequently. The manner in which tests are given may be changed: the usual order of items on intelligence tests may be altered to mix hard items with easy ones, items may be repeated on a number of different occasions, items may be omitted and ceilings estimated to avoid repeated failures, or appropriate inquiries may be curtailed to reduce anxiety or frustration. More important, with almost all borderline children, psychologists find themselves constantly trying to use their words, actions, tone of voice, expression, and general manner to check propensities for impulsive actions, to counteract attention problems, to alleviate anxiety, to provide support and reassurance, to offer encouragement, or otherwise to help youngsters stay with the test tasks. Often no more than an innocuous comment, a look, or a small nuance in the way in which a test item is presented, these actions may be so subtle that they easily escape notice. Indeed, frequently they are not even a response to children's overt actions but rather an effort to prevent behavior from occurring. For example, in working with unusually anxious, highly impulsive, or easily frustrated youngsters, psychologists may orient their testing around coping with these vulnerabilities and keeping them from becoming manifest. Significantly, since such actions are largely automatic and intuitive and since psychologists concentrate chiefly on test responses themselves, the nature and extent of these activities often go unnoticed apart from the sense of fatigue and relief felt when testing is over.

Because of the defensiveness of borderline children, their resistances, and their propensity to redefine the tests and the test relationship according to their own ends, "maintaining the structure of the tests" may also require constant work on the part of psychologists. Often, children present blatant problems in these respects. They may define particular test tasks in their own idiosyncratic ways or make the testing into a kind of play session; they may be so concerned with playing out roles or enacting battles with surrogate parents that the tests are treated chiefly as stage props; or they may so need to get away from the tests or vent their frustrations that psychologists must be constantly alert if they are to keep test equipment from being bent, folded, or mutilated. More often, attempts to change the tests or evade genuine involvement with them are subtle and involve such a mixture of motives that they may be difficult to spot and deal with. For example, the impulsivity and distractibility so characteristic of many borderline children reflect not only "ego weaknesses," they also serve as defenses as youngsters race through or ignore tasks which are difficult for them. Exaggeration of characterological problems may serve similar ends as youngsters give superficial, sarcastic, or perfunctory answers or otherwise go through the motions of taking tests in ways that provide little measure of their true abilities, concerns, or problems. At times, resistance may even take the form of "playing crazy" (Cain, 1964), as in the case of youngsters who exaggerate bizarre thoughts and behavior for defensive purposes and, in the process, produce test records far more florid than those of most psychotic children.

Psychologists differ greatly in how they deal with these problems at any given time: in some cases, no action is taken; in others, test items are simply repeated; and in still others, resistances are confronted and even interpreted. Moreover, each type of intervention may be made in any number of different ways (e.g., directly or indirectly, firmly or gently, seriously or humorously). Indeed, since such activities depend heavily upon the theoretical orientation, style, and skill of the individuals doing the testing and on their assessment of particular youngsters at any given moment, this aspect of testing is subject to the greatest variation among psychologists. This variability is only heightened by the fact that even what seem to be the best of these interventions are often far from successful. What remains constant is that, regardless of how they do so, psychologists find themselves constantly trying to cope with a variety of resistances to the test process throughout evaluations of these youngsters.

Finally, psychologists working with borderline children usually have to conduct a far more active inquiry process than they do with other youngsters. Borderline youngsters often give responses that are ambiguous or slightly off the mark and hence require clarification if they are to be understood and scored adequately. Many responses that are scorable contain odd phrasings, curious ideas, or unusual jumps in reasoning that, when explored, prove to be signs of more seriously disturbed thinking. Singer (1977) has suggested that one reason for the "purported" absence of odd reasoning on intelligence tests of borderline adults is that responses on these tests are taken for granted more readily and investigated less carefully than those on projective tests. Certainly, inquiry into intelligence test responses of borderline children frequently reveals pathological thinking. Careful inquiry and often repeating test items under altered conditions is also important with borderline children because their failures on test tasks or their unusual responses may arise for a variety of different reasons. For example, difficulties on tests of particular cognitive or visual-motor skills may reflect impulsivity, indifference, and/or organic problems. Similarly, peculiar Rorschach responses may reflect a tenuous hold on reality or simply the imperious treatment of reality on the part of a more intact youngster. However, while there is a greater need for inquiry with borderline children, their sensitivity to the problems they experience around tests, their anxiety in the face of disturbed ideation, and their limited capacity to tolerate the work involved in reflecting on their performance make decisions about whether and how to conduct such inquiries difficult and challenging ones.

PSYCHOLOGISTS' EMOTIONAL REACTIONS TO BORDERLINE CHILDREN

Not only are psychologists more active in their work with borderline children, they also experience a much more intense, much more personal emotional involvement with them. Establishing rapport with borderline children, helping them stay with tests, and trying to maintain the structure of the tests in the face of powerful resistance requires constant attention, intimate involvement with the children, and attunement to their emotional states on a moment-by-moment basis. The many problems the youngsters present in the course of testing may lead to fatigue, frustration, and anger in those working with them, while the anxiety and strain the children experience as a result of the tests may lead psychologists to feel guilty and deeply concerned. Indeed, Engel (1963, p. 433) notes that the "palpable suffering" of borderline children during the tests often makes psychologists ambivalent about maintaining a diagnostic attitude. Moreover, the extent to which borderline children themselves strive to establish primitive relationships that blur role boundaries only serves to amplify all of these reactions.

As a consequence of this combination of factors, psychologists may find themselves experiencing strong, bewildering reactions in the course of the testing. Commenting on the process of testing borderline children, Engel (1963) observes: "It may well be that the psychologist's own ego states shift more than he knows or remembers later, leaving him with the same feeling of discontinuity as the child is bound to experience." (p. 433) Even when not puzzled by their own reactions, psychologists are likely to experience and act upon powerful, conflicted feelings during the testing. For example, one report notes:

> During the testing, John often displayed an unusual combination of genuine and histrionic sadness which left me feeling, on the one hand, annoyed at being controlled and manipulated and, on the other, deeply concerned about helping a seriously hurt and deprived child. . . . Although I was initially inclined to adopt a highly supportive approach toward him, after repeated provocation I found myself taking a more stern, distant, authoritarian stance to which he responded with less anxiety and better cooperation.

In addition to strong reactions during the testing of borderline children, psychologists often feel fatigued and drained at the end of sessions, experiencing continuing emotional reverberations long after sessions are over and finding it more difficult to assume an objective stance in evaluating data, writing reports, and participating in conferences on these youngsters (Engel, 1963).

DIAGNOSTIC IMPLICATIONS

The nature and extent of psychologists' activities and emotional involvement in the process of testing borderline children have important diagnostic implications. On the one hand, where interventions have been extensive and unusual and where involvement with youngsters is intense, psychometric treatments of test data should be approached cautiously and the influence of these factors on the tests should be considered carefully. On the other hand, in addition to complicating and even confounding the interpretation of test data, these unusual aspects of the test process can make invaluable diagnostic contributions. The extent of the interventions it is necessary to make in order to test borderline children and the strength and character of psychologists' reactions to the children in the course of their evaluations are themselves global measures of the severity of the pathology involved. More important, different facets of the examiner's activities and experience of the test process can make quite specific contributions to an understanding of the problems borderline children face and to the planning of their treatment.

As we noted in an earlier paper (Leichtman & Shapiro, 1980a), in trying to "maintain rapport" and help youngsters sustain their involvement with tests, psychologists function as "auxiliary egos." The changes they introduce into the testing and even slight alterations in their behavior frequently represent responses intended to help youngsters cope with problems they are experiencing in the test situation. Consequently, by reflecting on the implicit rationale for their own largely automatic and intuitive actions in the course of testing, psychologists may for the first time appreciate fully the extent to which youngsters' impulsivity, distractibility, fears of failure, anxiety, and/or a host of other factors have interfered with their ability to deal effectively with the world around them.

Psychologists' efforts to maintain the structure of the testing can be an equally important source of information. While there may be considerable variation in the particular strategies psychologists adopt in dealing with resistances to testing, in each case their behavior points to some set of problems youngsters are experiencing—that is, to particular anxieties, conflicts, defensive strategies, and/or patterns of externalizing conflicts. Moreover, in each case, regardless of the particular actions psychologists have taken, there is an opportunity to observe youngsters' responses to some effort to help them deal with these problems.

The inquiry process and the children's responses to it are also significant sources of information. They provide opportunities to observe youngsters' abilities to explore particular problems, their tolerance for such explorations, and particular strategies of working with them that make such explorations harder or easier. Even what psychologists later recognize as mistakes in the inquiry process have diagnostic import. For example, reflecting on cases in which they have investigated responses less vigorously than usual or in which questions that should have been asked have been missed, psychologists may come to recognize the extent to which they have been intimidated by an angry child's threats to blow up or have become excessively concerned about a vulnerable child's seeming fragility.

The psychologists' emotional reactions in the course of testing can be used in a variety of ways. These reactions frequently contain clues to the meaning of particular test responses or behaviors. For example, in working with children who repeat the same inadequate strategy over and over again on intelligence test problems such as block designs, psychologists may find that they typically respond with patience to youngsters functioning at the limits of their ability, feel a strong impulse to help children who are being over-whelmed by anxiety, and react with impatience and annoyance to youngsters who are resisting the tasks or tying themselves in knots masochistically. Confronted with three similar Rorschach responses involving peculiar, aggressive percepts with poor form level, psychologists may feel relatively unconcerned, angry, or anxious depending on whether they sense the attitudes behind the response to be ones of "playful regression," hostility and devaluation, or anxiety and fear of decompensation. In such cases, an understanding of the meaning of particular test responses and the attitudes and emotional states responsible for them is to be found through a consideration not only of the content of the response but also of the examiner's reaction to it. Viewed in a broader perspective, the feelings, thoughts, and fantasies borderline children elicit in psychologists in the course of the evaluation may reflect a playing out of one or more affect-laden roles that complement ones the children are living out (Leichtman & Shapiro, 1980a). As noted previously the psychologist's reaction to and interactions with John would suggest that the test process can provide insights into characteristic patterns of transference and countertransference with borderline children.

In addition to contributing to the diagnosis of borderline children, consideration of the test process can play a major role in planning treatment. First, at the very least, that process provides psychologists with some understanding of the experience of parents, teachers, therapists, and others to whom recommendations are to be made. Second, because aspects of the test process resemble situations in which treatment will take place, the strategies psychologists adopt in the course of the testing and youngsters' responses to them provide information that has a direct bearing on recommendations. For example, intelligence and achievement tests resemble schoolwork sufficiently that factors which interfere with or facilitate youngsters' performances on these tests will be of considerable interest to special education teachers and tutors. Similarly, how testers are able to be of support to youngsters, how they are able to deal with resistances to the testing, and the nature of the relationships which evolve in the course of the testing can all contribute to recommendations to therapists and others who work with the children. Finally, the experience of testing borderline children provides a means of translating the powerful insights derived from the tests themselves into meaningful treatment recommendations. Because test data are dependent on particular instruments and often embedded in theoretical schemes, inferences made from them often seem to touch on the concrete behavior of borderline children only in an overly abstract and overly general manner. By allowing psychologists to understand how these inferences illuminate their own interactions with the children, attention to the test process offers a means of translating what is learned from the tests into the kind of specific recommendations that can be of immediate help to those who live and work with borderline children.

TESTS OF INTELLIGENCE, ABILITIES, AND ACHIEVEMENT

The test batteries most commonly used with borderline children are composed of two general types of tests: relatively "structured" tests of intelligence, mental abilities, and academic achievement, and "projective" tests. In our practice, the former group includes tests of general intellectual functioning such as the Wechsler Intelligence Scale for Children, Revised, and the Stanford-Binet Intelligence Scale; specialized tests of visual-motor and language functioning such as the Bender-Gestalt, the Developmental Test of Visual-Motor Integration, Frostig's Developmental Test of Visual Perception, the Peabody Picture Vocabulary Test, and/or items from the Merrill-Palmer Scale of Mental Tests; and, if a separate educational evaluation is not being done, a brief school achievement test such as the Wide Range Achievement Test, the Peabody Individual Achievement Test, or a combination of the two. Tests of this kind provide measures of general intelligence, specific cognitive abilities and disabilities, and the effectiveness with which these abilities are used in solving problems and mastering basic academic skills. They also provide insights into styles of thought, attitudes, and motivations that bear on all aspects of a youngster's life. In the diagnosis of borderline conditions, tests of mental abilities make especially significant contributions in a number of areas: (1) assessment of organic disturbances and learning disabilities; (2) evaluation of disturbances in thought organization and reality contact; (3) demonstration of difficulties in adaptation; (4) differentiation among types of borderline children; and (5) discovery of potential strengths and talents that can be utilized in treatment.

ORGANICITY AND LEARNING DISABILITIES

A number of investigators have suggested that organic factors can contribute to problems in at least some borderline children. Many of the disturbances in intelligence, language, motor development, and perception described by Rosenfeld and Sprince (1963) suggest such difficulties may be present; Rausch de Traubenberg and Boizou (1980) find marked lags in motor development in their group of borderline children; Rinsley (1980a) observes that at least one group of borderline children exhibits symptoms of "minimal brain dysfunction" currently described under the Attention Deficit Disorders of DSM-III; and we (Leichtman & Shapiro, 1980b) have noted that approximately one-third of the youngsters with borderline diagnoses seen at The Menninger Foundation Children's Division exhibit neurological soft signs or learning disabilities not readily attributable to emotional factors alone. While the absence of controlled empirical studies makes such estimates crude at best, clinicians generally recognize a high incidence of these types of problems in borderline children.

Because of the range of intellectual functions they sample, the controlled conditions under which observations of these functions can be made, and the norms against which children's performance can be measured, psychological tests are particularly useful in detecting organic and learning problems. However, the extensive emotional and behavioral problems borderline children exhibit at times when they experience difficulty or frustration often interfere with such assessments. The manner in which tests are selected, administered, and interpreted can help disentangle the cognitive and behavioral problems these children manifest. First, the use of tests with items ordered in a clear developmental progression, such as the Developmental Test of Visual-Motor Integration, are especially helpful in this regard because they provide a sample of children's work on easier items before difficulties have begun, help locate levels at which difficulties start, and, when youngsters have problems with items usually mastered at much earlier ages, offer graphic demonstrations of basic cognitive deficits. In areas of functioning where tests do not provide such a clear developmental progression, introduction of selected items from tests for younger children may be fruitful. For example, the difficulties a nine-year-old experiences with simple motor coordination or perceptual matching tasks at a four- or five-year level on the Merrill-Palmer Scale of Mental Tests can highlight areas of notable dysfunction. Second, where questions arise about whether youngsters' difficulties on test items reflect cognitive or psychological problems, items can be repeated later or under altered conditions. For example, with youngsters whose haste, wildness, or seeming indifference have contributed to poor performance on figure copying tasks, repetition of tasks with the examiner acting to counter impulsivity and distractibility may either result in the substantial improvement in performance or highlight motor problems or problems in the analysis and synthesis of spatial relations. Finally, rather than relying chiefly on test scores in making inferences about organic problems or learning disabilities, a careful analysis of errors made by the youngsters is essential. For example, whether a child's poor performance on a spelling or arithmetic item is due to carelessness and relatively minor errors or to failure to master basic operations obviously has a direct bearing upon determining the causes and treatment of such difficulties.

Patterns of test performance likely to be associated with organic problems in borderline children include (1) marked problems in gross and fine motor coordination; (2) difficulties in the analysis and synthesis of spatial relations such as those reflected in letter reversals, rotations, or gross distortion of figures on age-appropriate figure-copying tasks; (3) significant disturbances in language functions such as sound omissions, word-finding difficulty, and primitive grammatical structures; (4) mental retardation; and (5) striking variation in intellectual skills in different areas (e.g., major discrepancies in verbal and performance IQ's) that cannot be directly linked to patterns of adaptive and defensive functioning or environmental factors. The presence of marked hyperactivity, distractibility, and emotional lability during the tests may also raise questions about organic contributions to problems, although, in the absence of signs of organic dysfunction in cognitive areas, psychological tests do not currently provide a firm basis for determining whether these particular problems have a neurological or purely psychological basis. When a youngster's mastery of basic academic skills is two years below what would be anticipated on the basis of intelligence and schooling, questions may be raised about learning disabilities with possible organic roots. However, because of the extent to which the emotional and behavioral problems of borderline children interfere with their academic progress, such inferences should be made more cautiously with these youngsters than with others. Regardless of etiological considerations, careful description of intellectual functioning and academic skills and, particularly, attention to areas of notable dysfunction make signficant contributions to the development of educational remediation programs.

"STRUCTURED" TESTS AND THE ASSESSMENT OF BORDERLINE THINKING

As a group, tests of intelligence and achievement have two properties that are of particular importance in the diagnosis of borderline conditions: they are "highly structured," and they are reality-oriented. In contrast to the more ambiguous, open-ended, projective tests with their subjective orientation, mental tests have a relatively clear and unambiguous structure, call for responses of an objective and conventional nature, and rarely leave subjects in doubt about the direction their responses are expected to take. From the early work of Rapaport, Schafer, and Gill (1945–1946) and Knight (1953) to the recent work of Kernberg (1967), Gunderson and Singer (1975), and Singer (1977), authorities have held that the most distinctive characteristic of test performance by borderline adults is that they exhibit relatively adequate, intact thinking on "structured" tests and serious pathological thinking on less structured projective tests.

A similar pattern of test performance has been described in borderline children. For example, Rausch de Traubenberg and Boizou (1980) note that the children with whom they work function within the normal range on tests of mental skills ". . . demonstrating the capacity to adapt to objective reality in the context of a relatively structured situation." (page 400) However, in brief references to performance on intelligence tests, Engel (1963) suggests borderline schizophrenic children feel confronted by "insurmountable demands" and implies that concerns with maintaining the tenuous hold on reality may appear on all tests. In our experience, commonly noted differences between performance on "structured" and projective tests are usually found with borderline children but are less pronounced. Most borderline children display signs of less serious disturbances in thinking on tests of mental abilities, and younger and more severely disturbed members of this group are often exceptions to the rule, giving some evidence of impairments in formal thought processes and reality testing on these tests.

In an earlier paper, we (Leichtman & Shapiro, 1980b) argued that the thinking of borderline children is best conceptualized along a continuum rather than in terms of dichotomous categories of adequate reality contact and loss of reality testing. Between these extremes fall (1) playful modes of thought in which reality considerations are bracketed; (2) egocentric, arbitrary modes of thought in which reality is ignored or redefined according to personal wishes, interests, and fantasies; and (3) areas of slippage in formal thought processes and tenuous reality testing which can be seen as youngsters begin to decompensate. The thinking of borderline children, we suggested, characteristically oscillates around the middle of this continuum. All of these middle range phenomena are exhibited in their performance on intelligence tests.

A preference for playful regressive modes of thought is commonly seen. Rausch de Traubenberg and Boizou (1980) note that the youngsters with whom they work greatly prefer tests allowing "free expression and fabulation to those requiring pursuit of an objective goal." (p. 400) We have found that many borderline children try to convert intelligence tests into these kinds of tests. Material from the Block Design subtest may be used as toys and the test may be changed into a game; responses on the information or comprehension subtests of the WISC-R may have a high degree of self-reference and, indeed, serve simply as a jumping off point for real or fantasied accounts of events or interests in the child's life; and a readiness to indulge in regressive fantasies is evident throughout the tests. For example, the Comprehension subtest question about why brick houses are better than wooden ones can easily lead to thoughts of the three little pigs rather than the relative merits of the building materials.

Arbitrary, egocentric modes of thought in which there is an utter disregard of reality are also commonly seen on tests of intelligence and achievement. Youngsters with learning disabilities may perform arithmetic operations such as borrowing or carrying in odd, ineffective ways, insisting that their own mathematics is better than that of their teachers; youngsters may elaborate on highly esoteric interests, such as prehistoric times or space, mixing fact and fantasy, yet presenting them as the gospel; or children may reveal highly idiosyncratic views of the world in their unusual ordering of cards or odd stories on the WISC-R Picture Arrangement subtest. Intelligence tests also provide examples of the absolute refusal of many borderline children to recognize unpleasant realities. Unable to define the word *nuisance,* one youngster insisted desperately: "There is no such thing. There is no such word!"

Tendencies toward lapses in reality testing and impairments in formal thought processes can also occasionally be seen on these tests. Items of the WISC-R Vocabulary and Comprehension subtests that elicit associations around aggression, danger, or loss may lead to loose associations, peculiar ideation, odd verbalizations, or autistic logic. For example, asked why houses made of bricks are better than ones of wood, one youngster launched into a long description of how the former are impervious to attacks by hatchets. Another boy, in response to a question about what one should do upon seeing smoke coming from a neighbor's house, began to give an adequate response, only to jump from the notion of fire to fire extinguishers to caustic chemicals in extinguishers to thoughts that he might burn a hole in his stomach. On the Picture Completion subtest of the WISC-R, one youngster noted that the comb was missing "needles" rather than teeth; in defining the word *contagious* on the Vocabulary subtest, another suggested that "Clorox is contagious"; and, in telling what one should do if he has lost a friend's ball, a third gave a series of odd associations about how he could not retrieve the ball if it had fallen across a border into a different country. At times, the particular stimulus for peculiar thinking may not be readily apparent. Asked the similarity between a ball and a wheel, one boy replied that "the world is round" and responded to efforts to clarify the thought with an elaborate, confused explanation about how the sun gives off light that travels at 160,000 miles a second. To be sure, lapses in reality testing and disturbances in formal thought processes on "structured" tests are present in blatant forms in only some borderline youngsters. They are usually present in only subtle forms, and they are, in any case, seen far more clearly in projective test material. Nonetheless, such disturbances do intrude into the performance of borderline children on these tests and are of diagnostic significance.

INTELLECTUAL FUNCTIONING AND ADAPTATION

In addition to contributing to educational and vocational planning, measurements of intelligence and academic achievement are of broader significance in the assessment of borderline children. These tests are essentially "reality-oriented": they examine a number of significant, so-called "autonomous" ego functions (Hartmann, 1958) as well as the manner in which these functions subserve important aspects of adaptation such as gaining information about the world, solving intellectual problems, and mastering academic skills which society views as the basic work of childhood. Consequently, the nature and extent of the problems borderline children exhibit on these tests provide important insights into the manner in which their pathology has interfered with adaptation.

Psychological tests usually document the observations in the literature that borderline children experience significant problems in dealing with basic developmental tasks. For example, even while asserting that the performance of the borderline children with whom they worked demonstrated a "capacity to adapt to objective reality" on intelligence tests, Rausch de Traubenberg and Boizou (1980) note a range of intellectual quotients for these youngsters (61–113) that is quite low and a mean (93) that is at the 32nd percentile for the general population. In individual cases, mental tests are particularly helpful in tracing the nature and extent of interference with the development and utilization of particular adaptational skills since patterns vary considerably among borderline children. In some cases, children experience difficulties in all areas of intellectual functioning; in other cases, they exhibit uneven patterns of development; and, in still others, basic intellectual functions are intact but are used ineffectively or idiosyncratically. Perhaps of greater importance, these tests provide concrete demonstrations of the variety of factors that interfere with the development and use of intellectual skills. Among the factors commonly implicated are: (1) chronic anxiety; (2) impulsivity and hyperactivity; (3) distractibility and attentional problems; (4) poor frustration tolerance; (5) marked emotional lability; (6) specific cognitive deficits; (7) fear of failure and efforts to maintain precarious self-esteem; (8) pronounced narcissistic and egocentric attitudes and thought styles; (9) limited investment in learning and performance; (10) exaggerated defensive styles, regardless of whether these involve essentially alloplastic (e.g., avoidance, externalization, and action) or autoplastic (e.g., marked constriction or compulsivity) defenses; (11) intrusions of interpersonal conflicts into work; and (12) intrusive ideation, shifts in levels of formal thought processes, and/or efforts to stave off decompensation.

While patterns of test scores provide one basis for making inferences about the influence of these various factors, the most fruitful bases for such inferences are analyses of youngsters' failures on age-appropriate tasks and of unusual or idiosyncratic responses, examination of behaviors that disrupt the test process, and consideration of psychologists' efforts to work with youngsters at particular tasks. For example, while the Arithmetic and Digit Span subtests of the WISC-R are particularly vulnerable to the disruptive effects of anxiety, with borderline children anxiety may be seen in graphic form throughout the tests. Children who have done half the items on the Block Design subtest rapidly and adeptly may, upon hitting the first design that presents them with any difficulty, become so upset that they tie themselves in knots, repeatedly trying ineffective strategies or spoiling the beginning of good solutions because of their doubts. While youngsters exhibiting chronic ego weaknesses combined with a largely alloplastic, infantile defensive style may generally have performance IQ's that are well above verbal ones, their haste, impulsivity, and carelessness can be seen as readily in their manner of executing designs on figure-copying tasks as in any verbal subtests. Concerns about intrusive ideation manifested both in marked constriction and in the periodic emergence of peculiar ideas most often affect verbal subtests, but they may appear in striking fashion elsewhere. One child, for example, had difficulty with an Object Assembly subtest because puzzles consisting of parts of human figures triggered fantasies of dismemberment. Similarly, the sharp shifts in affects, defenses, and ego states so characteristic of borderline youngsters occur throughout the tests. For example, one ten-year-old, relieved to find that the first dozen items on the Information subtest at the beginning of the WISC-R were easy for him, quickly became confident and expansive in his responses. He noted not one but a number of explorers who could have been said to have discovered America and made side comments such as, "Heh, heh, that was too easy . . . way too easy!" However, two items later, unable to remember who invented the light bulb, he became deeply upset by his first failure and, after another two items, was angrily attacking the examiner and struggling to hang onto his own sense of competence by countering test questions with: "Why do you want to know that? I don't know if a grownup would know that! I dare you to try space on me! Ask me any questions about space!" In short, the pervasive problems borderline children experience may appear in striking forms at almost any point in the testing.

DIFFERENCES AMONG BORDERLINE CHILDREN

In addition to highlighting characteristics shared by most borderline children, tests of mental abilities also contribute to an appreciation of significant differences among this group of youngsters. As has been noted, these children may vary greatly in their intelligence, patterns of cognitive ability, and mastery of basic academic skills. Furthermore, while a host of emotional and behavioral problems interferes with the development and use of these skills and intellectual capacities, borderline children differ considerably in which factor or combination of factors are most salient. In some cases, impulsivity and hyperactivity play a major role in interfering with intellectual performance; in other cases, these factors are relatively absent, but children struggle with distractibility and attention problems; in still other cases, difficulties tolerating frustration or coping with anxiety may appear to be central. The particular nature of the anxiety that interferes with performance on intelligence tests may also vary. In some cases, it centers on fears of failure and concerns about the maintenance of self-esteem; in others, it centers on efforts to block out disturbing thoughts and maintain a hold on reality. Some youngsters strive to perform well on intelligence tests and are deeply troubled by their inability to do so, whereas others resent and resist what they perceive as demands upon them and affect an indifference to any standards other than their own. Moreover, in some borderline children, attitudes toward and approaches to intelligence tests remain relatively constant, while in others, their abrupt shifts result in quite different levels of functioning on tests at different times. Clearly, these kinds of specific differences among borderline children have an important bearing on understanding many of their presenting problems and on making treatment recommendations, especially regarding academic programs.

A consideration of the patterns of problems borderline children experience in taking mental tests, the attitudes and cognitive styles revealed in the course of these tests, and the character of their relationships with psychologists during the tests can also contribute to the broader diagnostic task of differentiating among types of borderline children. Perhaps the most common pattern found among borderline children is that in which a mixture of "chronic ego deficits" and impulsive, infantile character features predominate. The performance of these children on intelligence and achievement tests is distinguished above all by distractibility, impulsivity, and low frustration tolerance which are so inextricably bound with defensive strategies involving denial, avoidance, externalization, and action that it is difficult to distinguish between ego "weaknesses" and a style of life. A second group of youngsters experiences difficulty with intelligence tests less because of ego "weaknesses" or "deficits" than because of their predominantly narcissistic orientation. Treating psychologists as an audience, their "performance" on tests combines efforts to look good and sound impressive with utter indifference to the substance or accuracy of their answers. Their test responses have a high degree of self-reference, and they seem able to stay with test tasks only so long as they are entertaining and interesting. In contrast to the indifference to the adequacy of performance characterizing this group, borderline children with prominent depressive features may be obsessed with these matters. Such youngsters constantly need to check whether their answers on tests are correct; they strive desperately to match a standard of performance that is beyond them; and they comment frequently on their inadequacy. With another group, "schizotypal" features are central. Most salient in their test performances are their concerns about maintaining a hold on reality, their efforts to block out intrusive ideation through constriction or desperate obsessive maneuvers, and the shifts in formal thought processes and periodic disturbances in reality testing that come in spite of these efforts. Both the content of responses on mental tests and styles of taking the tests can also point to paranoid or antisocial tendencies that may be mixed with these other features. To be sure, there is a danger in seeking overly refined typologies for borderline children. Because character is less crystallized in children in general and because of the marked regressive shifts and lability in functioning characteristic of many borderline youngsters, it is often inappropriate to think in terms of fixed character types. Furthermore, many individuals exhibit a mixture of characteristics. Nonetheless, when different patterns of functioning are described carefully and viewed as developmental trends or tendencies, they may be of considerable help in understanding youngsters and planning for their treatment.

STRENGTHS AND TALENTS

While it is the problems borderline children experience in the development and utilization of intellectual skills that stand out on tests of mental abilities, these tests can also call attention to accomplishments, talents, and areas of potential strength that are especially important in treatment. By pointing to good general intelligence, mastery of particular academic areas, visual-motor abilities, physical prowess, artistic talents, or any other interests, skills or accomplishments, regardless of how esoteric they may be, these tests can be of enormous service to teachers, therapists, and others working with borderline children. If focused upon, such areas of strength provide opportunities for less conflicted relationships, contribute to a building of esteem-enhancing skills, and help children establish some firmer anchor in reality. Indeed, because of their narcissistic vulnerabilities, their many problems and disabilities, and their readiness to withdraw into fantasy, borderline children desperately need not only recognition for actual accomplishments but also faith in areas of potential talent before these become manifest.

PROJECTIVE TESTS

The second broad group of tests commonly used with borderline children is the projective tests. In our battery, these tests include (1) the Rorschach Test, (2) one or more story-telling tests such as the Thematic Apperception Test (TAT), the Children's Apperception Test (CAT), and the Tasks of Emotional Development Test (TED); and (3) brief projective instruments such as the Human Figure Drawing, the Animal Choice Test, and the Three Wishes.

Projective tests have three sets of characteristics with significant bearing on the diagnosis of borderline conditions. First, in contrast to tests of mental abilities, they are relatively unstructured. They do not have "right" answers, and conventional responses are neither readily apparent nor encouraged. Because of the absence of objective guides to thinking and communication and the anxiety and regression that may be generated by their absence, projective tests are well suited to elicit signs of disturbed thinking in predisposed individuals. Second, in contrast to the objective orientation of tests of mental abilities, projective tests have a subjective orientation and draw heavily upon creativity and imagination. Individuals are asked to give form to diffuse inkblots, make up stories, create metaphors, or draw imaginary figures. Because such tests have the potential for tapping into personal fantasy systems, both the content and structure of responses to them can contribute significantly to an understanding of impulse-defense configurations, predominant conflicts, affect states, self-experience, and object relationships (Sugarman, 1980). Finally, in contrast to the largely conventional orientation of tests of intelligence and achievement, projective tests are structured in ways that maximize individual differences. Test tasks are open-ended, give individuals wide latitude in how they may be approached, and lend themselves to an almost infinite variety of responses. As a result, these tests can highlight not only differences between borderline children and other youngsters but also differences among borderline children.

The attitudes and approaches borderline children take to projective tests are quite varied. Engel (1963) suggests that the projective test performance of the children with whom she worked is distinguished, above all, by their vulnerability to regression and their desperate efforts to maintain a hold on reality. In contrast, dealing with what appears to be a broader group of borderline children, Rausch de Traubenberg and Boizou (1980) observe that their youngsters prefer projective tests to more structured ones and exhibit playfulness and enthusiasm on them as well as fearfulness and regression. They note:

> Participation was far livelier and more enthusiastic in projective situations, be it the Rorschach or thematic tests, than in the more structured efficiency test situations. The need for expression burst out, so to speak, as the specific character of the material stimulated fantasizing, and allowed fabulation as well as regression. . . . For the observer it was like watching a game, a game pushed to the extreme, in which there was a constant shifting between fantasy and reality with a precarious balance maintained between both. (p. 400)

Our experience with borderline children has been similar (Leichtman & Shapiro, 1980b): in working on projective tests these youngsters may alternate within a matter of moments between playfulness, highly arbitrary egocentric thinking, and periods of serious regression and disorganization.

Just as there is considerable variation in how individual borderline youngsters approach a test from moment to moment, so too are there significant differences among these children in their approach to and performance on different projective tests. Because of this variability, Rausch de Traubenberg and Boizou (1980) recommend including many projective tests in batteries because ". . . the degree of the impact of the material is impossible to predict, as some tests may well inhibit certain children and intensely liberate the fantasies in others." (p. 398) We (Leichtman & Shapiro, 1980a, 1980b) have also called attention to this variability in performance on projective tests and have stressed that it is the aggregate of the material the tests produce rather than any particular test signs or patterns that is most significant in the diagnosis of borderline conditions. Recognizing this variability, it is nonetheless possible to describe some of the ways in which particular projective tests, notably the Rorschach and the thematic tests, typically contribute to such diagnoses.

THE RORSCHACH TEST: APPROACHES TO THE TASK

Because it most often elicits evidence of serious regressive potential, signs of pathological thinking, and evidence of disturbances in object relationships, the Rorschach Test frequently occupies a central place in test batteries for borderline children. The distinctive quality of their approach to this test is best appreciated through an example. Beginning the Rorschach in a relatively playful way, Tom, a seven-year-old youngster, took the second card and almost immediately reported that it looked like the face of a clown with his tongue sticking out. During the later inquiry, he indicated that the quality of human movement and the red and black colors were important in determining this response. In the 40 seconds following this initial response, Tom poured out in an increasingly agitated fashion a series of responses that made use of the same area of the blot, the same colors, and the same animation. The clown with his tongue sticking out became a man with his tongue cut open and his eyes bleeding; the man became a black cat with red eyes and a red tongue; and this percept gave way to that of an evil figure from *Star Wars* "shooting hot red fire from his tongue and hot flames from his eyes and liquid, hot liquid from his eyes."

As the example suggests, the typical approach of borderline children to the Rorschach is one of intense involvement in which rich, multidetermined responses are given in a rapid and fluid manner. While children may begin responses with enthusiasm, primitive fears and anxieties emerge abruptly and percepts laden with disturbing fantasies pour forth. Thus, for example, in a matter of moments the percept of the potentially cute, defiant clown gives way to images in which offending organs are mutilated and in which the injured parts become destructive weapons used by a malevolent figure to scourge adversaries. In the midst of such a train of associations, the formal quality of responses may deteriorate sharply, and youngsters may have great difficulty taking an objective stance toward percepts which appear to have become almost real to them.

Although borderline children usually produce Rorschach responses with ease, they have little tolerance for inquiry into location or determinants. Not only are they anxious about the test and about what a close look at their thinking will reveal, but they also dislike the work involved in the task. It is thus best to inquire into responses after each card rather than waiting until the end of the test in order to make this work more tolerable and to compensate for the rapidity with which the memory of these youngsters for their responses fades. Even if inquiry is conducted at the end of responses to each card, many borderline children may simply deny having given threatening or unpleasant responses mentioned only moments before. Under the best of circumstances, it is often hard to elicit the particular determinants of responses because this task is more difficult for children than for adults, because of the rich, multifaceted nature of the responses borderline children produce, and because of their general lack of reflectiveness.

Significant exceptions to this general mode of intense participation in the Rorschach are found among young, limited, frightened, and/or avoidant youngsters who may give sparse perseverative records; among highly impulsive, action-prone youngsters who may resist the test in general; and among youngsters trying to hold together through constriction who strive to give only banal, obvious, popular responses to the test and take no chances on opening up further.

RORSCHACH: LOCATION AND DETERMINANTS

The only extensive treatment of Rorschach scores of borderline children in the literature is that of Rausch de Traubenberg and Boizou (1980), although our own work (Leichtman & Shapiro, 1980b) comments on determinants in passing. Among the most significant points noted in these papers are: (1) the number of responses is usually well above average; (2) reaction times tend to be brief; (3) responses tend to be to the whole blot or common details, although whole responses often have a poorly differentiated, syncretistic quality; (4) form is usually the primary determinant, although it typically has a highly fabulized or dynamic quality (e.g., rather than seeing bats, borderline children may see "a big, blood-sucking bat coming at you," and rather than a cat skin, "a smashed cat that's been run over by a steamroller"); (5) there is a higher than average number of human and animal movement responses, typically involving themes of aggression or danger; (6) inanimate movement responses, responses frequently associated with the experience of internal and external forces beyond one's control, are common; (7) although less prevalent than movement responses and fabulization, color responses are often present, especially responses in which color predominates over form (C and CF), a pattern suggesting relatively unmodulated affective experience and a propensity for action; (8) arbitrary integrations of color and form (e.g., "it's a blue bat") are occasionally seen; and (9) other determinants such as shading and achromatic color responses are less frequently present.

RORSCHACH: SIGNS OF PATHOLOGICAL THINKING

More than any other test in the battery, the Rorschach is distinguished by its power to elicit and highlight signs of disturbances in formal thought processes and reality contact. Its use in the assessment of borderline thinking is discussed by Meyer and Caruth (1964) and Rausch de Traubenberg and Boizou (1980) and described most fully in our own work (Leichtman & Shapiro, 1980b). Among the signs of pathological thinking evident in Rorschach protocols of borderline children are the following: (1) the ready emergence of primary process ideation and bizarre and peculiar ideas (e.g., responses such as "a squirrel computer," "two chickens pulling a nostril apart," or "the American idea of hammering a hammerhead shark"); (2) fluidity of associations and intrusive thoughts that disrupt and redirect thinking (e.g., Tom's responses following the percept of a clown's head); (3) perseverations that result not from a paucity of ideas, but from repetition of highly cathected, emotion-laden ideas (e.g., ghosts, monsters, or tornadoes seen early in the Rorschach may be repeated five or even ten times); (4) poor or erratic form level, especially where there is a high number of F-spoil responses in which initially good percepts deteriorate in the process of elaboration and DW responses in which poor responses to the whole blot are based, in fact, upon a single adequately perceived detail; (5) odd phrasings, neologisms, clang associations, and other peculiar verbalizations (e.g., "those are different colors and paints and poots, not poodles, that saved America," "a cat with pitter paws," or "Devil Island, Skull Island, Spook Island, Vampire Island, Stampire Island, Ampire Island . . . . "); (6) contaminations or condensations in which percepts and ideas lose their boundaries and fuse or in which different levels of meaning are superimposed on one another (e.g., an area that looks like a skull and an island is called "Devil Island" or part of a blot is seen as a rocket and Jesus and made into a "rocket-Jesus"); and (7) indications of thinking dominated and distorted by fantasy including (a) a high number of fabulized or dynamic responses, (b) fabulized combinations in which distinct, otherwise adequate, percepts are combined in unusual and inappropriate ways on the basis of fantasies (e.g., "two people holding a butterfly down," "two giant crabs crawling out of the rotting carcass of a dinosaur," or "people pounding rotting skulls together"), and (c) outright confabulations in which the perceptual characteristics of Rorschach blots serve as little more than springboards into elaborate fantasies (e.g., a line down the center of a card is used as the basis for a description of two unseen people angrily tearing something apart, red areas seen as blood trigger involved fantasies of aggressive acts, or a small area of a blot that looks like a throne leads to a detailed description of a banquet hall set up in such a way that people cannot get too close to the king and kill him). It is this last set of characteristics, signs of the extent to which their experience of the world can be pervaded by fantasy, that is the most distinctive quality in the thinking of borderline children.

In evaluating responses suggestive of serious thought disorder, it is important to consider not only the content of the responses but also the attitudes behind them. As a group, borderline children manifest a wider range of thought disorder signs than borderline adults. For example, they exhibit contaminations which in adults are typically found in psychotic records. Even more important, because many borderline children may, in a defensive way, plunge headlong into anxiety-arousing thoughts and loose thinking and even "play crazy," they can produce Rorschach records that appear far more disturbed than those of most psychotic youngsters. While significant lapses in reality testing are present in borderline youngsters (Engel, 1963), analysis of disturbed responses often indicates a less pathological basis for such responses than that encountered in psychotic children. Many of the peculiar verbalizations of borderline youngsters turn out to be little more than the playful babble of a preschooler; strange ideas prove to reflect arbitrary thinking, an indifference to reality constraints, or partially controlled defensive maneuvers rather than serious decompensation; and contaminations often result from what Rausch de Traubenberg and Boizou (1980) call "associative rapidity and intensity of participation" (p. 402) rather than more pathological processes. As has been noted, children's behavior in producing these responses and, even more, the emotional reactions the responses elicit in examiners are critical in evaluating their meaning.

RORSCHACH: THEMES AND IMAGERY

While the themes and imagery of Rorschach responses can be used to illuminate all aspects of the pathology of borderline children (Leichtman & Shapiro, 1980b), their bearing on two areas, drives and their regulation and object-relations issues, are especially noteworthy.

The content and quality of Rorschach imagery of borderline children are determined chiefly by pregenital drives of a largely aggressive nature. For example, human and animal figures are frequently seen attacking or being attacked, and claws, mouths, teeth, jaws, pincers, and other weapons are often elaborated on figures or seen in isolation. Although such imagery is predominantly of an oral-aggressive nature, anal themes similarly suffused with aggression occasionally appear (e.g., "crap," "messes," or "a monster shooting torpedoes and bombs out of all of the openings of his body"). Themes of natural or instinctual forces out of control such as floods, explosions, earthquakes, fires, erupting volcanoes, and tornadoes are common. Typically, these images have a raw, vivid, highly personalized, fantasy-laden quality, and often the very process of giving the response seems suffused with the quality of the drives being represented. For example, sexual imagery may be described in highly excited, sexually charged ways, or aggressive themes may be described angrily and youngsters may even attack the Rorschach card. In short, the Rorschach imagery of borderline children speaks to a fantasy world pervaded by primitive drives, fears, and anxieties that are barely held in check.

The content of Rorschach responses of borderline children also points to marked disturbances in the experience of self and others. Although human figures are seen frequently, they are rarely seen under ordinary circumstances. Rather, they are described as in agony, enraged, weird, damaged, deteriorated, or endangered. Human movement responses often portray people engaged in or threatened by aggressive actions of a bizarre nature. Quasi-human and humanoid responses (e.g., witches, wizards, devils, werewolves, monsters, robots, or creatures from outer space) are common as are images combining human and animal features (e.g., "people with rats' heads" or "men in gorilla suits"). Percepts involving animals and animals in movement have many of the same vivid, fantasy-laden qualities as human percepts and often involve aggressive predators, loathsome reptiles, or helpless, threatened, or damaged creatures. Responses frequently portray conflicts around early object-relations issues dramatically. One finds concerns around fusion and merger (e.g., images of two-headed people, Siamese twins, animals or people joined together, Martians capable of fusing together to eat and protect themselves, or figures magically bound together or doing odd things in unison), concerns around distancing and isolation that are directed toward warding off fears of engulfment (e.g., astronauts alone in space, hermits, robots, or computers), or images combining wishes for union and distance (e.g., an astronaut floating in space with a long life-support cord attaching him to the mother ship). One also finds images of small, helpless, endangered beings or individuals on the verge of disintegration alternating with identifications with omnipotent, other-worldly figures (superheroes, aliens, wizards, and monsters). Particularly common are percepts involving either extreme danger and threats of annihilation or primitive, sadistic, aggressive assaults on others, themes that also alternate with astonishing rapidity as in the initial example in which the image of a damaged bleeding man quickly gives way to that of an evil figure using damaged organs to wreak destruction. In general, then, what emerges from Rorschach imagery and fantasies of borderline children are concerns with early object-relations issues embodied in fantasy systems that are stark, primitive, and utterly fantastic in nature and that contain few elements of ordinary human interactions or reflections of the more conventional social world.

THEMATIC TESTS

It is more difficult to generalize about the responses of borderline children to tests such as the TAT, CAT, and TED than about their responses to most other tests in the battery for a number of reasons. First, this difficulty arises from the wide range of stimuli involved in these tests. The mixed, at times ambiguous, pictures on the TAT and the animal pictures on the CAT more often evoke regressive material than the TED, which consists of photographs of youngsters in everyday life situations; on the TAT itself, relatively ordinary pictures such as a boy looking at a violin are not as likely to produce such material as pictures with less realistic content or forms like a murky, seemingly prehistoric scene or pictures with gothic overtones. Second, the variability of responses to these tests reflects the fact that they occupy a middle position in the test battery with regard to their degree of structure. On the one hand, by requiring that children make up stories about affect-laden interpersonal themes and providing relatively few guidelines about how this task is to be accomplished, thematic tests are likely to elicit more original and disturbing responses than tests of mental abilities; on the other hand, because they usually involve relatively clearly structured stimuli, these tests are less likely to elicit disturbed thinking and archaic fantasies than the Rorschach. This intermediate degree of structure accentuates differences between youngsters who are especially vulnerable to disorganization and those who are less prone to regression or more defensive. Finally, borderline children differ considerably in their responses to thematic tests because they differ considerably in their perceptions of the tests and attitudes toward them. Relieved by the degree of structure in the tests and pleased by the opportunity to indulge in fantasy, some youngsters find them less threatening than the Rorschach with its ambiguous stimuli or intelligence and achievement tests with their demands for performance. In contrast, other youngsters, seeing thematic tests as calling more directly for self-revelation, experience greater anxiety on them than on the Rorschach, which can be treated as a game having little connection with "real life." Among the latter group of children, anxiety may contribute to disorganization in some cases, while resulting in greater constriction and defensiveness in others. Hence, there is considerable variability in the manner in which borderline children approach thematic tests and, indeed, in the way in which individual children approach particular tests or test cards.

From a clinical standpoint, the range of stimuli involved in thematic tests and the variability in youngsters' approaches to them can be helpful in highlighting differences among borderline children. For example, the content of stories and the manner in which they are told can point to differences in character organization. Impulsive, infantile youngsters may display their intolerance for looking at relationships and dealing with feelings in the ways in which the main characters in their stories constantly act out in the face of dysphoric affects and in their own difficulty tolerating the task and their propensity to act out in the face of it; narcissistic youngsters may make their stories into plays that run on for two and three pages as they dramatize each role; and youngsters with pronounced "schizotypal" tendencies may underline their struggle to hold onto reality in the plights of the characters in their stories and their own proneness to regression and disorganization in the course of the test. Equally important, thematic tests can also contribute to an understanding of particular aspects of individual children's personalities or life situations. Both specific stories and recurrent themes in stories can give glimpses of predominant affects or conflicts, marked inhibitions, antisocial tendencies, or other character traits, and of family alliances, feelings about parents and siblings, relationships with peers, or related issues.

In spite of this variability, four general issues arise with sufficient frequency in the thematic tests of borderline children to warrant special consideration. First, the stories of borderline children frequently center on separation, loss, and thwarted dependency needs, revealing the enormous difficulties these youngsters have in handling such feelings. Central characters in their stories, especially children, are portrayed as hungry, needy, rejected, abandoned, poor, misunderstood, or otherwise hurt and deprived. Often, not only children but whole families are described in these terms. Typically, borderline children have difficulty tolerating simply confining their stories to these themes. In some cases, recognition of such feelings in stories is immediately followed by impulsive actions on the part of their main characters. For example, to a TAT card of a figure huddled by a couch (card 3BM), a ten-year-old boy told the following story:

> This boy was waiting for his father to come home and didn't realize that his father was in jail for doing something he shouldn't have done. He gets so mad that he finally got up and killed himself because he was so mad.

In other cases, characters in stories or plots undergo abrupt changes; for example, a figure mourning by a graveside may suddenly be attacked by or transformed into a monster. In other cases, themes of hurt or loss in stories may lead to a shift in youngsters' attitudes toward the task or toward the examiner: their stance toward a story may change from serious involvement to one of sarcastic devaluation of characters within it, or they may ignore the story itself and seek to provoke or battle with the psychologist. In still other cases, youngsters may be able to tolerate one story about loss or deprivation, only to follow it with another in which aggressive, antisocial, or regressive tendencies are striking. The particular responses of borderline children to themes of thwarted dependency needs and separation are diverse; what tends to be constant is the prevalence of such themes and the great difficulty youngsters experience in dealing with them.

Second, the stories of borderline children are filled with aggression. They involve vividly described fights, injuries, murders, suicides, and threats of annihilation. Significantly, such aggression often occurs within families. Not only are parents or children often killed "off-stage" ("this is a boy whose mom and dad died in an accident. . . ."), but often this type of aggression is a main theme of the story. For example, the TAT picture of a woman holding another figure at the bottom of a staircase (card 18GF) is frequently seen as a mother throttling or even strangling her child.

Third, borderline children produce many stories in which main characters undergo or fear they will undergo major transformations. Changes in figures with whom children identify at times have clearly defensive connotations (e.g., hurt or lonely children suddenly become robbers or aggressors or helpless vulnerable children develop magical powers); at times, such changes speak to their concerns about being overwhelmed by powerful affects and unable to control their actions (e.g., main characters engage in inexplicable acts or commit crimes when upset); and, at times, they reveal concerns about going crazy or the loss of self in some other way. For example, an eleven-year-old told the following story to a picture of a man holding his hand over a sleeping boy (card 12M):

> The boy was sleeping and then this phantom came for him. He needed the boy to help him in his phantom house to get all the people to be phantoms, so when he was asleep, the phantom came up with bad power in his hand to make his mind drift away and the boy died of it and he became a phantom and spread it around the town.

Supporting characters in stories, usually ones representing parental figures, undergo sudden and unexplained changes as well. For example, a kind man in a graveyard may turn out to be digging up corpses with which he intends to rule the world or a benevolent grandmotherly figure may suddenly try to strangle a youngster. In some cases, the roles or attitudes of characters shift in confusing and unpredictable ways. Roles of aggressor and victim may alternate so rapidly that they cannot be differentiated, and characters may seem to represent children and their parents simultaneously or in rapid succession (Rausch de Traubenberg & Boizou, 1980). While some contradictions or shifts in character for defensive reasons are found in the stories of less disturbed youngsters, the stories of borderline youngsters tend to be distinguished by both the extent and the instability of the transformations of character that occur within them.

Finally, many borderline children tell at least one story on thematic tests centering on archaic fantasies which point to a capacity for marked regression. Such stories frequently combine primitive and bizarre fantasies of the kind more often seen on the Rorschach with a breakdown of spatial and temporal organization and signs of disturbances in formal thought processes. For example, one nine-year-old, after performing in a relatively organized fashion throughout most of the testing, told the following story on the next to the last card of the TAT (card 18GF):

> This lady, she's mad at this boy, her son. She's mad and he's mysterious, so she puts him on the bench and decides to tear off his head. So she tears off his head, pokes out his eyes. I'm making these last stories good! She cuts off his hair. So she puts his head in the roasting pan and roasts his head. So after she's finished roasting his head, she takes it out, puts it on her plate, sticks her fork in his face, and starts cutting and eating away [laughs]. It's a good story.

On the last card (12M), he follows this story with "an even better one" in which a boy cuts off a woman's head, cooks and eats it, and scoops out the brains to share with his friends, the rabbits and dogs. Drawing on a reservoir of ideas provided by fairy tales, Saturday morning cartoons, and horror movies, far less seriously disturbed children are also capable of giving ghoulish and, at times, blood-curdling stories with gothic overtones to TAT pictures. Borderline children differ from others not only in the extent of their attraction to these stories but in the vividness with which they tell the stories and in the idiosyncratic and unusual twists they give them. The stories of borderline children seem far less determined by cartoons or movies than by the emergence of primary process ideation.

OTHER PROJECTIVE TESTS

As in the case of the thematic tests, great variability exists in the approach of borderline children to other projective tests such as Human Figure Drawings and Brief Projective Questions. For example, in drawing people, some youngsters produce relatively primitive figures which point chiefly to cognitive limitations; others produce quite charming pictures of children younger than themselves, reflecting strong regressive wishes; others draw angry figures with teeth or claw-like hands accentuated, reflecting their own preoccupation with aggression; and still others sketch unusual or bizarre figures and share disturbing fantasies or concerns about bodily integrity related to them. The Animal Choice Test (Leichtman, 1980a), a series of brief projective questions in which children are asked to choose animals they would most like to be and least like to be and animals to represent themselves, parents, and other family members, is often helpful in understanding ways in which borderline children experience themselves and significant figures in their lives. The choices made and the rationale given for them typically reflect early conflicts, especially oral-aggressive wishes and fears of annihilation, include odd or idiosyncratic ideas, and often involve blatant attacks and devaluation in the very act of giving the responses. Again, rather than any single pattern of responses being encountered in the performance of borderline children on any of these tests, these tests are significant chiefly because they provide another opportunity to see a wide range of phenomena of the kind already noted with regard to the Rorschach and the thematic tests.

INTEGRATION AND USE OF DIAGNOSTIC INFORMATION

After diagnostic information has been gathered in the test situation and after it has been processed on a test-by-test basis, psychologists possess a wealth of data on borderline youngsters. Produced by a heterogeneous group of children who approach tests in an erratic and idiosyncratic fashion and who are tested under many different circumstances, the data vary considerably from case to case. As a result, it is hard to find single test signs or test behaviors that distinguish the group of children as a whole. The difficulty this state of affairs poses for diagnosis, however, is more than offset by the sheer abundance of clinical material that evaluations provide. The problem facing clinicians at this point is that of translating this material into an understanding of presenting symptoms, a meaningful diagnosis, and a useful treatment plan.

Rather than focusing on an analysis and report of diagnostic findings on a test-by-test basis, we favor an approach to this task that centers on the integration of material from diverse sources into "middle-level" descriptions of psychological functioning (see Appelbaum, 1972). As tests are scored and as individual responses and behaviors are analyzed, inferences can be made and grouped according to their bearing on questions about areas of psychological functioning deemed significant on both practical and theoretical grounds. Among questions we ask are: What are the predominant needs, wishes, and conflicts youngsters experience? What is the nature of their affective experience? What can be said about their intellectual functioning? Are there disturbances in formal thought processes and reality testing and, if so, what kinds? What patterns of defenses and coping strategies are used? What other ego strengths and weaknesses are present? How do youngsters experience themselves and others and how are these experiences manifested in interpersonal relationships? After diagnostic information has been processed in this manner, patterns can be sought in each grouping of data and answers to these and similar questions formulated in ways which provide the best fitting, most coherent treatment of that data. Given the quantity of rich material that borderline children produce in the course of the testing and the frequent convergence of inferences from a wide variety of sources, what emerges from this process is a comprehensive picture of such matters as an individual's central conflicts, defensive organization, thought style, and experience of self and others. It is this picture that provides a basis for general diagnostic formulations, explanations of presenting symptoms, and development of treatment plans.

To be sure, this account of the integration of diagnostic material simplifies a complex process. While data on borderline children from a variety of sources often converge to support particular inferences, equally frequently those data suggest that youngsters can function in very different ways at different times. For example, a child may appear markedly constricted and inhibited at some times and wild and impulsive at others, or may exhibit relatively organized, intact thinking on "structured" tests and loose, bizarre thinking on projective tests. The task at this point becomes one of trying to understand different patterns of behavior in terms of the conditions under which they occur. Even more important, this account of the diagnostic process gives little attention to the extent to which each step in the gathering and processing of diagnostic information is influenced by theoretical orientations, existing theory and research, and levels of clinical skill. Because these factors play such a large role in clinical practice, psychologists may differ greatly in how they approach and carry out diagnostic tasks. For the present purposes, we will simply note that the following discussion of issues in the diagnosis of borderline children represents a psychoanalytically oriented approach to an area in which research is still limited and basic theoretical questions are far from settled.

PATTERNS OF PSYCHOLOGICAL FUNCTIONING IN BORDERLINE CHILDREN

The literature on the testing of borderline children has focused almost exclusively on aspects of psychological functioning common to the group as a whole. In an earlier paper (Leichtman & Shapiro, 1980b), we describe the manner in which data from different aspects of the psychological evaluation converge to produce the following picture of personality development in six different, though clearly overlapping, areas.

First, as a group, borderline children exhibit abundant evidence of early fixations in libidinal development and significant problems in drive regulation. The thoughts, fantasies, and actions of these youngsters as seen in test behavior and test reponses reflect predominantly oral and anal wishes which are heavily colored by aggression. Phallic and Oedipal wishes may be present and even acted on blatantly, but they are more heavily influenced by perverse, pregenital drives. In behavior and, even more, on projective tests, borderline youngsters present drives in raw, vivid, unmodulated forms rather than tamer, more derivative, reality-oriented ones. These drives tend to be manifested in labile, shifting combinations rather than more predictable, organized need-states. However, while primitive drives enter consciousness readily and are acted upon impulsively, they do not have the same disorganizing and disintegrative potential with borderline children that they do with psychotic youngsters. Rather, borderline youngsters frequently seem to plunge into drive-related activities as a means of gaining some measure of control and relief.

Second, borderline children give evidence of experiencing affect in relatively primitive, unmodulated forms. Their test behavior and test responses typically reflect dysphoric affects, chiefly depression, rage, and anxiety. They have great difficulty tolerating such feelings, experience abrupt mood swings, and are prone to act out and/or regress in the face of strong affect. Shifts in affect may also utterly transform their perceptions of themselves and their world. Chronic anxiety, often centering on issues of separation, survival, and annihilation, is especially common. This anxiety frequently escalates into panic rather than serving as a signal function and more often leads to regression and desperate action than the mobilization of higher level defenses.

Third, the test performance of such youngsters suggests that represssion and higher level defenses where present tend to be rigid and tenuous. One frequently finds indications of more primitive defenses, notably early forms of projection and projective identification, splitting and dissociation, withdrawal into fantasy, and/or blatant forms of denial, externalization, and action.

Fourth, in the course of psychological evaluations, borderline children display modes of thinking associated with early developmental arrests and transitory regressions in which more serious disturbances in formal thought processes and reality testing may be seen. In contrast to psychotic children, these youngsters rarely give the impression of "being out of contact with reality"; however, their stance toward reality differs significantly from that of less disturbed children. Reality-oriented, secondary process thinking does not seem firmly established, and their thinking is heavily colored by wishes and fantasies. They typically interpret the world in highly egocentric, arbitrary ways; they readily withdraw into fantasy; and they frequently superimpose fantasies on their interactions with others. In less structured situations, notably on projective tests, they frequently exhibit evidence of primary-process ideation, impairments in formal thought processes, and transitory disturbances in reality testing.

Fifth, in the course of testing, borderline youngsters display either constant or periodic disturbances in ego functioning consisting of poor frustration tolerance, distractibility, impulsivity, and/or difficulty in sustaining goal-directed activity. Disturbances in "autonomous" ego functions such as perception, language, motility, and intelligence may be present and, even when such functions are intact, they are typically not used in effective, productive, reality-oriented ways. Chronic underachievement in school and difficulty in handling other normal adaptive tasks of childhood such as those represented by tests of mental ability and achievement are frequently evident.

Finally, the test performance of borderline children reveals marked disturbances in interpersonal relationships and in the experience of self and others. In their behavior in the test situation, these youngsters tend to react to examiners as need-satisfying objects or enter into intense, controlling, dependent or hostile-dependent relationships. Their experience of themselves and others as seen in tests is heavily colored by needs, moods, and fantasies; that experience is relatively unintegrated and subject to rapid alterations between contradictory, univalent images; and, in periods of regression, it is often bizarre and fantastic. Signs of a tenuous sense of identity and shifts between grandiose, omnipotent self-images and helpless, impotent ones are common. However, these youngsters are able to maintain more effective relationships with others than psychotic youngsters in that they do not impress them with a sense of "otherness" and are frequently successful in engaging others in interactions heavily colored by their own fantasy systems.

In addition to pointing to general characteristics shared by borderline children as a group, careful descriptions of the psychological functioning patterns seen in each area can highlight important differences among these children. Such differences include: (1) the presence of a variety of forms of brain dysfunction and learning disabilities in some youngsters; (2) variations in intelligence, patterns of cognitive abilities, levels of academic achievement, and special talents and abilities; (3) differences in self-concept and the experience of significant others related to identifications with particular family members, family constellations, and life circumstances; and (4) varying patterns of needs, defenses, thought styles, ego strengths and deficits, and self- and object representations associated with nascent infantile, narcissistic, depressive, antisocial, schizoid, and/or paranoid character traits.

THE BORDERLINE DIAGNOSIS

"Middle-level" descriptions of psychological functioning of this kind provide the basis for more general diagnostic formulations, although in advancing diagnoses, psychologists, like other clinicians, must struggle with problems inherent in current nosological schemes.

The psychiatric literature on borderline conditions in children has been written almost exclusively from a dynamic as opposed to a descriptive standpoint (Sugarman & Lerner, 1980). In contrast to Kraepelinian approaches to diagnosis that seek to establish distinct syndromes based on observable signs and symptoms clustered in precise, clearly delimited groups, psychoanalytic approaches conceptualize psychopathology in terms of developmental disturbances that, because they involve the interaction of a multiplicity of factors, may have a wide variety of dynamic and structural consequences. From this perspective, borderline disorders are viewed as distortions or arrests in development centering on a period in which separation and individuation from the mother have begun, but in which the achievement of a stable sense of identity and "object constancy" have yet to be established (Weil, 1953; Rosenfeld & Sprince, 1963; Chethik, 1980; Rinsley, 1978, 1980a, 1980b). As a consequence, these youngsters, while not psychotic, exhibit severe disturbances in libidinal development, ego development, and object relations. In psychological evaluations in settings such as our own, the diagnosis of borderline disorders in children has been advanced when, in considering diverse areas of psychological functioning (e.g., central conflicts, affect organization, ego development, thought organization, object relations), one finds patterns such as those described in the preceding section. In each area one encounters signs of early fixations and marked disturbance in functioning that, nonetheless, stop short of those found in psychotic children.

This approach to the diagnosis of borderline disorders in children has both advantages and limitations. On the positive side, it has called attention to a group of children insufficiently recognized in the past, provided a label that conveys information about the degree of their pathology, and pointed to a body of literature bearing on understanding and treating their problems. At the same time, the concept and the manner in which it has been used in clinical practice have had significant problems associated with them. Because borderline conditions are conceptualized in terms of a continuum of psychopathology, and because there have been no clear and accepted demarcations of the boundaries that set these conditions apart from more and less severe psychopathology (Pine, 1974; Leichtman & Shapiro, 1980a), there may be considerable variations in labeling practices with youngsters who differ in either direction from the modal characteristics of borderline conditions upon which clinicians can agree. As a consequence, authorities on borderline conditions such as Rosenfeld and Sprince (1963) freely acknowledge that many of the youngsters they describe as manifesting borderline conditions would be considered "frankly psychotic" by other clinicians. Equally important, although as early as the 1950s Anna Freud (1957) suggested that the term "borderline children" be applied to a series of disorders between the boundaries of established neurotic and psychotic conditions, apart from the work of Pine (1974) and Rinsley (1980b) little has been written on differentiating among such children. Indeed, not only is there no commonly accepted typological scheme for categorizing different types of borderline children, but, until recently, even the need for such a scheme has not been appreciated enough. Hence, at best, in working with individual youngsters, diagnosticians have to try to underline pronounced infantile, narcissistic, depressive, antisocial, or schizotypal characteristics in their reports on borderline children in the hope that these significant differences among the children will receive sufficient attention in treatment planning.

The recent introduction of DSM-III with its descriptive approach to diagnosis is likely to lead to significant changes in the labeling of youngsters who have heretofore been described as manifesting borderline conditions. On the one hand, by using multiple diagnoses and highlighting the range of problems people can experience, this new diagnostic system offers the possibility of a richer formal description of characterological differences among borderline children and of secondary features (e.g., attentional disorders, hyperactivity, and learning disabilities) often found among them. On the other hand, at least in the immediate future, this system may result in less rather than greater agreement among clinicians on the labeling of the central disturbances in this group of children.

Indeed, such problems may be inevitable because these conditions involve two of the most controversial areas of DSM-III—the concept of borderline disorders in general and the characterization of psychopathology in childhood. Some of the difficulties that arise are relatively minor: many of the youngsters who have until now been described as manifesting borderline conditions would be either classified as Schizotypal Personality Disorders on DSM-III or given multiple diagnoses. More important, perhaps recognizing the reluctance of many clinicians working with children to identify borderline conditions in children with those found in adults (see Leichtman & Shapiro, 1980a), DSM-III discourages, but does not entirely proscribe, the use of borderline diagnoses before the age of eighteen. While the substitution of the diagnosis of Identity Disorders is encouraged with adolescents, it is clearly less satisfactory with children. At present, in the absence of clear conventions regarding their diagnoses, children who exhibit the characteristics noted in the preceding section and who have been described as manifesting borderline disorders in the past may now be variously diagnosed as manifesting Schizotypal Personality Disorders, Borderline Personality Disorders, or Atypical Pervasive Development Disorders, or they may simply be diagnosed on the basis of predominant symptomatology (e.g., as Conduct Disorders or Phobic Disorders) either with or without borderline features being noted as an uncoded personality trait.

In the future, the use of the term borderline disorders with children will undoubtedly change even further. Not only does the current situation with regard to DSM-III call for clarification of conventions governing such labeling, but as more research is done on the nature, etiology, and outcome of these conditions in children, classification systems are likely to change substantially. Subtypes of borderline conditions may be more clearly delineated, or what is now viewed as a family of disorders may come to be recognized as distinct syndromes that have some similar surface manifestations. For the present purposes, it is perhaps sufficient to note that psychological testing, like all other forms of diagnosis, is done within a nosological framework and cannot help but change and improve as that framework changes and improves.

EXPLANATIONS OF PRESENTING SYMPTOMS

Given the controversies around the use of the term "borderline disorders" and the limitations in our present knowledge of such conditions, it is important to recognize that a decision regarding labels is only one step in the diagnostic process and, at least in current clinical practice, by no means the most significant step. The most important steps in that process are those of providing an understanding of the problems which have brought youngsters to evaluations and developing plans to help them and those who work with them deal with these problems. Diagnostic categorization is of some assistance with these tasks, but its contributions are limited, since youngsters with similar labels may manifest seemingly similar symptoms that, nonetheless, have different causes. It is "middle-level" descriptions of psychological functioning, descriptions typically formulated with thoughts of their bearing on presenting problems already in mind, that contribute most to these tasks because these descriptions allow referral questions to be answered with the kind of specificity necessary for developing differentiated treatment plans.

For example, although academic and behavioral difficulties at school are common presenting symptoms of borderline children, the reasons for these difficulties may vary considerably from child to child. In some cases, the picture that emerges from test data points to intellectual limitations that have interfered with academic progress and exacerbated all other problems the youngsters are experiencing in school; in other cases, youngsters have adequate intelligence, yet struggle with particular organically based learning disabilities; and in still other cases, youngsters may be of average intelligence and exhibit no learning disability, yet have failed to master so many basic academic skills in the past that they are unable to keep up with current work, a situation which in itself contributes to disinterest and acting up in class. In these and other cases, classroom behavior and school performance can also be affected by different patterns of ego weaknesses, defensive and coping styles, the degree of investment in learning, narcissistic orientations, anxiety, preoccupations with severe psychological conflicts, and/or interpersonal difficulties. It is not the diagnostic category, but, rather, the kind of comprehensive picture of a youngster's psychological functioning noted earlier that provides psychologists with the basis for making educated judgments about the particular constellation of factors that is most significant in explaining school problems in any given case.

Other presenting symptoms of borderline children can be approached in the same way. When borderline youngsters have been referred because of delinquent acts, in some cases the picture that emerges from the analysis of test data is that of impulsive, needy children who are prone to act out when hurt; in other cases, that of highly impressionable youngsters eager to impress peers and easily swayed by them; in other cases, that of children with deeply rooted antisocial attitudes; and in still other cases, that of youngsters whose seeming antisocial attitudes, in fact, represent a desperate effort to hold onto an identity that disguises and staves off decompensation. Where disturbed thinking or bizarre actions are major referral problems, the picture that emerges from the evaluation can help clarify the circumstances under which such thinking or acts are likely to occur and the degree to which they reflect genuine disorganization and loss of reality testing as opposed to highly arbitrary, egocentric modes of thought or unusual defensive maneuvers. Similarly, using the context provided by conceptualizations of modes of intellectual functioning, affective patterns, conflicts and defenses, and object relationships, psychologists are able to offer explanations that can help clarify the particular meaning of a youngster's hyperactivity, distractibility, conflicts with family members, or other presenting problems.

TREATMENT RECOMMENDATIONS

A number of constraints affect recommendations for the treatment of borderline children based upon psychological evaluations, like those based on other types of evaluations. One constraint is how little is known about the treatment of borderline children and the effects of that treatment. The literature in these areas is surprisingly meager, consisting chiefly of descriptions of psychotherapy processes. In a recent review of borderline syndromes in children, for example, Chethik (1980) confines his discussion of treatment almost exclusively to psychotherapy and notes significant differences of opinion among authorities in this area. The most comprehensive discussion of treatment modalities, that of Rinsley (1980b), is a highly schematic one. Moreover, there are few follow-up studies on the treatment of borderline children and even fewer that have clear implications for how treatment should be conducted. For example, while Szurek and colleagues (Szurek & Berlin, 1973) strongly advocate outpatient treatment for borderline children, Wergeland (1979) suggests that inpatient treatment may be as valuable to many of these children. However, on the basis of the fullest recent follow-up study of the latter group of borderline children, Wergeland concludes:

> In our study it was also impossible to decide which part of the therapy was most effective. Was it the individual psychotherapy, the milieu-therapy, the separation from home, or the quality of the professionals at the clinic—or was it simply a result of natural maturation over so long a time? (p. 474)

A second constraint on recommendations based upon psychological evaluations is that testing provides only one perspective on youngsters who display complicated problems with neurological, psychological, and social roots. Treatment recommendations are best made on the basis of a combination of perspectives on youngsters including those provided by clinical interviews, developmental histories, assessments of families, neurological evaluations, and educational assessments. Finally, plans for treatment are also affected heavily by practical considerations such as what families can accept, the psychological and financial resources they have available, and the treatment available in the community.

Despite such constraints, the concluding step of the diagnostic process remains that of using the data available to make practical recommendations which can help children and those who care for them deal with the problems they are experiencing. Because of the severity and complexity of these problems, treatment plans for borderline children are usually multifaceted. The following represent some of the ways psychological evaluations can contribute to decisions regarding treatment in six general areas.

First, while psychological evaluations alone are rarely the decisive factor in determinations of whether treatment should be conducted on an inpatient or outpatient basis, they can contribute to decisions regarding whether residential treatment is needed and how it may best assist youngsters. Rinsley (1980b) notes three criteria for recommending residential treatment: (1) the youngster's symptomatology is so strange, bizarre, disruptive, or destructive that it causes social ostracism or endangers life; (2) despite repeated treatment efforts, there is significant deterioration in basic areas of psychosocial adaptation such as school; and (3) the family situation is not only pathogenic, but does not provide sufficient structure and support for the child and the family as a whole to change and grow. Information from psychological evaluations about the degree of disorganization youngsters are experiencing, their propensity for acting out, and the extent to which their pathology has interfered with negotiation of age-appropriate development tasks have an important bearing on the first two of these points. At the same time, information from sources other than testing on such matters as youngsters' behavior at home, at school, and in the community as well as family circumstances have as much or more importance in final decisions regarding placement. However, regardless of whether treatment is conducted on an inpatient or outpatient basis, psychological evaluations can contribute significantly to recommendations about how those living with borderline youngsters can work with them. In particular, information about the degree and kinds of difficulties in impulse control that borderline children experience, their response to structure, their capacity to form attachments, the transference and countertransference patterns encountered with them, their readiness to accept help, their strengths, and the adaptive aspects of their defenses all provide a basis for helpful suggestions to primary caretakers.

Second, psychological testing can be of considerable help in making recommendations to those conducting psychotherapy with borderline children. To be sure, it should be noted that, at present, there is no consensus in the field on how such therapy is best done. While most of the literature on psychotherapy with these children notes the need for support and containment in the therapy process, there are significant differences of opinion between those who recommend "ego-supportive" approaches in which interpretation is used only in limited ways and emphasis is placed on containing impulsivity, managing anxiety, strengthening defenses, and developing coping skills (Rosenfeld & Sprince, 1965; Chethik, 1980) and those who advocate more active interpretive techniques (Ekstein, 1966; Rinsley, 1980b). In the absence of general agreement about technique, psychologists' recommendations regarding psychotherapy depend heavily on their own positions on such issues. Nonetheless, even given this state of affairs, evaluations can point to particular techniques having better or poorer chances of success with particular youngsters. For example, children with chronic ego weaknesses and infantile character organizations manifest a lack of reflectiveness and a proneness to regress or act out in the face of anxiety that suggest they will require a more supportive and structured form of therapy and will have great difficulty making use of expressive techniques. Regardless of therapists' particular techniques, psychological assessments can provide them with information about the nature of youngsters' inner worlds, their capacity to form relationships, patterns of transference and countertransference, degrees of reflectiveness, central conflicts, and a host of other issues bearing on the treatment. Moreover, we have noted, the ways in which youngsters respond to psychologists in the course of testing, the kinds of support and confrontation they require, their response to efforts to be of help to them, and their handling of the inquiry process can all be of assistance in making recommendations regarding psychotherapy.

Third, by providing information on children's perceptions of their families and revealing pathological processes of attachment and identification, psychological evaluations often highlight the need for casework or family therapy. However, tests reflect only the children's perspective and decisions about the nature of these processes are best made on the basis of other evaluations, notably those of the family's functioning. Indeed, with borderline children in particular, great caution should be exercised in making inferences from test material to actual family situations because the children's portrayals on tests of significant figures in their lives are heavily colored by their needs and by primitive pathological fantasies.

Fourth, psychological tests can be especially helpful in planning school programs for borderline children. Information about intelligence, patterns of abilities, and mastery of basic academic skills can help school personnel become aware of mismatches between youngsters' abilities and their current placements and can help in determining appropriate education programs; signs of organic dysfunction and learning disabilities can lead to further educational testing and referral to special classes; and an appreciation of emotional and behavioral problems interfering with intellectual performance and techniques used to cope with these problems in the course of the testing can be of help to teachers and tutors.

Fifth, although little has been written on the use of medication with borderline children, Rinsley (1980b) suggests that youngsters displaying "attention deficit disorders," depressive characteristics, and schizotypal features may respond to particular medications. If these suggestions prove correct, testing can contribute to decisions about medication by helping in the delineation of such disorders.

Finally, a variety of secondary recommendations can be made on the basis of observations made in the course of the evaluation. For example, youngsters from single parent families may reveal a hunger for contact with interested adults and benefit considerably from a "big brother" or "sister." Isolated children with poor social skills may be able to make good use of participation in Scouts, clubs, or activity groups. In addition, as areas of special skill, talent, or interest are noted, educational, vocational or artistic programs can be recommended to help develop these areas and build esteem-enhancing skills.

In certain respects, psychological evaluations can be of greatest help to those working with borderline children *after* treatment has begun. Although recommendations made at the outset of treatment are, of course, valuable, therapists, treatment institutions, and schools have their own distinct ways of working with children, ways that differ considerably, depending upon the institutions involved. For example, Rosenfeld and Sprince (1965), observe: "Working with borderline children appears to produce as many techniques as there are children and this figure can probably be multiplied by the number of therapists concerned." (p. 495) Frequently, only after they have begun working with borderline children and experienced success in some areas and frustration and confusion in others do therapists, child care workers, teachers, and others involved with treatment develop their own questions about what youngsters are like and how they may be treated. It is at this point that a dialogue around the testing is most useful because those doing the treatment now know the children, know what they want to know, and are in a better position to appreciate answers given to those questions. For example, in our own institution, rethinking issues discussed in test reports written two or three years earlier has often proved helpful in working with teachers who find they have run into an impasse with borderline children in some aspect of their educational programs.

CONCLUSION

The diagnosis of children described in the psychiatric literature as manifesting borderline disorders is among the most challenging tasks confronting clinical psychologists today. In part the challenge of the task lies in the obstacles these children present in the test process. Many approach tests in so erratic and idiosyncratic a fashion and create so many problems for test administration that often there are reasons to question whether the assumptions underlying standard psychometric procedures have been met. In part the challenge of the task lies in the fact that diagnosis must be done amidst crosscurrents of shifting views about how such conditions are to be understood, classified, labeled, and treated.

If diagnosis is viewed chiefly as a process of categorization and labeling based on particular test signs, accounts of the psychological assessment of borderline children would have to emphasize the limitations of current techniques and theories. Yet if diagnosis is viewed from a broader perspective, if it is seen as a process of asking and seeking answers to questions about how the children and those who live and work with them may be helped in dealing with these problems, it is possible to be far more optimistic about present practices and future prospects. From this perspective, psychological testing may be seen, above all, as a way of gathering information bearing on these questions, a way, it has been suggested, that provides a wealth of data from a wide range of sources. While problems may be encountered in gathering such data and questions raised about their meaning under certain circumstances, these very problems and circumstances represent additional sources of rich clinical material. From this perspective, existing theory and research can be appreciated for their contributions to delineating conditions unrecognized in the past and for their provision of ways to view the behavior of children manifesting these conditions that offers some basis for understanding their problems and formulating treatment plans. As more is learned about borderline conditions in children, new ways of understanding, classifying, and treating these disorders will undoubtedly supersede older ones. However, such changes can be viewed as an improvement rather than as a repudiation of current practice. The fundamental task confronting practicing clinicians in the future will remain the same: that of using the techniques and knowledge available to understand the problems which have brought children to the evaluation and to make recommendations that have the greatest promise of making a difference in their lives.

R E F E R E N C E S

American Psychiatric Association. *Diagnostic and statistical manual of mental disorders* (DSM-III) (3d ed.). Washington, D.C.: 1980.

Appelbaum, S. A method of reporting psychological test findings. *Bulletin of the Menninger Clinic,* 1972, *36,* 535–545.

Beres, D. Ego deviation and the concept of schizophrenia. *The Psychoanalytic Study of the Child,* 1956, *11,* 164–235.

Cain, A. On the meaning of "playing crazy" in borderline children. *Psychiatry,* 1964, *27,* 278–289.

Chethik, M. The borderline child. In J. Noshpitz, (Ed.), *Basic handbook of child psychiatry* (Vol. 2). New York: Basic Books, 1980.

Chethik, M., & Fast, I. A function of fantasy in the borderline child. *American Journal of Orthopsychiatry,* 1970, *40,* 756–765.

Chiland, C., & Lebovici, S. Borderline or prepsychotic conditions in childhood—A French point of view. In P. Hartocollis (Ed.), *Borderline personality disorders: The concept, the syndrome, the patient.* New York: International Universities Press, 1977.

Ekstein, R. *Children of time and space, of action and impulse.* New York: Appleton-Century-Crofts, 1966.

Ekstein, R., & Wallerstein, J. Observations on the psychology of borderline and psychotic children. *The Psychoanalytic Study of the Child,* 1954, *9,* 344–369.

Engel, M. Psychological testing of borderline children. *Archives of General Psychiatry,* 1963, *8,* 426–434.

Fast, I., & Chethik, M. Some aspects of object relationships in borderline children. *International Journal of Psycho-Analysis,* 1972, *53,* 479–485.

Freud, A. The assessment of borderline cases. In *The Writings of Anna Freud* (Vol. 5). New York: International Universities Press, 1969. (Originally published, 1957.)

Frijling-Schreuder, E. Borderline states in children. *The Psychoanalytic Study of the Child,* 1969, *24,* 307–327.

Fuller, D., Escudero, M., Mandelbaum, A., & Hirschberg, J. Some research implications in the evaluation of a borderline child. *Bulletin of the Menninger Clinic,* 1954, *18,* 72–79.

Geleerd, E. Borderline states in childhood and adolescence. *The Psychoanalytic Study of the Child,* 1958, *13,* 279–295.

Gunderson, J., & Singer, M. Defining borderline patients: An overview. *American Journal of Psychiatry,* 1975, *132,* 1–10.

Hartmann, H. *Ego psychology and the problem of adaptation.* New York: International Universities Press, 1958.

Kernberg, O. Borderline personality organization. *Journal of the American Psychoanalytic Association,* 1967, *15,* 641–685.

Kernberg, O. A psychoanalytic classification of character pathology. *Journal of the American Psychoanalytic Association,* 1970, *18,* 800–822.

Kernberg, O. Early ego integration and object relations. *Annals of the New York Academy of Science,* 1972, *193,* 233–247.

Knight, R. Borderline states. *Bulletin of the Menninger Clinic,* 1953, *17,* 1–12.

Leichtman, M., & Shapiro, S. An introduction to the psychological assessment of borderline conditions in children: Borderline children and the test process. In J. Kwawer et al. (Eds.), *Borderline phenomena and the Rorschach test.* New York: International Universities Press, 1980a.

Leichtman, M., & Shapiro, S. An introduction to the psychological assessment of borderline conditions in children: Manifestations of borderline phenomena on psychological testing. In J. Kwawer et al. (Eds.), *Borderline phenomena and the Rorschach test.* New York: International Universities Press, 1980b.

Mahler, M., Ross, J., & DeFries, Z. Clinical studies in benign and malignant cases of childhood psychosis. *American Journal of Orthopsychiatry,* 1949, *19,* 295–305.

Marcus, J. Borderline states in childhood. *Journal of Child Psychology/Psychiatry,* 1963, *4,* 207–218.

Meyer, M., & Caruth, E. Inner and outer reality on the Rorschach. In R. Ekstein (Ed.), *The challenge: Despair and hope in the conquest of inner space.* New York: Brunner/Mazel, 1971. (Originally published, 1964).

Olesker, W. Early life experience and the development of borderline pathology. In J. Kwawer, et al. (Eds.), *Borderline phenomena and the Rorschach test.* New York: International Universities Press, 1980.

Pine, F. On the concept "borderline" in children. *The Psychoanalytic Study of the Child,* 1974, *29,* 341–368.

Rapaport, D., Gill, M., & Schafer, R. *Diagnostic psychological testing* (2 vols.). Chicago: Year Book, 1945–1946.

Rausch de Traubenberg, N., & Boizou, M. Prepsychotic conditions in children as manifested in their perception and fantasy experiences on Rorschach and thematic tests. In J. Kwawer, et al. (Eds.), *Borderline phenomena and the Rorschach test.* New York: International Universities Press, 1980.

Rinsley, D. Borderline psychopathology: A review of aetiology, dynamics, and treatment. *International Review of Psycho-Analysis,* 1978, *5,* 45–54.

Rinsley, D. The developmental etiology of borderline and narcissistic disorders. *Bulletin of the Menninger Clinic,* 1980a, *44,* 127–134.

Rinsley, D. Diagnosis and treatment of borderline and narcissistic children and adolescents. *Bulletin of the Menninger Clinic,* 1980b, *44,* 147–170.

Rosenfeld, S., & Sprince, M. An attempt to formulate the meaning of the concept "borderline." *The Psychoanalytic Study of the Child,* 1963, *18,* 603–635.

Rosenfeld, S., & Sprince, M. Some thoughts on the technical handling of borderline children. *The Psychoanalytic Study of the Child,* 1965, *20,* 495–517.

Shapiro, E. The psychodynamics and developmental psychology of the borderline patient: A review of the literature. *American Journal of Psychiatry,* 1978, *135,* 1305–1315.

Singer, M. The borderline diagnosis and psychological tests: Review and research. In P. Hartocollis, (Ed.), *Borderline personality disorders: The concept, the syndrome, the patient.* New York: International Universities Press, 1977.

Stone, M. *The borderline syndromes: Constitution, personality, and adaptation.* New York, McGraw-Hill, 1980.

Sugarman, A. The borderline personality as manifested on psychological tests. In J. Kwawer, et al. (Eds.), *Borderline phenomena and the Rorschach test.* New York: International Universities Press, 1980.

Sugarman, A., & Lerner, H. Reflections on the current state of the borderline concept. In J. Kwawer, et al., (Eds)., *Borderline phenomena and the Rorschach test.* New York: International Universities Press, 1980.

Szurek, S., & Berlin, I. *Clinical studies in childhood psychoses.* London: Butterworth, 1973.

Terman, L., & Merrill, M. *Stanford-Binet intelligence scale: Manual for the third revision.* Boston: Houghton Mifflin, 1960.

Wergeland, H. A follow-up study of 29 borderline psychotic children 5 to 20 years after discharge. *Acta Psychaitrica Scandanavica,* 1979, *60,* 465–476.

Weil, A. Certain severe disturbances of ego development in children. *The Psychoanalytic Study of the Child,* 1953, *8,* 271–287.

Weil, A. Some evidence of deviational development in infancy and childhood. *The Psychoanalytic Study of the Child,* 1956, *11,* 292–299.

C H A P T E R 7

Neurological Dysfunction in Borderline Children

Joseph Marcus, M.D.
PROFESSOR OF CHILD PSYCHIATRY AND
DIRECTOR, UNIT FOR RESEARCH IN
CHILD PSYCHIATRY AND DEVELOPMENT
DEPARTMENT OF PSYCHIATRY
UNIVERSITY OF CHICAGO
CHICAGO, ILLINOIS

Fred Ovsiew, M.D.
FELLOW IN NEUROPSYCHIATRY
DEPARTMENT OF PSYCHIATRY
UNIVERSITY OF CHICAGO
CHICAGO, ILLINOIS

Sydney L. Hans, Ph.D.
RESEARCH ASSOCIATE (ASSISTANT PROFESSOR)
DEPARTMENT OF PSYCHIATRY
UNIVERSITY OF CHICAGO
CHICAGO, ILLINOIS

As is clear from discussion in previous chapters, the concept of the borderline child as used in psychiatry has evolved out of a tradition of psychoanalytic thinking that emphasizes the ego functioning of these children. The principal author of this chapter himself once urged the study of such children with an emphasis on ego functioning (Marcus, 1963). At that time and today, most analytically oriented therapists dealing with borderline children have conceded that an underlying constitutional weakness or an "anlage" of some sort disturbs the proper ego development of these children. However, researchers interested in treating and studying the borderline child have focused almost exclusively on the behavioral study of ego functioning— specifically on the analysis of object relationships and narcissism—reflecting adult psychiatry's strong analytic interest in these conceptualizations. As a result, there is today a total absence of studies of neurological or neurophysiological functioning in children diagnosed as "borderline."

During the years that the concept of the borderline child has gained importance in psychiatry, many advances have been registered in the study of the neurological, neurophysiological, and neuropsychological functioning of other groups of children. For many groups, outward behavior seems to be very similar, if not identical, to that of children diagnosed "borderline" by psychoanalytically oriented clinicians. In fact, we suspect that many children identified by terms such as minimal brain dysfunction, learning disabilities, hyperactive child syndrome, offspring of schizophrenics, offspring of substance abusers, obsessional disorders, Gilles de la Tourette Syndrome, and various forms of childhood psychosis, might in fact be labeled "borderline" children if their ego functioning were assessed analytically.

In this chapter, we describe the research literature on neurological and neurophysiological functioning in children similar to borderline children, in hopes that such a review will both yield information relevant to the constitutional deficits possible in borderline children and stimulate research specifically addressing this issue. To achieve an integrated understanding of children whose disturbed behavior results from an interacting system of brain dysfunction and personality development, the work of analysts and neuroscientists must begin to converge. Ultimately, such research would lead to better

The authors are affiliated with the Department of Psychiatry, University of Chicago.

Many of the ideas presented in this paper developed out of work done under a grant from the National Institute on Drug Abuse (#PHS5R18 DA-01884-03). The authors gratefully acknowledge the editorial assistance of Amy Morris and Patricia Huetteman.

understanding of the borderline child and the etiology of the deviance, thus providing a stronger basis for the designation of proper and effective therapy.

A COMPARISON OF DESCRIPTIONS:
"EGO DISTURBANCES" IN BORDERLINE CHILDREN
AND "BEHAVIORAL DISTURBANCE" IN
RELATED SYNDROMES

Clinically, borderline children do not meet the criteria necessary for the diagnosis of childhood psychosis; nevertheless they manifest symptomatology that extends well beyond neurosis. Commonly described symptoms include extreme anxiety, obsessions, phobias, problems with impulse control, and low self-esteem. Chethik (1979), in his review of borderline psychopathology, acknowledged the contribution of hereditary and constitutional factors. As evidence of disturbed organic functioning, he cited reports of deviant physiological patterning in infancy, including phenomena such as hypertonic states and intense difficulty in inhibiting stimuli. Early psychoanalytic descriptions of children who would now probably be called "borderline" actually emphasized such organic features. Thus Weil (1956) observed a variety of physiological disturbances in "deviational, ego-disturbed, atypical" children that included hypertonic states, excessive crying, erratic patterns of eating and sleeping, apathy, sleeplessness, restlessness, hyperactivity, and aggressiveness." She noted neurological abnormalities such as prolonged athetosis, thrashing movements, and convulsion-like phenomena, and said that "such children look like primarily organic, sometimes even like defective organic, children for a long time." Attempting to better define the concept "borderline," Rosenfeld and Sprince (1963) recorded similar observations in a number of their cases, including a boy who "cried almost constantly during the night, until he was two years old, while he was unusually quiet during the day," and another boy of low-average intelligence with "the possibility of a minimal organic lesion which, however, was never medically diagnosed." Marcus (1963) described borderline children whose symptoms of ego dysfunction included mild disorientation, poor judgment, impulsivity and generally poor control of desires, and "awkward, excessive, non-directed, or incoordinate motor discharge"—all symptoms that could be closely tied to organic dysfunction.

Psychiatric diagnosis is not yet a finely tuned science: many diagnostic categories describe heterogeneous symptoms and diverse etiologies that overlap with descriptors for other diagnostic categories. The parallels between the borderline child and the psychotic child are most obvious, borderline pathology having usually been defined in terms of symptoms that are similar to but do not quite meet the stringent requirements necessary for diagnosis of psychosis.

Another group with symptomatology similar to borderline children is the offspring of schizophrenics. A sizeable proportion of these children have psychotic breakdowns later in life; others who never actually have psychotic breakdowns manifest a variety of disturbed behaviors during childhood. Clinically, there seem to be two types of pathological behaviors in offspring of schizophrenics: a withdrawn, schizoid type, and a hyperactive, asocial delinquent type (Rieder, 1973; Rieder & Nichols, 1979). The asocial children have been described by Mednick and Schulsinger (1968) as being "class disciplinary problems, domineering, aggressive, and creating conflicts, or disturbing the class with chatting." Bender (1937) extends this description to include hyperkinesis and learning difficulties. The contrasting withdrawn type was described by Kestenbaum (1981) as manifesting "extreme shyness and introversion, magical thinking not commensurate with age nor intelligence, anhedonia, phobias, attentional problems, and maladaptive defense mechanisms such as projection and denial." Similarly, Cowie (1961) reported "undue sensitivity, irritability, over-excitability, solitariness, timidity, excessive daydreaming and a tendency to retreat into a fantasy world." It is likely that many of these children from both groups would be given a borderline diagnosis by an analyst.

Another principal group is those chidren who have been classified "minimal brain dysfunction" or, more recently, "attention deficit disorder." Clements and Peters (1962) formulated the concept of minimal brain dysfunction (MBD) and described its central symptoms under the categories of specific learning deficits, perceptual-motor deficits, general coordination deficits, hyperkinesis, impulsivity, emotional lability, and short attention span and/or distractibility. The very name of this syndrome reflects the underlying assumption that neurophysiological or neurochemical dysfunctions are present. The organic nature of this syndrome is supported by data suggesting that: there is a strong familial component to MBD (Cantwell, 1975b), many MBD children have minor craniofacial anomalies (Rapoport, Quinn, & Lamprecht, 1974), and many MBD children respond well to drug therapy (see Wender, 1978). MBD symptoms manifest themselves differently across children and at different ages. In latency-age children the most salient symptoms seem usually to be those most likely to interfere with classroom performance—hyperactivity and learning disabilities. In adolescence, the list of most salient symptoms expands to include poor social skills, low self-esteem, depression, and delinquency (see Wender, 1979). The overlap between MBD and borderline symptomatology is great; and in fact, follow-up studies of MBD children indicate that a significant number in late adolescence and adulthood are diagnosed borderline (Milman, 1979). Hartocollis (1979) suggests that the common symptoms of MBD and borderline individuals include "labile affective dispositions . . . low self-esteem and a defective sense of identity, which create . . . a sense of emptiness, loneliness, or narcissistic hurt . . . ."

Similarity between the borderline child syndrome and these other syndromes can easily be found at the behavioral level. Proceeding with this assumption that the population of borderline children overlaps considerably with populations receiving other diagnoses, the remainder of this paper presents a selective review of neurological and neurophysiological functioning in children with these related syndromes. We describe four types of assessment used in diagnosing these children—clinical neurological examinations, attentional assessment, neuroradiological examinations, and electrophysiological examinations. Immediately following each description, we discuss test results in reference to pertinent childhood psychopathological syndromes.

CLINICAL NEUROLOGICAL EXAMINATIONS

The clinical neurological examination of children can and should include a classical neurological examination for focal lesions in the central nervous system. An excellent description of such an examination has been outlined by Kinsbourne (1979). However, the types of clinical neurological dysfunctions seen in children with MBD and related disorders are generally not due to focal lesions. Neurological examinations appropriate for such groups must also assess maturation of motor control, muscle tone, perceptual development, and patterned behaviors. Details of such examinations have been developed for infants and toddlers (see Marcus, 1979) and school-age children (e.g., Touwen & Prechtl, 1970; Rutter, Graham, & Yule, 1970). While the specific measures used in such examinations (e.g., clumsiness, motor overflow or associated movements, "primitive responses," right-left confusion, dysarthria) have misleadingly been described as "soft" or "equivocal" signs (Bender, 1956; Rutter et al., 1970; Shaffer, 1978), their consistency and validity have been demonstrated empirically (Werry et al., 1972; Shapiro et al., 1978) and problems with their use are related primarily to their interpretation (Touwen & Sporrel, 1979). Cox and Ludwig (1979) recently proposed a system for interpreting these signs according to probable types of cortical lobe dysfunction. "Soft" signs do clearly indicate minor neurological dysfunction or dysmaturation. With increased research, we may come to an improved understanding of the meaning of specific signs or sets of signs.

SCHIZOPHRENIA

Bender (1953) was the first to note that soft neurologic signs are pervasive in young, schizophrenic children. These signs are not specific to childhood schizophrenia and include delayed acquisition of motor skills, poor motor coordination, and poor integration of visual, auditory, and proprioceptive perceptions. Other studies have reported the existence of such signs in schizophrenic adolescents (Hertzig & Birch, 1966, 1968) and adults (Quitkin, Rifkin, & Klein, 1976; Cox & Ludwig, 1979; Bellak, 1979).

MINIMAL BRAIN DYSFUNCTION

Neurological "soft" signs are so frequently identified in MBD children that they are listed as an "associated feature" of the syndrome in the most recent *Diagnostic and Statistical Manual* (1980) of the American Psychiatric Association. In a study comparing hyperactive children with neurotic and normal children, Werry et. al. (1972) found in the hyperactive children an excess of "soft" signs reflecting sensorimotor incoordination. Other studies also found that children with hyperactive behavior disorders and learning problems had more signs than normal children (Cohen et al., 1967; Wolff & Hurwitz, 1973; Adams, Kocsis, & Estes, 1974). These signs included involuntary movements of a choreiform or athetoid type, motor overflow (mirror movements), dysdiadochokinesia and general clumsiness, as well as sensory abnormalities such as dysgraphesthesia.

OFFSPRING OF SCHIZOPHRENICS

Another area in which the clinical neurological examination has proved revealing is in the study of children "at risk" for schizophrenia (usually the offspring of schizophrenics). In this area of research, investigators have used neurological soft signs as tools in their search for behavioral markers of genetically determined vulnerability in the central nervous system that can be observed prior to the onset of clinical psychopatholoy.

In the first work of this type, Fish (Fish, 1957; Fish & Alpert, 1963) identified a subgroup of infants born to schizophrenic mothers who demonstrated irregular development with lags in physical growth, gross motor development, and visual motor coordination. As young adults, some of these children became schizophrenic and others showed disorders within the "schizophrenic spectrum" that might be considered "borderline" by some observers.

In a study started in 1965, Marcus and others (Marcus, 1974) found that approximately half of the school-age offspring of chronic schizophrenic parents (mothers and fathers) showed deficits on tasks of motor coordination, visual-motor coordination, and perception. They also had more associated movements ("motor overflow"), but as we see later, this may not be specific to their particular "anlage." Five of these offspring of schizophrenic parents have had psychotic breakdowns during late adolescence.

More recently, other investigators (Erlenmeyer-Kimling et al., in press; Orvaschel et al., 1979), examining school-age children in New York and Denmark, found similar difficulties in motor development. Pollin, Stabenau, Mosher, and Tupin (1966), in a retrospective study of adult monozygotic twins discordant for schizophrenia, found that the psychotic adults had had more neurologic problems in childhood than did their nonpsychotic twins. Rieder and Nichols (1979) reported similar findings (as well as hyperactivity) in seven-year-old offspring of "continuous schizophrenic" patients. Other studies of infant offspring of schizophrenics have found motor and sensorimotor deficits in the first year of life (Marcus et al., 1981; McNeil & Kaij, in press; Ragins et al., 1975).

Most studies of "soft signs" have used an "overall score" of optimal functioning. Such overall scores sum across all measures on a test, losing the information value of specific items. Marcus and Mednick (Marcus et al., in press), in an on-going analysis of their Israeli and Danish data, have used a multidimensional data analysis technique (see Shye, 1978) to arrive at a more exact definition of which types of dysfunction are specific to the schizophrenic offspring and which only add "noise" to the overall score. These analyses have shown that associated movements, for instance, seem to exist in the offspring of schizophrenics but are not specific to them. On the other hand, problems of coordination (both motor and sensorimotor) are more specific to the offspring of schizophrenics. We feel that such types of analyses may lead, in the future, to a clearer understanding of the various "soft signs," their specific meanings in terms of functions, and possibly to a better understanding of their underlying causes.

ATTENTIONAL ASSESSMENT

During the last decade, the construct of attention has been one of the major topics of investigation within the field of psychopathology. Volumes of theoretical and empirical papers have been published on attentional disturbances of schizophrenia. In DSM-III (American Psychiatric Association, 1980), the hyperactive child syndrome and minimal brain dysfunction have been renamed "attentional deficit disorders." Despite the wide usage of the term "attention," its conceptualization as a unitary scientific concept has proven impossible. Attention is actually a set of psychological constructs (Boring, 1970), two of which have been used in a substantial body of research in psychopathology.

The first type of attention, selective attention, is the filtering aspect of information processing. Selective attention is the process by which one isolates a small aspect of the environment on which to focus as protection against becoming overwhelmed by all of the competing stimuli in the environment. Experimentally, selective attention can be assessed by dozens of different laboratory tasks that require a person to isolate a stimulus from the environment. However, only two laboratory paradigms have been used in the study of childhood psychopathology to assess selective attention: reaction time tests and the orienting response. The orienting response is the involuntary, reflexive aspect of selection. When certain novel stimuli are contrasted with background stimuli, subjects respond behaviorally with brightening of the eyes, inhibition of gross body movements, and orientation of the head toward the stimulus; they respond physiologically with heart rate deceleration, a galvanic skin response, and EEG desynchronization.

The second commonly studied type of attention is sustained attention, or vigilance. Like selective attention, sustained attention assumes that some aspect of environment (either present or expected) has been selected on which to focus—but also that this focus is maintained through time. Laymen usually identify sustained attention as "attention span" (although experimental psychologists have reserved the word "span" to mean "span of apprehension," the number of perceptual events one can identify during a very brief exposure). Physiological responses during sustained attention, while less well studied than those in the orienting response, certainly include EEG desynchronization and suppression of heart rate variability. Of the many behavioral tasks used to assess sustained attention, there is one test that has dominated research in psychopathology—the Continuous Performance Test developed by Rosvold and colleagues (Rosvold et al., 1956). A subject must watch for a long period of time a series of stimuli flashing rapidly on the screen, and push a button whenever a particular stimulus appears. Attention is measured by the number of errors (both of omission and commission), the speed of response, and decrease in performance over time. Note also that selection of the appropriate stimulus is involved in this task as well as maintenance of focus across time.

AUTISIM

In clinical reports, autistic children are described as frequently avoiding focusing attention, then suddenly fixating for long periods. They often have unpredictable patterns of orientation, sometimes showing no response to strong environmental stimuli and then producing excessive responses to minor, irrelevant stimuli. A host of studies have reported that in learning tasks with redundant cues, autistic children are much more likely than normal children to attend selectively to only one component of a stimulus (Lovaas & Schreibman, 1971; Lovaas et al., 1971; Koegal & Lovaas, 1978). This extreme overselectivity of attention has been the focus of most empirical work with autistic children.

MINIMAL BRAIN DYSFUNCTION

Children with MBD have been described clinically as having a short attention span, being impulsive and distractable, failing to follow through on instructions and to complete work, and being disorganized and inattentive. Much experimental work has been done in the last several years on children diagnosed with either the hyperactive child syndrome or minimal brain dysfunction. Studies of the orienting response have generally found that hyperkinetic children can be differentiated from controls by their degree of physiological responsiveness. Skin conductance responses and cardiac responses are both of smaller magnitude in hyperactive children (Cohen & Douglas, 1972; Satterfield & Dawson, 1971; Spring et al., 1974; Zahn et al., 1975; Porges et al., 1975; Dykman et al., 1971). Reaction-time research has frequently found that hyperkinetic, minimal brain dysfunction and learning-disabled children have slower simple reactions times than do controls (Cohen & Douglas, 1972; Porges et al., 1975; Spring et al., 1973; Zahn et al., 1975). Some of these studies also suggest that hyperkinetic and learning-disabled children have more intraindividual variation in reaction times than controls (Cohen & Douglas, 1972; Sroufe et al., 1973) and that their reaction times become poorer across repeated trials (Cohen & Douglas, 1972; Spring et al., 1973), indicating that these children may not only be poorer at selectively attending to the reaction-time stimuli, they may also be poorer at sustaining attention to the task across time. Experiments on distractibility in hyperkinetic children has thus far yielded surprising results (Sykes et al., 1971; Dykman et al., 1970; Worland, North-Jones, & Stern, 1973; Browning, 1967). The presence of background noise during vigilance tasks either has no effect on performance or sometimes actually improves performance. Types of distractors used have ranged from obnoxious noises, to flashing lights, to attractive objects present in the room. These experimental findings are in such sharp contrast to reports by teachers and parents of the tremendous distractibility of hyperactive children that more empirical studies need to be conducted before any definitive statements can be made about the distractibility of hyperactive children.

OFFSPRING OF SCHIZOPHRENICS

In recent years, studies of the children of schizophrenics have begun to incorporate attentional measures into their test batteries, reflecting the excitement that has been generated by studies of attention in adult schizophrenics. Marcus (Marcus et al., in press), in the Jerusalem study of infants born to schizophrenic women, found a subgroup of offspring who at two weeks of age showed poor behavioral orienting responses. The most frequently used test of attention with older children has been the Continuous Performance Test. In four samples now, children at risk for schizophrenia have been given various forms of the Continuous Performance Test (Asarnow et al., 1977— the McMaster-Waterloo Project; Rutschmann, Cornblatt, & Erlenmeyer-Kimling, 1977—the New York High-Risk Project; Nuechterlein et al., in press; Nuechterlein, in press—the Minnesota High-Risk Project; Grunebaum et al., 1974; Herman et al., 1977—Boston study). In three of these studies, differences were reported between the offspring of schizophrenics and controls, with a trend especially toward more errors of omission. The two studies that used signal detection analyses reported that poorer performance in the schizophrenic offspring was due to poorer discriminability of the stimulus and not to response bias (New York, Minnesota). None of these studies reported a decline in performance across time in the Continuous Performance Test.

All three of the groups discussed demonstrate deficits in attention. The available data, however, do not allow one to conclude whether the same types of deficits are present in each of the groups. Few of the studies with the different groups used the same measues of attention, and only one study (Nuechterlein et al., in press) directly compared attentional functioning in two clinical groups. This study found slightly different patterns of responding on the Continuous Performance Test between hyperactive boys and the offspring of schizophrenics. It is highly likely, given the heterogeneity of these diagnostic categories, that members of these groups may have varying types of attentional deficits. None of the studies cited combined behavioral measures of attention with brain measures that might point to the physiological basis of the attentional problems. And finally, again, none of the studies were done with children actually diagnosed as "borderline." Thus it is difficult to state with certainty whether such children would demonstrate attentional deficits and if so, of what sort.

NEURORADIOLOGICAL EXAMINATIONS

One of the most important, indeed revolutionary developments in brain research in recent years has been the advent of brain imaging by the use of computed tomography, or CT-scanning (also called computerized axial tomography, CAT-scanning, or occasionally after the name of the earliest manufacturer, EMI-scanning). The principle behind CT-scanning is simple, even though the technology is impressively complex and correspondingly expensive. At several levels ("slices") in the brain, a large number of X-ray pictures are taken, each from a slightly different angle. A computer is then able to combine the information from all the pictures to give, for each slice, a high-resolution image of the brain, allowing one to distinguish gray and white matter, ventricles, cisterns, and some nuclei, such as basal ganglia. This process is analogous to taking photographs of a forest from several different perspectives, so that one can see what is behind all the trees. CT-scanning thus provides an enormously powerful, as well as quite safe and noninvasive way, to look at the structure of the living human brain.

Although the impact of CT-scanning on clinical neurology has been enormous, its effect on clinical psychiatry has been less striking. With a safe and noninvasive tool for identification of structural brain lesions, the diagnostician may be less likely to prescribe psychological treatment for a medical or surgical conditon, but this has never been a common difficulty. The real impact of CT-scanning in psychiatry is likely to be in research fields. Treatment of psychiatric patients may not be altered, but our knowledge of etiology and pathogenesis may be increased.

SCHIZOPHRENIA

Most psychiatric research using CT-scanning has so far focused on adult schizophrenic populations. Several findings have emerged. First, the brains of adult schizophrenics have shown ventricular enlargement (Weinberger et al., 1979a; Johnstone et al., 1978). Careful planimetric measurement of the ratio of ventricles to total brain size revealed an increase in ventricular size, presumably due to a subcortical atrophic process. It should be noted, however, that the pathological basis of this abnormality is not known and cannot be easily inferred from the nonspecific finding of ventricular enlargement. Further, the two research series involved chronic patients: whether ventricular enlargement could be observed at presentation of symptoms or whether the abnormality is present even before the onset of clinical symptoms is unknown.

Cortical atrophy (Weinberger et al.,1979b), and atrophy of the cerebellar vermis (Weinberger, Torrey, & Wyatt, 1979) also appeared in CT-scans of schizophrenics. Again, one must note that the histopathology here is unknown, although cerebellar atrophy has been noted in post-mortem investigations of schizophrenic patients (Weinberger et al., 1980). These two findings, while less well confirmed than that of ventricular enlargement, are of considerable interest in their implications for sites of neuropathology. Although abundant evidence exists that the cerebellum plays a role in psychomotor processes (Watson, 1978), cerebellar lesions are not generally thought of as contributing to psychopathology. There is a hint, however, (Weinberger, Torrey, & Wyatt, 1979) that the type of cerebellar lesions associated with schizophrenia may be associated with minor degrees of clumsiness. Poor motor coordination, as noted earlier, can be a "soft sign" of brain dysfunction or dysmaturation in a patient who lacks gross neurological disease. Because such dysmaturation has been related to various psychopathologies in childhood, its possible relationship to schizophrenia—and its anatomical basis in the brain—deserves further study.

All the above studies involved adults, and to our knowledge no studies of CT-scanning of schizophrenic children have been published. One remaining finding in adult schizophrenics does, however, have direct relevance to the development of psychopathology. Most normal right-handers have brains that are wider anteriorly on the right than on the left, and wider posteriorly on the left than on the right. Luchins, Weinberger, and Wyatt (1979) found a reversal of this pattern in certain schizophrenic adults, an anatomic abnormality presumptively developmental in origin and putatively related to deviant information processing.

MISCELLANEOUS CHILDHOOD PSYCHOPATHOLOGY

The finding of a reversal in hemispheric anatomy in adult schizophrenics replicates findings reported earlier by Hier and his colleagues involving chilren diagnosed with a variety of pathologies. For both autistic (Hier, LeMay, & Rosenberger, 1979) and dyslexic (Hier et al., 1978) children a reversal of cerebellar asymmetry has been identified in a larger proportion of patients than would be expected in a group of normal children. The abnormality does not seem to be specific to any one diagnostic category. In the only other study to investigate reversal of anatomical hemispheric differences,

Damasio, Maurer, Damasio, and Chui (1980) could not replicate the finding in a small group of autistic children. (Several of these children did have gross structural lesions identified by CT-scan.)

The findings to date demonstrate that, in schizophrenic adults as well as in children with other behavioral disorders, the CT-scan may uncover subtle structural brain abnormalities—even in so-called "functional disorders"—and may do so even with no other indication of "organic disease."

Other neurological imaging techniques are fast approaching clinical utility. The technique nearest to fruition is positron emission tomography, or PET-scanning (also called emission computerized axial tomography, or ECAT-scanning). This technique produces a radiograph from the inside out, so to speak. The patient is given a compound labeled with an atom that emits positrons; the positrons combine with nearby electrons to produce gamma rays which are then recorded by an apparatus very similar to the CT-scanner. The unique power of PET-scanning is that labeled compounds can be chosen which will proceed along specific metabolic pathways. Thus PET-scanning can reveal functional activity, not just anatomic structure. One can map glucose utilization, or regional blood flow, or the uptake of a particular drug. The technique is already in limited use at several centers. What it may ultimately reveal to us is unknown, but the possibilities are tantalizing.

ELECTROPHYSIOLOGICAL EXAMINATIONS

If CT-scanning offers a new way to look at brain structure, then electrophysiological techniques must be counted as our most powerful way to examine brain function. A complete review of the technology and findings within psychophysiology is beyond our scope here, and the interested reader is referred to several excellent and recent reviews of the topic (Vaughan, 1978; Spohn & Patterson, 1979; James & Barry, 1980).

The oldest and most widely used method of electrophysiologic assessment is electroencephalography (EEG). This is, of course, a method of recording the rhythmic and paroxysmal electrical activity of the brain through a matrix of electrodes placed on the scalp. Because it is simple, painless and noninvasive, electroencephalography has been widely applied to many populations of psychiatric patients, with confusing and often contradictory results. In our opinion, the confusion results from two sources.

First, electrodes on the scalp may be several centimeters away from the actual site of action in the brain. The cortex is separated from the electrodes by a thick layer of meninges, skull, and skin; and subcortical structures are even further removed. In the 1950s, Heath and his colleagues (Hodes, Heath,

& Miller, 1954) were able (and permitted) to implant electrodes in deep brain structures of schizophrenics. Their findings were intriguing but, because of the obvious clinical limitations of such an invasive technique, they have not been replicated.

The second cause of confusion in scalp EEG recording is more remediable. Because an EEG recording is a very complex set of waveforms containing a great deal of data, interpreting all the data in an EEG tracing by inspection alone is impossible. For this reason, the application of computer techniques, such as power-spectrum or coherence analysis, has increased the value of electroencephalography as a research tool.

A second technique improving EEG validity is that of event-related potentials (ERPs) or evoked potentials (EPs). EEG responses to repeated presentation of a stimulus are recorded. The responses are then averaged across presentations to obtain a pure wave form of the evoked response. This technique, which also requires computer methods, has the advantage that the stimulus can be tailored to probe a particular brain area or function of interest. ERPs and EEGs have often been combined in recent electrical studies of psychiatric disorders.

Again, we find no studies of borderline children using electrophysiological techniques. Rather, there are studies of groups of children bearing some connection to borderline children, We shall summarize some of the results, focusing on the way such techniques might be used to investigate a diagnostic group lacking obvious brain disorder.

SCHIZOPHRENICS AND OFFSPRING OF SCHIZOPHRENICS

A number of studies of EEGs in both adults and children with psychoses, especially schizophrenia, have been conducted. However, the research results are far from clear; Shagass's (1976) summary indicates that in adult schizophrenics, "the one finding that seems consistent across studies is that central frequency tends to be lower in chronic schizophrenics"; further, these patients tend to have a low-variability, "hyperstable" EEG. Reports of EEG abnormalities in psychotic children complicated by varying diagnostic criteria and varying criteria for abnormality of the EEG are even less conclusive. A number of investigators, however, have found abnormalities in the EEGs of those psychotic children with autism and those with childhood schizophrenia (e.g., James & Barry, 1980).

In a recent investigation using analysis by inspection alone, Waldo, Cohen, Caparulo, Young, Prichard, and Shaywitz (1978) found a number of

EEG abnormalities in children with severe psychiatric disorders; about 25 percent of their schizophrenic group and just over a third of their autistic group showed abnormalities. Through discriminant analysis of specific EEG features, they found it possible to differentiate diagnostic subgroups, such as the autistic and schizophrenic children, with high accuracy. Interestingly, however, EEGs did not clearly discriminate patients with and without "organic" features. Thus the EEGs of primary autistic children looked like those of secondary autistic children (so defined by the presence of "neurologic or organic substrate or association"). This work raises hopes that the EEG can reveal an abnormality in cerebral functioning, the presence of which may not be suspected on clinical grounds.

Itil and his colleagues have published a series of studies, in which several groups were investigated according to the various computerized EEG techniques. For example, in a study of psychotic children which did not distinguish between autism and schizophrenia (Itil, Simeon, & Coffin, 1976), they found more slow as well as more very fast activity in the EEG. Their findings for both schizophrenic children and adults were strikingly similar. They suggest that this pattern may indicate a state of hyperarousal. Shagass, Ornitz, Sutton, Tueting (1978) point out in turn that this finding may possibly be a manifestation of bursts of increased muscle tension. Whether the Itil results indicate abnormal central neurophysiological functioning or peripheral secondary effects of psychosis is still an open question.

Evidence that bears on the issue of interpretation of schizophrenic EEG patterns—and which also may contribute to our understanding of the borderline child—can be found in studies of offspring of schizophrenics. Itil, Hsu, Saletu, and Mednick (1974), studying a sample of Danish children with schizophrenic mothers, found EEG patterns similar to those of adult schizophrenics and psychotic children and significantly different from those of normal controls. If children at high risk for schizophrenia, but lacking the clinical state, show abnormal electrophysiology, then the finding would more likely be attributable to some fundamental neurophysiological process. Follow-up studies are not yet available, but on genetic grounds one would expect "borderline schizophrenia" to appear in some of these children. In a different sample, Herman, Mirsky, Ricks, and Gallant (1977) found no significant EEG abnormalities in children at risk for schizophrenia.

Unfortunately, ERP studies have not been of major help in clarifying the neurophysiology of childhood psychosis. Shagass et al. (1978) summarized ERP studies of autistic children by saying that they have revealed "inconclusive or minimal results." They felt that the report of Lelord, Laffont, Jusseaume, and Steffant (1973) of abnormally large potentials produced by stimulus coupling was an exception. These waves resemble those normally produced by movement, and they may be in some way associated with the abnormal motility observed in autistic children.

Itil and his colleagues (Simeon & Itil, 1975) also studied ERPs in their psychotic children. They did find shorter latencies and smaller amplitudes; however, their results are reported without discriminating autistic from schizophrenic subjects. In a separate study (Saletu et al., 1974) neuroleptic drugs reversed ERP abnormalities concurrently with clinical improvement. These associations between brain electrical activity and behavior, however, do not prove the existence of a fundamental neurophysiological abnormality.

A few studies have examined evoked potentials in the offspring of schizophrenics. Itil et al.(1974) found shorter ERP latencies in high-risk children than in controls. But Friedman, Vaughan, and Erlenmeyer-Kimling (1979) and Herman, Mirsky, Ricks, and Gallant (1977) found longer latencies in separate samples. Similarly, while Itil's group found no abnormalities in amplitude, Herman et al. (1977) found larger amplitudes at 100–200 msec, and Friedman, Vaughan, and Erlenmeyer-Kimling (1980) found smaller amplitudes at 340–400 msec. With so many inconsistencies, any conclusions as to which patterns of ERP characterize the offspring of schizophrenics—or subgroups of these offspring—are premature. Likewise, it is too early to speculate as to what specific cognitive processes may be associated with specific abnormalities in brain physiology.

MINIMAL BRAIN DYSFUNCTION

Children with minimal brain dysfunction have also been studied extensively using electrophysiologic methods. Unfortunately, results are again inconclusive. As is generally recognized, children grouped together under the category MBD are a heterogeneous lot. One would expect, however, that different subgroups might show different abnormalities. Duffy, Denckla, Bartels, and Sandini (1980) therefore used highly specific defining criteria for MBD in their study, together with an especially sensitive electrophysiological measurement technique. Through computer EEG mapping, the authors were able to identify differences between "dyslexia-pure" children and age-matched controls in the functioning of four cortex areas involved in language processing. Studies of evoked potential considering a broader range of MBD children show findings considerably less clear-cut. Results conflict as to the effect of age, the prediction of drug response, and even the nature of the abnormalities found. This area is well reviewed by Shagass et al. (1978).

In addition to these electroencephalographic studies, electrical measures of autonomic nervous system response, especially electrodermal and cardiac response, have been employed with some of these clinical groups. Most work concentrates on MBD children, and the pattern of results is mixed. There is some evidence, however, that hyperactive children have lower tonic skin conductance (Satterfield & Dawson, 1971) and lower heart rate levels (Conners, 1975; Porges et al., 1975), as well as smaller electrodermal responses to stimuli (Cohen & Douglas, 1972; Satterfield & Dawson, 1971; Spring et al., 1974; Zahn et al., 1975) and smaller cardiac responses (Sroufe et al., 1973; Porges et al., 1975; Zahn et al., 1975). Experimental reports of psychotic children have also shown them to have lower electrodermal responses (Bernal & Miller, 1970). Studies of the electrodermal responses in the offspring of schizophrenics have yielded conflicting results (Mednick & Schulsinger, 1968; Erlenmeyer-Kimling et al., in press).

SUMMARY AND DISCUSSION

Extensive progress has been made in recent years in the development of neurobehavioral and neurophysiological assessments of children. Equally impressive advances have been made in related fields (which we have not even attempted to review), such as neuropsychological testing. These advances have caused neurological techniques to be widely applied in research studies on many types of childhood psychopathology, including some types closely related to the borderline child syndrome. In this chapter, we described some of the neurological findings for childhood psychosis, childhood minimal brain dysfunction, and children of schizophrenics. Given the similarity of the borderline child to these categories, and the availability of a wide range of assessment techniques in neurology and related disciplines, the time is certainly ripe for direct study of neurological functioning in borderline children in order that the nature of organic deficits can be precisely clarified.

The state of our knowledge concerning neurological functioning in the borderline child reflects the basic problems now facing psychiatry. The terms we use to describe human psychopathlogy were generated by scientists with diverse and divergent theoretical perspectives. The borderline syndrome is but one example of a syndrome whose relationship to a variety of similar categories has not yet been clarified. The diagnostic categories themselves are often insufficiently defined: within almost any given diagnostic category, a heterogeneous collection of individuals can be found. Children diagnosed as borderline offer vastly different behavioral profiles and almost certainly different biochemical and neurological characteristics as well.

The way the problem of heterogeneous populations and the overlapping nature of diagnostic categories is handled influences our understanding of basic pathology and, ultimately, the treatment of that pathology. Descriptions of clinical case studies play an important part in the early exploration of a syndrome: such a case study approach has already been well utilized with the borderline child. Unfortunately, researchers too often believe the only other alternative is to study large populations using a very limited range of measures. Research focusing exclusively on one diagnostic category does nothing either to integrate our understanding of psychopathology or to bring together knowledge from different disciplines. Work that compares only average behaviors of different groups of people (as do most of the studies reviewed in this paper) both denies the heterogeneity of people assigned to diagnostic categories and makes identification of subgroups within diagnostic categories impossible. As a result, the view taken of the patient is a very narrow one.

A broader understanding of the borderline child requires both a synthesis of psychological thinking with biological concepts and clarification of the relationship between borderline and similar syndromes. We propose that research on borderline children take this step toward multidisciplinary, in-depth assessment of borderline and related problems. Such work should

Table 7-1
MAPPING SENTENCE FOR A COMPREHENSIVE STUDY OF THE BORDERLINE CHILD.

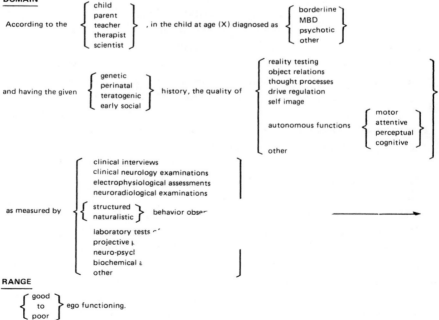

involve collaboration among practitioners from different fields, with each field attempting to add to a comprehensive description of the children under examination. The following paragraphs offer some specific proposals for conducting this type of research.

Such complex research requires careful conceptualization in advance. One process we have found useful in structuring this type of research is facet design. Facet design is a process that requires a scientist to conceptualize *a priori* the domain of observations relevant to a particular study. The heuristic tool used in facet design is a mapping sentence. Table 7-1 shows a mapping sentence of how a very comprehensive multidisciplinary study of borderline child could be designed and conducted. A mapping sentence describes a range of common interest for all measures in a study, in this case, the ego functioning of the child. All measures used in such a study should be indicators of ego functioning. The domain of a mapping sentence defines in terms of facets the stimuli, conditions, and procedures inherent in the measures used in a particular study. (For more on facet theory, see Shye, 1978.) Our particular sentence for the study of the borderline child has six facets: (1) the person providing information about the child, (2) the age of the child being assessed, (3) the diagnosis of the child, (4) the history of the child, (5) the type of ego function being assessed, and (6) the type of instrument used for making assessments.

In reality, no study could be so comprehensive as to have measures covering every element of each facet; that would involve an enormous research staff with unlimited time and equipment. A multidisciplinary study would, however, sample widely from elements within each facet. It would not rely on reports from only one source or about only one type of ego function or about early social interactions to the exclusion of medical events surrounding the birth period, nor would it rely on electrophysiological measures to the exclusion of material available from interviews. We offer this mapping sentence as a source of the types of measures to be considered when planning assessments of the borderline child.

Studies with many measures, and by necessity limited numbers of subjects, obviously need to employ very special data analysis methods. Data analysis should be appropriate to the goals of the study and the limitations of the data. The goals of the type of research we have described are to construct clinical profiles from many measures in order to identify those measures that fit together in patterns and thereby identify subgroups of children with different patterns. The limitations of the data include categorical level of measurement and a disproportion of measures to subjects. For this purpose, we recommend nonmetric multidimensional techniques (see Shye, 1978; Marcus et al., 1981) or techniques such as cluster analysis.

A second type of research paradigm that would help us to understand the borderline child is the longitudinal study of children at risk. In psychiatric illness where organic and early social factors are suspected causes of illness, it is very useful to understand behaviors from earliest infancy. Given the notorious inaccuracy of mothers' retrospective accounts of their children's behavior, observations made as the child develops are invaluable data. The at-risk study paradigm involves selection of those children who for genetic or other reasons are believed to be at increased risk for displaying pathology in later life. Studies of offspring of schizophrenics were earliest in the at-risk research field and may, in fact, also be yielding valuable information about the early behavior of children who later develop borderline symptomatology. We feel that another group who may be at risk for later borderline symptomatology are the offspring of substance abusers. For example, some reports in the literature indicate increased incidence of childhood hyperactivity and attentional disorders in the offspring of drug addicts (Nichtern, 1973; Wilson, Desmond, & Verniaud, 1973; Blinick et al., 1975). We are presently engaged in just such a longitudinal at-risk study of the offspring of substance abusers (Marcus, Jeremy, & Hans, 1981). In the future, other populations at risk for borderline symptomatology can be identified and studied: perhaps offspring of parents with MBD, children with minor physical anomalies, children with certain birth complications, or—after our knowledge expands—children with certain biochemical markers. Again, longitudinal studies could sample broadly from the kinds of measures outlined in the mapping sentence.

The information gained from comprehensive studies will have important implications for therapy. Therapy is always best based on a thorough assessment and diagnosis. We suspect from the literature we reviewed on children with related syndromes that borderline children may have a variety of types of neurological deficits, each of which would indicate a specific type of therapy. As in the approach sometimes used to treat MBD children (Cantwell, 1975a), therapy could be based on a combination of special education techniques for specific deficits (such as reading difficulties or motor incoordination), drug therapy for other deficits (such as impulsivity or distractibility) and psychotherapy for secondary psychological problems. A complete understanding of all the deficient functions in a particular borderline child would lead to a complete therapeutic program capable of providing maximum benefit to the child.

R E F E R E N C E S

Adams, R.M., Kocsis, J.J., & Estes, R.E. Soft neurological signs in learning-disabled children and controls. *American Journal of Diseases of Children*, 1974, *128*, 614–618.

The American Psychiatric Association. *Diagnostic and statistical manual of mental disorders* (3d ed.). Washington, D.C.: 1980.

Asarnow, R.F., Steffy, R.A., MacCrimmon, D.J., & Cleghorn, J.M. An attentional assessment of foster children at risk for schizophrenia. *Journal of Abnormal Psychology,* 1977, *86,* 267–275.

Bellak, L. Schizophrenic syndrome related to minimal brain dysfunction: A possible neurological subgroup. *Schizophrenia Bulletin,* 1979, *5,* 480–489.

Bender, L. Behavior problems in the children of psychotic and criminal parents. *Genetic Psychology Monographs,* 1937, *19,* 229–339.

Bender, L. Childhood schizophrenia. *Psychiatric Quarterly,* 1953, *27,* 663–681.

Bender, L. *Psychopathology of children with organic brain disorders.* Springfield, Ill.: Charles C. Thomas, 1956.

Bernal M.E., & Miller, W.H. Electrodermal and cardiac responses of schizophrenic children to sensory stimuli. *Psychophysiology,* 1970, *7,* 155–168.

Blinick, G., Inturrisi, C.E., Jerez, E., & Wallach, R.C. Methadone assays in pregnant women and progeny. *American Journal of Obstetrics and Gynecology,* 1975, *121,* 617–621.

Boring, E.G. A short historical perspective. In D.I. Mostofsky (Ed.), *Attention: Contemporary theory and analysis.* New York: Appleton-Century-Crofts, 1970.

Browning, R.M. Effect of irrelevant peripheral visual stimuli on discrimination learning in minimally brain-damaged children. *Journal of Consulting Psychology,* 1967, *31,* 371–376.

Cantwell, D.P. A critical review of therapeutic modalities with hyperactive children. In D.P. Cantwell (Ed.), *The hyperactive child: Diagnosis, management, and current research.* New York: Spectrum, 1975(a).

Cantwell, D.P. Genetic studies of hyperactive children. In R.R. Fieve, D. Rosenthal, & H. Brill (Eds.), *Genetic research in psychiatry.* Baltimore: John Hopkins University Press, 1975(b).

Chethik, M. The borderline child. In J.D. Noshpitz (Ed.), *The basic handbook of child psychiatry* (Vol. 2). New York: Basic Books, 1979.

Clements, S.D., & Peters, J.E. Minimal Brain Dysfunctions in the school-age child. *Archives of General Psychiatry,* 1962, *6,* 185–197.

Cohen, H.J., & Douglas, V.I. Characteristics of the orienting response in hyperactive and normal children. *Psychophysiology,* 1972, *9,* 238–245.

Cohen, H.J., Taft, L.T., Mahadeviah, M.S., & Birch, H.G. Developmental changes in overflow in normal and aberrantly functioning children. *The Journal of Pediatrics,* 1967, *71,* 39–47.

Conners, C.K. Minimal brain dysfunction and psychopathology in children. In A. Davids (Ed.), *Child personality and psychopathology: Current topics* (Vol. 2). New York: Wiley, 1975.

Cowie, V. The incidence of neurosis in the children of psychotics. *Acta Psychiatrica Scandinavica,* 1961, *37,* 37–87.

Cox, S.M., & Ludwig, A.M. Neurological soft signs and psychopathology. *The Journal of Nervous and Mental Disorders,* 1979, *167,* 161–165.

Damasio, H., Maurer, R.G., Damasio, A.R., & Chui, H.C. Computerized tomographic scan findings in patients with autistic behavior. *Archives of Neurology,* 1980, *37,* 504–510.

Duffy, F.H., Denckla, M.B., Bartels, P.H., & Sandini, G. Dyslexia: Regional differences in brain electrical activity by topographic mapping. *Annals of Neurology,* 1980, *7,* 412–420.

Dykman, R.A., Ackerman, P.T., Clements, S.D., & Peters, J.E. Specific learning disabilities: An attentional deficit syndrome. In H.R. Myklebust (Ed.), *Progress in learning disabilities* (Vol. 2). New York: Grune & Stratton, 1971.

Dykman, R.A., Walls, R.C., Suzuki, T., Ackerman, P.T., & Peters, J.E. Children with learning disabilities: Conditioning, differentiation, and the effect of distraction. *American Journal of Orthopsychiatry,* 1970, *40,* 766–782.

Erlenmeyer-Kimling, L., Cornblatt, B., Friedman, D., Marcuse, Y., Rutschmann, J., & Simmens, S. Neurological, electrophysiological and attentional deviations in children at risk for schizophrenia. In H.A. Nasrallah & F. Henn (Eds.), *Schizophrenia as a brain disease.* New York: Oxford University Press, in press.

Erlenmeyer-Kimling, L., Marcuse, Y.B., Cornblatt, B., Friedman, D., Rainer, J.D., & Rutsch-mann, J. The New York high-risk project. In N. Watt, E.J. Anthony, L. Wynne, J. Rolf (Eds.), *Children at risk for schizophrenia: a longitudinal perspective.* New York, Cambridge University Press. In press.

Fish, B. The detection of schizophrenia in infants. *The Journal of Nervous and Mental Disease,* 1957, *125,* 1–24.

Fish, B., & Alpert, M. Patterns of neurological development in infants born to schizophrenic mothers. In J. Wortis (Ed.), *Recent advances in biological psychiatry* (Vol. 5). New York: Plenum, 1963.

Friedman, D., Vaughan, H.G., Jr., & Erlenmeyer-Kimling, L. Event-related potential investiga-tions in children at high risk for schizophrenia. In D. Lehmann & E. Callaway (Eds.), *Human evoked potentials: Applications and problems.* New York: Plenum, 1979.

Friedman, D., Vaughan, H.G., Jr., & Erlenmeyer-Kimling, L. The late positive complex to unpredictable auditory events in children at high risk for schizophrenia. *Psychophysiology,* 1980, *17,* 310–311.

Grunebaum, H., Weiss, J.L., Gallant, D., & Cohler, B.J. Attention in young children of psychotic mothers. *American Journal of Psychiatry,* 1974, *131,* 887–891.

Hartocollis, P. Minimal brain dysfunction in young adults. In L. Bellak (Ed.), *Psychiatric aspects of minimal brain dysfunction in adults.* New York: Grune & Stratton, 1979.

Herman, J., Mirsky, A.F., Ricks, N.L., & Gallant, D. Behavioral and electrographic measures of attention in children at risk for schizophrenia. *Journal of Abnormal Psychology,* 1977, *86,* 27–33.

Hermelin, B., & O'Connor, N. Measures of the occipital alpha rhythm in normal, subnormal, and autistic children. *British Journal of Psychiatry,* 1968, *114,* 603–610.

Hertzig, M.E., & Birch, H.G. Neurologic organization in psychiatrically disturbed adolescent girls. *Archives of General Psychiatry,* 1966, *15,* 590–598.

Hertzig, M.E. & Birch, H.G. Neurologic organization in psychiatrically disturbed adolescents: A comparative consideration of sex differences. *Archives of General Psychiatry,* 1968, *19,* 528–537.

Hier, D.B., LeMay, M., & Rosenberger, P.B. Autism and unfavorable left-right asymmetries of the brain. *Journal of Autism and Developmental Disorders,* 1979, *9,* 153–159.

Hier, D.B., LeMay, M., Rosenberger, P.B., & Perlo, V.P. Developmental dyslexia: Evidence for a subgroup with a reversal of cerebral asymmetry. *Archives of Neurology,* 1978, *35,* 90–92.

Hodes, R., Heath, R.G., & Miller, W.H. Electroencephalograms and subcorticograms made before stimulation. In Tulane Department of Psychiatry (Eds.), *Studies in schizophrenia,* Cambridge, Mass.: Harvard University Press, 1954.

Itil, T.M., Hsu, W., Saletu, B., & Mednick, S. Computer EEG and auditory evoked potential investigations in children at high risk for schizophrenia. *American Journal of Psychiatry,* 1974, *131,* 892–900.

Itil, T.M., Simeon, J., & Coffin, C. Qualitative and quantitative EEG in psychotic children. *Diseases of the Nervous System,* 1976, *37,* 247–252.

James, A.L., & Barry, R.J. A review of psychophysiology in early onset psychosis. *Schizo-phrenia Bulletin,* 1980, *6,* 506–525.

Johnstone, E.C., Crow, T.J., Frith, C.D., Stevens, M., Kreel, L., & Husband, J. The dementia of dementia praecox. *Acta Psychiatrica Scandinavica,* 1978, *57,* 305–324.

Kestenbaum, C. The child at-risk for major psychiatric illness. In S. Arieti & H.K.H. Brodie (Eds.), *The American handbook of psychiatry* (2d ed., Vol. 7). New York: Basic Books, 1981.

Kinsbourne, M. Principles of the neurological examination. In J.D. Noshpitz (Ed.), *The basic handbook of child psychiatry* (Vol. 1). New York: Basic Books, 1979.

Koegel, R.L., & Lovaas, O.I. Comments on autism and stimulus over-selectivity. *Journal of Abnormal Psychology,* 1978, *87,* 563–565.

Lelord, G., Laffont, F., Jusseaume, P., & Steffant, J.L. Comparative study of conditioning of average evoked responses by coupling sound and light in normal and autistic children. *Psychophysiology*, 1973, *10*, 415–425.

Lovaas, O.I., & Schreibman, L. Stimulus over-selectivity of autistic children in a two-stimulus situation. *Behavior Research and Therapy*, 1971, *9*, 305–310.

Lovaas, O.I., Schreibman, L., Koegel, R., & Rehm, R. Selective responding by autistic children to multiple sensory input. *Journal of Abnormal Psychology*, 1971, *77*, 211–222.

Luchins, D.J., Weinberger, D.R., & Wyatt, R.J. Schizophrenia: Evidence of a subgroup with reversed cerebral asymmetry. *Archives of General Psychiatry*, 1979, *36*, 1309–1311.

McNeil, T.F., & Kaij, L. Offspring of women with nonorganic psychoses. In N. Watt, E.J. Anthony, L. Wynn, and J. Rolf (Eds.), *Children at risk for schizophrenia: A longitudinal perspective*. New York: Cambridge University Press, in press.

Marcus, J. Borderline states in childhood. *Journal of Child Psychology and Psychiatry*, 1963, *4*, 207–218.

Marcus, J. Neurological findings in children of schizophrenic parents. In A. Koupernick (Ed.), *The child in his family—children at psychiatric risk*. New York: Wiley, 1974.

Marcus, J. Examination of the infant and toddler. in J.D. Noshpitz (Ed.), *The basic handbook of child psychiatry* (Vol. 1). New York: Basic Books, 1979.

Marcus, J., Auerbach, J., Wilkinson, L., & Burack, C.M. Infants at risk for schizophrenia: The Jerusalem infant development study. *Archives of General Psychiatry*, 1981, *38*, 703–713.

Marcus, J., Jeremy, R.J., & Hans, S.L. Developmental patterns of state and motor functioning in neonates born to methadone users. Unpublished paper, 1981.

Mednick, S.A., & Schulsinger, F. Some premorbid characteristics related to breakdown in children with schizophrenic mothers. In D. Rosenthal & S.S. Kety (Eds.), *The transmission of schizophrenia*. London: Pergamon, 1968.

Milman, D.H. Minimal brain dysfunction in childhood: Outcome in late adolescence and early adult years. *Journal of Clinical Psychiatry*, 1979, *12*, 371–380.

Nichtern, S. The children of drug users. *Journal of the American Academy of Child Psychiatry*, 1973, *12*, 24–31.

Nuechterlein, K.H. Sustained attention among children vulnerable to adult schizophrenia and among hyperactive children. In N.F. Watt, L.C. Wynn, E.J. Anthony, L. Erlenmeyer-Kimling, & J.E. Rolf (Eds.), *Children at risk for schizophrenia: A longitudinal perspective*. New York: Cambridge University Press, in press.

Nuechterlein, K.H., Phipps-Yonas, S., Driscoll, R.M., & Garmezy, N. The role of different components of attention in children vulnerable to schizophrenia. In M.J. Goldstein (Ed.), *Preventive intervention in schizophrenia: Are we ready?* Government Printing Office, Wash. D.C. In press.

Orvaschel, H., Mednick, S., Schulsinger, F., & Rock D. The children of psychiatrically disturbed parents: Differences as a function of the sex of the sick parent. *Archives of General Psychiatry*, 1979, *36*, 691–695.

Pollin, W., Stabenau, J.R., Mosher, L., & Tupin, J. Life history differences in identical twins discordant for schizophrenia. *American Journal of Orthopsychiatry*, 1966, *36*, 492–509.

Porges, S.W., Walter, G.F., Korb, R.J., & Sprague, R.L. The influences of methylphenidate on heart rate and behavioral measures of attention in hyperactive children. *Child Development*, 1975, *46*, 727–733.

Quitkin, F., Rifkin, A., & Klein, D.F. Neurologic soft signs in schizophrenia and character disorders. *Archives of General Psychiatry*, 1976, *33*, 845–853.

Ragins, N., Schachter, J., Elmer, E., Preisman, R., Bowes, A.E., & Harway, V. Infants and children at risk for schizophrenia. *Journal of the American Academy of Child Psychiatry*, 1975, *14*, 150–177.

Rapoport, J.L., Quinn, P.O., & Lamprecht, F. Minor physical anomalies and plasma dopamine-beta-hydroxylase activity in hyperactive boys. *American Journal of Psychiatry*, 1974, *131*, 386–390.

Rieder, R.O. The offspring of schizophrenic parents: A review. *The Journal of Nervous and*

Mental Disease, 1973, *157,* 179–190.

Rieder, R.O., & Nichols, P.L. Offspring of schizophrenics III: Hyperactivity and neurological soft signs. *Archives of General Psychiatry,* 1979, *36,* 665–674.

Rosenfeld, S.K., & Sprince, M.P. An attempt to formulate the meaning of the concept "borderline." *Psychoanalytic Study of the Child,* 1963, *18,* 603–635.

Rosvold, H.E., Mirsky, A.F., Sarason, I., Bransome, E.D., Jr., & Beck, L.H. A continuous performance test of brain damage. *Journal of Consulting Psychology,* 1956, *20,* 343–350.

Rugel, R.P., & Rosenthal, R. Skin conductance, reaction time, and observational ratings in learning-disabled children. *Journal of Abnormal Child Psychology,* 1974, *2,* 183–192.

Rutschmann, J., Cornblatt, B., & Erlenmeyer-Kimling, L. Sustained attention in children at risk for schizophrenia: Report on a continuous performance test. *Archives of General Psychiatry,* 1977, *34,* 571–575.

Rutter, M., Graham, P., & Yule, W. *A neuropsychiatric study in childhood.* Philadelphia: Lippincott, 1970.

Saletu, B., Simeon, J., Saletu, M., Itil, T.M., & DaSilva, J. Behavioral and visual evoked potential investigations during trihexyphenidyl and thiothixene treatment in psychotic boys. *Biological Psychiatry,* 1974, *8,* 177–189.

Satterfield, J.H., & Dawson, M.E. Electrodermal correlates of hyperactivity in children. *Psychophysiology,* 1971, *8,* 191–197.

Shaffer, D. "Soft" neurological signs and later psychiatric disorder: A review. *Journal of Child Psychology and Psychiatry,* 1978, *19,* 63–65.

Shagass, C. An electrophysiological view of schizophrenia. *Biological Psychiatry,* 1976, *11,* 3–30.

Shagass, C., Ornitz, E.M., Sutton, S., & Tueting, P. Event related potentials and psychopathology. In E. Callaway, P. Tueting, & S.H. Koslow (Eds.), *Event-related brain potentials in man.* New York: Academic Press, 1978.

Shapiro, T., Burkes, L., Petti, T.A., & Ranz, J. Consistency of "nonfocal" neurological signs. *Journal of The Academy of Child Psychiatry,* 1978, *17,* 70–79.

Shye, S. *Theory construction and data analysis in the behavioral sciences.* San Francisco: Jossey-Bass, 1978.

Simeon, J., & Itil, T.M. Computerized electroencephalogram: A model of understanding the brain function in childhood psychosis and its treatment. *Journal of Autism and Childhood Schizophrenia,* 1975, *5,* 247–265.

Spohn, H.E., & Patterson, T. Recent studies of psychophysiology in schizophrenia. *Schizophrenia Bulletin,* 1979, *5,* 581–611.

Spring, C., Greenberg, L., Scott, J., & Hopwood, J. Reaction time and effect of Ritalin on children with learning problems. *Perceptual and Motor Skills,* 1973, *36,* 75–82.

Spring, C., Greenberg, L., Scott, J., & Hopwood, J. Electrodermal activity in hyperactive boys who are methylphenidate responders. *Psychophysiology,* 1974, *11,* 436–442.

Sroufe, L.A., Sonies, B.C., West, W.D., & Wright, F.S. Anticipatory heart rate deceleration and reaction time in children with and without referral for learning disability. *Child Development,* 1973, *44,* 267–273.

Sykes, D.H., Douglas, V.I., Weiss, G., & Minde, K.K. Attention in hyperactive children and the effect of methylphenidate (Ritalin). *Journal of Child Psychology and Psychiatry,* 1971, *12,* 129–139.

Touwen, B.C.L., & Prechtl, H.F.R. *The neurological examination of the child with minor nervous dysfunction.* Philadelphia: Lippincott, 1970.

Touwen, B.C.L., & Sporrel, T. Soft signs and MBD. *Developmental Medicine and Child Neurology,* 1979, *21,* 528–530.

Vaughan, H.G., Jr. Toward a neurophysiology of schizophrenia. *Journal of Psychiatric Research,* 1978, *14,* 129–154.

Waldo, M.C., Cohen, D.J., Caparulo, B.K., Young, J.G., Prichard, J.W., & Shaywitz, B.A. EEG profiles of neuropsychiatrically disturbed children. *Journal of the American Academy of Child Psychiatry,* 1978, *17,* 656–670.

Watson, P.J. Nonmotor functions of the cerebellum. *Psychological Bulletin,* 1978, *85,* (5), 944–967.

Weil, A.P. Some evidences of deviational development in infancy and early childhood. *Psychoanalytic Study of the Child,* 1956, *11,* 292–299.

Weinberger, D.R., Kleinman, J.E., Luchins, D.J., Bigelow, L.B., & Wyatt, R.J. Cerebellar pathology in schizophrenia: A controlled post-mortem study. *American Journal of Psychiatry,* 1980, *137,* 359–361.

Weinberger, D.R., Torrey, E.F., Neophytides, A.N., & Wyatt, R.J. Lateral cerebral ventricular enlargement in chronic schizophrenia. *Archives of General Psychiatry,* 1979a, *36,* 735–739.

Weinberger, D.R., Torrey, E.F., Neophytides, A.N., & Wyatt, R.J. Structural abnormalities in the cerebral cortex of chronic schizophrenic patients. *Archives of General Psychiatry,* 1979b, *36,* 935–939.

Weinberger, D.R., Torrey, E.F., & Wyatt, R.J. Cerebellar atrophy in chronic schizophrenia. *Lancet,* 1979, *1,* 718–719.

Wender, P.H. Minimal brain dysfunction: An overview. In M.A. Lipton, A. Dimasio, & K.F. Killam (Eds.), *Psychopharmacology: A generation of progress.* New York: Raven, 1978.

Wender, P.H. The concept of adult minimal brain dysfunction. In L. Bellak (Ed.), *Psychiatric aspects of minimal brain dysfunction in adults.* New York: Grune & Stratton, 1979.

Werry, J.S., Minde, K., Guzman, A., Weiss, G., Dogan, K., & Hoy, E. Studies on the hyperactive child-VII: Neurological status compared with neurotic and normal children. *American Journal of Orthopsychiatry,* 1972, *42,* 441–450.

Wilson, G.S., Desmond, M.M., & Verniaud, W.M. Early development of infants of heroin-addicted mothers. *American Journal of Diseases of Children,* 1973, *126,* 457–462.

Wolff, P.H., & Hurwitz, I. Functional implications of the minimal brain damage syndrome. *Seminars in Psychiatry,* 1973, *5,* 105–115.

Worland, J., North-Jones, M., & Stern, J.A. Performance and activity of hyperactive and normal boys as a function of distraction and reward. *Journal of Abnormal Child Psychology,* 1973, *1,* 363–377.

Zahn, T.P., Abate, F., Little, B.C., & Wender, P.H. Minimal brain dysfunction, stimulant drugs, and autonomic nervous system activity. *Archives of General Psychiatry,* 1975, *32,* 381–387.

Borderline Syndromes and Attention Deficit Disorders of Childhood: Clinical and Neuro-chemical Perspectives

Donald J. Cohen, M.D.

PROFESSOR OF PEDIATRICS, PSYCHIATRY, AND PSYCHOLOGY AND CO-DIRECTOR
YALE MENTAL HEALTH CLINICAL RESEARCH CENTER
YALE UNIVERSITY SCHOOL OF MEDICINE & CHILD STUDY CENTER
NEW HAVEN, CONNECTICUT

Sally E. Shaywitz, M.D.

ASSISTANT PROFESSOR OF PEDIATRICS AND CHIEF,
LEARNING DISORDERS CLINIC
YALE UNIVERSITY SCHOOL OF MEDICINE
NEW HAVEN, CONNECTICUT

J. Gerald Young, M.D.

ASSOCIATE PROFESSOR OF PEDIATRICS AND PSYCHIATRY
DIRECTOR OF LABORATORY FOR DEVELOPMENTAL NEUROCHEMISTRY
YALE UNIVERSITY SCHOOL OF MEDICINE AND CHILD STUDY CENTER
NEW HAVEN, CONNECTICUT

Bennett A. Shaywitz, M.D.

ASSOCIATE PROFESSOR OF PEDIATRICS AND NEUROLOGY AND CHIEF OF
PEDIATRIC NEUROLOGY
YALE UNIVERSITY SCHOOL OF MEDICINE
NEW HAVEN, CONNECTICUT

THE REIFICATION OF DIAGNOSTIC ENTITIES tends to create a particular type of epistemological problem. When a child with serious personality disturbance is also found to have attentional and learning difficulties—as is often the case—there may be the temptation to diagnose *two* disorders, for example, attention deficit disorder (ADD) and borderline syndrome. This type of approach, however useful it may be for some clinical purposes, may impede the search for deeper, psychobiological understanding of the mechanisms involved in disorders of development. The areas of difficulty in ADD and borderline syndromes—disturbances in attention, activity, learning, impulse control—are also characteristic of other neuropsychiatric disorders of childhood, ranging from autism to obsessive-compulsive neurosis. For clinical research and care, it is thus important to look at constellations of clinical findings and dimensions of disturbance rather than discrete syndromic classifications. From this perspective, it is possible to conceptualize ADD as a constellation of behavioral dysfunctions which becomes manifest in phenotypically divergent disorders or which leads to different syndromes depending on the interaction of other genetic, constitutional, familial, and experiential factors. The predisposition to ADD may appear as relatively circumscribed attentional difficulties in one child; in another child who is additionally burdened by environmental distress and a genetic endowment leaning toward psychosis, ADD may be but one facet or determinant of a more ominous disorder, such as a borderline syndrome.

To explore this hypothesis and sort out the relations between the various clinical presentations of ADD and borderline syndromes will require systematic research, utilizing various methods of study. In turn, further understanding of attentional mechanisms and the biology of ADD may suggest new approaches to the treatment of perplexing borderline syndromes. In this chapter, we describe neurochemical concepts, strategies, and results of studies of ADD, highlighting aspects of ADD that appear of particular relevance to the more severely impaired borderline child. The extension of these concepts and methods to children with diagnosed borderline syndromes remains an unmet empirical challenge.

From the Child Study Center and the Departments of Pediatrics, Neurology, and Psychiatry, Yale University School of Medicine.

These studies were supported, in part, by MHCRC grant MH 30929, NICHD grant HD-03008, CCRC grant RR 00125, NS 12384, AA 03599, the Thrasher Research Foundation, the Ford Foundation, the Baker Foundation, and Mr. Leonard Berger.

CLINICAL BACKGROUND

The concept that there is a distinctive pattern of psychopathology occupying the borderlands between childhood neurosis and psychosis emerged from the care and study of a diverse group of seriously ego-impaired children. From the first, clinical descriptions of the borderline syndrome in childhood have emphasized the instability of psychological organization and the disruption of multiple development lines. Ekstein and Wallerstein (1954), A. Freud (1956), Geleerd (1958), Mahler (1952, 1971), Pine (1974), Weil (1953), and others have described the unevenness, lags, and distortions in the borderline child's development of capacities for relating to others, recognizing and coping with anxiety and sadness, regulating self-esteem, and modulating and discharging aggressive impulses. In etiological formulations, constitutional and genetic factors are frequently noted as possible contributing factors, but relatively more weight has been placed on adverse experiences, particularly with primary caregivers, than on inborn vulnerabilities. Systematic psychobiological research into these conditions has been inhibited by the limitation of available methods, the nature of the clinical interests of the major investigators, and absence of well-defined diagnostic criteria. Research and theory have focused, instead, on important areas of emotional development, such as the vicissitudes of mother-child relations, self-object differentiation, individuation, and other intrapsychic processes.

No formal diagnostic criteria for borderline disorders of childhood have, as yet, achieved general acceptance; thus, clinicians and investigators must indicate the definition guiding their thinking (see Shapiro, 1983; and Vela, Gottlieb, & Gottlieb, 1983). In our clinical research, borderline children are considered as suffering from a persistent, stable pattern of developmental deviations, usually apparent by the fourth year of life. This pattern or profile includes disturbances in the following sectors of development:

1. *Cognitive processes:* difficulties in organizing thoughts rationally and sequentially and sorting fantasy from reality; shifting delusions involving grandiose, paranoid, and aggressive themes; overinvolvement with fantasy; learning disorders.

2. *Social relations:* isolation from peers; rapidly alternating and perplexing combinations of immature, disinhibited, and ambivalent feelings toward adults, with extremes of hateful attack and positive affection directed at the same person or split between adults; oversensitivity to nuances of behavior, particularly felt rejection of others, and insensitivity to the impact on others; darting or piercing gaze.

3. *Anxiety regulation:* irrational anxiety, panic, separation anxiety, phobias, counterphobic behavior, and obsessions.

4. *Neuromaturation:* uneveness in fine and gross motor development; odd posturing and gait; hyper- or hypotonia; atypicalities on neurological examination, with disturbances in body image, sequencing, and coordination.

5. *Activity and attentional regulation:* impulsivity, distractibility, hypo- or hyperactivity.

Conceptualized in this manner, the borderline diagnosis carries no etiological significance; however, the early onset, family history of psychiatric disorder (personality disorder and psychosis), suggestions of neuromaturational difficulty, and association with organic disorders (such as seizure disorders, central language disorders, and organic encephalopathies with retardation) suggest diverse constitutional factors, often in interaction with environmental experiences (Fish, 1977). And in this manner, the diagnosis may be applied, today, to some of those children considered on the "atypical spectrum" or schizophrenic during the 1950s and 1960s. Of particular interest are those children with early-onset developmental language disorders who progressively manifest features of the borderline disorder as they mature and acquire increasing language competence. Their difficulties in internal representation of complex human interactions, regulation of anxiety, separating fantasies from reality, and regulating attention and action reveal the close relations between cognitive and affective development in the broader class of borderline children (Caparulo & Cohen, 1982; Cohen, Caparulo, & Wetstone, 1981).

The *Diagnostic and Statistical Manual* (DSM-III, 1980) criteria for the diagnosis of a borderline personality disorder in adults are not suitable for children, especially young children, for several reasons. The adult criteria of intolerance of being alone, uncertainty about several issues relating to identity, and affective instability may be normative in childhood; other criteria are generally outside of the realm of childhood experience (spending, sex, gambling) or are satisfied in too many disorders to be of differential use (intense anger, self-damaging acts, boredom). In some respects, the disorders closest to childhood borderline conditions, as defined above, are designated as pervasive developmental disorders (PDD) in DSM-III. Their definitions, however, raise difficulties and, in some instances, are inconsistent with clinical experience. For example, childhood autism is not always characterized by a pervasive *lack of responsiveness,* as DSM-III requires, but, instead, by a failure of normal attachments, lack of appreciation of mutuality, or social withdrawal (Cohen, Caparulo, & Wetstone, 1981; Cohen, 1980). Nor does the language of autistic children always manifest gross deficits; instead, autistic children may have linguistically more interesting, circumscribed impairments, e.g., normal syntax but semantic limitations. DSM-III thus draws autism in overly broad terms which rule out the higher functioning children.

The problems raised in this approach to the diagnosis of autism are not solved by the availability of the category of childhood onset PDD which essentially portrays higher functioning autistic children along with a heterogeneous group who, in earlier periods, would have been called atypical. Here, the difficulty lies with the criterion that the full syndrome must appear after thirty months of age; this timetable is inconsistent with the common situation where children who satisfy the criteria for this disorder often have suffered from quite serious difficulties since the first or second year of life (e.g., impaired social relations manifested in clinging or aloofness, excessive anxiety, inappropriate fearfulness, resistance to change, odd speech and movements, and hyper- or hyposensitivity to stimuli). Because of these difficulties in the nosology, many children with early onset serious disorders will have to be classified in the DSM-III "remainder" category of atypical pervasive developmental disorder. Unfortunately, this category has been deprived of the richness of description associated with the term in the past without being provided with operational specificity in DSM-III. Better delineated, it might encompass children whom clinicians would diagnose as borderline. Similarly, the absence of a diagnostic category for childhood schizophrenia, except where the childhood disorder is isomorphic with the adult, requires that these children, too, be placed in the atypical PDD category along with distinctly different children.

In future revisions, DSM-III criteria for the early onset disorders will require extensive reworking to become more attuned to clinical knowledge and the range of severity within the spectrum of developmental neuropsychiatric disorders (which occasionally, but not always, are pervasive). If DSM-IV is appropriately revised, borderline children could very well be assimilated into a new typology close to what are now labeled PDDs. A good deal can be learned about borderline children seen from the perspective provided by the more disabling, pervasive conditions. However, in this chapter we highlight how, on their other side, borderline children come into contact with those who inhabit the nosological domain of attention deficit syndromes (ADD). The correspondences between aspects of the borderline and ADD conditions will appear particularly vivid for those ADD syndromes which are embedded in, or found in association with, major and sustained behavioral or personality difficulties.

Alongside the growing interest in borderline syndromes has been the increasing interest and research on an equally heterogeneous group of children designated by various names, such as minimal brain dysfunction (MBD), hyperactive child syndrome, and, most recently, attention deficit disorder (ADD) (Cohen, 1976; Shaywitz, Cohen, & Shaywitz, 1979; Wender, 1971). When the characteristics of children with borderline syndromes are compared with those of ADD children, there are remarkable overlaps. "Typical" ADD children are inattentive, impulsive, hyperactive, and intolerant of frustration, as are ego-impaired borderline children; they are oblivious to instructions, unconcerned about the consequences of their actions or the feelings of others, and centered on the satisfactions of their own desires, thus sharing traits with other children with immature object relations. Acting as if driven by a motor, the ADD child may leave a trail of chaos and then feel bewildered and hurt if reprimanded. Like a borderline child, he or she may seem impervious to criticism and then, in a flash, reveal the loneliness, hopelessness, sadness, and exquisite sensitivity to rejection which usually lie concealed under the camouflage of action. The ADD child, as the borderline child, frequently has problems in academic achievement even when intellectual endowment is satisfactory. Thus, it seems conceivable that the ADD and borderline syndromes might represent, at least in part, similar clinical entities with some common underlying biological dysfunctions.

While there has been little explicit research on the relevance of ADD to borderline syndromes, clinicians often confront this issue. In clinical discussions, the question is often raised as a dichotomy. Do the rapid shifts in the child's associations indicate the thought disorder of one variety of borderline syndrome, or are the wandering speech and out-of-context, intrusive ideas a reflection of difficulties in maintaining a sustained, inner focus of attention as in ADD? Should the child be treated with some combination of approaches to ADD (behavior modification, special education, stimulant medication, parental guidance) or with intensive, individual psychotherapy, perhaps augmented by neuroleptics? The experienced clinician will, of course, escape from nosological dilemmas by considering the individual child's special needs. Yet questions are raised by the process of differential diagnosis. Does the child more closely approximate ADD or a borderline syndrome? Does he suffer from both? And does one contribute to or "cause" the other? Finding the answers to these questions raises fundamental research problems in developmental psychopathology.

Research, theory, and treatment of borderline and ADD disorders have, however, progressed in parallel, with little mutual enrichment. ADD has been the province mainly of psychologists, educators, pharmacologists, psychiatrists, and other investigators whose major concerns have been overt behavior and conduct. By contrast, borderline children have been studied by psychoanalysts and other clinicians devoted to understanding the dynamics of a child's inner life. This splitting has had unfortunate results in relation to both syndromes. First, attentional, learning, and cognitive difficulties of some borderline children may not be fully appreciated as important, and perhaps primary, areas of dysfunction and as generative of other social and affective disabilities. Furthermore, the emotional problems of children categorized as ADD may receive insufficient recognition in programs geared toward the modification of behavior and enhancement of learning skills. Finally, research on borderline syndromes has not benefited from rigorous biological, psychological, and epidemiological methods which have arisen from studies on ADD, and, on the other hand, studies of children with ADD have not gained from current theories of object relations, self-representation, and self-esteem regulation.

Studies of natural history may provide an important bridge between the two childhood syndromes and between developmental difficulties and later adult psychiatric disorder. Difficulties in school achievement, in the modulation of activity and attention, and in forming meaningful and stable peer relations are typical of young adult patients with borderline personality disorder. Formal retrospective, clinical evaluations and assessments of adolescents and young adults diagnosed as suffering from borderline syndromes repeatedly have revealed earlier diagnoses or current manifestations of ADD (or MBD) (see Andrulonis et al., 1981, for review). In contrast, fewer of these adult patients appear to have suffered from full-blown childhood borderline syndromes. Instead it appears that the borderline child may have a more ominous natural history (e.g., toward psychosis) or one leading to disorders such as schizotypal personality disorder. Improved diagnostic and clinical research methods are now available for addressing complex questions of natural history; in turn, clarification of the relations between the childhood ADD and borderline syndromes and later schizophrenic, borderline, schizotypal, and other conditions may greatly clarify diagnostic issues and underlying processes.

NEUROCHEMISTRY AND ADD

During the past decade, neurochemically oriented research has provided a framework for investigations of childhood neuropsychiatric disorders, particularly childhood psychosis and ADD (Cohen & Young, 1977; Young et al., 1982). No formal studies have been performed using currently available methodologies with borderline children. The neurochemical understanding of ADD, however, may be of relevance to borderline disorder for two reasons. First, as noted above, aspects of the two disorders overlap, and these resemblances may reflect, at least in part, involvement of similar neurochemical mechanisms. Further understanding of the biological bases of inattention and impulsivity may have direct relevance to the etiology of certain sectors of the childhood borderline syndrome. Second, research methods developed in relation to ADD (and psychosis) can now be applied to borderline children. In the following sections, as we review studies on ADD, we do not conceptualize ADD as a specific disease but as a pattern of psychobiological dysfunction which may be found in relative isolation or embedded in more complex disorders, such as borderline syndromes.

Evidence from several lines of investigation has converged to support the belief that the disturbances in activity, attention, and learning which together characterize the clinical entity currently designated as attention deficit disorder (ADD) with hyperactivity (Shaywitz et al., 1979) may be understood as reflecting alterations in brain neurochemical mechanisms, in particular those involving the catecholamines, dopamine (DA), and norepinephrine (NE). Clinical investigations incorporating measurements of monoamines or their metabolites in populations of children with ADD have supplemented and strengthened the epidemiological, pharmacological, and genetic studies that led to the notion that brain monoaminergic mechanisms may be involved in the pathogenesis of the disorder. Most recently, the development of an animal model with many striking similarities to the clinical disorder has provided a unique opportunity to approach ADD, utilizing more detailed and sophisticated pharmacological methodology than is possible in human investigations (Shaywitz, Cohen, & Shaywitz, 1978).

Our understanding of the neurochemical influences in ADD reflect in large measure both basic and methodological advances in the pharmacology of brain monoamines (Cohen & Young, 1977; Young & Cohen, 1979; Hunt et al., 1982). For example, present techniques have made it possible to reliably measure concentrations of the monoamines, their metabolites, and related synthetic and degradative enzymes in urine, plasma, and cerebrospinal fluid (CSF).

Tyrosine hydroxylase (TH), the rate-limiting step in catecholamine metabolism catalyzes the formation of 1-dihydroxyphenylalanine (1-DOPA) from the amino acid tyrosine; aromatic acid decarboxylase (AAAD) catalyzes the formation of DA from 1-DOPA. Both synthetic enzymes are located intracellularly and are not presently measurable in clinical studies, except at autopsy (McGeer & McGeer, 1973; Robinson et al., 1977). Formation of NE from DA is dependent upon dopamine-β-hydroxylase (DBH), which is present in serum (see below). Catabolism of DA proceeds by one of two routes: deamination via monoamine oxidase (MAO, which may be determined in platelets and has been extensively examined), resulting in the formation of dihydroxyphenylacetic acid (DOPAC, which most recently has been assayed in plasma), or O-methylation by catechol-O-methyltransferase (COMT, a more difficult enzymatic assay and one that has only recently been utilized in clinical investigations) to 3-methoxytyramine (MTA). DOPAC is subsequently O-methylated (via COMT), and MTA is deaminated (via MAO) to yield homovanillic acid (HVA, a compound studied extensively in human disorders). For NE, the combined actions of COMT and MAO result in an O-methylated, deaminated glycol, 3-methoxy-4-hydroxyphenethyleneglycol (MHPG), a compound which may be assayed in plasma, urine, and CSF. (Leckman & Maas, 1982; Young et al., 1982).

BRAIN CATECHOLAMINES AND ADD: EARLY STUDIES

Following the pandemic of von Economo's encephalitis in the early part of this century, the pediatric literature of the 1920s and 1930s described symptoms of hyperactivity, impulsivity, short attention span, and school learning difficulties in many of the survivors (Bond & Partridge, 1926; Ebaugh, 1923; Hohman, 1922). This finding, taken together with the occurrence of Parkinson's disease in many adults who recovered from von Economo's encephalitis led Wender (1971, 1978) to speculate that the virus causing von Economo's encephalitis damaged the nigroneostriatal DA system in both adults and children. Although reasonable, such a suggestion is difficult to substantiate since the pandemic occurred in an era before methods for culturing viruses had been developed, and thus the virus of von Economo's encephalitis was never isolated. Nevertheless, Lycke and Roos have demonstrated that if mice are innoculated with herpes simplex virus, they exhibit hypermotility, behavioral excitation, and increased turnover and synthesis of brain DA and serotonin (Lycke & Roos, 1974, 1975). Thus it is reasonable to believe that infection with a viral agent such as that causing von Economo's encephalitis may produce a response in the human brain similar to that observed by Lycke and Roos in animal investigations.

Pharmacological studies of the effects of stimulants in children with ADD provide further evidence supporting a role for brain catecholamines in the genesis of the disorder. As early as 1937, Bradley observed that the hyperactivity and attentional difficulties in ADD could be ameliorated by administration of amphetamines, and numerous studies over the last two decades have confirmed this observation. Amphetamines (and the closely related agent, methylphenidate) appear to exert their effect by influencing at least three distinct central catecholamine mechanisms. Amphetamines stimulate the release of neurotransmitter (both DA and NE) from neuronal terminals, reduce reuptake of transmitter by the neuronal membrane, and inhibit MAO (and thus degradation). The net effect of these mechanisms is an increase in concentration of both DA and NE at the synaptic cleft. Since amphetamines (and methylphenidate) act via brain catecholaminergic mechanisms, and since both stimulants ameliorate the symptoms of ADD, this commonality between ADD and the stimulants suggests that brain catecholaminergic mechanisms may play a role in the disorder (Wender, 1971, 1978).

Demonstration of an hereditary pattern for a clinical syndrome often is the first indication of a biochemical abnormality, and investigations of a genetic predisposition in ADD may provide indirect evidence of a biochemical influence in the disorder. To date, investigations employing family studies (Cantwell, 1972; Morrison & Stewart, 1971), twin studies (Willerman, 1973), and adoptive methods (Cantwell, 1975; Morrison & Stewart, 1973; Safer, 1973) all support genetic contributions to the ADD syndrome. Similarly, genetic contributions have been recognized as relevant to the etiology of borderline syndromes in childhood, as exemplified by the clinical reports and studies of Bender (1942), Fish (1977), and Goldfarb (1961) on the prevalence of psychiatric disorders in the parents and families of children with childhood psychosis (see Fish & Ritvo, 1979, and Shapiro, 1983, for reviews). In some respects, the family histories of children with ADD—characterized by parents with impulsivity, alcoholism, sociopathy, attentional problems, and other psychiatric difficulties—overlap with those of some children with borderline syndromes. It is also of interest to consider ways in which the childhood family dynamics reconstructed for adult patients with borderline syndromes may reflect, at least in part, genetic contributions which are expressed in both the parents and the defined patient (see Gunderson & Englund, 1981). Sophisticated studies of the transmission of psychiatric disorder will need to consider the multiple synergistic, environmental, biological, and genetic factors which increase vulnerability.

CLINICAL STUDIES

Documentation of an abnormality of amines, their metabolites, or the enzymes concerned with their formation and degradation in clinical populations may serve as a basis for linking brain catecholaminergic mechanisms to either ADD or borderline syndromes. One strategy is to examine the concentrations of those enzymes which influence the formation and catabolism of the catecholamines and which might serve as a useful index of monoaminergic function. Tyrosine hydroxylase, the rate-limiting step in catecholamine synthesis, and aromatic acid decarboxylase, another synthetic enzyme, are located intracellularly and are not measurable in serum or CSF. The enzyme has been assayed at autopsy, and its activity appears to decrease (McGeer & McGeer, 1973) or not to change with age (Robinson et al., 1977), but there have been no determinations of this enzyme in the children with ADD.

Dopamine-β-hydroxylase (DBH), the enzyme which catalyzes the formation of NE from DA, is extruded from the presynaptic neuron into the circulation where it may be assayed. A major problem in interpreting population studies of DBH activity is the wide range of activity varying up to over one hundredfold in a normal population. Furthermore, serum DBH activity increases with age, particularly during the first few years of life (Freedman et al., 1972; Weinshilboum et al., 1973; Young et al., 1980). Despite these reservations, Rapoport et al. (1974) investigated plasma DBH levels in 72 hyperactive boys between ages six and twelve but failed to detect any relationship between DBH levels and hyperactivity, results confirmed as well on a group of children with ADD investigated by our group (Shaywitz et al., 1980).

While the catabolism of the catecholamines is influenced by the activity of both monoamine oxidase (MAO) and catechol-O-methyltransferase (COMT), by far the largest number of studies have examined MAO, and much information is available for this enzyme. Several isoenzymatic forms of MAO exist: Type A, found in plasma, is specific for the oxidation of NE and 5-HT but does not act on DA. Type B, found in platelets and other tissues, oxidizes phenylethylamines such as DA (Youdim et al., 1972). Studies in our laboratories indicate that platelet MAO activity is greater in girls than boys, but in both sexes it tends to decrease during childhood and adolescence in control subjects and children with a variety of psychiatric disorders (Young et al., 1979). MAO activity in platelets and plasma then increases during adult years (Belmaker et al., 1976; Robinson et al., 1977; Robinson & Nies, 1980), a result which parallels that observed for MAO in brain (Robinson & Nies, 1980). Although extensively studied in adult populations because of its potential importance in schizophrenia, MAO has only begun to be carefully examined in children. Studies in our laboratory indicate that platelet MAO in autistic children is similar to that observed in a normal population (Cohen et al., 1977). Although preliminary, studies of MAO in a group of children with ADD indicate that the great majority demonstrate normal concentrations of MAO, however there may exist subgroups of children within the ADD population who exhibit abnormally reduced concentrations of the enzyme.

Although COMT has been examined in human autopsy material (Robinson et al., 1977), methodology for examining activity of COMT in plasma has only recently been developed, and, to date, no data are available on its activity in children.

Determination of the urinary concentrations of monoamine metabolites would intuitively seem to represent an ideal strategy for documenting biochemical abnormalities in affected clinical populations. Historically, the earliest attempt to utilize such a procedure was the study by Wender et al. (1971). These investigators examined urinary concentrations of HVA, the principal metabolite of DA, but did not detect differences between groups of children with ADD compared to normals. However, urinary HVA reflects the concentration of DA in both the central and peripheral (including autonomic) nervous systems, as well as its concentration in other body organs. Thus any small differences in brain DA might be overlooked because of the overwhelming amount of DA originating in other tissues.

In contrast, determination of the urinary concentrations of the principal metabolite of NE may offer insights into the activity of the parent amine in brain. Metabolism of NE (and epinephrine, E) results in the formation of two major metabolites, vanillylmandelic acid (VMA) and 3-methoxy-4-hydroxyphenylethylene glycol (MHPG). Investigations in both animals and man indicate that while VMA is a product of peripheral sympathetic activity, approximately 60 percent of urinary MHPG is derived from brain metabolism (Maas et al., 1976). Concentrations of MHPG, a measure of central noradrenergic activity, increase during childhood (McKendrick & Edwards, 1965; Young et al., 1982). Shekim et al. (1979) has demonstrated that urinary concentrations of MHPG are reduced in a population of children with ADD, adding further support for the belief that central catecholaminergic mechanisms are involved in the pathogenesis of ADD. However, these studies are complicated by methodological and diagnostic questions (Young et al., 1982). It is possible that some of the heterogeneity in neurochemical findings in ADD may reflect, in part, the problems in diagnosis of ADD and the inclusion of children with more complex personality disorders who also satisfy the diagnostic criteria for ADD. Such questions can be clarified through the application of similar, noninvasive studies with borderline children, and much research needs to be pursued.

It is reasonable to believe that examination of the amines and their metabolites in CSF might provide a more reliable approach to catecholaminergic mechanisms within the brain than is possible utilizing solely measures of urinary metabolites or serum enzymes (Cohen et al., 1980). For a number of years, it has been possible to determine concentrations of 5-

hydroxyindole-acetic acid (5-HIAA) and HVA, the major metabolites of serotonin (5-HT) and DA, respectively, in samples of CSF, and most recently, the development of high performance liquid chromatographic (HPLC) techniques have permitted these analyses on microliter quantities of CSF. Considerable evidence indicates that the concentrations of these metabolites in CSF reflect the activity of their parent amines in brain (Moir et al., 1970).

To date, two investigative groups have examined CSF monoamine metabolite concentrations in children with ADD. Shetty and Chase (1976) noted that while baseline concentrations of HVA and 5-HIAA were similar in normal and hyperactive children, administration of amphetamine resulted in a significant reduction in CSF concentrations of HVA but not 5-HIAA in the hyperactive group.

Evidence utilizing several experimental methods demonstrates that the concentration of HVA and 5-HIAA in CSF following probenecid administration reflects the turnover of the respective amines DA and 5-HT within the brain (Bowers, 1972; Goodwin et al., 1973). Utilizing this technique, our investigative group (Shaywitz et al., 1977) has reported that the levels of HVA in CSF were significantly reduced in children with ADD when compared to controls, although 5-HIAA levels were no different. Thus, our findings, like those of Shetty and Chase, suggest that central catecholaminergic mechanisms play a role in ADD. More impressive and consistent findings on CSF metabolites have emerged from studies of children with Tourette's syndrome (TS). Perhaps the majority of patients with TS suffer from ADD, a phenomenon which we have attributed to the broad-gauged dysfunction in psychomotor inhibition which may precede the onset of motor and phonic symptoms and coexist with them (Cohen, 1980a; Cohen et al., 1980a; Cohen et al., 1980b; Cohen, Detlor, Shaywitz, and Leckman, 1982). Many also have more serious personality disorders and anxiety syndromes. Several investigatory groups have confirmed the observation of reduced CSF levels of 5-HIAA in TS (Cohen et al., 1978; Butler et al., 1979). This finding has also been observed in depressed patients more prone to suicide and in young adults with impulsivity, suggesting the involvement of serotonergic inhibitory mechanisms in a variety of psychiatric disorders. Similar studies of borderline children would help to clarify the relationship of this syndrome to other neuropsychiatric disorders as well as perhaps to suggest approaches to treatment. For example, the clinical effectiveness of clonidine in reducing the impulsivity, irritability, and attentional problems in TS (in addition to motor and phonic symptoms) suggested its potential value in the treatment of ADD, where it has also proven of benefit in pilot studies with selected children. Clinical research on the neurochemistry of borderline syndromes may suggest alternative approaches to pharmacotherapy in these syndromes; response to medication, in turn, may delineate subgroups and clarify aspects of the underlying pathophysiological processes.

Psychopharmacology of Attention Deficit Disorders

While examination of monoamine metabolites in CSF is of great value in documenting central catecholaminergic influences in ADD and other disorders, the invasive nature of lumbar puncture limits to a great extent a role for such techniques in any practical clinical setting. Any reasonable diagnostic neurochemical index of catecholaminergic function in ADD should exploit the recently developed methodology for determining plasma concentrations of monoamines and their metabolites.

For example, recent studies indicate that plasma NE has a brief half-life of two minutes and tends to increase with stress. Particular care must be exercised in obtaining samples because a variety of seemingly innocuous maneuvers (change in posture, temperature, and so on) may influence NE levels (Young et al., 1980). In recent investigations (Shaywitz et al., 1980), we have examined not only the plasma concentrations of the catecholamines (DA, NE, E) in children with ADD but their relationship to prolactin and growth hormone, hormones closely linked to central catecholaminergic functions. Furthermore, all these parameters were themselves studied during administration of the stimulant methylphenidate (MPH). In the first study, we examined MPH levels, prolactin, growth hormone, and MAO in twelve children during chronic administration of the stimulant at a dose of 0.3 mg/kg body weight. MPH concentrations averaged 11 ng/ml at one hour and 9 ng/ml at two hours after administration. Plasma MPH was also significantly correlated with oral dose. However, no relationship existed between drug concentration in plasma and prolactin, growth hormone, or MAO level. Interestingly, MPH concentrations in those children whose behavior rating scales improved on medication were significantly higher than those found in children judged to be nonresponders to the drug.

In a complementary study, prolactin, growth hormone, MAO, NE, DA, and E concentrations were all determined continuously in plasma (at approximately thirty-minute intervals) following acute administration of 0.3 mg/kg of MPH. Concentrations of MPH peaked at ninety minutes, with a half-life of approximately four hours. Growth hormone concentrations increased significantly at the same time as the peak MPH, and the plasma catecholamines tended to decline following administration of the stimulant. Prolactin was not altered.

Clearly, such studies are still in their infancy, and much more investigation is necessary before we are able to reliably determine normal from abnormal concentrations of monoamines and their related enzymes and metabolites in plasma. However, these preliminary data suggest that it may be possible to differentiate clinical syndromes utilizing biochemical markers that may be assayed in plasma. The advantages of such a procedure are readily apparent—the noninvasive nature of the technique and the ease of its application offer promise that we may at last have available a practical and readily applicable technique that can be applied to large numbers of children with ADD, borderline, and other disorders in an effort to understand the pathogenesis of their disorder better (Hunt et al., 1982).

ANIMAL MODELS OF ADD

Both ethical and scientific considerations provide a cogent rationale for the development of an animal model of ADD. For example, it is permissible to perform certain types of experiments on animals that would never be considered in clinical investigations. Even more important, investigations on animals may be much more precisely controlled and particular parameters examined in greater detail than is possible in human studies. Of special relevance to investigations on developing organisms is the ease with which the entire course of maturation from prenatal life through adulthood may be examined using a relatively brief and certainly more convenient span than one measured in years that is the case in clinical studies.

A suitable animal model of ADD should represent a simplified replica of the human disorder, with similar phenomenology, similar etiology, and similar response to pharmacological agents that are effective in children (Alpert et al., 1978; Murphy, 1976). Necessary criteria include:

1. Production of the syndrome in a developing animal, rather than in the neurologically mature adult. Furthermore, behavioral characteristics should follow a chronology similar to the time course of the symptoms in affected children. For example, an important and striking feature of the human disorder is hyperactive motor behavior, most prominent in the younger school-age child (this behavior tends to abate as the child approaches adolescence). In order to simulate ADD, the hyperactive motor behavior produced in an animal model should be observed only in the immature organism—it should not be apparent in the neurologically mature adult.

2. Replication of specific features of the ADD syndrome in the animal model—for example, such features might include hyperactive motor behavior, cognitive difficulties, and deficits in habituation (which may be considered as an animal counterpart of impulsivity).

3. Production of the animal model by methods which bear some relationship to the presumed pathogenesis of the disorder. For ADD, this means that the procedures should involve those that influence central catecholaminergic mechanisms.

4. Response to administration of pharmacologic agents in animals that parallels that observed in the clinical syndrome. As noted earlier, administration of stimulants such as amphetamine or MPH to children with ADD frequently results in a reduction in hyperactivity, an effect characterized as "paradoxical" but also seen with normal children who are performing specific cognitive tasks (Rapoport et al., 1978, 1980). A similar stimulant-induced reduction in hyperactivity should be observed in an animal mode. Furthermore, although their long-term effect on learning remains controversial, administration of both amphetamines and MPH improve performance on attentional and cognitive tasks in affected youngsters, an effect we would also like to duplicate in any animal model. Morever, the similarity in response in children and animals should not be limited solely to the stimulants. For example, clinical experience suggests that administration of barbiturates, generally considered to be sedative agents, often exacerbates hyperactivity and further interferes with cognitive ability of children with ADD. One might expect a parallel response to phenobarbital in an animal model. Clearly, the response to newer pharmacological agents that might possess some therapeutic efficacy provides one of the most potent stimuli for the development of an animal model.

While a number of animal models of hyperactivity have been developed previously (Shaywitz et al., 1978), their use has been limited by a failure to meet these criteria for an animal model. Although several have been described in which not only was hyperactivity produced but a hyperactivity that was reduced by amphetamine or MPH, this effect was observed in the mature animal rather than in the developing organism. Most recently, we have employed an animal model of ADD that utilizes the neurotoxin 6-OHDA in the developing rat pup. This model not only satisfies our criteria and is convenient, it has also been confirmed and replicated by a number of independent investigators throughout the world (Eastgate et al., 1978; Erinoff et al., 1979; Shaywitz et al., 1976; Sorenson et al., 1977; Stoof et al., 1978).

The model is effected in the five-day-old rat pup by first pretreating the animal with desmethylimipramine (DMI) followed one hour later by the intracisternal administration of 6-OHDA. Because DMI acts to prevent incorporation of 6-OHDA into noradrenergic terminals, the neurotoxin is selectively taken up by dopaminergic neurons, where it is converted to a peroxide which destroys the DA terminal. This occurs rapidly, over the course of approximately two days, and the DA terminals do not regenerate (Smith et al., 1973). Such treatment results in a reduction of whole-brain DA to values 10–14 percent of controls, while NE is essentially unchanged. Assays of brain regions utilizing either enzymatic or HPLC techniques (Anderson et al., 1979) indicate that DA concentrations are profoundly reduced in neostriatum and nucleus accumbens, and to a lesser extent in hypothalamus, results confirmed histologically as well. In a typical experiment, the behavior of pups treated in this fashion is examined throughout infancy and adolescence, utilizing a variety of measures.

We, as well as others, have demonstrated that rat pups treated in this manner exhibit a characteristic spectrum of behaviors with many similarities to the ADD and borderline syndromes observed in children. For example, pups treated with 6-OHDA as neonates are significantly more active than their littermate controls during the period of behavioral arousal observed between two and three weeks of age (Shaywitz et al., 1976). However, as is the case in the childhood disorder, the hyperactivity appears to abate as the animals mature, so that by the end of the first month of postnatal life (adolescence in the rat), normal and 6-OHDA pups exhibit comparable activity. Cognitive difficulties represent still another area of similarity between the 6-OHDA pup and the child with ADD, reflected in the marked impairment of 6-OHDA pups for conditioned odor preference, T-maze, and shuttle-box tasks. Amelioration of these deficits in 6-OHDA pups by the stimulants amphetamine and MPH represents a further parallel to ADD. Administration of amphetamine exacerbates the activity of normal rat pups but results in a reduction in the hyperactivity of 6-OHDA animals (Shaywitz et al., 1976). Furthermore, MPH will improve the markedly impaired avoidance performance of 6-OHDA pups in the T-maze and shuttle-box tasks (Shaywitz et al., 1978), and amphetamine will ameliorate the impaired conditioned odor preference as well. Conversely (Shaywitz & Pearson, 1978), chronic administration of phenobarbital will reduce activity in normal pups but will exacerbate the already abnormal hyperactivity in 6-OHDA-treated animals. Still another behavioral similarity between the animal model and the human disorder is provided by the observation that normal rat pups tend to exhibit a reduction in activity over the hour-long observation period. Most interestingly, the parents of children with ADD frequently describe exacerbation of hyperactivity and distractibility resulting from a sudden change in milieu—for example, that occurring when the child goes from one classroom to another during a school day. This inability to adjust to change appears to be a reflection of impulsivity and has its counterpart in the impaired ability of the 6-OHDA rat pup to modulate his activity when placed in a new environment, an effect described experimentally as impairment in habituation of activity (Shaywitz et al., 1979).

Increasing evidence suggests that the complex interaction between genetic endowment and environmental determinants combine to produce a result that we observe as the behavioral repertoire of the organism. Clinical experience, as well as controlled observations (O'Leary & Pelham, 1978; Satterfield et al., 1979) indicate that environmental manipulations may be effective in treating children with ADD. Such frequently utilized procedures as placing children in a "one-to-one" setting, limiting the possibility for distractions, and "mainstreaming" ADD children in regular classrooms exemplify the role environmental factors play in ADD. In this context, it is of great interest that recent studies in our laboratory provide experimental verification of the importance of environmental factors on behavior (Pearson et al., 1980). We examined activity and avoidance learning in normal pups reared only with normal or with 6-OHDA pups and 6-OHDA pups reared with normal or similarly treated animals. Both biological factors (represented by 6-OHDA-induced depletion of brain DA) and environmental influences (embodied in alterations in litter composition) combine and interact to produce significant effects on activity and avoidance performance. Thus both hyperactivity and deficits in avoidance performance in 6-OHDA pups are significantly improved by allowing the 6-OHDA pups to be reared with normal littermates rather than confining them solely with other impaired animals. By "mainstreaming" the 6-OHDA animals, we effectively improved their impaired cognitive performance and reduced their hyperactivity. Such findings in an experimental paradigm provide support for the notion that environmental manipulations may be effective in treating abnormal behaviors which result from primary biological factors.

While we have utilized this animal model to explore such factors as the role of food colorings (Goldenring et al., 1980; Shaywitz et al., 1979) and the effect of potential therapeutic agents, such as bromocriptine (Shaywitz et al., 1979), the value of such experiments does not depend solely upon the mimicry of a human disorder in another species. Rather, such animal models have heuristic value in generating principles and generalizations about the organization of children's behavior and the ways in which discrete biological and environmental factors influence specific aspects of functioning. Such an approach is not limited by the methodological restrictions inherent in human investigations and offers the potential of defining neurochemical mechanisms utilizing technology clearly not possible in clinical investigations. If we are able to discover something of the mechanisms involved in the evolution of a specific behavioral parameter in our model system, then we have taken a significant step in increasing the understanding of the mechanisms involved in the production of this behavior in other model systems as well.

OVERVIEW

The developmental histories of children with borderline syndromes are often rich in symptoms pointing to early difficulties in the modulation of arousal, the focusing of attention, and the regulation of anxiety; such difficulties have been considered by psychoanalytic researchers as reflections of constitutional disturbances (Hartocollis, 1968; Weil, 1953). However, even for a young child it is difficult to specify what aspects of behavior reflect pure endowment and what modes of action and reaction are already shaped through interaction with primary caregivers and other experiences. For the older child, such clarity is rarely possible. Instead, the child's developmental achievements and emotional troubles must be seen as the result of a multitude of forces— constitutional endowment, the maturing of the agencies of the mind, the timing and nature of interventions, the intensity of normative and pathological conflicts, and the child's unique pattern of defense and compromise (A. Freud, 1981).

The complementary series of interactions between a child's psyche and soma and between a child and his or her world requires an interactive, rather than a linear model of development (Cohen, 1980; Dibble & Cohen, 1981). Endowment shapes experience and, in turn, experience modifies the expression of endowment. The clinical study of borderline adolescents and young adults presents opportunities for reconstructing one type of development pathway in which early psychobiological difficulties, often in conjunction with particular types of environmental provision, may lead to serious psychiatric disorder. In this progression, a child who has difficulty in muting inner tensions and habituating to stimulation experiences recurrent anxieties and is irritable with caregivers; this tension generates troubles in parenting, and that interaction leads to distortions in the child's creation of the internal representation of the mother as caring and good, in the establishment of transitional objects, and in the maturation of methods for modulation of anxiety. Based on the shaky foundations of early ego deviations, superego functioning predisposes such children to difficulties in self-control, narcissistic balance, and sublimation. In turn, their impulsivity and thoughtlessness evoke hostility from adults. As their self-esteem is battered and they see themselves as defective, they turn to projection and paranoid defenses or toward withdrawal and splitting. Anxious fragmentation and pyschological defenses distort such children's sense of reality and confidence in their own inner integrity. Finally, with the upsurge of sexual and aggressive impulses in puberty, they withdraw, break down, or strike out (Cohen, 1976; Cohen & Frank, 1975).

Faced with an adolescent with a borderline condition who has followed this prototype of one line of development, a clinician might reconstruct aspects of constitutional endowment and environmental experience. However, the child's functioning represents not the summation of factors but the unique result of their interaction. In our description of the current status of research of ADD, we emphasized biological alterations—particularly those involving catecholamines—that may predispose toward ADD in children or suggests models of ADD in animals. But these inborn or early biological alterations must be seen in the context of the child's, or animal's, experience, as demonstrated by the studies of the impact of environment on the hyperactivity of dopamine-depleted rat pups. In our research, constitutional variables have been the major domain of intervention, and we have shown that specific manipulations of catecholamines may lead to prolonged disorders of attention, habituation, and learning as well as transitory, phase-specific disturbances of activity. Parallels between animal studies and what is known about the organization and ontogeny of neurotransmitters in humans, and the known response of children to medication, make it plausible that catecholaminergic mechanisms may also be involved in the pathobiology of certain types of ADD and borderline symptomatology in children. However, it is equally possible that the attentional difficulties of some children arise on the basis of quite different types of constitutional difficulties, or none at all. And particular styles of parenting, stress, and other experiences in a child's life, in interaction with biological endowment, may lead to temporary or prolonged alterations in neurotransmitter metabolism.

Biological investigation of borderline children does not depreciate the important role of experiential factors, particularly early parent-child relations, in the origin of the syndrome. Nor does placing borderline syndromes in the context of ADD imply that all, or even a majority, of children with these disorders have disturbances in the ontogeny or regulation of neurotransmitters or other biological systems. Rather, contemporary clinical investigations reinforce psychoanalytic conceptions of the mutual effects of biological and experiential factors. Future studies of ADD will be enhanced by more refined analysis of the inner lives of children who justify this diagnosis. Some of these children will be seen to suffer the emotional pains of borderline syndrome. In turn, research on borderline syndrome and other serious developmental disorders of childhood will advance by the consideration of new hypotheses, drawn from fields which may be distant from clinical observation, and by the systematic application of new methods of biological and psychological inquiry.

Future clinical research will help clarify diagnostic criteria and assess the continued usefulness of currently accepted syndromes and operational definitions. Advancing knowledge of phenomenology, natural history, psychobiology, and genetics of childhood disorders should be expected to lead to new ways of organizing clinical data and syndromes. In the process of clinical inquiry, it will be particularly useful to study a range of childhood disorders in parallel or complementary studies. Pervasive developmental disorders, ADD, Tourette's syndrome, language disorders, and borderline syndrome, among others, share certain clinical features and yet have their own hallmarks. By comparing similarities and delineating differences between these disorders, using clinical and biological approaches, both the essential and nonspecific factors in vulnerability will be highlighted. Based on empirical findings, clinical research should aim at replacing syndromes such as ADD and borderline conditions, which reflect phenotypic profiles of developmental deviations, with more specific etiologies and more effective treatment.

REFERENCES

Alpert, J. E., Cohen, D. J., Shaywitz, B. A., Piccirillo, M., & Shaywitz, S. E. Animal models and childhood behavioral disturbances: Dopamine depletion in the newborn rat pup. *Journal of the American Academy of Child Psychiatry,* 1978, *17,* 239–251.

American Psychiatric Association. *Diagnostic and statistical manual of mental disorders* (3d ed). Washington, D.C.: American Psychiatric Association, 1980.

Anderson, G. M., Batter, D. K., Young, J. G., Shaywitz, B. A., & Cohen, D. J. Simplified liquid chromatographic electrochemical determination of norepinephrine and dopamine in rat brain. *Journal of Chromatography,* 1980, *181,* 453–455.

Andrulonis, P. A., Glueck, B. C., Stroebel, C. F., et al. Organic brain dysfunction and the borderline syndrome. *Psychiatric Clinics of North America,* 1981, *4,* 61–66.

Belendiuk, K., Freedman, D. X., Young, J. G., Sternstein, G., & Cohen, D. J. Hyperserotonemia in infantile autism. Submitted for publication, 1981.

Belmaker, R. H., Ebbesen, K., Ebstein, R., & Rimon, R. Platelet monoamine oxidase in schizophrenia and manic-depressive illness. *British Journal of Psychiatry,* 1976, *129,* 227–232.

Bender, L. Childhood schizophrenia. *Nervous Children,* 1942, *1,* 138–140.

Bond, E. P., & Partridge, C. E. Post-encephalic behavior disorders in boys and their management in a hospital. *American Journal of Psychiatry,* 1926, *6,* 25.

Bowers, M. B., Jr. Clinical measurements of central dopamine and 5-hydroxytryptamine metabolism: Reliability and interpretation of cerebrospinal fluid acid monoamine metabolite measures. *Neuropharmacology,* 1972, *11,* 101–111.

Butler, I. J., Koslow, S. H., Seifert, W. E., Caprioli, R. M., & Singer, H. S. Biogenic amine metabolism in Tourette's syndrome. *Annals of Neurology,* 1979, *6,* 37–39.

Cantwell, D. Psychiatric illness in the families of hyperactive children. *Archives of General Psychiatry,* 1972, *27,* 414.

Cantwell, D. P. Genetic studies of hyperactive children: Psychiatric illness in biologic and adopting parents. In R. R. Fieve, D. Rosenthal, & H. Brill (Eds.), *Genetic research in psychiatry.* Baltimore: Johns Hopkins University Press, 1975.

Caparulo, B. K., & Cohen, D. J. Developmental language studies in the neuropsychiatric disorders of childhood. In K. E. Nelson (Ed.), *Children's language.* New York: Gardner Press, 1982.

Cohen, D. J. The diagnostic process in child psychiatry. *Psychiatric Annals,* 1976, *6,* 404–416.

Cohen, D. J. Competence and biology: Methodology in studies of infants, twins, psychosomatic disease, and psychosis. In S. I. Harrison & J. F. McDermott, Jr. (Eds.), *New directions in childhood psychopathology: Developmental considerations* (Vol. 1). New York: International Universities Press, 1980a.

Cohen, D. J. The pathology of the self in primary childhood autism and Gilles de la Tourette syndrome. *Psychiatric Clinics of North America*, 1980b, *3*, 383–402.

Cohen, D. J., Caparulo, B. K., Shaywitz, B. A., & Bowers, M. B., Jr. Dopamine and serotonin metabolism in neuropsychiatrically disturbed children: CSF homovanillic acid and 5-hydroxyindoleacetic acid. *Archives of General Psychiatry*, 1977, *34*, 545–550.

Cohen, D. J., Caparulo, B. K., & Wetstone, H. The emergence of meanings and intentions. *Psychiatric Clinics of North America*, 1981, *4*, 489–508.

Cohen, D. J., Detlor, J., Shaywitz, B., & Leckman, J. F. Interaction of biological and psychological factors in the natural history of Tourette's syndrome: A paradigm for childhood neuropsychiatric disorders. In T. N. Chase & A. J. Friedhoff (Eds.), *Tourette's Syndrome*. New York: Raven Press, 1982.

Cohen, D. J., Detlor, J., Young, J., & Shaywitz, B. Clonidine ameliorates Gilles de la Tourette's syndrome. *Archives of General Psychiatry*, 1980a, *37*, 1350–1357.

Cohen, D., & Frank, R. Preadolescence: A critical phase of biological and psychological development. In D.V.S. Sankar (Ed.), *Mental Health in Children* (Vol. 1). Westbury, N.Y.: PJD Publications, Ltd., 1975.

Cohen, D. J., Shaywitz, B. A., Caparulo, B. K., Young, J. G., Bowers, M. Chronic, multiple tics of Gilles de la Tourette's disease: CSF acid monoamine metabolites after probenecid administration. *Archives of General Psychiatry*, 1978, *35*, 245–250.

Cohen, D. J., Shaywitz, B. A., Young, J. G., & Bowers, M. B., Jr. Cerebrospinal fluid monoamine metabolites in neuropsychiatric disorders of childhood. In J. H. Wood (Ed.), *Neurobiology of cerebrospinal fluid* (Vol. 1). New York: Plenum, 1980b.

Cohen, D. J., & Young, J. G. Neurochemistry and child psychiatry. *Journal of the American Academy of Child Psychiatry*, 1977, *16*, 353–411.

Cooper, J. R., Bloom, F. E., & Roth, R. H. *The biochemical basis of neuropharmacology* (3d ed.). New York: Oxford University Press, 1978.

Dibble, E. D., & Cohen, D. J. Personality development in identical twins: The first decade of life. *The Psychoanalytic Study of the Child*, 1981, *36*, 45–70.

Eastgate, S. M., Wright, J. J., & Werry, J. S. Behavioural effects of methylphenidate in 6-hydroxydopamine-treated neonatal rats. *Psychopharmacology*, 1978, *58*, 157.

Ebaugh, F. G. Neuropsychiatric sequelae of acute epidemic encephalitis in children. *American Journal of Diseases of Childhood*, 1923, *25*, 89.

Erinoff, L., MacPhail, R. C., Heller, A., & Seiden, L. S. Age-dependent effects of 6-hydroxydopamine on locomotor activity in the rat. *Brain Research*, 1979, *164*, 195.

Fish, B. Neurobiological antecedents of schizophrenia in children: Evidence for an inherited, congenital neurointegrative defect. *Archives of General Psychiatry*, 1977, *34*, 1297–1313.

Fish, B., & Ritvo, E. Psychoses of Childhood. In J. Noshpitz (Ed.), *Basic handbook of child psychiatry*. New York: Basic Books, 1979.

Freedman, L. S., Ohuchi, T., Goldstein, M., Axelrod, F., Fish, I., & Dancis, J. Changes in human serum dopamine-β-hydroxylase activity with age. *Nature*, 1972, *236*, 310–311.

Freud, A. The assessment of borderline cases. In *The writings of Anna Freud* (Vol. 4). New York: International Universities Press, 1969. (Originally published, 1956.)

Freud, A. Child analysis as the study of mental growth, normal and abnormal. In *The writings of Anna Freud* (Vol. 8). New York: International Universities Press, 1981.

Geleerd, E. R. Borderline states in childhood and adolescence. *The Psychoanalytic Study of the Child*, 1958, *13*, 279–295.

Goldenring, J. R., Wool, R. S., Shaywitz, B. A., Batter, D. K., Cohen, D. J., Young, J. G., & Teicher, M. H. Effects of continuous gastric infusion of food dyes on developing rat pups. *Life Sciences*, 1980, *27*, 1897–1904.

Goldfarb, W. *Childhood schizophrenia.* Cambridge: Harvard University Press, 1961.

Goodwin, F. K., Post, R. M., Dunner, D. L., & Gordon, E. K. Cerebrospinal fluid amine metabolites in affective illness: The probenecid technique. *American Journal of Psychiatry,* 1973, *130,* 73–79.

Gunderson, J., & Englund, D. W. Characterizing the families of borderlines. *Psychiatric Clinics of North America,* 1981, *4,* 159–168.

Hartocollis, P. The syndrome of minimal brain dysfunction in young adult patients. *Bulletin of the Menninger Clinic,* 1968, *32,* 102–104.

Hohman, L. B. Post encephalitic behavior disorders in children. *Johns Hopkins Bulletin,* 1922, *380,* 372.

Hunt, R., Cohen, D. J., Shaywitz, S., & Shaywitz, B. A. Strategies for study of the neurochemistry of attention deficit disorder in children. *Schizophrenia Bulletin,* 1982.

Leckman, J. F., & Maas, J. Preliminary characterization of plasma MHPG in man. In J. W. Maas (Ed.), *MHPG and psychopathology.* New York: Academic Press, 1982.

Lycke, E., & Roos, B. F. Influence of changes in brain monoamine metabolism on behavior of herpes simplex-infected mice. *Journal of Neurological Sciences,* 1974, *22,* 277.

Lycke, E., & Roos, B. F. Virus infections in infant mice causing persistent impairment of turnover of brain catecholamines. *Journal of Neurological Sciences,* 1975, *26,* 49.

Maas, J. W., Hattox, S. E., Landis, D. J., & Roth, R. H. The determination of a brain arteriovenous difference for 3-methoxy-4-hydroxyphenethyleneglycol (MHPG). *Brain Research,* 1976, *118,* 167–173.

Mahler, M. S. On child psychosis and schizophrenia. *The Psychoanalytic Study of the Child,* 1952, *7,* 286–305.

Mahler, M. S. A study of the separation-individuation process and its possible application to the borderline phenomena in the psychoanalytic situation. *The Psychoanalytic Study of the Child,* 1971, *26,* 403–424.

McGeer, E. G., & McGeer, P. L. Some characteristics of brain tyrosine hydroxylase. In A. J. Mandell (Ed.), *New concepts in neurotransmitter redulation.* London: Plenum, 1973.

McKendrick, T., & Edwards, R. W. The excretion of 4-hydroxy-3-methoxy-mandelic acid in children. *Archives of Diseases of Children,* 1965, *40,* 418–425.

Moir, A. T. B., Ashcroft, G. W., Crawford, T. B. B., Eccleston, D., & Guilberg, H. C. Cerebral metabolites in cerebrospinal fluid as a biochemical approach to the brain. *Brain,* 1970, *93,* 357–368.

Morrison, J., & Stewart, M. A family study of hyperactive child syndrome. *Biological Psychiatry,* 1971, *3,* 189–195.

Morrison, J., & Stewart, M. The psychiatric status of the legal families of adopted hyperactive children. *Archives of General Psychiatry,* 1973, *28,* 888.

Murphy, D. L. Animal models for human psychopathology: Observations from the vantage point of clinical psychopharmacology. In G. Serban & A. Kling (Eds.), *Animal models in human psychobiology.* New York: Plenum, 1976.

O'Leary, S. G., & Pelham, W. E. Behavior therapy and withdrawal of stimulant medication in hyperactive children. *Pediatrics,* 1978, *61,* 211.

Pearson, D. E., Teicher, M. H., Shaywitz, B. A., Cohen, D. J., Young, J. G., & Anderson, G. M. Environmental influences on body weight and behavior in developing rats after neonatal 6-hydroxydopamine. *Science,* 1980, *209,* 515–717.

Pine, F. On the concept "borderline" in children: A clinical essay. *The Psychoanalytic Study of the Child,* 1974, *29,* 341–368.

Rapoport, J. L., Buchsbaum, B. S., Weingartner, H., Zahn, T. P., Ludlow, C., & Mikkelsen, E. Dextroamphetamine: Its cognitive and behavior effects in normal and hyperactive boys and normal men. *Archives of General Psychiatry,* 1980, *37,* 933–943.

Rapoport, J. L., Buchsbaum, M. S., & Zahn, T. P., et al. Dextroamphetamine: Cognitive and behavioral effects in normal prepubertal boys. *Science,* 1978, *199,* 560–563.

Rapoport, J. L., Quinn, P. O., & Lamprecht, F. Minor physical anomalies and plasma dopamine beta hydroxylase activity in hyperactive boys. *American Journal of Psychiatry*, 1974, *131*, 386.

Robinson, D. S., & Nies, A. Demographic, biologic, and other variables affecting monoamine oxidase activity. *Schizophrenia Bulletin*, 1980, *6*, 298–307.

Robinson, D. S., Sourkes, T. L., Nies, A., Harris, S., Spector, S., Bartlett, D. L., & Kay, I. S. Monoamine metabolism in human brain. *Archives of General Psychiatry*, 1977, *34*, 89–92.

Safer, D. J. A familial factor in minimal brain dysfunction. *Behavior Genetics*, 1973, *3*, 175.

Satterfield, J. H., Cantwell, D. P., & Satterfield, B. T. Multimodality treatment: A one year follow-up of 84 hyperactive boys. *Archives of General Psychiatry*, 1979, *36*, 965.

Shapiro, T. The borderline syndrome in children: A critique. In K. S. Robson (Ed.), *The borderline child: Approaches to etiology, diagnosis, and treatment*. New York: McGraw-Hill, 1983.

Shaywitz, B. A., Klopper, J. H., & Gordon, J. W. Methylphenidate in 6-hydroxydopamine treated developing rat pups. *Archives of Neurology*, 1978, *35*, 463.

Shaywitz, B. A., Yager, R. D., & Klopper, J. H. Selective brain dopamine depletion in developing rats: An experimental model of minimal brain dysfunction. *Science*, 1976b, *191*, 305.

Shaywitz, B. A., Klopper, J. H., Yager, R. D., & Gordon, J. W. Paradoxical response to amphetamine in developing rats treated with 6-hydroxydopamine. *Nature*, 1976a, *261*, 153–155.

Shaywitz, B. A., & Pearson, D. E. Effects of phenobarbital on activity and learning in 6-hydroxydopamine treated rat pups. *Pharmacology, Biochemistry, and Behavior*, 1978, *9*, 173.

Shaywitz, B. A., Cohen, D. J., & Shaywitz, S. E. New diagnostic terminology for minimal brain dysfunction. *Journal of Pediatrics*, 1979a, *95*, 734–736.

Shaywitz, B. A., Goldenring, J. R., & Wool, R. S. Effects of chronic administration of food colorings on activity levels and cognitive performance in developing rat pups treated with 6-hydroxydopamine. *Neurobehavioral Toxicology*, 1979b, *1*, 41–47.

Shaywitz, B. A., Cohen, D. J., & Bowers, M. B., Jr. Cerebrospinal fluid monoamine metabolites in neurological disorders of childhood. In J. H. Wood (Ed.), *Neurobiology of Cerebrospinal Fluid* (Vol. 1). New York: Plenum, 1980.

Shaywitz, B. A., Cohen, D. J., Leckman, J. F., Young, J. G., & Bowers, M. B., Jr. Ontogeny of dopamine and serotonin metabolites in the cerebrospinal fluid of children with neurological disorders. *Developmental Medicine and Child Neurology*, 1980, *22*, 748–754.

Shaywitz, S. E., Cohen, D. J., & Shaywitz, B. A. The biochemical basis of minimal brain dysfunction. *Journal of Pediatrics*, 1978, *92*, 179–187.

Shekim, W. O., Dekirmenjian, H., Chapel, J. L., Javaid, J., & Davis, J. M. Norepinephrine metabolism and clinical response to dextroamphetamine in hyperactive boys. *Journal of Pediatrics*, 1979, *95*, 389–394.

Shetty, T., & Chase, T. N. Central monoamines and hyperkinesis of childhood. *Neurology*, 1976, *26*, 1000.

Smith, R. D., Cooper, B. R., & Breese, G. R. Growth and behavioral changes in developing rats treated intracisternally with 6-hydroxydopamine: Evidence for involvement of brain dopamine. *Journal of Pharmacology and Experimental Therapeutics*, 1973, *185*, 609–619.

Sorenson, C. A., Vayer, J. S., & Goldberg, C. S. Amphetamine reduction of motor activity in rats after neonatal administration of 6-hydroxydopamine. *Biological Psychiatry*, 1977, *12*, 133.

Stoof, J. C., Dijkstra, H., & Hillegers, J. P. M. Changes in the behavioral response to a novel environment following lesioning of the central dopaminergic system in rat pups. *Psychopharmacology*, 1978, *57*, 163.

Vela, R., Gottlieb, H., Gottlieb, E. Borderline syndromes in childhood. In K. S. Robson (Ed.), *The borderline child: Approaches to etiology, diagnosis, and treatment*. New York: McGraw-Hill, 1983.

Weil, A. M. Certain severe disturbances of ego development in childhood. *The Psychoanalytic Study of the Child,* 1953, *8,* 271–287.

Weinshilboum, R., Raymond, F. A., & Weidman, W. H. Serum dopamine-3-hydroxylase activity: Sibling-sibling correlation. *Science,* 1973, *181,* 943–945.

Wender, P. M. *Minimal brain dysfunction in children.* New York: Wiley, 1971.

Wender, P. M. Minimal brain dysfunction: An overview. In M. A. Lipton, A. DiMascio, & K. F. Killam (Eds.), *Psychopharmacology: A generation in progress.* New York: Raven Press, 1978.

Wender, P. M., Epstein, R. S., Kopin, I. J., & Gordon, E. K. Urinary monoamine metabolites in children with minimal brain dysfunction. *American Journal of Psychiatry,* 1971, *127,* 1411.

Willerman, L. Activity level and hyperactivity in twins. *Child Development,* 1973, *44,* 288.

Youdim, M. G. H., Collins, G. G. S., Snadler, M., Bevan Jones, A. B., Pare, C. M. B., & Nicholson, W. J. Human brain monoamine oxidase: Multiple forms and selective inhibitors. *Nature,* 1972, *236,* 225.

Young, J. G., & Cohen, D. J. The molecular biology of development. In J. D. Noshpitz (Ed.), *Basic handbook of child psychiatry* (Vol. 1). New York: Basic Books, 1979.

Young, J. G., Cohen, D. J., Anderson, G. A., & Shaywitz, B. A. Neurotransmitter ontogeny as a perspective for studies of child development and pathology. In B. Shopsin & L. Greenhill (Eds.), *The psychobiology of childhood: A profile of current issues.* New York: Spectrum, 1982a.

Young, J. G., Cohen, D. J., Caparulo, B. K., Brown, S.-L., & Maas, J. W. Decreased 24-hour urinary MHPG in childhood autism. *American Journal of Psychiatry,* 1979, *136,* 1055–1057.

Young, J. G., Cohen, D. J., Shaywitz, B. A., Anderson, G. M., & Maas, J. W. Clinical studies of MHPG in childhood and adolescence. In J. W. Maas (Ed.), *MHPG and psychopathology.* New York: Academic Press, 1982b.

Young, J. G., Cohen, D. J., Waldo, M. C., Feiz, R., & Roth, J. A. Platelet monoamine oxidase activity in children and adolescents with psychiatric disorders. *Schizophrenia Bulletin,* 1980, *6,* 324–333.

Issues in the Psychotherapy of Borderline Conditions in Children

Paulina Kernberg, M.D.
DIRECTOR, CHILD AND ADOLESCENT PSYCHIATRY
THE NEW YORK HOSPITAL, CORNELL MEDICAL CENTER
WESTCHESTER DIVISION
ASSOCIATE PROFESSOR OF PSYCHIATRY
CORNELL UNIVERSITY MEDICAL COLLEGE
NEW YORK, N.Y.

THIS CHAPTER PRESENTS an overview of the treatment of borderline personality organization in children with particular emphasis on individual psychoanalytic psychotherapy.

TREATMENT CONSIDERATIONS

A major goal in the treatment of all borderline children is the resolution of primitive defense patterns with the establishment of integrated and stable self- and object representations. The achievement of individuation in turn strengthens the ego. Also important are the attainment of reliable reality testing, facilitation of sublimatory channels, and the increased external adjustment. To increase their tolerance for affects, especially anxiety and depression, is another goal.

At latency age, the borderline child's failure to achieve a sense of self and role identity stands out. Unlike normal latency-age children, they do not show improved impulse control with predictable ego states, nor is there increased independence from parents with a relative growth in importance of peers. These children, for the most part, do not openly enjoy peer interaction or competitive games. Awareness of the world at large, understanding of birth and death issues, and the sense of belonging to an extended collective community are all greatly restricted.

SEPARATION-INDIVIDUATION DIFFICULTIES

As we have seen, many authors place the origins of borderline conditions in the separation-individuation phase, in particular the rapprochement crisis. Settlage (1977) has underlined the importance of this phase in normal development, and his observations carry implications for understanding and empathizing with the reenactment of derivatives of this phase in the therapeutic interaction. According to Settlage, the mirroring function of the mother entails: (1) interest in the child's developing skills, (2) attribution of meaning to the child's activities, (3) sharing power, (4) affirmation of the child's expanding sense of self and identity, (5) validation of the child's continuing importance to the mother, (6) acceptance and management of the child's urges, (7) being available when needed, and (8) tolerance for regression, as well as for the child's increasing autonomy. Each of these components of mirroring is also an important function of the therapist as he or she enables the patient to become aware of early wishes and needs through verbalization.

With the young child, it is possible to handle problems in separating from the mother in a way that differs technically from work with adolescents, where family therapy is sometimes indicated. The task is to resolve the pathological clinging, shadowing, and darting away through joint work with the mother-child pair. More often than not the pathological attachment to the mother belies an asymmetrical symbiosis-like relationship, in which the child may be much more ready to leave the mother than the mother is to leave the child. In working with the mother-child dyad, the therapist systematically explores and brings out the anxiety around individuation—the fears of abandonment and total loss or annihilation. These fears need to be verbalized by both the mother and the child and to be empathized with by the therapist. In this way, the separation-individuation process may be allowed to proceed toward self- and object constancy.

The following vignette describes this approach with a six-year-old child, suffering from an elevator phobia, who was reluctant to come to the office without his mother. At first, neither the child nor his mother took off their coats while visiting the therapist. Whenever the child began to play, the mother turned her back, yawned, fell asleep, or threatened to leave the room. Frequently they were absent from the sessions. As the threat of intrusion by the therapist increased, this was verbalized and dealt with openly. Eventually the mother agreed to participate in the sessions.

Through his play the child portrayed the various difficulties in separation. In one session, for example, he initially left the therapist outside, in the corridor, while he and his mother entered the room. Then he allowed the therapist to come into the room. Next, he himself remained outside while the therapist went into the room with his mother. Later on, he put a chair at the threshold of the door and asked the therapist to sit there; then he himself sat there. In the next session, he left the mother alone inside the room, checking on her from time to time. He then went to the elevator, threw some pieces of paper inside, and asked the therapist to step into the elevator while he waited outside. Later, he took elevator rides while the therapist waited outside in the lobby.

Slowly and painfully, both mother and child had a second chance, under the facilitating influence of the therapist, to work through the vicissitudes of separation-individuation.

COMPLICATIONS OF MINIMAL BRAIN DYSFUNCTION

The importance of identifying possible MBD impairments in treating border-line children and adolescent patients cannot be stressed enough, for it allows the clinician to combine the necessary pharmacological, educational, and psychotherapeutic interventions. Target symptoms can then be chosen for psychopharmacological treatment, in conjunction with a focused psychotherapeutic approach.[1] More generally, the patient must be informed about his or her deficits and learn to accommodate to them. By becoming conscious of and accepting these particular limitations, the patient will be less prone to anxiety and depression and may begin to establish better contact with peers and relevant adults. In conjunction with this, working with the parents to acquaint them with the child's particular difficulties may facilitate their empathic responses. This approach complements quite well the approach used to deal with conflict-based difficulties, namely, work in the here-and-now, interpretation of primitive defense mechanisms and negative transference, and the provision of external structure in cases of acting out.

Here it is interesting that Frosch (1971) and Greenson (1954) intuitively arrived at the need to work psychotherapeutically not only with these patients' conflicts but also with clarifying their perceptions and attitudes toward the therapist's interventions. What these two psychoanalysts propose may be a *must*, given that the patient's distorted perceptions of the therapist may be due not only to resistance but also to difficulties in attention and memory, as well as in perceiving social interactions—all hallmarks of the MBD syndrome.

Discontinuities in the perception of the object further facilitate the use of splitting. For instance, an object may be realistically perceived as different if it is presented from different angles; there may be no capacity to abstract common features. Here the advantage of a psychoanalytically oriented approach lies in the therapist's use of both observation and empathy to elucidate some of the perplexing manifestations of MBD and its possible contributions to borderline functioning.

AN OUTLINE OF TECHNICAL CONSIDERATIONS

The treatment approach we are advocating is a multimodal one with attention both to the child and to the environment. It may, for instance, be necessary to work directly with the family to provide a stable and predictable home life and correct pathogenic intrafamilial interactions supporting splitting projection and denial.

If these arrangements do not suffice to contain the child's destructive behavior towards self and others, a day hospital or inpatient setting are

---

[1]Imipramine, for instance, may be effective for both depression and MBD (see Petti, 1981). A trial methylphenidate or dextroamphetamine may be indicated for a child who is hyperactive and destructive.

indicated—the latter especially in the case of suicidal behavior, runaway behavior, severe school refusal accompanied by regression, anorexia, or lack of minimal family support. Individual psychotherapy with the child can then take place within this structured environment.

The psychoanalytically oriented psychotherapy takes place two or three times a week for a minimum of one to two years. The play materials should be simple and lend themselves to gross motor activities—sponge balls, bowling equipment—or to fantasy play—dolls, soldiers, puppets, superheroes, rubber monsters of all kinds. Games and videogames are much less useful because they do not promote person-to-person interaction or the elaboration of primitive dissociated fantasies into the fantasy life of play and creativity.

The psychoanalytically oriented psychotherapy with the child involves a number of special considerations.

1. Stress should be placed on the here-and-now. It is important that the child become aware of the actual ongoing interactions with the therapist. One can foster the child's reality-testing capacity and minimize distortions, as well as increase the necessary affective convictions about interpretations. Specifically, one should continually test these children's perceptions and their use of what they perceive in terms of the reality of the therapist's actions and verbal interventions. Despite these patients' tendency to distort reality through their use of primitive defense mechanisms, one must always remember that they do in fact have the capacity to test reality; in this respect, the therapist acts as an observing ego. Fantasy distortions need to be verbalized and shared to allow for secondary-process reasoning. It is through identification with the therapist's capacity to tolerate these primitive fantasies that the patient comes to feel less anxiety, while he develops the capacity to express them through play, dreams, or daydreams.

2. Working with the lack of ego and superego integration requires thorough discussion of contradictory behaviors in the therapeutic interaction. Splitting should be dealt with when it occurs within the session, as well as by contrasting information received from outside to what is observed in the session itself.

If the child is an outpatient, ongoing contact with the parents and/or joint family play sessions to assess nonverbal interactions are indicated.

Family work should aim at supporting and clarifying generational and sex boundaries and roles. This is needed for the parental couple to be able to include the siblings while maintaining their tie as a couple. We have observed that parents of borderline children more frequently relate to the children as siblings or as if they were single, that is, the mother or father relates to the child to the exclusion of the other parent.

If the patient is hospitalized, the therapist works alongside the interdisciplinary team which also receives impressions of the various splittings of the patient-self and object world. With direct information from the staff of their different perceptions of the patient, the therapist integrates and *synthesizes* them. Team meetings with the child to discuss everyday interactions can prove quite useful in working against splitting and other primitive defense mechanisms. The therapist's role is in turn important to keep the team aware of the patient's projections onto the staff which occur in subtle ways, making the staff feel anxious or hopeless about the patient while the latter keeps "cool" and challenging, for example.

3. With borderline children, one must recognize that the self-representation, although allowing for the separateness of the object, is not yet integrated. For instance, a seven-and-a-half-year-old boy was loving and friendly on Mondays and Wednesdays but a whining tyrant on Saturdays (when he was brought by his parents instead of his housekeeper). He grinned, saying, "You don't know what I am like on Tuesdays and Thursdays"! In such cases, making for the continuity and integration of the self-representation is an ongoing task which takes place both through the containment offered by the sessions and through verbalization of the contradictory self-images.

4. Another focus is work on the superego directly. While one child with superego lacunae was playing pick-up-sticks, I asked him to watch whether he moved the sticks to see if he could tell me whether he had moved the sticks before I said anything. I could thus evaluate the functioning of his conscience by the promptness of his reports; at the same time, I challenged him to check whether my conscience was working better or worse than his. This game was a very concrete way of practicing superego functions.

5. The borderline child's lack of empathy for others is reflected in poor peer relations. In the therapeutic context, it is important to articulate what is happening to the relationship at all points, as if the therapist were an actual playmate. While there are certainly countertransference risks in doing this, it is extremely useful in enabling the child to begin to work on social skills. Activity groups may beneficially be added for this purpose.

6. The negative effects of the not-infrequent incidents of overt maternal rejection must be clarified and understood by the child in the attempt to sort out reality, fantasy, and the implications for perceptions of self and mother.

7. Borderline children's perceptions of different aspects of the maternal relationship, such as their expectations of unpredictability or rejection, should also be explained. Frequently these patients need to assess their parents' reality, including the parents' limitations as separate from themselves. In that way, they can come to grips with the parental environment without feeling that they are the cause or the victims of it. This is particularly crucial in work with children who come from chaotic home environments. Grief for family deficits should be dealt with in therapy.

8. The various vicissitudes of pathological symbiosis and the conflicts around differentiation, practicing, and rapprochement need to be dealt with as they unfold in the transference. These difficulties correspond to the so-called pre-Oedipal conflicts around issues of trust or distrust, remaining the same or becoming different, shadowing or darting away, coercing or being coerced, autonomy or dependence, being a boy or a girl or an undifferentiated neuter. These conflicts, their attendant anxieties (e.g., annihilation fears), and the primitive defenses (e.g., projection, denial, and splitting) should be spelled out in the treatment in the same way that neurotic conflicts with neurotic defenses are in less severe psychopathology. Anxiety is marked in these children and needs to be articulated in terms of their omnipotent and magical fantasy thinking.

9. Any potentially disruptive experience needs to be anticipated and verbalized, since these children lack signal anxiety and thus are easily overwhelmed. Moves, hospitalizations, and impending parental divorces should be discussed as early as possible.

10. Borderline children may need help with their body ego. Those children with MBD or other handicaps need to recognize the nature of their handicap, their thoughts about it, and its implications for their functioning and their self-esteem.

By talking realistically about the child's deficit, the therapist enables the child to acknowledge it, to share the knowledge with a trusted person, and to grieve. The child can then elaborate and resolve the fantasy systems in connections with the deficit. These fantasies usually are concerned with guilt or the child's feeling of being defective. They have thus contributed to the child's low self-esteem. Such a child needs to learn how to compensate for the deficit by using intact capacities.

11. As borderline children are prone to various somatizations because of their dissociative tendencies and splitting, their use of body language needs to be clarified to them.

12. Lack of impulse control seems to be a hallmark of borderline functioning, as well as instability in the levels of ego organization. What is important, however, is that this lack of control, as in adults (Kernberg, 1975), may not necessarily represent an ego defect in the sense of lack of capacity to control, but may be used defensively to control anxiety. Clarification and interpretation of the *purposes* of these reactions may resolve what only seemingly appear as ego defects.

CASE ILLUSTRATION

N., the older of two siblings, came for consultation at the age of seven-and-a-half after one year of treatment with a psychiatrist who saw him on a twice-weekly basis, in addition to seeing the mother once a week. His previous psychotherapy had emphasized the verbalization of feelings to such an extent that he had been forbidden to play while in the treatment setting. He became worse. By the time he came to consultation, he suffered from severe separation anxiety marked by an inability to sleep in his own room and an inability to be left alone day or night. In addition, N. had no friends. Peer interaction was so bad that he was shunned by everybody in his elementary school. A school transfer was necessary because he was continually scapegoated and called names. N. refused to bathe, put on his clothes backwards, and chewed his shirts. He presented occasional soiling and swallowed his nasal mucus as a matter of habit. He was depressed and moody. Although he was doing well academically in his new school, he frequently talked about suicide, about trying to get himself run over by a car, getting himself asphyxiated, taking pills, or falling off a building—all to the great distress of his parents.

There was severe marital tension between his parents, a professional couple. At the time of my consultation with the patient, they were talking about divorce, although they kept this from the child.

N. had been a planned child and an unusually "lovely baby." At the age of two years, two months, however, he had been seen by a specialist for developmental evaluation, as he showed accelerated development in certain areas and retardation in others. His verbal functions, including vocabulary, comprehension, and complexity of speech were quite advanced (as measured by the Bailey Scales and Stanford-Binet). In these areas he at times scored as high as three years. His perceptual and visual motor coordination (measured by form boards and similar tasks) were also accelerated. On tasks involving fine motor coordination, as well as items requiring prolonged attention, patience, and willingness to engage in activities not of his own choosing, his performance was more at the normal level. In contrast, his gross motor-control coordination was not well-developed. He encountered difficulty in adapting his movement to different spatial configurations. For example, when his foot got caught beneath the walking board, despite earnest efforts he did not know to free it. Nor did he know how to put his arms into the proper sleeves of his coat.

Although his intellectual ability placed him in the superior range, he differed from the majority of two-year-olds in the way he used his abilities. His special interest in letters, shapes, writing, and reading was unusual, but from a developmental point of view it was as much a liability as an asset. For one thing, his central nervous system had not matured to the point at which integrated and adaptive use of reading, writing and even phonetic spelling could take place. He wrote with his left hand, reversed letters, and proceeded from right to left as well as vertically and randomly on the page. There was no clear-cut dominance with respect to a right/left preference of feet or eyes. In addition, certain features of N.'s behavior directly reflected tension and pressure. His writing and reciting of letters, for instance, became increasingly intense and erratic as his excitement mounted; the very fact that he turned to these activities when he was displeased or mildly frustrated for any reason indicated more than optimal tension.

Much could be said about N.'s disproportionate interest in shapes. It was as though he selectively perceived the form of the word at the expense of its functional meaning. In other words, he abstracted and conceptualized his environment to such a degree that his response to things did not match the perceptions and interests of other children. For him, blocks were primarily columns, triangles, and the like, or a means of constructing letters. While for other children blocks do have this property, they are primarily potential houses, tunnels, or whatever. Nor was N. able to use board games or rhythmic movement for imaginative play, although he could use them if these activities were supported by another person.

In summary, N. showed precocity and age-appropriate development in certain areas. Yet lags in physical, social, and emotional development created an imbalance and made ego adaption more difficult. He responded strongly to certain kinds of sensory and cognitive stimulation, but to what extent that illustrated special vulnerability could not be assessed at the time. Already at two years, two months, he was considered to be at risk.

After his lack of response to treatment as a six-year-old, N. started at seven-and-a-half on a three-times-a-week basis with me. The parents received counseling every two or three weeks, a necessary course of action as this was a typical case of alternating parental neglect and indulgence. Another issue addressed was the parents' belief that the children could be protected from their marital tension by their secretiveness. For instance, part of N.'s insomnia stemmed from his overconcern about trying to keep his parents together and his conflicts about that issue. (The father would watch until he fell asleep.)

N. began therapy in a rather apprehensive mood. During the first session, he expressed his regret about not being allowed to play during the sessions; he thought I would treat him in the same way as his previous therapist. I clarified this by saying that I wanted to get to know him so that I could make him understand his worries—it didn't matter whether he did this by talking or playing. He then proceeded in the first few sessions to build a city with blocks. In the first version, the city contained a very narrow house which one could hardly get into and a saloon next door with a man watching through the window and a police truck in it. The second version included a wider, much more comfortable house in which two people could live, and a helicopter entering a garage. The man in the saloon continued to watch through the window, but sometimes he came to the house to "relax." These, indeed, were the first indications of a therapeutic alliance with the therapist.

I shall now describe a period of particular interest in some detail. For several sessions, we had played "Monopoly," which I interpreted as his way of controlling the amount of things we could say or do. As he was setting up the pieces, he spontaneously remarked that he had tried to go to sleep between 8:30 and 9:30 P.M. the night before, but that he had had to wait for three hours before his father came to his room to put him to bed. (Having his own bedroom was a new development, initiated at my suggestion.) I mentioned to N. that I felt that he needed to see that he could fall asleep on his own and that his father or mother could only help him by keeping him company in the beginning. In turn, he replied that his father had been watching TV, but when his father came he could fall asleep; he did not need to have his father all night. His father could "go" once he fell asleep. "What happens when he doesn't come?" I asked. Here N. mentioned seeing ghosts in the room. I wondered what they looked like. Well, according to N., they had see-saw mouths, dark eyes, were all black, and they could stretch like chewing gum. When I asked him whether they were men or women, he answered they were women ghosts. This response made me wonder where his mother was in all this. He said that his mother was playing with the housekeeper, working on crossword puzzles. N. paused and then added, "It makes me feel sad that she would prefer the puzzles better than me." I then interpreted that he was probably afraid to be angry at her because she might really leave him. Instead he made up these ghosts to be angry at. But he forgot that the ghosts were pretend and started thinking that the ghosts were angry at him, which of course frightened him. I then said that he was hoping his mother would come, sticking to this wish year after year, not giving up. He wanted her to be available to him when he needed her, and it was hard and painful to see when she failed to do that. What was so hard to accept was that she didn't come of her own wishes. He said then that he was finished with his mother and wanted to play "Monopoly."

At the end of the session, N. went through the back door and asked me for the first time to count until he whistled, indicating that his housekeeper was there to accompany him, which I did. I told him that if he didn't find the housekeeper he could come back. He ventured into the relatively dark part of the patio, hopping along without fear, and did not need to return.

N.'s mother acknowledged that she had never had a moment of peace with N. since the birth of his sibling when N. was two years old. N. had become so controlling, demanding, clinging, and negativistic that on many occasions she had told him she would send him away or that she would leave the home, and she did so from time to time.

Comment During the session, I provided continuity through the playing of "Monopoly." N. had displaced his wish for someone to put him to sleep onto the father instead of the mother. (In fact, he had said that should his parents divorce, he would prefer to go with his father.) I then observed that he had a hallucinatory experience with his ghosts. Knowing that he had the capacity to test reality, I insisted on his elaborating on this experience and sharing his thoughts with me. When I reacted to his fanstasy with interest and without anxiety, his primary-process thinking could be replaced by secondary-process thinking. Specifically, I asked him where his mother was in all this, and he indicated what he was defending himself against, namely, his depressed feeling about being second in importance to his mother's doing puzzles. After I interpreted that he did this with his ghosts, I became the target of the transference, namely, the mother of the rapproachement crisis. He was then able to ask me, not his father or anybody else, to accompany him— symbolically—fulfilling his wish, without coercion, that I be available to him. He refueled by looking back briefly on his way out, but he could go through the dark part of the patio without any help, hopping along with an increased sense of autonomy and less anxiety. Joint sessions with him and his mother were later instituted to deal with the stalemate of their relationship and his grief for it, work which is still in process but which has had a positive effect on his depression and on the disappearance of a number of symptoms.

SUMMARY

Therapeutic intervention requires a careful assessment of organic and psychological determinants in order to institute an appropriate treatment plan. This is particularly important in children with borderline personality organization because of the frequent association of MBD and depression.

I am recommending a type of psychoanalytic psychotherapy that focuses on clarification and confrontation in the areas of transference, external reality, and the communicative process between therapist and patient. This includes making the child cognizant of his or her organic deficits, if any.

The interpretation of primitive defense mechanisms includes clarification by verbalizing their functions and the purposes for their use. The particular role of the therapist in facilitating the resolution of conflicts deriving from the separation-individuation stage are all important facets of this psychotherapeutic approach.

R E F E R E N C E S

Frosch, J. Techniques in regard to some specific ego deficits in the treatment of borderline patients. *Psychoanalytic Quarterly,* 1971, *45,* 216–220.

Greenson, R. R. The struggle against identification. *Journal of the American Psychoanalytical Association,* 1954, *2,* 200–217.

Kernberg, O. *Borderline conditions and pathological narcissism.* New York: Jason Aronson, 1975.

Petti, A. T. Imipramine treatment of borderline children: Case reports with a controlled study. *American Journal of Psychiatry,* (1981), *138,* 515–518.

Settlage, C. F., The psychoanalytic understanding of narcissistic and borderline personalities: Advances in developmental theory. *Journal of the American Psychoanalytical Association,* 1977, *25,* 805–833.

CHAPTER 10

Psychopharmacologic Treatment of Borderline Children

Theodore A. Petti, M.D.

ASSOCIATE PROFESSOR OF CHILD PSYCHIATRY
UNIVERSITY OF PITTSBURGH SCHOOL OF MEDICINE
DIRECTOR, CHILD AND YOUTH SECTION
OFFICE OF EDUCATION AND REGIONAL PROGRAMMING
WESTERN PSYCHIATRIC INSTITUTE & CLINIC
PITTSBURGH, PENNSYLVANIA

PREVIOUS CHAPTERS IN THIS BOOK have detailed current concepts regarding nosology, etiology, diagnosis, and treatment of the borderline child. This chapter attempts to synthesize material concerning psychopharmacologic approaches to treating borderline symptomatology and symptom complexes in children. Issues concerned with the psychopharmacologic treatment of borderline adults are addressed as they relate to specific categories of psychotropic agents in order to provide a sense of continuity with the adult syndromes. Stone (1980) provides a most comprehensive overview of the adult borderline syndromes but devotes little attention to pharmacologic therapies. One explanation for this oversight may be that past diagnoses of borderline disorders in both children and adults were most often made with a predominant affinity for psychoanalytic, rather than biological, conceptions of psychopathology. A second may be that many borderline schizophrenic (schizotypal) patients have been considered schizophrenic and treated accordingly.

The literature to date is virtually nonexistent regarding psychopharmacologic interventions with borderline children. Lewis (1976) suggests that medication, when coupled with intensive psychotherapy and milieu therapy, might alleviate the deterioration seen in some borderline children. Rinsley (1980) briefly reviews the unsettled nature of child psychopharmacology and the failure of our knowledge concerning borderline and narcissistic disorders in children and adolescents. He offers the following generalizations about such children.

1. Those with "attention deficit disorder" (DSM-III), "minimal brain dysfunction," or "hyperkinetic reaction" often respond to psychomotor stimulants and a smaller number of phenothiazines.

2. Those with "separation anxiety disorder" to imipramine.

3. Those with "chronic motor tic disorder" (Gilles de la Tourette's Syndrome) to Haldol.

4. Those with multiple symptoms show differential response to the range of antipsychotic and antidepressant (tricyclic and MAO inhibitor) medications, depending on the predominant symptomatology.

Petti and Unis (1981) provide a short overview of the related literature and three case descriptions with a controlled single case study of the use of imipramine in the treatment of borderline children. The use of medications has been briefly addressed for children identified as borderline psychotic and fitting into either Schizotypal or Borderline Personality DSM-III, Axis II Disorders (Petti & Law, 1981).

236

Symptoms that have been commonly described for borderline children include the following: anxiety, neurotic symptomatology, impulsivity, and deviant character traits (Chethik, 1979). Other symptoms frequently associated include borderline psychotic or micropsychotic episodes, aggressive outbursts, masochistic behavior, uneven cognitive development, bizarre behavior and depression (Petti & Unis, 1981). (These are described throughout other chapters of this book.) Because so few studies directly address the psychopharmacologic treatment of borderline children, and because diagnostic criteria are just being formulated, the following chapter discusses the use of medications for symptoms similar to those commonly reported in borderline psychotic children. Each section is devoted to a specific class of drugs and to its use with related childhood and adult disorders.

ANXIOLYTIC AGENTS (MINOR TRANQUILIZERS)

Anxiety, often of panic dimensions, frequently occurs in borderline children. Various psychotropic agents have been recommended for the treatment of anxiety in children, but the targeted anxiety is usually assumed as the etiology for diverse symptomatology (Gittelman-Klein, 1978; Petti et al., 1981). Anxiety has been inferred as the underlying cause of behavior disorders, "neurotic" disorders, sleep disturbance, and school phobia. Koch et al. (1976) illustrate this point in their treatment and broad definition of anxiety for twenty-five children newly admitted to a university hospital who were of diverse diagnoses.

Drugs used to treat anxiety include, but are not limited to, the following classes: anxiolytic (chlordiazepoxide, diazepam, dipotassium chlorazepate); antihistaminic (diphenhydramine); sedative-hypnotics (phenobarbitol, meprobamate); tricyclic antidepressants (imipramine/Tofranil, amitriptyline/Elavil) and the major tranquilizers (Thorazine, Stelazine, Haldol). Though the benzodiazepines have been among the most widely prescribed psychotropics for children and adolescents, recent pronouncements note that they be limited to symptoms suggestive of anxiety (Silver, 1979) or that they have dubious value in treating the emotional disorders of children (Greenblatt & Shader, 1974). However, Gittelman-Klein (1978) notes that the benzodiazepines may be underrated as antianxiety agents for children because clinical reports consistently depict their positive effect on uncomplicated (neurotic) children with uncomplicated anxiety disorders.

Skynner (1961), in contrast, describes the effective use of chlordiazepoxide in children with school refusal and other forms of separation anxiety based on hypothesized repressed hostility and anxiety, phobic and obsessional states, withdrawn children, and children who are paranoid and masochistic. Skynner believes that the effect of chlordiazepoxide is to reduce the intensity of hostile and aggressive feelings so that they are rendered acceptable to conscious awareness. However, he cautions that children who are already hyperactive, rebellious, impulsive, or antisocial demonstrate an increase in their undesirable behavior and overt aggression.

In a small, double-blind, controlled crossover pilot study, Petti et al. (1981) have demonstrated statistically significant improvement in language production and affect during treatment with chlordiazepoxide as compared to placebo. The children were noted to become less depressed, anxious, or hostile, as well as more verbal and sociable while on the drug. These were the most severely disturbed boys, aged eighty-four to one-hundred thirty-two months, hospitalized on the Psychiatry Unit at Bellevue at that time, and four showed definite borderline features. The children who were most impulsive and the one child with schizophrenia tended to worsen on the drug. Increases in excitability, confusion, impulsivity, or sleepiness occurred with doses at or above the optimal level. Side effects occurred at doses from 15 to 120 mg/day (0.7 to 5.28 mg/kg/day) and one child had no ill effects from the latter dose. It must be cautioned that this was a preliminary, small pilot study conducted in a hospital setting. Though marked improvement was noted in two of the boys and improvement in four, of the three with no change or worsening in condition, one boy became floridly more delusional and the other two more impulsive and aggressive. Further clinical trials of chlordiazepoxide in controlled settings are definitely indicated to determine their practical use for borderline children.

Gelenberg (1980) relates the role for antianxiety agents in the treatment of adult patients with severe personality disturbances as perhaps adjunctive. These agents are considered ineffective at therapeutically acceptable doses in ameliorating the severe anxiety often experienced by borderline patients. It is interesting to note that though anxiety is a frequently reported symptom in borderline states, Stone (1980) does not refer to the use of anxiolytic agents, the benzodiazepines, in the borderline syndromes. Similarly, Pariser et al. (1979) fail to deal with the anxiety and periodic panic of the borderline conditions when discussing the diagnosis and management of anxiety symptoms and syndromes.

TRICYCLIC ANTIDEPRESSANTS

Depression, as manifest by lowered self-esteem, self-punitive physical actions, chronic feelings of emptiness and boredom, and constricted affect, has been found to be a frequently occurring component of the borderline picture in children (Petti & Unis, 1981; Petti & Law, 1981b) and adolescents (Rinsley, 1980). Reviews that detail the psychopharmacologic treatment of depressed children (Rapoport, 1977; Gittelman-Klein, 1978; Petti, 1981), individual case reports (Petti & Wells, 1980; Petti et al., 1980), and group studies (Weinberg et al., 1973; Puig-Antich et al., 1978; Puig-Antich et al., 1979) of imipramine treatment of depressed children are available.

Generally, the tricyclic antidepressant group of drugs, particularly imipramine, have been reported as highly effective. Unfortunately, most of the studies have been open or uncontrolled (Gittelman-Klein, 1978; Petti, 1981). However, many workers feel that imipramine and related compounds are useful in the treatment of depression and related symptoms for a wide range of disorders. Controlled and uncontrolled studies employing the tricyclic and monoamine oxidase inhibitor antidepressants have been fully reviewed elsewhere (Gittelman-Klein, 1978; Campbell, 1979; Petti, 1981). Symptom complexes such as mixed disorders, schizophrenia, psychosis, aggression, hyperkinesis, and school refusal are considered under the rubric of depression-related disorders treated with the tricyclic antidepressants.

Lucas and associates (1965) treated a diagnostically heterogeneous group of children who demonstrated a major depressive component in their behavior. The fourteen children, ranging in age from ten to seventeen years, participated in a twelve-week placebo-controlled, double-blind crossover study comparing amitriptyline and placebo. The children were at the same time provided with a total milieu program. Statistically significant differences ($p < .001$) were found in individual patients regarding symptoms related to borderline disorders such as response to controls, need for controls, spontaneous relationships, participation in activities, and settling at bedtime. The dosage levels were comparatively low (30–75 mg/kg/day). Some of the children showed a deterioration in condition as well, which is not surprising, considering that some of the children were diagnosed as schizophrenic. Moreover, those who showed the poorest response had chronically poor adjustment histories and inadequate control of negativism and hostility.

Although Campbell et al. (1971) report worsening of the clinical condition, as a group, of preschool autistic/schizophrenic children treated with imipramine, Petti and Campbell (1975) describe the improvement of one of these children who was clearly depressed. Kurtis (1966) reports on the successful treatment of children diagnosed as schizophrenic or postencephalitic syndrome with nortriptyline. In this uncontrolled study of children four to fifteen years of age, 76 percent demonstrated improvement in depression, aggression, destructiveness, and self-destructiveness.

Aggression, hostility, hyperactivity, and poor school performance have also been described for borderline children. A number of studies (Huessy & Wright, 1970; Winsberg et al., 1972; Ryback et al., 1973; Brown et al., 1973; Watter & Dreifuss, 1973; Waizer et al., 1974) have demonstrated the response of such children to imipramine and to amitriptyline (Yepes et al., 1977).

School refusal, another area felt to be related to both anxiety/avoidant disorders (Gittelman-Klein, 1978) and depression, is frequently found in borderline children, and some consider it to be an early sign of schizophrenia when it first occurs in adolescence. A double-blind placebo-controlled study (Gittelman-Klein & Klein, 1973) clearly demonstrated the superiority of imipramine over placebo. Of particular significance was the well substantiated observation that the children on medication felt and looked better and happier, whether they attended school or not. Imipramine is generally considered an appropriate part of the therapeutic regime for such children after the diagnostic work-up is completed. Enuresis and encopresis, both considered signs of either immaturity, psychic conflicts, or both, have also been reported and found to be helped by tricyclic treatment.

Case reports of children who met criteria for either schizotypal or borderline personality disorders and who were treated with imipramine for depression are available (Petti et al., 1980; Petti & Unis, 1981; Petti & Law, 1981a). Each of these children met research criteria for depression (Petti, 1978). The medication was expected to allow the children to experience more meaningful contact with their affect and feelings and, as a rule, to be more accessible to other therapeutic modalities. Each of those cases and previous others (Petti & Davidman, 1977; Pallmeyer & Petti, 1979; Petti & Wells, 1980) provide poignant descriptions of such an occurrence. We have usually found that six to eight weeks of medication accompanied by intensive treatment is sufficient for good results.

Potential serious side-effects and toxic reactions to tricyclic antidepressant treatment can occur, particularly with borderline or psychiatrically disturbed children. Cardiovascular and central nervous system reactions are the most serious and require special attention. Fatalities related to these two systems have resulted from overdosages, accidental or deliberate, and in one case an excessive prescribed dosage (Saraf et al., 1974). Precautions concerning the cardiovascular changes resulting from imipramine doses of greater than 5 mg/kg/day have been issued (Robinson, 1975; Hayes et al., 1975). These include monitoring of the EKG when dosage approximates 5 mg/kg/day or when patients with preexisting cardiac disease of cardiographic abnormalities require tricyclic treatment. Seizures as a response to moderate imipramine dosage have been reported. Preexisting organic brain damage or particular susceptibility, as with schizophrenic children (Petti & Campbell,

1975), are described as potential contraindications. These issues are extensively reviewed elsewhere (Petti, 1981).

One major concern in the short-term use of high doses of imipramine involves withdrawal side effects. We have found that abrupt cessation over one to three days leads to dramatic increases in symptomatology with imipramine (Petti & Law, 1981a). Even withdrawal of the drug over a week's time results in significant symptomatology, including gastrointestinal distress, irritability, and agitation (Law et al., 1981). Slowly decreasing the dosage over two week's time seems almost to eliminate this as a problem.

Antidepressant medications have been used in adult borderline disorders because depression has been a frequently reported symptom or an integral component of the borderline syndrome (Grinker et al., 1968; Klein, 1975; Rinsley, 1978, 1980a; Stone, 1980).

Klein (1975) reviews the psychopharmacology of the borderline patient and specifically the role of drug treatment for the groups of borderline patients described by Grinker (Grinker et al., 1968). The Group I classification of angry, withdrawn, hostile, and depressed patients were noted to resemble the hysteroid dysphoric patients who respond to monoamine oxidase inhibitors (Klein & Davis, 1969). The schizoid, obsessional, withdrawn patients making up Grinker's Group 3 classification, Klein (1975) suggests, may "represent a phasic depression in a relatively well-integrated person" and be helped by antidepressants. The Group 4 patients who manifest anxious, clinging, and depressed behavior are similar to the phobic anxious patients who show a good response to imipramine. Group 2 patients are the only group without depression as a major feature. Klein (1975) notes that their response to antidepressants is highly variable, ranging from mood stabilization to irritability, aggressiveness, and, in some cases, mania. Moreover, Siris et al. (1978), in reviewing the use of antidepressant drugs in treating "pseudoneurotic schizophrenics" (patients who share many common features with the borderline syndromes), note that these patients respond to tricyclic antidepressant treatment without concomitant treatment with a major tranquilizer.

The combined adult and child literature regarding the tricyclics provides substantial support for their use with borderline individuals and support for delineating subgroups based on response to such treatment.

PSYCHOMOTOR STIMULANTS

Many borderline children have signs and symptoms suggestive of minimal cerebral dysfunction or immature development of the central nervous system. Hyperactivity and situational inattentiveness, agitation, and impulsivity frequently accompany the borderline picture for both schizotypal and borderline personality disorder children. The psychomotor stimulant group of medications (dextroamphetamine, methylphenidate, and pemoline) are presently the most commonly prescribed psychotropic drugs for hyperactive children.

Though presently considered to be appropriate only for attention deficit disorder, with or without hyperactivity, stimulants were originally applied to a very heterogeneous group of children (Bradley, 1937).

Bradley (1937), in what may have been the first reported controlled psychotropic drug study, described the effect of Benzedrine (d-1-amphetamine) on thirty children, ages five to fourteen years, residing in a hospital. They had severe behavior disorders, including aggressive and schizoid disturbances. Two boys and one girl were thirteen or older, and one child was five years of age. There were twenty-one boys and nine girls. The most impressive change occurred in fourteen of the children who became much more interested and involved in their school work. Of the fifteen school-age children who did not show such dramatic changes, eight showed some improvement in school behavior and in their personal characteristics. Five others showed significant changes in other behaviors, though no change in school behaviors. No response to Benzedrine was found in two of the children.

Distinctly subdued emotional responses were demonstrated by fifteen of the children. This consisted of a decrease in mood swings and placid easygoing behavior replacing noisy, aggressive, irritable, domineering group behavior. In the other fifteen, seven described and evidenced a sense of well-being, a widening interest in their surroundings, and a decrease in self-preoccupation. These children responded by crying easily and being more sensitive, two others seemed to be more preoccupied with worrying, and only one child became more hyperactive, irritable, and aggressive. Half of the children with improvement in mood were among those with dramatic improvement in school. Bradley (1950) later reported that some children responded to both Benzedrine and d-amphetamine.

Scholarly and extensive reviews concerning the use of the stimulant medications are available (Cantwell & Carlson, 1978; Campbell, 1979). Their positive short-term effect on hyperactive/inattentive behavior has been generally accepted. Recent work relating clinical efficacy to cognitive factors such as attributional style (Bugental et al., 1977, 1978) should prove of great help to the clinician in sorting out the children who are likely to respond from those who will probably be poor responders.

Hyperactive children, like borderline children, frequently behave inappropriately in particular situations or under certain stresses. Whalen and associates (1978) successfully and objectively discriminated stimulant drug effects in the overt behavior of hyperactive children. By employing a coding system which included both quantitative and qualitative judgments of behavior, they found that the behavior of medicated hyperactive boys was not significantly different from that of their "normal" classmates. However, the hyperactive boys on placebo differed significantly by showing the highest rates of inappropriate, noisy, and disruptive behavior, the most motor movement, and the least attention to tasks. The children on medication tended to be less impulsive and better able or motivated "for response inhibition in the service of task performance" (Whalen et al., 1979).

Much has been made of the problematic relationship between borderline psychotic children and their mothers, particularly related to separation-individuation issues. Though hyperactive/attentional deficit-disordered children infrequently are reared in "environments where a high level of social pathology . . . [is] part of the everyday life" (Pine, this volume), observations concerning the effect of stimulant medication on the mother-child dyad may be related. Barkley and Cunningham (1979) employed a triple-blind methylphenidate-placebo crossover design to study the drug's effect on twenty hyperactive boys observed in free play and task-oriented periods and in their interactions with their mothers. When the children were on medication, the percentage of time in which the mothers did not initiate any interaction or play with the child during any part of the 15-second coding interval significantly increased. Significant decreases in interactions initiated by the child and increase in both mothers' responses to initiations by their children and facilitation of the play were found. Other significant changes in the drug period included decreases in direct commands and negative behavior by the mothers and competing behavior of the child. The children complied more frequently on the drug and showed significant increases in the duration of their compliance to a direct request by their mothers in the free-play setting.

Similar findings were demonstrated during the structured task period. In addition, the mothers attended to their child's compliant behavior with significantly greater positive social interactions or attention. In other words, methylphenidate appears to have reduced the interactions that were perceived as inappropriate by the mothers and the children were more likely to pay attention to their mothers. This decreased the need for the mothers to control their children's activities or to scold them. The relationship was able to move in a less ambivalent, more positive direction with medication as compared to the placebo condition. The stimulant medication thus seems to set the stage for positive change, and the mothers, in turn, must modify the punitive controlling styles often forced upon them by the children's previous deviant behavior if long-term positive gains are to be effected (Barkley & Cunningham, 1979).

Though hyperactivity and inattentive behavior are the predominantly accepted criteria for the use of stimulant medication at this time, Winsberg et al. (1974) note that hyperactive and/or aggressive children respond with significant improvement to both d-amphetamine and methylphenidate as compared to placebo. In a seminal paper, Fish (1971) broke down the categories of "hyperkinesis" and related historical as well as future directions for the field. She described the type of disorders which respond to amphetamines as follows:

> Children with behavior disorders and even some with schizoid personality characteristics may respond but not usually those with borderline or grossly psychotic symptoms. The behavior disorders which responded included those with a predominance of anxiety and neurotic mechanisms (now characterized in the DSM II as "overanxious reaction"), and those predominantly manifested by negativism, belligerence, and aggressive behavior (now termed "unsocialized aggressive reaction" in the DSM II).
>
> Children with these two major types of behavior disorders may respond to amphetamine whether hyperactivity is present or not, and whether or not there is associated mental retardation, organic brain syndrome or lesser defects characterized as "minimal brain dysfunctions."

Arnold and associates (1973) tested out some of these impressions by employing both levo- and dextroamphetamine in disturbed children. They found that both the d- and l-amphetamines were about equal in helping unsocialized aggressive children; however, d-amphetamine was more effective in the overanxious and hyperkinetic children. Both were significantly more effective than placebo.

Bender and Cottington (1942) found that psychomotor stimulants with children who are irritable, emotionally unstable, and depressed can lead to grossly disorganized behavior. Geller et al. (1981) describe two severely disturbed children with borderline psychotic behavior and DSM-III diagnoses of both Childhood Onset Pervasive Developmental Disorder and Attention Deficit Disorder with Hyperactivity. The latter disorder was found to improve for both boys with relatively low doses of dextroamphetamine. The boys demonstrated neither worsening nor improvement in their bizarre ideation.

Returning to levoamphetamine, Campbell et al. (1976) report a general worsening of young schizophrenic children on the drug. However, a few of the children did improve. Arnold and associates (1973) describe the successful treatment of a fourteen-year-old with paranoid obsessions, intense anxiety, depression, and compulsive rituals with levoamphetamine. The anxiety had responded to chlordiazepoxide. The other symptoms persisted. After four months of hospitalization, low-dose thioridazine was used unsuccessfully. He then demonstrated dramatic improvement with 21 mg b.i.d. of l-amphetamine as indicated by a decrease in his florid symptomatology, by the ability to discuss his conflicts in therapy, and by more appropriate social functioning. Employing a five-day double-blind, random crossover study between the two amphetamine isomers and placebo, the results unequivocally supported l-amphetamine as the therapeutic agent.

The psychomotor stimulants, perhaps more than any of the other group of psychotropics for children, have been criticized, maligned, overprescribed, and extolled. This brief review provides some flavor for a rich literature regarding their use, particularly around some of the behaviors related to borderline psychotic behavior. Even more, it suggests the need for more controlled single case studies to determine the profiles of children who are most likely to be responders to this group of drugs and perhaps to assist in delineating one subgroup from another.

My own personal experience in treating a graduate student in her mid-twenties may provide a transition between the borderline conditions of children and adults and aid in supporting consideration of the stimulants for borderline patients. This patient had been diagnosed as a childhood schizophrenic in a number of private, university, and public hospital settings. She had received trials of numerous medications, predominantly the major tranquilizers or neuroleptics and had always done marginally well with recurrent psychiatric hospitalizations. Fortunately, her IQ was in the genius range and she progressed academically. During her college years, she found that Dexedrine (5 mg b.i.d.) was sufficient to keep her thoughts coherent and organized for effective study. Though she remained eccentric and isolated, she was able to develop superficial but intense relationships. A previous attempt to withdraw her from the psychomotor stimulant and to institute a trial of Haldol resulted in an intense but transient psychotic episode. Two of my fellow residents had treated similar patients and reported similar experiences.

Bellak (1976) describes individuals who fall within a subgroup of the schizophrenias. These patients present with a "low stimulus barrier," many nonfocal neurological signs, and poor impulse control. He reports that their condition deteriorates with the major tranquilizers but improves with Dilantin, Valium, Ritalin, and Tofranil. Huessy (1974) has noted anecdotally that a group of young adults diagnosed as schizophrenic responded to either psychomotor stimulant medication or to tricyclic antidepressant treatment. Mann and Greenspan (1976) describe two cases of "adult brain dysfunction" as a counterpart to the minimal brain dysfunction described in children. They note that they and their colleagues had observed over twenty similar cases in the previous two years, many of whom would have fit into the category of borderline psychotic states. They also found that medication, either tricyclics or the stimulants, allowed the patients to become more organized with focused attention without experiencing dysphoria or increased excitement, and to use psychotherapy "to begin altering characterologic and neurotic problems."

Parenthetically, acute improvement in "schizophrenic symptoms" has been reported in well-controlled studies with some chronic schizophrenic patients following d-amphetamine infusion. Many demonstrated "increased alertness trust and openness," and a decrease in withdrawal, motor retardation, blunted affect, and psychotic symptoms (Van Kammen & Bunney, 1979; Van Kammen et al., 1981). These findings also provide parallels to the work with children and future avenues for research with borderline children.

NEUROLEPTICS (MAJOR TRANQUILIZERS, ANTIPSYCHOTICS)

As with adult psychotic schizophrenic patients, the neuroleptics or major tranquilizers are more frequently the drugs of choice for treating the psychoses of children and adolescents. The most popular, based on an international survey of pediatric psychopharmacology outside the United States (Simeon et al., 1974), were chlorpromazine, thioridazine, haloperidol, and trifluoperazine. A number of outstanding reviews are available concerning the use of neuroleptics in children (Solow, 1976; Campbell, 1978; Winsberg & Yepes, 1978; Campbell, 1979). Campbell (1978) has cautioned that little is truly known concerning the overall effectiveness of psychotropics in autistic and schizophrenic children or even when a drug should best fit into the overall treatment for such children; she does provide concrete recommendations for future research. It is generally suggested that the neuroleptics for children are best used in treatment of acute psychotic reactions, disorders such as organic brain syndrome, and in mental retardation when psychomotor excitement or agitation are major features. However, the FDA (1980) has cautioned that chlorpromazine has not been demonstrated as effective "for the treatment of moderate to severe agitation, hyperactivity, or aggressiveness in disturbed children." Similarly, the effectiveness of trifluoperazine "for the control of excessive anxiety, tension and agitation as seen in neurosis or associated with somatic conditions" is questioned.

Nevertheless, in terms of general usage, thioridazine was the first (21.2%) and chlorpromazine the fourth (14.1%) most popular drugs in use for

TABLE 10-1
(Abstracted from Simeon et al., 1974)

INTERNATIONAL POPULARITY OF NEUROLEPTICS OVER OTHER PSYCHOTROPICS IN TREATING CHILDHOOD DISORDERS

DISORDER	DRUG*					
Hyperkinetic Reaction	thioridazine (1) (21.2)	chlorpromazine (4) (14.1)	periciazine (6) (5.3)			
Unsocialized Aggressive Reaction	chlorpromazine (1) (26.5)	thioridazine (2) (22.0)	periciazine (4) (9.1)	haloperidol (7) (4.6)		
Overanxious Reaction	thioridazine (3) (18.8)	chlorpromazine (4) (9.0)				
Withdrawing Reaction	thioridazine (1) (14.5)	chlorpromazine (2) (12.0)	trifluoperazine (3) (10.1)	haloperidol (7) (7.2)		
Psychosis	chlorpromazine (1) (26.6)	thioridazine (2) (23.7)	haloperidol (3) (12.2)	trifluoperazine (4) (9.6)	fluphenazine (5) (3.6)	perphenazine-amitriptyline (6) (3.6)
Nightmares	thioridazine (3) (10.3)					
Insomnia	chlorpromazine (4) (10.8)	thioridazine (5) (8.3)				
Sleepwalking	chlorpromazine (4) (8.5)	thioridazine (5) (7.5)				
Phobic Neurosis	thioridazine (2) (17.5)	chlorpromazine (4) (8.8)				
Obsessive-Compulsive Neurosis	chlorpromazine (4) (12.4)	haloperidol (7) (6.7)				

*Under each drug is the ranking given that neuroleptic for the particular disorder by an international group of child psychiatrists and the percent of respondents who would employ that particular drug for the particular disorder

the hyperkinetic reaction, and with surprising frequency in other disorders (see Table 10-1, taken from Simeon et al., 1974).

The widespread use of this class of drugs may be related to their global spectrum of action which includes a long duration of action and "a complex admixture of dopaminergic, alpha-adrenergic and cholinergic blocking actions on the central and autonomic nervous systems, plus in some cases a weak adrenergic action due to block of reuptake of monoamines. . ." (Winsberg & Yepes, 1978, p. 241).

Serrano and Forbis (1973) treated sixty children aged six to eleven years by randomly assigning thirty to haloperidol and thirty to fluphenazine under double-blind conditions. These children had received previous treatment and in all but one case were judged to be static or deteriorating clinically (60 percent had been unsuccessfully treated with other psychotropic agents). The diagnoses varied but nonpsychotic organic brain syndrome with problem behavior and adjustment reaction of childhood predominated. Statistically significant superiority was demonstrated for haloperidol over fluphenazine. Especially striking was the improvement in all twelve children with hostility and all fourteen children with anxiety who took haloperidol. Similarly, 94 percent of the Haldol-treated children with aggression, 88 percent with unpredictability, 78 percent with regression, 93 percent with impulsivity, and 82 percent with hyperactivity improved moderately or better. The results with fluphenazine were far less dramatic. Academic improvement "tended to improve" during the drug period.

It is clear that the neuroleptics have enjoyed widespread popularity. However, many feel that this may not be appropriate, and such drugs should not be routinely used by clinicians. Winsberg et al. (1976) argue that they should be the very last used for hyperactive or aggressive children. Each of the reviews cited above documents and discusses the serious side-effects of such drugs. A recent review (Gualtieri et al., 1980) notes that dyskinesias do occur in children and youth with varying diagnoses and ages treated with neuroleptics. These dyskinesias are not always reversible, are present in both chronic and low-dose short-term drug treatment, and include the range of abnormal movements and severity. Withdrawal-emergent symptoms and acute extrapyramidal symptoms are also frequently occurring complications of neuroleptic treatment. These workers caution clinicians that neuroleptics put children at risk for the dyskinesias and should be employed "with great discretion."

We rarely employ the neuroleptics in children because, aside from their acute sedating effect, they seem to have little to balance the possibility of cognitive impairment and other more serious complications. Even for acutely and moderately disturbed and disturbing children admitted to a psychiatric hospital, the neuroleptics are infrequently required. Of the first fifty-five children, only three admitted to a highly therapeutic unit (Petti, 1980) required a trial of neuroleptic treatment as the first drug of choice. Three of the five children discharged on a neuroleptic were diagnosed as Childhood Schizophrenic (DSM-II).

We did treat one depressed, borderline psychotic child with chlorpromazine after he had failed to respond to imipramine. Among the first admitted to the unit, this eight-year-old boy was referred for outbursts of temper, rage reactions, and uncontrollable behavior. He manifested anxiety and depression, suicidal ideation, low self-image, poor expressive speech, tangential thinking and confusion under stress, poor social skills, multiple nonfocal neurological and developmental signs, and provocative, masochistic behavior. All routine lab studies, including a sleep-deprived EEG, were unremarkable.

All-night sleep EEG studies (Kupfer et al., 1979) were more consistent with what would be considered an organic syndrome, neurologic disorder, or schizophreniform process. His depression cleared with imipramine (150 mg/d; 5 mg/kg/d) and he seemed somewhat less anxious. Realistic perceptions of rejection by or, at best, ambivalence on the part of his mother and step-father did not improve. After three weeks on this dosage of imipramine, repeat all-night EEG studies were more consistent with the type of results found in adults who responded poorly or not at all to the drug. A trial of chlorpromazine (175 mg/d) resulted in mild improvement, a decrease in his rage reactions and anxiety, and better academic functioning. The child remained moderately impaired in all spheres.

Because borderline adult patients, particularly the schizotypal, resemble the schizophrenic syndrome, neuroleptics (major tranquilizers) have been considered the drugs of choice (Hollister, 1980). Patients who resembled Grinker and associates' (1968) Group 1 Borderline patients (angry, hostile, withdrawn, and depressed) and were labeled "hostile depression," responded well to major tranquilizers (Overall et al., 1964). Moreover, Klein and Davis (1969) have argued for thioridazine as the most efficacious agent for patients who resemble Grinker's Group 2, emotionally labile borderline patients. Many clinicians caring for borderline children have employed neuroleptics based on their experience with drug management of schizophrenic adults and the limited literature cited above. It is important that neuroleptics have been proven efficacious in only one subgroup of borderline adults. The model for their use should be intensively scrutinized before prescribing neuroleptics for borderline children. We have seen a number of children who have been unsuccessfully treated with varying doses of these drugs.

LITHIUM

Lithium has been used infrequently in the treatment of symptoms related to borderline children. Rapoport el al. (1978) summarize the literature related to controlled trials of lithium in children, noting both the small numbers of such studies and the diverse nature of the target symptoms. They comment that emotionality, outbursts of aggressive behavior, and mood swings may respond to lithium, while hyperactivity and childhood psychosis do not. Individual case studies suggest promise for lithium in the treatment of manic-depressive-like disorders of children or of children with moderately severe conduct problems whose parent(s) have responded to lithium. Replication attempts have been negative.

DeLong (1978) reports on the beneficial effect of lithium on twelve children (four to fourteen, mean 9.5 years) treated over a six-to-thirty-three-month period. All had chronic behavior disorders with hostility, aggression, and distractibility, and nine of the twelve had extreme mood swings with withdrawal and depression alternating with manic excitement. This latter condition was marked by overenergetic, hypervoluble, giddy, bizarre behavior and confusion. The depression was characterized by self-deprecation and physically damaging self-abuse. The cycles were usually of hours or days in duration but of months of time in two girls. The hostile and aggressive behavior transcended the cycles and "affective instability, when present, showed itself in extremes of mood, generally encompassing hostile, depressive and manic features." (p. 690)

Improvement in mood was striking in the responders as the children began to demonstrate warmth and affection (some for the first time) and a decrease in "hostility, anger, rage, frustration and aggressive outbursts." The extremes of behavior and neurovegetative symptoms diminished and school performance markedly improved for five of the children. A double-blind, placebo-controlled crossover study conducted with four of these children demonstrated continued improvement and maintenance of positive gains on the lithium and significant deterioration on placebo. We have administered lithium to two hospitalized children similar to those described by DeLong, but our results were equivocal, and certainly not indicative of such positive results. Since positive results have been reported in several studies (Rapoport et al., 1978; Campbell, 1979) and since some of these children were borderline adolescents (Rifkin et al., 1972) or psychotic (Gram & Rafaelsen, 1972), further consideration should be given to lithium as an agent for a class of borderline children.

This view is supported by a number of reports which suggest that lithium salts might be effective in the treatment of borderline states (Rifkin et al.,

1972) and the nonaffective symptoms in schizophrenics (Small et al., 1975; Biederman et al., 1979). In related studies, prisoners who had a recurring pattern of anger and violent behavior to the slightest provocation were studied by Tupin et al. (1973). Most were diagnosed as explosive personality disorder, schizophrenia, or possible schizophrenia. As a response to lithium, the number of aggressive episodes and disciplinary action for violent behavior decreased markedly. The prisoners reported greater control over their anger, with episodes experienced as less intense. Kellner and Rade (1979) review other studies which found lithium to be an effective agent in treating personality disorders and patients whose clinical pictures resemble borderline disorders.

SUMMARY

Few studies have directly reported the use of psychotropic medications with borderline children. In part, this may be related to the previous body of literature that emanated, almost completely, from those investigators and clinicians with a psychoanalytic orientation to patients. There are notable exceptions (Lewis, 1976; Rinsley, 1980; Petti & Unis, 1981; Petti & Law, 1981). It is important to realize that there are several subtypes of borderline children (Pine, this volume), and medication may be of assistance in both treatment and differential diagnosis; psychopharmacology may play a major role in learning more about the disorder. It is of vital importance to be aware that medication is only one facet of the total treatment of borderline children. It is evident from this review that medications have been used for many symptoms related to the borderline disorders of children. At times they may be overused or used well beyond the duration of need. Some medications are used excessively and some inappropriately (e.g., the use of neuroleptics for mild anxiety and many behavior or conduct disorders). In many instances, medication is underutilized or not used at all by psychiatrists treating or supervising the care of children and adolescents.

Psychotropic medication for borderline children should follow the guidelines laid down for treatment of similarly disturbed adults. Sarwer-Foner (1976) labels the total therapeutic endeavor "global treatment."

> It [medication] can usually only deal with the emergency or emergent aspect of certain disruptive symptoms or acute psychotic states, and this in itself is not always enough to help the borderline patient with the fundamental aspects of borderline disorder over time. Its use, however, in adequate doses is often essential in staving off decompensation in an emergency situation or in helping a

patient achieve mastery over unacceptable impulses, mastery which helps the patient progress in his defenses to at least an acceptable level or to return to his usual state or to be able to decide whether he wants to have further, more intensive therapy.

Donlon (1980) and Klein (1975) offer similar advice. It is vital to good treatment that psychotropic agents be discontinued as quickly as clinically warranted. It is critical that the clinician be aware of the nuances of drug effects, indications and, more important, contraindications, toxic effects, and the meaning of the return of old or development of new symptoms upon discontinuation of pharmacologic agents. More and more young investigators and clinicians are developing interest in borderline psychotic phenomena. In the next five years, we can expect a burgeoning of reports that should open new vistas of understanding. Contributions from psychopharmacology and physiology should assist us in these endeavors.

This chapter has highlighted a number of issues related to treating symptoms and symptom complexes. Very little systematic work has been done which addresses the use of medication and other therapies for borderline children. Once the symptom and clinical pictures of these disorders are better defined, perhaps employing adult criteria (Petti & Law, 1981b), then a more rational discussion of drug treatment of the various types of borderline children should be possible. At present, an overview of related symptoms found in borderline children was necessary.

R E F E R E N C E S

Arnold, L. E., Kirilcuky, V. & Corson, S. A. (1973), Levoamphetamine and dextroamphetamine: Differential effect on aggression and hyperkinesis in children and dogs. *Am. J. Psychiat.*, 130:165–169.

Arnold, L. E., Krebs, G., Knopp, W. (1974), Amphetamine treatment of paranoid obsessions: Case report and biochemical implications. *Pharmakopsychiatrie*, 35:322–327.

Barkley, R. A. & Cunningham, C. E. (1979), The effects of methylphenidate on the mother-child interactions of hyperactive children. *Arch. Gen. Psychiat.*, 36:201–208.

Bellak, L. (1976), A possible subgroup of the schizophrenic syndrome and implications for treatment. *Am. J. Psychother.*, 30:194–205.

Bender, L. & Cottington, F. (1942), The use of amphetamine sulfate (benzedrine) in child psychiatry. *Am. J. Psychiat.*, 99:116–121.

Biederman, J., Lerner, Y., Belmaker, R. H. (1979), Combination of lithium carbonate and haloperidol in schizo-affective disorder. *Arch. Gen. Psychiat.*, 36:327–333.

Bradley, C. (1937), The behavior of children receiving benzedrine. *Am. J. Psychiat.*, 94:577–585.

———(1950), Benzedrine and Dexedrine in the treatment of children's behavior disorders. *Pediatrics*, 5:24–37.

Brown, D., Winsberg, B. G., Bialer, I., & Press, M. (1973) Imipramine therapy and seizures:

Three children treated for hyperactive behavior disorders. *Am. J. Psychiat.,* 130:210–212.

Bugental, D. B., Collins, S., Collins, L. & Chaney, L. A. (1978), Attributional and behavioral changes following two behavior management interventions with hyperactive boys: A follow-up study. *Child Develpm.* 49:247–250.

———, Whalen, C. K. & Henker, B. (1977), Causal attributions of hyperactive children and motivational assumptions of two behavior change approaches: Evidence for an interactionist position. *Child Develpm.* 48:874–884.

Campbell, M. (1978), Use of drug treatment in infantile autism and childhood schizophrenia. In: *Psychopharmacology,* eds. M. A. Lipton, A. Dimascio & K. F. Killam. New York: Raven Press, pp. 1451–1461.

———(1979), Psychopharmacology for children and adolescents. In: *Basic Handbook of Child Psychiatry,* ed. J. K. Noshpitz. New York: Basic Books, pp. 367–396.

———, Fish, B., Shapiro, T., Floyd, A. (1971), Imipramine in preschool autistic and schizophrenic children. *J. Aut. Childh. Schizo.* 1:267–28.

———, Small, A. M., Collins, P. J., Friedman, E., David, R. & Genieser, N. (1976), Levodopa and levoamphetamine: A crossover study in young schizophrenic children. *Current Therapeutic Research,* 19:70–86.

Cantwell, D. P., & Carlson, G. A. (1978), Stimulants. In: *Pediatric Psychopharmacology,* ed. J. S. Werry. New York: Brunner/Mazel, pp. 171–207.

Chethik, M. (1979), The borderline child. In: *The Basic Handbook of Child Psychiatry,* II, ed. J. Noshpitz. New York: Basic Books, pp. 304–321.

DeLong, G. R. (1978), Lithium carbonate treatment of select behavior disorders in children suggesting manic-depressive illness. *Pediatrics,* 93:689–694.

Donlon, P. T. (1980), Special pharmacologic management problems. Presented at 133rd Annual Meeting of the American Psychiatric Association. In: *Transient Psychosis,* McNeil Laboratories, pp. 11–14.

Federal Drug Administration (1981), Prescription drug products currently classified by the food and drug administration as lacking adequate evidence of effectiveness.

Fish, B. (1971), The "one child, one drug" myth of stimulants in hyperkinesis. *Arch. Gen. Psychiat.* 25:193–203.

Gelenberg, A. J. (1980), A role for antianxiety agents. Presented at the 133rd Annual Meeting of the American Psychiatric Association. In: *Transient Psychosis,* McNeil Laboratories, pp. 15–19.

Geller, B., Guttmacher, L. B. & Bleeg, M. (1981), Coexistence of childhood onset pervasive developmental disorder and attention deficit disorder with hyperactivity. *Am. J. Psychiat.* 138:388–389.

Gittelman-Klein, R. (1978), Psychopharmacological treatment of anxiety disorders, mood disorders and Tourette's disorder in children. In: *Psychopharmacology,* eds. M. A. Lipton, A. DiMascio & K. F. Killam. New York: Raven Press, pp. 1471–1480.

——— & Klein, D. F. (1973), School phobia: diagnostic considerations in the light of imipramine effects. *J. Nerv. Ment. Dis.,* 156:199–215.

Greenblatt, D. J., & Shader, R. I. (1974), *Benzodiazepines in clinical practice.* New York: Raven Press.

Grinker, R. R., Werble, B., & Brye, R. C. (1968), *The Borderline Syndrome.* New York: Basic Books.

Gualtieri, C. T., Barnhill, J., McGimsey, J. & Schell, D. (1980), Tardive dyskinesia and other movement disorders in children treated with psychotropic drugs. *This Journal,* 19:491–510.

Hayes, T., Panitch, M., & Barker, E. (1975), Imipramine dosage in children: A comment on imipramine and electrocardiographic abnormalities in hyperactive children. *Am. J. Psychiat.,* 132:546–547.

Hollister, L. E. (1980), Transient psychoses and personality disorders. Presented at the 133rd Annual Meeting of the American Psychiatric Association. In: Transient Psychosis, McNeil Laboratories, pp. 26–31.

Huessy, H. R. (1974), The adult hyperkinetic. *Am. J. Psychiat.*, 131:724–725.

—— & Wright, A. L. (1970), The use of imipramine in children's behavior disorders. *Acta Paedopsychiatrica*, 37:194–199.

Kellner, R., & Rade, R. T. (1979), Pharmacotherapy of personality disorders. In: *Psychopharmacology Update*, eds. J. M. Davis & D. Greenblatt. New York: Grune and Stratton, 29–63.

Klein, D. F. (1975), Psychopharmacology and the borderline patient. In: *Borderline States in Psychiatry*, ed. J. E. Mack. New York: Grune and Stratton, 75–91.

——(1977), Psychopharmacological treatment and delineation of borderline disorders. In: *Borderline personality disorders: The concept, the syndrome, the patient*, ed. P. Hartocollis. New York: International Universities Press, 365–383.

Koch, M., Duffy, J. C., Zimmerman, R. (1976), Treatment of anxiety in children: A controlled chemical trial of dipotassium chlorazepate (tranxene). In: *Psychopharmacology of Childhood*, ed. E. V. Siva Sankar. New York: PJD Publication, Inc., pp. 69–73.

Kupfer, D. J., Coble, P., Kane, J., Petti, T. A., Conners, C. K. (1979), Imipramine and EEG sleep in children with depressive symptoms. *Psychopharmakology*, 60:117–123.

Kurtis, L. B. (1966), Clinical study of the response to nortriptyline on autistic children. *International Journal of Neuropsychiatry*, 298–301.

Law, W., Petti, T. A., Kazdin, A. E. (1981), Withdrawal symptoms after graduated cessation of imipramine in children. *Am. J. Psychiat.*, 138:647–650.

Lewis, M. (1976), Transitory or pseudo-organicity and borderline personality in a 7-year-old child. *J. Am. Acad. Child Psychiat.*, 15:131–138.

Lucas, A. R., Lockett, H. J., Grimm, F. (1965), Amitriptyline in childhood depressions. *Diseases of the Nervous System*, 26:105–111.

Mann, H. B. & Greenspan, S. I. (1976), The identification and treatment of adult brain dysfunction. *Am. J. Psychiatry*, 133:1013–1017.

Overall, J. E., Hollister, L. W., Meyer, F., Kimbell, L., Shelton, J. (1964), Imipramine and thioridazine in depressed and schizophrenic patients. Are there specific antidepressant drugs? *JAMA*, 189:605–608.

Pallmeyer, T. & Petti, T. A., (1979), Effects of imipramine on aggression and dejection in depressed children. *Am. J. Psychiat.*, 136:1472–1473.

Pariser, S. F., Pinta, E. R., Jones, B. A., Young, E. A. (1979), Diagnosis and management of anxiety symptoms and syndromes. In: *Psychopharmacology Update*, eds. J. M. Davis & D. Greenblatt. New York: Grune and Stratton, 145–172.

Petti, T. A. (1978), Depression in hospitalized child psychiatry patients: Approaches to measuring depression. *J. Amer. Acad. Child Psychiat.*, 17:49–59.

——(1980), Residential and inpatient treatment of children and adolescents. In: *The treatment of emotional disorders in children and adolescents*. eds. G. P. Shoevard, R. M. Benson and Blinder. Spectrum Publications, Inc. 209–228.

——(1981), Imipramine in the treatment of depressed children. In: *Childhood depression*, eds. D. Cantwell and G. Carlson. New York: Spectrum Publications, In Press.

——, Bornstein, M., Delamater, A., Conners, C. K. (1980), Evaluation and multi-modality treatment of a depressed pre-pubertal girl. *J. Amer. Acad. Child Psychiat.*, 19:690–702.

—— & Campbell, M. (1975), Imipramine and Seizures. *Am. J. Psychiat.*, 132:538–540.

—— & Davidman, L. (1977), Homicidal school-age children: Cognitive style and demographic features. Paper presented at the 24th Annual Meeting of the American Academy of Child Psychiatry, Houston, October 21, 1977.

——, Fish, B., Shapiro, T., Cohen, I. L., Campbell, M. (1981), Chlordiazepoxide treatment of disturbed children—A pilot study. Paper presented at the Annual Meeting of the American Academy of Child Psychiatry, Dallas, Texas, 1981.

—— & Law, W. (1981a), Abrupt cessation of high-dose imipramine treatment in children. *JAMA*, 246:768–781.

—— ——(1981b), Borderline psychotic behavior in hospitalized children: Approaches to assessment and treatment. *J. Amer. Acad. Child Psychiat.*, In Press.

—— & Unis, A. (1981), Treating the borderline child with imipramine: A controlled study. *Am. J. Psychiat.*, 138:515–518.

—— & Wells, K. (1980), Crisis treatment of a preadolescent who accidentally killed his twin. *Am. J. Psychother.*, 34:434–443.

Pine, F. (1981), Borderline syndromes in childhood: A working nosology and its therapeutic implications. *This Volume.*

Puig-Antich, J., Blau, S., Marx, N., Greenhill, L., Chambers, W. (1978), Prepubertal major depressive disorder: A pilot study. *J. Amer. Acad. Child Psychiat.*, 17:695–707.

——, Perel, J. M., Lupatkin, W., et al. (1979), Plasma levels of imipramine (IMI) and desmethylimipramine (DMI) and clinical response in prepubertal major depressive disorder. *J. Amer. Acad. Child Psychiat.*, 18:616–627.

Rapoport, J. L. (1977) Pediatric psychopharmacology and childhood depression. In: *Depression in childhood: Diagnosis, treatment and conceptual models,* eds. J. G. Schulterbrandt & A. Raskin, New York: Raven Press, 87–100.

——, Mikkelsen, E. J., Werry, J. S. (1978), Antimanic, antianxiety, hallucinogenic and miscellaneous drugs. In: *Pediatric Psychopharmacology,* ed. J. S. Werry, New York: Brunner/Mazel, 316–356.

Rifkin, A., Quitkin, F., Carillo, C., Blumberg, A., Klein, D. (1972), Lithium carbonate in emotionally unstable character disorders. *Arch. Gen. Psychiatry,* 27:519–523.

Rinsley, D. B. (1980), Diagnosis and treatment of borderline and narcissistic children and adolescents. *Bulletin of the Menninger Clinic.* 44:147–170.

Robinson, D. S. (1975), Official minutes and chairman's report: Ad Hoc Committee on tricyclic antidepressant activity. Bureau of Drugs, Food and Drug Administration, Rockville, Md.

Ryback, W. S., Jorgensen, A., Gorgensen, S. (1973), Sensitivity reaction to imipramine. *Am. J. Psychiat.*, 130:940.

Saraf, K. R., Klein, D. F. (1974) Imipramine side effects in children. *Psychopharmacologia,* 37:265–274.

Serrano, A. C., & Forbis, O. L. (1973), Haloperidol for psychiatric disorders in children. *Diseases of the Nervous System,* 34:226–231.

Silver, L. B. (1979), Drug therapy with children and adolescents. In: *Drugs and the special child.* ed. M. J. Cohen, New York: Gardner Press, 33–62.

Simeon, J., Utech, C., Simeon, S., Itil, T. M. (1974), Pediatric psychopharmacology outside the U.S.A. *Diseases of the Nervous System,* 1974, 35:37–47.

Siris, S. G., Van Kammen, D. P., Docherty, J. P. (1978), Use of antidepressant drugs in schizophrenia. *Arch. Gen. Psychiat.*, 35:1368–1377.

Skynner, C. R. (1961) Effects of chlordiazepoxide. *Lancet,* 1:1110.

Small, J. G., Kellams, J. L., Milstein, V., Moore, J. (1975) A placebo controlled study of lithium combined with neuroleptics in chronic schizophrenic patients. *Am. J. Psychiat.*, 132:1315–1317.

Solow, R. A. (1976) Child and adolescent psychopharmacology in the mid-seventies: Progress or plateau? *Psychiatry Digest,* 15–38.

Stone, M. H. (1980), *The borderline syndromes: Constitution, personality, and adaptation.* New York: McGraw-Hill.

Tupin, J. P., Smith, D. B., Clanon, T. L., Kim, L. I., Nugent, A., Groupe, A. (1973), The long-term use of lithium in aggressive prisoners. *Comprehensive Psychiatry,* 14:311–317.

Van Kammen, D. P., & Bunney, W. E. (1979), Heterogeneity in response to amphetamine in schizophrenia: effects of placebo, chronic pimozide and pimozide withdrawal. In: *Catecholamines: Basic and clinical frontiers.* eds. E. Usdin, I. J. Kopin, J. Barchas. Oxford: Pergamon Press, 1896–1898.

——,Docherty, J. P., Marder, S. R., Ebert, M. H., Rosenblatt, J. E., Rayner, J. N. (1981), d-Amphetamine induces heterogeneous changes in psychotic behavior in schizophrenia.

Waizer, J., Hoffman, S. P., Polizos, P., Engelhardt, D. M. (1974), Outpatient treatment of hyperactive school children with imipramine. *Am. J. Psychiatry*, 131:587–591.

Watter, N., & Dreifuss, F. E. (1973), Modification of hyperkinetic behavior by nortriptyline. *The Virginia Medical Monthly*, 100:123–126.

Weinberg, W. A., Rutman, J., Sullivan, L., Penick, E. C., Dietz, S. G. (1973), Depression in children referred to an educational diagnostic center: Diagnosis and treatment. *Pediatrics*, 83:1065–1072.

Whalen, C. K., Collins, B. E., Hender, B., Alkus, S. R., Adams, D., Stapp, J. (1978), Behavior observations of hyperactive children and methylphenidate (Ritalin) effects in systematically structured classroom environments: Now you see them, now you don't. *J. Pediatric Psychology*, 3:177–187.

———, Hender, B., Collins, B. E., McAuliffe, S., Vaux, A. (1979), Peer interaction in a structured communication task: Comparisons of normal and hyperactive boys and of methylphenidate (Ritalin) and placebo effects. *Child Development*, 50:388–401.

Winsberg, B. G., Bialer, I., Kupietz, S., Tobias, J. (1972), Effects of imipramine and dextroamphetamine on behavior of neuropsychiatrically impaired children. *Am. J. Psychiat.*, 128:1425–1431.

———, Press, M., Bialer, I., Kupietz, S. (1974), Dextroamphetamine and methylphenidate in the treatment of hyperactive/aggressive children. *Pediatrics*, 53:236–241.

——— & Yepes, E. W. (1978), Antipsychotics. In: *Pediatric psychopharmacology*, ed. J. S. Werry. New York: Brunner/Mazel, 234–273.

———, ———, Bialer, I. (1976), Psychopharmacological management of children with hyperactive/aggressive/inattentive behavior disorders: A guide for the pediatrician. *Clinical Pediatrics*, 15:471–477.

Yepes, L. E., Balka, E. B., Winsberg, B. G., Bialer, I. (1977), Amitriptyline and methylphenidate treatment of behaviorally disordered children. *J. Child Psychology and Psychiatry*, 18:39–52.

CHAPTER 11

The Day and Residential Treatment of the Borderline Child

Graeme Hanson, M.D.
ASSISTANT CLINICAL PROFESSOR OF PEDIATRICS & PSYCHIATRY
UNIVERSITY OF CALIFORNIA AT SAN FRANCISCO
AND DIRECTOR OF PEDIATRIC MENTAL HEALTH SERVICES
SAN FRANCISCO GENERAL HOSPITAL

Jules R. Bemporad, M.D.
DIRECTOR OF CHILDREN'S SERVICES
MASSACHUSETTS MENTAL HEALTH CENTER
ASSOCIATE PROFESSOR OF PSYCHIATRY
HARVARD MEDICAL SCHOOL
BOSTON, MASSACHUSETTS

Henry F. Smith, M.D.
CLINICAL INSTRUCTOR IN PSYCHIATRY
HARVARD MEDICAL SCHOOL
STAFF PSYCHIATRIST
DIVISION OF CHILDREN'S SERVICES
MASSACHUSETTS MENTAL HEALTH CENTER
BOSTON, MASSACHUSETTS

INTRODUCTION

THIS CHAPTER FOCUSES on the important aspects of treating the borderline child in a residential or day-treatment program. We deal primarily with children of latency age. The borderline child and his or her family present major challenges to mental health and social service agencies, frequently requiring more extensive therapeutic efforts than would ordinarily be expected in light of their presenting symptomology. In a number of cases, placement in a day- or residential treatment center is the treatment of choice.

We outline certain characteristics which we consider typical of the borderline child and then address the ways each of these characteristics could be handled in a residential or day-treatment setting.

In our experience the major areas of psychopathology in the borderline child are:

1. Fluctuations occur in ego functioning with rapid decompensations in functioning secondary to objectively minimal emotional stress followed by equally rapid reintegration, often after a reaction from the environment. Brief shifts from neurotic to psychotic ideation and recurrent intrusions of bizarre fantasies and preoccupations are intermittently present.

2. Serious difficulties in the management of anxiety manifested by an inability to contain anxiety with rapid escalations from a state of anxiousness to panic are common. There is also a limitation in the child's ability to use anxiety as a signal to mobilize defensive maneuvers to deal with the anxiety. The basis of the anxiety resides in a fear of destruction, mutilation, or total annihilation rather than in the more usual latency-age courses of anxiety—superego anxiety, castration anxiety, fear of loss of love, and so on.

These children also experience greater suffering from anxiety because of the inadequacy and unreliability of neurotic defenses. On the other hand, they do not stabilize at a chronically psychotic level.

3. These children often have serious difficulties in thought content and process. There is an excessive fluidity of thought between fantasy and reality with an inability to control potentially frightening avenues of association. There is a short "reality span" with recurrent but transient intrusions of grotesque and bizarre fantasy themes. There is an exaggerated concern with survival which is dealt with by defenses such as severe obsessions, phobias, extreme dependency, merging fantasies, and so on, in the service of warding off the possibility of catastrophic destruction. These children may be quite proficient in obscure areas of knowledge with a lack of awareness of practical everyday matters, especially in the areas of social functioning. For instance, an intelligent boy of nine had an intense preoccupation with, and a prodigious knowledge of, dinosaurs and reptiles, which reflected his primitive oral destructive conflicts, but he was relatively "dumb" in regard to common everyday events and customs.

We have also found that a number of borderline children have a range of cognitive and intellectual deficits which appear to reflect organic central nervous system dysfunction. These difficulties become important, especially in planning for education for these children as well as in designing the overall treatment approach for each child. In the therapeutic interaction, the style and complexity of interpretations must take into account the child's cognitive capacities and difficulties. Frequently these children have neurological "soft" signs with a general lack of body integration and an overall awkwardness in their relationship to their body. They lack the usual graceful, secure, well-integrated use of their body so typical of latency children.

4. These children often have disturbed relationships with others, as might be expected from the areas of pathology described above. In particular, they have immature attachments to need-fulfilling adults. Unlike the typical latency child, there is an excessive reliance on others to maintain inner security. They function best with a trusted adult. They have poor relationships with peers and are unable to utilize intellectual talents in group situations. Reports from outside observers often stress that these children have great difficulty functioning in a group of peers without adult supervision.

5. Again unlike most latency children, these children have major difficulties in the area of self-control, with an inability to delay gratification or to tolerate frustration.

6. Other symptoms frequently found in these children which are important to address in a residential or day-treatment program include social awkwardness, a lack of adaptability, and an inflexibility in normal play activities which constitute such a significant part of the latency child's life.

OVERALL TREATMENT PLANNING

Each individual child will, of course, present his or her own unique combination of difficulties in a number of areas of functioning. Therefore each treatment plan will be tailored to the child's individual combination of special needs (Rosenfeld & Sprince, 1965). As Anna Freud (1956) emphasized in her paper "The Assessment of Borderline Cases" these children do not present a symptom complex within an otherwise appropriately developing personality structure; rather, their overall development is disturbed in a variety of areas. Generally speaking, we feel that nearly all borderline children need a broad spectrum of approaches to address their difficulties; this may include individual therapy, special education, and parental counseling and guidance, as well as group therapy, recreational therapy, and other modalities. In our experience, child mental health professionals tend initially to underestimate the degree and extent of disturbance in these children because the borderline child is capable of higher level, age-appropriate functioning which leads the therapist to assume that the child can be treated with less extensive therapeutic approaches.

The parents of the borderline child are usually not capable of coordinating the various aspects of the child's treatment and the wide variety of agencies involved. Thus one person, often the individual therapist, must take on the role of case manager. The smooth coordination of various services offered to the child is an important aspect of the overall treatment. If a trained professional takes on this role, it minimizes the fragmentation of therapeutic efforts and the disorganization that often results if the coordination is left to the parent.

Since the major pathology of the borderline child consists of deviations, delays, and distortions in a wide variety of ego vulnerabilities, and poorly resolved internal conflicts, the major thrust of treatment is to enhance the development and stabilization of a range of ego functions. This is done by a variety of means, including learning with social reinforcement, identifications, corrective emotional experiences, and the successful resolution of internal developmental conflicts. A first and important step is to interrupt the chronic and ongoing developmental interferences which result from the child's negative relationship with the environment, especially with his or her parents.

DAY OR RESIDENTIAL TREATMENT

Day or residential treatment may be the treatment of choice for a number of borderline children. The rationale for this recommendation is based on an understanding of the deeper dynamics of the child's psychopathology and his family's social and psychological functioning. Of special importance are the child's problems with (1) the establishment of a separate and stable core identity, (2) the parents' difficulty in separating themselves psychologically from the child, and (3) the intensity of the negative and destructive relationship which the borderline child has often established with his environment—home, school, social life, peers, and so forth.

There are no hard and fast criteria for the decision to admit a child to a day- or residential treatment program. In some cases, there is little choice: the child's violent and destructive behavior is so severe that he is dangerous and unmanageable at home, in special classes, or in a more open, eclectic day program. These children, for their own safety and the safety of others, need an environment that is physically capable of managing their serious regressions in a therapeutic milieu staffed by personnel experienced to deal with children in such regressed, panic-stricken states. Other children whose behavior may not require urgent behavioral management may also be treated most efficiently and successfully in a day- or residential treatment program. Perhaps the most important determining factors in these cases are the nature of the child's pathology, the parent-child relationship, and the parents' personality structure and their ability to change with counseling. In later sections we discuss in detail some of our observations on the parents of borderline children. If in the initial assessment of the borderline child it becomes clear that the parent has a significant and relatively fixed pathological relationship with the child, then separation and inpatient treatment should be considered.

Certain specific areas of difficulty of the borderline child can be especially addressed by separating the child from his usual environment and placing him in a residential or day-treatment program. For instance, it is not uncommon to find a borderline child who has few or no peer relationships; he is scapegoated and alienated at school, failing academically and socially, has a reputation of being "weird," and is extremely difficult to manage. Of even greater importance, however, is the negative, ambivalent relationship between the child and his or her parents in which the child stimulates regressive and destructive tendencies in the parents which then further intensify the child's difficulties. In other words, rather than being able to utilize a positive growth-promoting relationship with the parent, these children are often locked into a vicious cycle of mutual regression with their parents. For example, a boy of eight, whose parents were divorced, lived with his father and younger sister after having been kidnapped back and forth by both parents in a custody battle. This boy, although intelligent, had serious academic problems, in part on the basis of a specific perceptual-motor difficulty. He also had major behavior problems, was scapegoated, disliked by his peers and teachers, and would provoke the father and other adults to be excessively punitive with him. The father, who was an intelligent and socially sophisticated man with a degree of psychological awareness, would allow his son to go to school dressed in his younger sister's clothing even though he, the father, was aware that the child had major conflicts over his sexual identity. The mother would often take the boy to bed with her when he visited for the weekend. On occasion during these times, the boy would bite her. She would retaliate by biting him back. This particular child could at times be quite age-appropriate and manifest typical latency concerns. He could also deal with his environment in a sophisticated way on many occasions. At other times, he would regress rapidly and become infantile and mentally and behaviorally disorganized.

These constant fluctuations of functioning are quite characteristic. A trial of outpatient treatment was initiated. This was followed by day treatment when outpatient treatment proved unsuccessful. Eventually, the boy was placed in an inpatient treatment program. A drastic intervention was necessary to protect the child by interrupting the downhill spiral in the child's relationship to his family and his outside environment. In addition, the separation served to help the child establish a clear sense of his own separate identity and to develop more adequate and successful defenses. It also allowed his parents to obtain and maintain some objectivity about their child and not to become involved in the mutually regressive relationship with him that had developed before admission to the program.

The importance of the effect of the separation of the child, especially in the most severe cases, depends on practical as well as dynamic considerations. If the situation becomes increasingly destructive and the usual outpatient interventions are not sufficient to interrupt this cycle, separating the child from that environment is a practical solution to the destructive course of the child's life. From a psychotherapeutic standpoint, the separation from the family confronts the child and his parents with the unresolved conflicts around issues of separation and individuation (Gair & Salomon, 1962). Day or residential treatment of the child emphasizes his separateness. It also confronts the parents with their having to entrust their child to other people and helps them to acknowledge and to relinquish some of their fantasied omnipotent hold on the child. In our experience, the separation especially helps the parents to be aware of their projections onto the child. The decrease in involvement of the child in everyday interactions with the parents and the realistic assessment of the child by the therapeutic team helps the parents put their projections in perspective.

A second advantage of separating the child from his or her family by admission to a residential or day-treatment program is having the various therapeutic interventions coordinated in one overall program with a consistent approach and philosophy. When this is the case, there is less tendency to split the various therapeutic interventions or to pit one agency against another as often happens in the treatment of these difficult and perplexing children. It also helps the child integrate various aspects of his or her difficulties. The specific learning disorder, the internalized developmental conflicts, the problems with peer relationships can all be dealt with in an integrated program rather than being handled by a variety of agencies, a strategy that tends to encourage splitting and compartmentalization.

A third important reason for treating some of these children in a residential or day-treatment program is that it offers a significant opportunity to work with the parents since by necessity and/or design they are more involved with the program. (We recommend strongly that at least initially parental involvement be a prerequisite of the child's admission to a program.) Being able to deal with the child in the all-important aspects of everyday life—eating, toileting, bedtime, peer relationships, school, and so on—provides an opportunity for the staff to know this child in great depth and to understand in a more subtle way his or her deeper concerns. This also enables the staff to discover ways to help children master their various crises and confrontations. The staff is then in a much better position to help the parents by advice and by example based on a more in-depth knowledge of the child. The often powerful yet subtle everyday events that trigger major fluctuations in functioning of the child can be understood by the staff. This understanding can be translated and conveyed to the parents in terms that they can comprehend and accept.

As Lewis and Brown (1979) point out, it is extremely important for these children who have fragmented egos and who tend to compartmentalize to have a constancy in the people who care for them. The opportunity for the child to form positive identifications is greater if the people working with him or her are involved in an intensive everyday way.

OPTIMUM INPATIENT OR DAY-PATIENT SETTING

Because these children have important needs in many areas of their lives, it is important that a multidisciplinary team approach be taken with personnel trained to understand and to deal therapeutically with the broad spectrum of emotional, behavioral, and cognitive difficulties that these children present. Ideally, the program includes staff to work sensitively as everyday caretakers in the milieu, who can be adequate parent substitutes as well as models for identification for both the child and the parents. The staff should include trained personnel who can act as individual psychotherapists to deal with the more complex internalized problems. It includes special education teachers, social workers or other professionals who can work with the families, recreational and occupational therapists who can play an important role in helping the child develop skills that may help develop sublimations, especially if there are specific cognitive or perceptual motor difficulties as is often the case with these children.

The physical setting should be warm, homelike, and well structured with a consistent arrangement set up to deal with children. However, because many borderline children have serious problems with impulse control and can become violent quite rapidly with severe temper tantrums, the space needs to be set up in a way that when a child does lose control, the risk of serious harm to himself or others is minimized. This may mean that breakable items are kept to a minimum, that certain areas are strictly off-limits to children, that the physical arrangement is such that a child can be quickly secured and protected if in danger. We have found that in special cases a "quiet room" that is relatively bare but safe, with visual and auditory access to the rest of the milieu, can be very helpful. We discuss this particular aspect when we deal with the child who is out of control.

When a recommendation is made for a residential or day-treatment program for a child, it is very helpful diagnostically and practically to have the child and the parents visit the ward before an acceptance of the recommendation. If the family agrees, it helps to have the treatment team visit the child at home. There are many reasons for this. Often these children and their families have very vivid and frightening fantasy lives, and their fantasies of the physical plant, the other children, and the personnel can be quite unrealistic. Visiting the ward can be reassuring. The home visit not only gives the staff information about the home and some of the family interactions, but also symbolically indicates to the parents that they are considered a part of the treatment team and that they are encouraged to participate in the treatment of their child. The self-esteem of many of these parents is vulnerable, and they are often threatened with the idea that their child will be taken away from them or that someone else can do a better job as a parent than they can. It is important to understand these considerations when recommending inpatient treatment for a child and to deal with these concerns directly with the parent by reassuring the parent that admitting their child to an inpatient facility is not taking the child away from the family. It is, rather, an addition to the ongoing life of the child, and the family will be very much a participant in the treatment program.

We have also found that the way the child and the family deal with the admission of the child to the program, particularly if it is a residential program, can reveal significant aspects of the nature of the underlying pathology. It can also elicit the defenses and coping mechanisms that the child and the family can bring to bear at this very important and often traumatic time. It is a very poignant experience for a family to leave their child in a residential program, and some of the underlying dynamics of the relationship between the child and the family can be brought out in stark vividness at the time the family has to say "good bye" to the child (Gair & Salomon, 1962). One brief case example illustrates this.

A boy of eight who had been severely school phobic for two years and who had been tried in an outpatient program in his hometown with no success was referred to our program for evaluation. A recommendation was made for inpatient treatment, particularly when it was discovered that the boy had been locking himself in the bathroom or bedroom with knives and threatening to kill himself and his parents if they tried to take him to school or make him go out of the house. The parents accepted the recommendation for inpatient treatment. When it came time for the parents to leave on the day that the boy was admitted to the facility, the mother became remarkably pale, started shaking, and looked as if she might faint or die. Her fear and anxiety were remarkable and noticeable to all the staff members. In a postadmission conference, the staff agreed that if they as adults felt the terror in the mother to the extent that they did, then the child himself must feel it even more powerfully on an everyday basis. Thus an important aspect of the dynamics of the school phobia became palpably clear to everyone.

This case illustrated another characteristic of borderline children that became clear as time went on. This child, for instance, was given the "honor" of choosing the name for his younger brother who was born when the patient was five. In addition, the mother had told her son several times that his anger might be so destructive that it could kill his father. The father had a heart condition, and the boy was reminded over and over that if he upset his father, the father would die. This sense of omnipotence and grandiosity in the child fostered by the family, particularly the mother, is common in borderline children. Having to leave their child in the hands of other people often confronts the family with the fact that they and their child are not omnipotent or grandiose and that their child is just a child and is going to be treated as such by responsible professional adults. This can be a very important and powerful intervention both for the child and his parents. The fact that the trained staff can recognize and understand the child's omnipotent fantasies and deal with them as fantasies and still treat the child realistically as a child can be a very valuable although sometimes painful lesson to the child as well as an important message to the parent that their child is a child and not the powerful monster of their projections. These are behavioral and symbolic interpretations to the child and family which are supported and elaborated in the individual counseling with the parents.

DEALING WITH OTHER ASPECTS OF BORDERLINE PATHOLOGY IN A RESIDENTIAL OR DAY-TREATMENT CENTER

Rapid fluctuations in various ego functions are most problematic for the child in his or her interactions with the environment. These children can move rapidly from dealing with themselves and the outside world in an age-appropriate way to being quite regressed, infantile, and at times transiently psychotic. They then with equal rapidity return to age-adequate functioning. These major fluctuations in behavior, thought process, defensive level, and fantasy can be troubling for the people dealing with the child and are most baffling to untrained professionals—parents, teachers, neighbors, peers, and others. One important function that the treatment staff can perform is to pay very careful attention to the changes in the child's ego functioning and try to understand what triggers these impulsive and rapid regressions and progressions. Ekstein and Wallerstein (1954, 1956), in their discussions of the psychopathology and psychotherapy of borderline children, comment that if it were possible to examine the moments before these changes in ego functioning occur, one would most likely see that there had been a subtle but important break in the empathic communication between the child and another person. We have observed this to be true. We have also observed that subtle injuries to the child's self-esteem set off major regressions in functioning. Borderline children in general seem to have poor regulation of their self-esteem which is especially vulnerable to the slightest insults or failures. At these times, it is not at all uncommon for the child either to withdraw into a psychotic, autistic-like state or to become very active, break things, have a temper tantrum, become provocative—behavior that forces people in the environment to intervene. If the staff can observe in great detail what happened just prior to the fluctuation in functioning, they can then understand whether or not it is primarily a self-esteem problem or whether it is a problem of empathic communication, and on subsequent occurrences they will be able to address this with the child verbally as well as behaviorally. It would also be very useful to communicate this understanding to the parents, that is, that the fluctuations in functioning are not mysterious or totally happenstance but that they are motivated by self-esteem injuries or a breakdown in communication. This understanding not only relieves the parents of their fears that their child is operating on some mysterious basis, it also helps to provide for the parent an empathic understanding of the child's difficulty which then may make it easier for them to deal with the fluctuations in functioning.

Another advantage of having a variety of people available rather than just one person to deal with the child is that for many of these children in the midst of a regression which results from a perceived injury or insult from one person, that person, in the child's mind, is now totally negative and destructive and to be feared. This person thus cannot be utilized to help the child reconstitute. Other trusted staff who are around can become involved and help the child recover. Further, trained staff members, sensitive to the emotional dynamics of these children, are much less likely to be drawn into regressive interactions with the child at those moments when the child resorts to primitive mechanisms. The staff can maintain an objective and neutral observing stance which can be reassuring to the child in contrast to what goes on more usually, which is that the parent regresses with the child and both of them lose their objectivity.

We have found that it can also be helpful to the child at the times of regression for the staff to put into words what they understand the child to be experiencing and to give the child a cognitive handle on the situation. This enables the child eventually to limit the frequency and degree of these fluctuations.

As we said at the outset, many of these children have major difficulties in managing anxiety and progress quickly from being anxious to becoming overwhelmed by panic. If the staff understands this, it gives them an opportunity both by their words and by their actions to reassure the child and to help the child diminish this anxiety by verbally reassuring the child that they, the staff, will allow nothing dangerous to happen. One has to have the clinical understanding that these children can go from a mild anxiety level to a major panic and fear of total annihilation, or of their own fantasied omnipotent destructiveness, or of being merged with someone else and a losing of themselves. If the staff understands this, they can say in words directly to the child that they the staff are not going to hurt him or her and will not allow the child to hurt or destroy anyone else, thus addressing the child's innermost fears which may be totally inappropriate to the original situation that triggered the anxiety. Often it is more helpful to distract the child and to engage him or her in some physical activity where strength and mastery can be used to interpret the underlying conflicts. Dynamic interpretations at these points often result in further regressions (Kitchener, Sweet, & Citrin, 1961). (A more complete discussion of the role of interpretation is presented in the chapter on individual psychotherapy, chap. 9, this volume.) To the untrained observer, this panic does not make much sense and most laypeople and parents would not understand how to intervene, or if they did, how to intervene in a way that promotes control of the regression.

Another way in which the milieu staff can be very helpful to the child is in the gradual development of the use of signal to anxiety or at least a cognitive recognition of those situations of most vulnerablity to losing control. The staff can help institute immediately some change in the course of action to help avoid the dangerous situation. For instance, as the staff becomes increasingly aware of what triggers a regression in the child and what the earliest manifestations of such a regression are, the staff can intervene, saying to the child, "I think you are about to lose control, that you are about to scare yourself again. Let's do something to change that." Or the staff may institute some discussion and/or activity which will help minimize the regressive pull and escalation to panic. We would like to emphasize that the understanding of these early warning signals often takes weeks if not months of careful observation and close living with the child before patterns become clear, and oftentimes this can best or only be accomplished in a day or residential setting.

The borderline child's problems with impulse control and his tendency to immediate action rather than using fantasy or displacement when threatened often lead to sudden and serious threats to others or to himself or herself. At these times, the child requires direct physical controls. Often removing the child to a safe, secure space where there is little stimulation is necessary. Going to the "seclusion" room is a most useful intervention, especially if used sensitively and with an understanding of the child's vulnerability at the time (Gair, Bullard, & Corwin, 1965). Geleerd (1945) observed that while most children in the midst of a temper tantrum will settle down if securely and firmly confronted by an adult, some children would instead escalate to a state of panic in the face of such an approach. She found that these children needed a much warmer, supportive approach, with affection and holding to help them come out of the temper tantrum. While we have found this a useful observation in handling some borderline children, others become more panic stricken when approached physically in the midst of a temper tantrum. It is as if during their outbursts their ego boundaries are even less well-defined and the physical closeness of another person seriously threatens their integrity. They need distance, safety, and security in order to reintegrate. They respond well to being removed to the quiet room quickly, with as little laying on of hands as possible. These children frequently eroticize any physical contact, so that controlling the child by holding him, which is often necessary, must be done with this concern in mind. Once in the quiet room, verbal and/or visual contact is maintained with the counselor, but at some distance. This helps the child keep contact with the outside world at a safe enough distance so that he or she can recover more mature defenses without being threatened by merging fantasies.

In the therapeutic milieu, a variety of methods can be employed to help the child develop better impulse control and increase the ability to delay gratification. A very reliable and consistent system of limits and rewards administered with objectivity is most important. Perhaps the most powerful therapeutic tool is the identification with a loved counselor who has been intimately involved with the child's everyday activities. We have seen children after a certain period in an inpatient program institute for themselves limits that had previously been set by their counselor, e.g., taking a "time out" in a chair or going to the quiet room on their own.

One of the major problems of these children is differentiating reality from fantasy, and although their reality testing is frequently intact in the general sense, in certain circumstances their reality testing is weak and breaks down completely. This can be transient, and they may become panic stricken momentarily. In other words, these children often scare themselves by their own thoughts and have trouble differentiating between thought and the outside world. This difficulty stems certainly in part from unresolved separation-individuation difficulties.

One of the most important aspects of treating borderline children lies in this area, in strengthening and shoring up their reality testing and their reality sense. This can be assisted in individual therapy sessions, but in everyday life in a treatment program it can be addressed by the staff from all disciplines as they become more and more aware of this aspect of the child's difficulties, whether in the school setting, in recreation therapy, or in the regular ward setting. The sensitive staff, constantly aware that the child may be having difficulty assessing his or her fantasy life and clear that it is just fantasy, can help by asking questions about the child's thoughts and by reassuring the child that fantasies and ideas are very different from reality. Oftentimes if the child is involved in play that symbolizes his innermost difficulty—annihilation, destruction, sexuality, for example—the sensitive counselor can emphasize from time to time that this is just play or make-believe and make sure that the child is aware of the distinction. This can be very useful in allaying the child's fears and stopping the potential for regression. We understand that this is a directive, teaching approach appealing to the child's cognitive function. It has limitations, but many children can make use of such direct cognitive information, especially if given by a trusted counselor.

In our experience with borderline children, to our suprise many of them had subtle but important cognitive deficits. It is quite easy to assume that their academic difficulties in school are primarily based on their emotional and behavioral problems because these are certainly quite extreme. However, specific learning disorders may thus be overlooked. We have therefore made it part of our routine to administer a battery of tests to pinpoint more clearly the specific nature of the learning disorder. This is especially important for these children who are very vulnerable in their self-esteem, who are very critical of themselves, who have great difficulty in coping with failure. When their grandiose fantasies are confronted with real-life failures of which there are often many in school, it leads to a devastating experience for them.

If through the special education system, and particularly through psychological and cognitive function testing, it is discovered that the child has specific cognitive problems, e.g., with auditory memory, sequencing, or certain aspects of reproductive language functioning, this information can be shared with the staff who deal with the child in an everyday way and incorporated in the techniques used to deal with the child. For instance, certain of these children have a difficulty in keeping a certain sequence of steps in mind, and it is difficult for them to remember more than two steps at once. This is something that many special education teachers are aware of; most parents do not understand this, however, and mental health personnel are often unsophisticated in this area.

This information could be shared with the staff so that when the child is given directions or is given tasks to do, the directions are given in the most simple way, one or two steps at a time, with the understanding that the child is cognitively incapable of processing more that that. It frequently happens that these children are given complicated instructions, partly because they appear mature enough to understand them and partly because at times they do function at a higher level. As they undertake the task, they may be able to remember the first two steps but not the others. They become confused, and in their confusion their self-esteem is injured. They cannot admit that they do not know, and frequently they do something in a disruptive way to call attention to themselves which distracts people from the task that they set out to do. They end up being punished or berated for some negative action. A good example of this is the child who was told to go into the office and get the red book that was on the table by the telephone. The child went into the office, remembered the red book, but forgot the next step. In the room he became confused, did not know what to do, and began to throw things on the floor. The staff then became angry with him and confronted him with his negative behavior. In this way, what he considered his "dumbness" was avoided.

Another way in which these cognitive deficits play a significant role in the psychological development of these children is that many of these children have major difficulties developing adequate sublimations. This is particularly true in school where the process of learning and the excitement and thrill of mastering academic studies is not part of the borderline child's experience. Even though they may be intelligent children and talented in some areas, the school experience becomes a very negative one and is lost as an avenue of sublimation for them. If their specific cognitive deficits and strengths can be outlined by special testing, other avenues toward the development of sublimatory channels can be developed. For instance, one child of eight was a severely disturbed borderline child with a significant learning difficulty in reading and writing which was more clearly identified in special testing. The same test showed that he was quite brilliant in spatial relations, and through the help of his therapist and school personnel who were alerted to this, he became quite an expert in activities that called upon his incredible capacities in spatial relations—paper folding, origami, architectural models, artistic creations, and other three-dimensional constructions.

Along the same lines, many of these children have poor body integration, with "soft" neurological signs and a rather uncomfortable relationship to their bodies which is quite unusual for the normal latency child. As Elizabeth Kaplan (1965) pointed out in her paper "Reflections Regarding Psychomotor Activities During the Latency Period," it is extremely important for the latency child to become the master of his body; it is one of the most impressive developmental accomplishments of latency. Many of these borderline children are awkward, clumsy, and not well-coordinated. Even though fine motor coordination may be adequate, their overall body integration is poor, thus limiting another avenue for successful sublimation. This makes it difficult for them to take a successful part in many everyday activities—sports, hopscotch, jumping rope, and other important competitive and self-rewarding physical activities that lead to a sense of mastery. With these children, a sensitive, patient, and understanding recreational therapist in the treatment milieu can be extremely valuable, and it may help them find some areas in which they can be skillful and provide some sense of mastery over their body. As there is improvement in therapy, their self-esteem, body image, and confidence increases, and their bodily integration subsequently improves.

These children often have significant difficulties in peer relationships. In a day- and residential treatment program, of course, they will have to deal directly with peers on an everyday basis, and the complex and frequently destructive way in which these children interact with other children can be brought into clear focus in the treatment program. We have found that it can be very useful to the children to have an opportunity to meet on a regular basis as a group with a group leader to help them observe and discuss their interpersonal problems as a group and to help the children understand each other's difficulties. The group leader functions as an observing ego for the children in the group. With the help of the leader, the child in the group can learn ways to negotiate his role with other members and to develop a sense of belonging to a group, another important aspect of normal latency development.

The use of medication with borderline children is discussed in another chapter, and we pass over that issue here except to comment that in our experience, one needs to keep in mind that both parent and child in these cases often have a rather primitive fantasy life with oral incorporative conflicts. More than in other cases, there is a tendency to develop magical fantasies regarding the medication and its side effects, and this has to be taken into account when administering medication to a borderline child.

WORK WITH PARENTS

Surprisingly little has been written about the parents and families of border-line children. At the Massachusetts Mental Health Center over the last ten years, we have treated a number of borderline children in a day and residential setting. Although the sample is relatively small—around twenty— we can draw some general though tentative conclusions about the parents of these particular children. In our setting, all parents of children in the program are seen weekly by a social worker in addition to frequent informal meetings with the child's counselors. The general consensus of the personnel working with the parents of borderline children is that these parents are among the most difficult to work with. They have little insight into their role in their child's difficulties, often use primitive mechanisms such as projection, denial, and splitting to deal with their conflicts, and often have strikingly fixed and distorted perceptions of their child. We have already mentioned the case of the boy whose father allowed him to wear his sister's clothing to school and whose mother would bite him when he bit her. Another mother had a fixed belief that her daughter was a witch. This conviction was immutable. The girl eventually acted out her mother's projections by trying to poison her younger brother, setting clothing on fire, and so on. After more than two years of intensive counseling with a social worker, this particular mother still believed her daughter to have been born "a bad seed."We have also observed that the parents themselves had difficulty with impulse control and a number of our borderline children had been battered as very young children. The parents tended to use splitting mechanisms, to see people and agencies as either all good or all bad, frequently shifting their perception rapidly and with little apparent cause. This tendency makes the child-guidance work extremely difficult, and one spends much of the therapeutic effort directed towards maintaining an alliance with the parent.

As we said, the parents have little insight into their role in the child's problem. They also seem to have little empathy for their child's plight. They often treat their child as an adult (usually a grandiose or debased component of themselves) or infantilize the child, trying to maintain a symbiotic relationship with him. Sometimes the parents have an uncanny sensitivity to the child's more primitive conflicts and play into these conflicts rather than help the child find a resolution. For instance, in the case of the boy who was mentioned above with significant bisexual and oral aggressive conflicts, on his ninth birthday his mother gave him a present of a necklace made of shark's teeth.

It is not uncommon to find that the parents encourage the child to sleep with them long past the time most children spend the night in their own beds. Several parents of borderline children allowed their latency-age child to have erotic direct physical contact with their bodies. A boy of eight would play with his mother's breasts; a girl of nine would take showers with her mother and would caress and fondle her mother's body.

Since it is difficult to use an insight-oriented approach with the parents of these children, the work with parents often then becomes mainly educational, giving them direct advice regarding the management of their child and their involvement in their child's activities. One of the principal aims of the work with the parent is to minimize their primitive involvement which perpetuates the child's difficulties. At the same time, one works constantly to maintain a positive alliance with the parent in order to keep the child in the therapeutic program. These parents, like their children, have very fragile self-esteem regulation and can feel narcissistically injured quite readily. When this happens, often they break off the relationship to the therapeutic program.

STAFF REACTIONS AND COUNTERTRANSFERENCE

One of the most important aspects of the day and residential treatment of the borderline child is the successful management of the powerful and often difficult feelings that these children invoke in the people working with them. Although some of these feelings fall into the general area of countertransference and can be dealt with in supervision as one ordinarily would with countertransference difficulties, much of the time these children confront the staff with fantasy material, behavior, and levels of relationship that elicit emotional reactions from the staff that are beyond countertransference, strictly speaking. The child's sudden shifts from age-appropriate functioning to primitive behavior place significant demands on the staff to shift their way of relating to the child equally suddenly. One has to think and act quickly in quite different modes, often without immediate understanding of what provoked the change. This constant need to be on guard and to shift the therapeutic stance is exhausting to the staff.

Because of their easy access to primitive fantasy, these children often confront staff with painful issues quite directly. Often they will ask very direct personal questions, or they will suddenly become physically very intimate, either with an erotic or an aggressive aim. They often have an uncanny capacity to sense another person's vulnerable areas of psychological difficulty and to play on these areas. In addition, the demands put on the staff at times for direct physical contact can be emotionally very trying for the staff. These children can be extremely provocative and stimulate considerable anger in the people dealing with them. If it is necessary to control the child physically, the counselor has to be able to accomplish this without the interaction becoming a vehicle for the counselor's sadistic and retaliatory wishes. Another area of difficulty for the staff working with the borderline child is in dealing with the parents, who, as we have mentioned, frequently use splitting and projection to deal with their conflicts. The possibility of the parent playing on staff members' vulnerabilities and pitting one member against the other is great. In addition, one has to be sensitive to the tendency to compete with the parents, to want to be the better parent, or to blame the parent for the child's problems, especially when the parents do indeed interact with the child in a primitive way.

For all these reasons, it is especially important for the staff working with borderline children to have good clinical supervision of their individual work with the child, as well as frequent staff conferences to share observations, to obtain support from peers, and to clarify each other's role and function with the child. As mentioned earlier, it is essential to have one person designated as a case manager who can coordinate the various aspects of the child's therapeutic program. Working with these children and their families is one of the most demanding and often frustrating roles that the children's mental health professional can encounter. A support structure providing for group meetings, in-service education, and opportunities to release and discuss feelings is essential to the operation of the program.

PLANNING FOR DISCHARGE

In reaching a decision to discharge a child from the program, the therapeutic team needs to assess the child's improvement in general, but especially in the major areas of pathology such as the management of anxiety and impulse control. The staff needs to see that these capacities have become stabilized and that the child is able to call upon new capacities independently or at least with less dependence on the presence of an adult figure. This can be observed in the child's independent functioning in school, in peer-group functioning, and in handling anxiety. Is he or she now able to use and institute more adaptive maneuvers rather than escalating to panic? Has he or she developed more capacity to master the school and social settings with some degree of personal gratification and enhancement of self-esteem? Does he or she have other healthy ways to bolster self-esteem? These are questions that need to be addressed in assessing the borderline child's readiness to leave a day or residential treatment program.

The day or residential treatment of a borderline child is usually only one phase of the overall treatment, and most of these children will need ongoing specialized help after leaving the program. Therefore, another important element in determining the child's readiness to leave the program is an assessment of the environment to which the child will return. Have the parents made sufficient gains, even if only at a behavioral level, to be able to maintain a reasonably appropriate relationship to the child and to support the continuation of therapeutic interventions on an outpatient basis? These outpatient therapeutic efforts often include intensive individual psychotherapy, special education, sometimes peer group therapy, and medication. Again, even for an outpatient it is important to have one professional person coordinate the overall program rather than leave the coordination to the parents. Occasionally the parents' and child's pathology is such that a long-term separation may be the best solution. If that assessment is made, we have found it possible to help the parent decide to place their child voluntarily in foster care or long-term residential schooling (Lewis & Brown, 1979).

CONCLUSION

In conclusion, the treatment of the borderline child and his family is usually complex and extensive, involving a variety of modalities. In certain cases, treatment in a day or residential therapeutic milieu is the treatment of choice in order to interrupt the destructive, mutually regressive relationship the child has with the environment and to enable the child to develop adequate defensive and coping mechanisms to deal with himself and the outside world. One important goal of placing a child in a day or residential treatment program is to help establish a supportive and growth-promoting environment to which the child can return. These children and their families are often among the most difficult, frustrating, and discouraging patients. A comprehensive multidisciplinary program with a coordinated, well-trained, and adequately supported staff can provide a chance for the child to develop the basic building blocks for recovery and for a successful future development.

REFERENCES

Ekstein, R., & Wallerstein, J. Observations on the psychology of borderline and psychotic children. *The Psychoanalytic Study of the Child,* 1954, *9,* 344–369.

Ekstein, R., & Wallerstein, J. Observations on the psychotherapy of borderline and psychotic children. *The Psychoanalytic Study of the Child,* 1956, *11,* 303–311.

Freud, A. The assessment of borderline cases. In *The writings of Anna Freud* (Vol. 5). New York: International Universities Press, 1969. (Originally published, 1956.)

Gair, D., & Salomon, A. Diagnostic aspects of psychiatric hospitalization in children. *American Journal of Orthopsychiatry,* 1962, *32,* 445-461.

Gair, D., Bullard, D., Jr., & Corwin, J. Residential treatment: Seclusion of children as a therapeutic ward practice. *American Journal of Orthopsychiatry,* 1965, *35,* 251–252.

Geleerd, E.R. Observations on temper tantrums in children. *American Journal of Orthopsychiatry,* 1945, *15,* 238-246.

Kaplan, E.B. Reflections regarding psychomotor activities during the latency period. *The Psychoanalytic Study of the Child,* 1965, *20,* 222-238.

Kitchener, H., Sweet, B., & Citrin, E. Problems in the treatment of impulse disorder in children in a residential setting. *Psychiatry,* 1961, *24,* 347–354.

Lewis, M., & Brown, T.E. Psychotherapy in the residential treatment of the borderline child. *Child Psychiatry and Human Development,* 1979, *9,* 181–188.

Rosenfeld, S.K., & Sprince, M.P. Some thoughts on the technical handling of borderline children. *The Psychoanalytic Study of the Child,* 1965, *20,* 495-516.

CHAPTER 12

The Borderline Personality Organization in Elementary School: Conflict and Treatment

Raymond Schimmer
DIRECTOR OF EDUCATION
PARSONS CHILD AND FAMILY CENTER
ALBANY, NEW YORK

A MAJOR PIECE OF BUSINESS in elementary school is the struggle to establish what Anna Freud (1974) calls "a reasonable agreement between the child's ego, the urge of his impulses, and the demands of society." (p. 84) "The demands of society" are presented by the school to the child, who often finds them in conflict with his instinctual desires. Most children, with varying degrees of difficulty, are able to repress or sublimate their desires and achieve some sort of accommodation with the school's demands. In the best of situations, the school may even become a stage for the display of new power and a vehicle for the attainment of rewards.

A child whose personality manifests traits described by Geleerd (1958), Kernberg (1967), Frijling-Schreuder (1970), Pine (1974), and others is at a severe disadvantage in an elementary school environment. Consider some basic characteristics of the school environment:

1. Its foremost subject of study is the external world and the child's relationship to it.

2. Success within it is dependent upon the repression and sublimation of instinctual drives, irrespective of the strength of those drives within the individual.

3. Much of its activity occurs in groups, which requires a subordination of individual will and desire.

4. The gratification derived from the activities depends upon the child's appreciation of other people and upon his good regard for his own growth.

The student must possess grossly healthy object relations and an increasingly reliable ability to organize behavior around environmental demands rather than primary, internal imperatives. But deficiencies in these areas are intrinsic to the borderline personality organization, and these may cause a wide range of school problems. They may be compounded by the presence of a physical handicap or an organically based learning disability.

The borderline syndrome has been described elsewhere in this volume, but certain salient aspects may be emphasized here to underscore the basic conflicts which exist between these children and the elementary school environment.

The borderline personality appears to represent a developmental disorder which is accompanied by an excess of aggression. The child is filled with rage of a pregenital nature, and with great anxiety as well. Two sources of anxiety may be an awareness and fear of rage and the dread of a serious failing of protection and nurturance. Instinctual desires continue to predominate as

278

major motivational forces long after this state has ceased to be developmentally appropriate. A distorted view of the world comes about which is often influenced by the ungovernable fears of deprivation and suspicions of persecution. A desperate concern with self-gratification leads to the classification of others as either potential self-objects—entities whose sole reason for being is the child's pleasure—or enemies.

Visible behavior disturbances attending the borderline organization may include temper tantrums, impulsivity, an inability to inhibit stimuli or control reactions to anxiety, motor disturbances, somatic complaints, and a variety of cognitive problems. Because the syndrome is broadly defined and the number of influential variables is large, it is impossible to describe a single representative behavioral pattern. The range extends from attention-disordered, violent children who appear to have serious learning impairments to superior students who appear to be passive or eccentric.

In spite of the manifest behavioral variations, a broad apprehension of the borderline child's possible school problems may be realized by comparing some basic, opposing characteristics of the school and the syndrome.

1. *The school is externally oriented; the child tends to be internally preoccupied.* The school's primary business is the orderly unfolding of information about the external world, much of which is not directly related to the individual student. The child is expected to accept the importance of the information and subjugate "irrelevant" desires to the task of acquiring it. While attending to formal study, he must also attempt to master a complex set of personal relationships. The second grader, for example, assesses his own importance with respect to first graders, third graders, teachers, principals, and classmates. Most children become marvelously adept at incorporating an understanding of these various strata, each of which has its own connotations of power, subordination, privilege, and inferiority.

The borderline child's appreciation of the outside world may be extremely impoverished. The importance of objects is determined by their immediate usefulness to the child. Relations with the outside world may consist of attempts to exploit, to justify feelings of persecution, to project rage, or to establish self-objects. Sources of motivation which sustain the normal child during elementary education are unavailable to the child with borderline features. Though in some cases an anxious desire to conform exists, the pleasing of parents and other adults may have little meaning because the child's feeling for the mental and affectual states of people is reduced. Ego skills may be unreliable, and in any event they are frequently of less concern than the achievement of gratification which derives from early stages of development.

2. *The school demands the supremacy of the reality principle, but the* *child adheres to the pleasure principle.* Schools rely upon the child's increasingly accurate ability to analyze situations in terms of objective reality and to act accordingly. This frequently involves endurance of discomfort and the delay of gratification. The borderline child may have difficulty with such analyses and activity. The degrees of need, rage, and anxiety are so great that affectual memory (Kernberg, 1967) or evocative memory (Adler & Buie, 1979) may be rendered ineffectual. Without trust in adults or an abiding memory of protection and provision, the child may not feel sufficient cause to deny or to restrain himself. This situation may be intolerable in many schools which are designed to promote growth at a quick pace rather than to cope with regression.

    3. *The school demands performance despite the child's ego deficiencies.* The school's high regard for growth and learning leads to the attachment of great importance to the timely development of ego strength. Where any definition of positive performance—e.g., skill acquisition or intellectual achievement—exists, there is also an implicit disapproval of opposing behavior. The borderline child who cannot generate adequate, consistent ego functioning may be unable to find esteem and tends to establish himself as an "enemy" of the institution and its highest goals. The consequences of fluctuating levels of performance or of chronic ego deviance may damage the foundation of order in the external environment as well as jeopardize the child's progress through it. The child may well be recognized by the school as behaviorally disturbed, cognitively impaired, or learning disabled.

MANIFESTATIONS OF BORDERLINE PERSONALITY ORGANIZATION IN SCHOOL

Manifestations of the borderline personality organization in school are numerous. For purposes of examination, these manifestations may be collected into two categories: behavior and learning style.

    Behavioral disturbances are evident in relationships with peers and adults. The provocation and alienation of others is directly related to characteristics which include idealization and devaluation, projection, absence of empathy, greediness, exploitation, and splitting. The following examples are taken from experiences at the day school of the Tufts-New England Medical Center's Division of Child Psychiatry.

> Buzz's class was engaged in a cooking activity with a new student teacher. Buzz was a proficient cook, and normally enjoyed these sessions. But on this occasion he was overactive and oppositional from the beginning of the period. He began to

complain loudly about the student teacher's deviation from established procedure, mocking her and responding to instructions by saying in a particularly provocative fashion "No way!" Eventually the entire class became disorderly and the activity had to be stopped prematurely. Before recounting the incident in supervision, the exasperated teacher blurted: "Just give me one reason why I should ever spend another minute with Buzz!"

Buzz's anxiety about the unfamiliar student teacher prevented him from deriving his usual pleasure from the activity. Unable to tolerate his anxiety and unable to empathize with the nervous adult, he devalued her publicly, thus raising her own anxiety and simultaneously enraging her. In the supervisory situation, the student was able to examine and profit from the event; but in the kitchen, under the strain of group leadership, she was quite vulnerable to Buzz's behavior.

> Throughout the rehearsals for the school play, Susan performed her small but crucial part with competence and enthusiasm. She had, in fact, been the major force in organizing the activity and in recruiting the cast. But on the day preceding the play, after invitations had been sent to parents, her teacher found her alone in the classroom, sobbing for no apparent reason. She hid her face, crying and moaning loudly. The teacher expressed concern and puzzlement. After some time, Susan collected herself in order to yell: "You never do nothing to those other kids when they tease me! I quit! I don't want to be in this dumb old play!"

The consternation of the teacher and Susan's classmates may well be imagined: at the last moment their weeks of work appeared destined to produce only disappointment and embarrassment. Although Susan eventually performed with distinction, relations with her peers had been severely strained.

In evidence here were those "'non-specific' aspects of ego weakness" referred to by Kernberg (1967), which include lack of anxiety tolerance, lack of impulse control, and lack of developed sublimatory channels. Susan's anxiety about the play induced a shift in ego functioning. Her statement was intended to depict herself as the hapless victim of group sadism which existed because of the teacher's incompetence, prejudice, and insensitivity. Susan's accusations and threat to resign at the last moment endeared her to no one and later marred her own memory of the actual performance.

Behaviors particularly damaging to peer relationships include greediness and exploitation. The child may be unable to accept gracefully the second place in line, or the slightly smaller pencil, or the corner piece of lasagna at lunch. Unremitting behavior of this sort serves to infuriate classmates who are struggling themselves to achieve mastery over the same sorts of wishes. Their angry reactions may strengthen the child's sense of isolation (Adler, 1979) and provoke additional anxiety. Exploitation has a similarly self-damaging outcome. The borderline child's sense of entitlement and search for self-objects leads to the manipulation of others; the absence of empathy for them removes the last barriers to selfish operations. Though not necessarily as obvious as greed, exploitation invariably produces an adverse effect in peer relations.

Splitting is a major issue in relationships with authority figures—usually teachers—at school. The teacher's traditional dual roles as repository and dispenser of information and as chief limit-setter are sources of trouble. In the child's eyes, the teacher may be like the "bad mother," capable of giving or withholding nurturance on a whim, the needs of the helpless child notwithstanding. No matter how responsive and generous the teacher may actually be over an extended period, when at last he or she sets limits, this may define the teacher as a depriver and persecutor. The child's perception of the teacher is then determined by the splitting mechanism; a long history of pleasant, nurturing interaction can be discarded from the child's memory. The mental image of the teacher becomes singularly evil, and the feeling of persecution may be supported. The teacher may be depicted as bad or inept and measured against an absent good or competent figure: "Just wait until my mother finds out what you did. . . ."; "I wish Mr. MacDonald was still our teacher. . . ." This type of assault is particularly telling if the teacher enters into the interaction with personal doubts, as Buzz's teacher did. The child is often uncommonly adept at charging the teacher with precisely those shortcomings he or she is most worried about.

Idealizing and then devaluing the teacher is another troublesome extension of splitting. In this instance, teacher and child enjoy a very good relationship initially. The teacher is viewed by the child as a special intimate and may naturally conclude that a genuine closeness exists between them. But ineluctably the pressure of daily activity produces a situation in which the teacher either cannot meet the child's demands or must insist upon a repression of behavior. The "honeymoon" then ends, often replaced by bitter strife. The teacher may search for his or her error, or attempt to reason with the child, convinced that the rapid deterioration of relations was caused by some specific accident. These efforts usually fail, because the child's behavior was not based upon a mutually shared understanding of objective fact accessible to discussion. Its roots are too deep, beyond the immediate context. The teacher is at best puzzled, and at worst angry and frustrated.

The term "power struggle" may be used to describe situations which evolve when the child challenges demands made by the teacher that are based on the teacher's authority within the institution. The child may declare the authority to be illegitimate, usually because in his or her view the teacher is acting in a prejudicial and persecutory fashion. Opposition to the oppression may be declared, and fierce resistance offered. The more forcefully the teacher repeats his or her demands, the more stubbornly the child may deny them, with an increasing sense of righteousness. The teacher, once embroiled, may quickly lose contact with the therapeutic role. A "tar-baby" scene may ensue, wherein the teacher's actions become increasingly punitive and ineffective. In the end, they serve only to reinforce the child's sense of persecution and conviction that he or she is entirely correct in opposing the "abuser." These struggles commonly arise from behavioral limit-setting or requests for academic production.

> Billy's teacher was absent, and the substitute was the school principal, with whom Billy had a friendly but superficial relationship. The day's assignment was to write or recount a fairy tale according to a definition formulated by the class after a long discussion. Billy began to write about a bloody fight between a boy and a dinosaur. When told that the story was not a fairy tale, Billy became obstreperous. He insisted it was a fairy tale. He offered a definition somewhat at variance with the class's. The principal rejected Billy's definition and demanded that Billy write as directed. Billy then sulked and refused to write at all. After a few minutes he yelled: "If you don't like it, why don't you rip it up?" He then shredded the paper himself.

These struggles are at least partly related to the child's reluctance to grant authority over himself to others. This reluctance is frequently acted out through petty, irritating behaviors which function to initiate this type of power struggle. These struggles often start during very ordinary interactions which flash into serious episodes before teachers are able to comprehend them.

> A child-care worker was showing films to a group of children which included Buzz. Buzz began making loud noises while the worker's back was turned. The worker demanded that Buzz stop. Buzz denied that the noises were loud and continued to make them until the worker ordered him out of the room. Buzz began to comply, but then shouted a racial epithet at the worker and started running about the area. When the worker took Buzz by the arm to lead him from the room, a prolonged tantrum took place during which the worker restrained Buzz. For several days thereafter, Buzz refused to speak with the worker and ate his lunch in a hall rather than near the worker who had previously been one of Buzz's favorites. His position was that "He had no right to put his hands on me."

Gross misbehavior, including tantrums, impulsive action, and periods of severely regressed behavior, is common. Its onset can be sudden, apparently without instigating antecedents, and it is very difficult to manage in the wrong setting.

Tony accompanied his class to the beach for the spring picnic. Just before leaving, he noticed that a small toy belonging to him was missing. Departure for the entire group was delayed while a futile search was conducted. Although assured that the toy would be replaced, Tony refused to re-enter the bus. His disconsolate crying turned into a screaming assault on teachers and classmates. The scene eventually drew the attention of a mounted policeman, who quickly became involved after Tony cursed him.

Shortly after departure was finally effected, Tony was chattering happily, apparently unaware of the disturbance he had caused.

Episodes such as Tony's tantrum or Susan's loss of control before the school play are often the result of a sudden increase in anxiety. This may occur in school following abruptly increased demands for performance (performing in the play) or a drastic change in routine (the beach trip) which stress the child beyond his or her ability to cope in the usual fashion.

LEARNING STYLES

The child's relationship to learning is also affected by borderline features, although the manifestations are not always obviously negative. If cognitive and sensory faculties are intact, the child may employ learning as another defense against some aspects of his inner and outer world. Long sessions of story writing or reading provide the child with socially acceptable methods of withdrawal from potentially dangerous personal interaction. Teachers beset by regular power struggles and gross misbehavior welcome such interludes and regret their passing. The motivation for the child's activity may not be preparation for life in the external world but rather relief from internal demands and the conflicts they bring about with that external world.

A variation of this "defensive learning" is common in children with healthy cognitive faculties. It involves the development of a large body of information about a particular subject, usually an esoteric one. The subject is frequently an annihilating force, such as dinosaurs, snakes, or sharks. The esoteric nature of the subject usually sets the child beyond competition within the peer group and beyond the range of the teacher's curriculum. These characteristics nurture the sense of omnipotence. Although the choice of subject is frequently the annihilating force, children may develop elaborately personalized cursive writing systems, an encyclopedic knowledge of Christopher Wren's architecture, or complete familiarity with the entire Hardy Boys series. The problematic aspect of this type of learning is not necessarily the subject but, instead, the way the knowledge is used to set the child off from his environment.

Another type of defensive learning described by Frijling-Schreuder (1970) is marked by a strongly felt need to conform with peers. This may favor good school performance, or actually inhibit progress.

> Nora's first reading teacher utilized a phonetic reading system for beginners, gradually switching to a more eclectic approach after the children were familiar with phonemes and blending. Nora was quite successful in her phonetic reading, but refused to employ the approach after Peter began reading complete words without blending phonemes first. Nora preferred to make erroneous guesses rather than to do accurate sound-blending. She invariably responded to the teacher's pleas to resume the successful method by saying: "No. I want to read like Peter."

Frijling-Schreuder attributes the striving for conformity to the desire to be like others despite the absence of a reliable feeling for them. An alternative explanation for the phenomenon is that the borderline child may accept education as an instrument of power and regard school as a desperate contest to maintain parity with potential aggressors. Once again, the need to be omnipotent in the face of threat is active.

More broadly, many children rely heavily on the structure offered by the school's routine. These are probably the children Pine (1974 and this volume) refers to as mimicking external organization. Although without an independent organizing capability, they are able to utilize an exostructure consisting of the teacher's vigorous management and the classroom's rigid routine. Tony was such a child. He rarely had behavioral trouble in class, so long as tight structure was available. But his learning activity was largely *pro forma*; he was not seriously interested in the content, which described the world outside of himself, but, instead, valued the regimen for the tranquility it conferred.

Other characteristics of the borderline child with respect to the learning task are not so well adapted to the environment. They render the child unable to participate regularly in school activities. Assignments are refused or executed desultorily. Some days the child is curious and active; others he is hostile and provocative. Several reasons for this irregular activity may be posited. The most serious is probably a tendency in many borderline children to conflict with the teacher.

The teacher has been described as having some qualities of the "bad mother." She is in possession of nurturance—the curriculum—and may give or withhold as she pleases. She may grant or deny small favors—going to the lavatory, getting a drink—which may sweeten the course of a day. The borderline child, beset by keenly felt desires which are perceived as vital needs, may find the teacher's position of power to be intolerable. By accepting instruction erratically, the child can establish him or herself as nondependent. By working inconsistently, he or she may be able to externalize this conflict through the teacher's angry reaction.

Inconsistent involvement frustrates another threatening function of schools, the gradual revelation of comparative talent and intelligence among students. Comparative evaluation is inherent whenever people work in groups, and many schools actually emphasize individual distinction as a motivational force. Many children cannot bear the outcome of such objective measurement which ultimately leads to the realization that powers larger than one's own exist. The measurement may be avoided by adopting unverbalized and unsubstantiated mental attitudes of superiority—described by E. Klein (1949)—and then refusing to produce anything which might be measured. Flashes of displayed competence fortify the child's belief in his superiority, but only on his terms, and only at a time of his choice. Nora, for example, would giggle or mumble when asked to read a word from the blackboard. When the word was assigned to another child, Nora would shout an answer at the precise moment that the other child spoke. Whether right or wrong, she would then say loudly: "I read it! I did it!"

One more source of learning difficulty is rooted in the delayed ascendance of the reality principle and the extended reign of the pleasure principle. Steady learning calls for more sacrifice of instinctual desire than the borderline child can usually bear. The conflict between present wishes and long duty is an unequal one. The borderline child fails at it far more frequently than does the normal child. Impulsive motor activity, flight into fantasy, and the urge to play are much more compelling than the several-times-removed pleasure of parental approval, an elevated sense of self, and the respect of one's peers.

The conflict with the teacher and inconsistent involvement with the school work is additionally harmful to the child whose cognitive functioning might be impaired by learning disability or developmental delay. A child with superior ability may succeed in spite of problematic behavior and may even excel because of "defensive learning." But less fortunate children will not, and their learning may be severely reduced in consequence. Teaching which helps children compensate for learning disabilities is frequently highly systematic and repetitious; the student must be highly motivated to use it effectively. The student must also be able to function depite the knowledge that others learn more quickly with much less effort. These demands may be overwhelming for the borderline child, who may then compound the degree of difficulty by reacting with behavior which is inimical to compensatory learning.

Negative aspects of a borderline child's learning style can be quite frustrating to school personnel and parents. The child appears to have the requisite cognitive ability, and is clearly not psychotic. He may display enthusiasm on occasion—"He did four pages of math in one day last week, but not a thing since then"—but generally fails to respond to the inducements and pressures which sustain most children. School personnel may feel with some justification that the child is being obstinate and provocative for reasons which have no obvious correlates in the immediate external context. Unless adjustments are made, the reaction by the school environment to the child may quickly provide those initially absent correlates.

SCHOOL AS A MODALITY OF TREATMENT

The many conflicts between the school and borderline child place the school in a unique position with respect to the pathology. The applied stresses of school often bring forth an abundance of difficult behavior in a setting which must address it, and in so doing they have some effect, for better or worse, on the underlying disturbance. The school's great advantages in the task are the presence of a potentially therapeutic community, a context of general structure, and an extended period in which both child and school can make complex statements of action. These advantages, in conjunction with the proximity to pathology, create a position of opportunity and danger. The child will act out within the school, and the school will reply. To some extent, the outcome of the case hinges on that reply. It may reinforce the defensive structure or offer the child an acceptable alternative to the disordered vision of self and the world about.

D.W. Winnicott, discussing what he calls the "anti-social tendency" (1958), describes the experience of maternal deprivation and consequent behavioral disturbance common to many borderline children. Winnicott sees the behavior as a "nuisance value" created by the child in a not entirely unconscious effort on the child's part to alert the environment about the ruthlessness of his desires. The child is seen as searching for the "good mother," and so long as he does search—that is, discomfit the environment— there is hope for change. Winnicott thus attributes a measure of power and responsibility to the child's living environment.

> Over and over again, one sees the moment of hope wasted, or withered, because of mismanagement or intolerance. This is another way of saying that the treatment of the anti-social tendency is not psychoanalysis but management, a going to meet and match the moment of hope. . . . When . . . the staff of a hostel carry a child through all the processes they have done a therapy that is surely comparable to analytic work. (pp. 309, 314)

To the extent that the child is susceptible to external activity, the school then is a powerful agency in the child's life. The opportunity to manage the "moment of hope" is significant in terms of time and intensity of experience.

The attainment of the general elementary school goals can have a strong positive effect upon the borderline child. If the school can act as an ambassador to the child from the outside world, it might diminish the consequences of the developmental disorder and enable the child to function capably in spite of those which remain. But the goals will probably not be attained without changes in the school's operation.

The school must achieve some diminution in the degree of distrust the child feels. This diminution should relieve a portion of the child's diffuse anxiety and provide readier access to reasoned behavior. The school must also illuminate the real, objective limits of desire and rage and define the unpleasant and unproductive qualities of defenses, particularly splitting. This illumination is achieved in the life of the school through action, repetition, and the external maintenance of memory as the school seeks to persuade the child that it is a benevolent, nurturing force embedded in a context of order.

The range of disturbance within the borderline syndrome is enormous, and the educational adjustment may be a slight change in classroom procedure or placement in a special day or residential setting. In any case, an important aspect of the school's intervention in a borderline personality disorder is the provision of sufficient supervision for teachers and other direct service personnel. This supervision is as essential to the prevention of additional harm as it is to the achievement of progress. Defenses employed by borderline children frequently result in the establishment of virulent interpersonal relationships. Teachers who tend to evaluate their professional performance in terms of their pupils' growth and productivity are quite susceptible to the regressive characteristics of the borderline child. Teachers who place faith in the power of their alliances with students may find themselves frustrated by the shallowness of the child's affectual capacity. All are vulnerable to the child's apparently personalized assaults in the forms of projected rage, feelings of inadequacy, and sense of aloneness.

The stress of dealing with behavior which follows abrupt shifts in ego functioning and gross reactions to anxiety takes a heavy toll from teachers. The worker trying to show movies, the student teacher in the kitchen, the counselor explaining Tony's behavior to a policeman on a horse, all were disturbed by the events to some degree, and all were forced to cope with feelings and doubts which were uncommon and unsettling. Supervision or consultation may be used to familiarize teachers with aspects of the syndrome and to help them obtain and retain objectivity in their interactions with the child. It must be clear to teachers that they belong to a therapeutic community which supports their work. Too frequently the teacher's long and close association with the child qualifies him or her for the lowest position in a hierarchy which ascribes most prestige to members furthest from direct service. In the school setting, nothing is more important to the child than the actions, reactions, and countless decisions of the staff.

The provision of both order and nurturance within the school is extremely difficult because of the characteristic borderline defense of splitting. The child has difficulty understanding how a school which denies or prohibits can be good and giving at the same time. The school's offerings may be rejected outright, or accepted and then devalued. Most commonly, the child may actually forget that positive transactions ever occurred. Gratitude may never be expressed because of the dependence it implies and the inevitable deprivation the child may believe it insures.

By virtue of long service—trial by fire—school personnel may overcome some of these problems. The creation and cultivation of child-school history is effective in preserving objective fact and undercutting splitting. Teachers may note aloud the transpiration of pleasurable interactions and begin to develop a mutually shared "memory" to supplement the child's own. Simply reminding the child, by referring to events, that the nurturing, nonpersecuting quality has been sustained over time despite interpersonal vicissitudes is an effective general technique.

> The principal expressed anger and disappointment when Billy destroyed the dinosaur story, but refrained from attempting to force the boy to write more that day. Some weeks later, a similar assignment was given to the class. Billy asked what would happen if he refused to write. The principal replied: "Probably the same thing that happened before. I'll get mad, you'll be unhappy, and then in a day or so things will be back to normal." Billy then wrote a four-page story, which he called "my masterpiece." The principal remarked that masterpieces were nice, but not necessary. He added that they would probably have trouble again sometime in the future, but that they would get by it again.

Occurrences recounted by teachers for children serve as homilies or fables. They may diminish splitting, give some perspective to rage and its expression, and detoxify personal relationships. Shared reminiscing about the pleasant experiences or competent performances also assists in the construction of a sense of self, deriving its power from the force of historical fact.

The advantages of the ordered context are chiefly concerned with keeping behavior manageable, permitting staff members to co-exist with children for long periods in a therapeutic manner, and providing a fertile climate for the growth of ego skills and self-concept. In reducing regressive behavior, the school improves the child's personal history, which is influential with respect to the nascent sense of self. The controlled nature of the setting also allows for modulated environmental reaction to behavior, and this, in turn, demonstrates to the child that the quantity of rage will have only a limited impact upon himself or herself and the world.

The creation of an ordered environment is made difficult because it invariably involves the setting of limits. The borderline child's behavior draws the particular attention of limit-setters. This reinforces the child's perception of them as persecutors and allows him or her to assign them a single, negative valence. Initially, the child may be completely unable to deal with the limit-setting teacher in any other way. A third person, one not connected with the frustrating incident and therefore neutral, is valuable in these early stages of treatment. That person may review a difficult incident with the child, sympathizing with the deprivation and regretting the unhappiness while at the same time representing the emotions of the absent "opponent," and maintaining for the child a memory of past good times with that person. The third party may also suggest strategies for mending the present situation and hold out hope for a renewal of good relations in the future.

> The worker who became involved with Buzz while showing the movie consulted his supervisor. After Buzz finished a week of lunch in the hallway, the supervisor asked him to stop by his office for a chat. He told Buzz that he had noticed him in the hall and asked how the situation had come about. Buzz presented a rather incomplete version which placed heavy blame upon the worker. Gentle questioning allowed Buzz to reconstruct a more realistic version eventually, and he was able to accept some responsibility for events. He agreed to confer with the worker to resolve matters between them.

Great care must be taken when using the third-person tactic to avoid contributing to splitting. Later in the treatment, the limit-setter should be able to join with the child in person to review these incidents after a firm and undeniable history of nurturance and good will has been established.

This same general technique of review in perspective may be applied to serious acting out, including tantrums. In managing such events, the teacher guides his or her actions on the basis of an understanding of the child's perception of them and by the requirements of the postincident interview. In some cases, the teacher may remain removed to reduce the child's chances of identifying the teacher as the sadistic source of trouble; at other times, the teacher may have to suffer such a characterization temporarily, relying on repeated demonstrations of benevolence to rectify the child's perception in the long run, a luxury inherent in the school setting. An example of the latter instance is seen in the case of Marky, a young boy who would ferociously assault other children when frustrated. He would then call the teacher who was forced to restrain him "Troublemaker" for nearly an hour. Peter, on the other hand, would tantrum upon frustration in a relatively "safe" fashion, screaming and stamping. His teacher could avoid contamination by remaining at a distance until Peter was calm. He was then in a much better position to conduct a review of the incident with Peter afterwards.

RESULTS OF TREATMENT

The broad nature of the borderline syndrome and the multiplicity of associated behaviors precludes simple, accurate formulations about outcomes of treatment. But some observations may be presented along with cautionary principles concerning their interpretation.

Treatment of borderline children within an adjusted school setting largely consists of manipulating the external environment in a purposeful manner. If the child is at all susceptible to the character of the environment, the results of the manipulation may be potent, because the school represents such a great part of the child's life. This is not to say that purposeful manipulation of the environment is easily achieved; the number of logistical and interpersonal factors at play is too great, and complete success is a chimerical goal. Significant improvement, on the other hand, is not.

But a review of the model of borderline theory indicates that the difficulties of many children will not be easily accessible, even in a remedial environment, because of the deeply seated nature of their instinctual needs and developmentally disordered motivations. Adjustments of the school setting may be of less consequence to these children. This rough dichotomy separating children according to their susceptibility to environmental activity is reflected in Pine's (1974) categories. Children suffering from chronic ego deviance or shifting levels of ego organization might be considered less likely to respond favorably to educational intervention, while those who mimic external disorganization or who manifest an incomplete internalization of psychosis may be more positively affected.

An incident involving Susan illustrates the interplay of environment and deeply rooted disorder. Susan's teacher drove his students home following an after-school play rehearsal. While dropping Susan off, he noticed the words "Susan sucks" spray-painted in large letters on the side of her apartment building. The graffito was an obvious environmental insult which was damaging to Susan's sense of self, but it was probably not gratuitous and may have represented a "neighborhood diagnosis" of Susan's capacity for regression to a particular stage of development. Her interactions with the community were marked by the same orality, infantile behavioral control, and vulnerability which were displayed at school. The core existed in some measure without reference to the environment.

Despite the probable existence of such a dichotomy, our experience indicates that most borderline children can use an adjusted school experience to achieve varying degrees of mastery over their behavioral symptoms and, in some cases, improvement in the tone of object relations. The general style of improvement seems to have involved a gradual extension of time between regressive episodes, although the intensity of the episodes may not appear to be diminished. This has the effect of smoothing the day-to-day existence of the child and those about him. The quality of life, if not normalized, is at least improved.

Specific changes observed in various cases include an increase in sublimated behavior, an awakening of interest in the external world, the acqustion of academic skills appropriate for age, and some ability to reflect upon and regret regressive episodes. The children's ability to cope with routine may increase, producing the semblance of increased frustration tolerance.

It is not possible to state with certainty that these behavioral observations indicate major shifts in pathological psychological structure. In the most promising cases, they may appear to be successful adjustments to chronic handicaps.

SUMMARY

1. Conflicts exist between the requirements of elementary schools and the borderline personality organization.

2. Disturbances in school functioning of the borderline child are evident in interpersonal relationships and in learning.

3. The general goals of the elementary school, the duration and intensity of the child's experience with it, and the school's ordered context afford it a unique therapeutic position.

4. Adjustments necessary in school operations include increased supervision for teachers, the development of a capacity to manage symptomatic behavior in a therapeutic manner, and the presentation of the school to the child as a benevolent agent.

5. Efficacy of intervention with an adjusted school model is dependent upon the child's susceptibility to the influence of the environment.

6. Improved functioning is evident in the development of forms of sublimation, increased interest in curriculum, an increased ability to acquire academic skills, and a reduction in the frequency of disruptive behavior.

R E F E R E N C E S

Adler, G. The myth of alliance with borderline patients. *The American Journal of Psychiatry,* 1979, *136,* 642–645.

Adler, G., & Buie, D. Aloneness and borderline psychopathology: The possible relevance of child developmental issues. *International Journal of Psychoanalysis,* 1979, *60,* 83–96.

Alpert, A. Reversibility of pathological fixations associated with maternal deprivation in infancy. *The Psychoanalytic Study of the Child,* 1959, *14,* 169–185.

Chethik, M. Borderline child. In J. Noshpitz (Ed.), *Basic handbook of child psychiatry* (Vol. 2). New York: Basic Books, 1979.

Freud, A. *Psychoanalysis for teachers and parents.* New York: Norton, 1979.

Frijling-Schreuder, E. C. M. Borderline states in children. *The Psychoanalytic Study of the Child,* 1970, *24,* 307–327.

Gerleerd, E. Borderline states in childhood and adolescence, *Psychoanalytic Study of the Child,* 1958, *13,* 279–295.

Kernberg, O. Borderline personality organization. *Journal of the American Psychoanalytic Association,* 1967, *15,* 641–685.

Klein, E. Psychoanalytic aspects of school problems. *The Psychoanalytic Study of the Child,* 1949, 3 and 4, 369–390.

Lustman, J. On splitting. *The Psychoanalytic Study of the Child, 32,* 1977, 119–154.

Pine, F. On the concept "borderline" in children. *The Psychoanalytic Study of the Child,* 1974, *29,* 341–367.

Rank, B., & MacNaughton, D. A clinical contribution to early ego development. *The Psychoanalytic Study of the Child,* 1950, *5,* 53–65.

Rosenfeld, S., & Sprince, M. An attempt to formulate the meaning of the concept "borderline." *The Psychoanalytic Study of the Child,* 1963, *18,* 603–635.

Winnicott, D. W. Hate in the countertransference. Also, The anti-social tendency. In *Collected papers: Through pediatrics to psychoanalysis.* New York: Basic Books, 1958.

INDEX

About the Editor

KENNETH S. ROBSON, M.D., is Director of Training in Child Psychiatry and Associate Professor of Psychiatry at New England Medical Center Hospital and Tufts University School of Medicine. The author and editor of numerous books and articles, Dr. Robson's clinical and research interests have related to the care and understanding of seriously disturbed infants and children.